Latino Crossings

Latino Crossings

*Mexicans, Puerto Ricans, and
the Politics of Race and Citizenship*

Nicholas De Genova and
Ana Y. Ramos-Zayas

ROUTLEDGE
NEW YORK AND LONDON

Published in 2003 by
Routledge
Taylor & Francis Group
270 Madison Avenue
New York, NY 10016

In memory of my grandfather, Francisco Zayas, who instilled in me the value of a real-life education and whose integrity, tenacity, and sense of hope resemble those of the people who inspired this book.
—*A.Y.R.Z.*

Printed in the United States of America on acid-free paper
10 9 8 7 6 5 4 3 2

International Standard Book Number-10: 0-415-93457-5 (Softcover)
International Standard Book Number-13: 978-0-415-93457-2 (Softcover)
Library of Congress Card Number 2003005104

Library of Congress Cataloging-in-Publication Data

De Genova, Nicholas.
Latino crossings : Mexicans, Puerto Ricans, and the politics of race and citizenship / Nicholas De Genova and Ana Yolanda Ramos-Zayas.
    p. cm.
Includes bibliographical references and index.
ISBN 0-415-93456-7 (alk. paper)—ISBN 0-415-93457-5 (pbk.: alk. paper)
1. Mexican Americans—Illinois—Chicago—Social conditions. 2. Puerto Ricans—Illinois —Chicago—Social conditions. 3. Hispanic Americans—Illinois—Chicago—Social Conditions. 4. Mexican Americans—Race identity—Illinois—Chicago. 5. Puerto Ricans—Race identity —Illinois—Chicago. 6. Intergroup relations—Illinois—Chicago. 7. Chicago (Ill.)—Race relations. 8. Citizenship—Social aspects—Illinois—Chicago. I. Ramos-Zayas, Ana Y. II. Title.
F548.9.M5D44   2003
305.868'7207731—dc21

2003005104

Visit the Taylor & Francis Web site at
http://www.taylorandfrancis.com

and the Routledge Web site at
http://www.routledge-ny.com

Table of Contents

Acknowledgments

If all ethnographies derive much of their substance from a combination of haphazard conversations and sustained collaboration, and ultimately emerge fundamentally from dialogue, then that is true of this one in a special sense and to an extraordinary degree. This is, after all, a book that stages a conversation between two discrete research studies, and which was produced through our own protracted dialogue, oftentimes side-by-side at the same computer. Whereas academic writing commonly appears to be the result of an individual scholar's isolation, therefore, such an illusion is simply not tenable in this case. Thus, we are so much the more acutely aware of, and deeply grateful to, the many people who have provided us with the intellectual, political, and emotional communities that have sustained this project, as well as the institutions that have materially facilitated our collaboration.

Our shared interests in the field of Latino studies, our mutual entanglement in the discipline of anthropology, and the happenstance that we had both conducted ethnographic studies in Chicago during the same time period, perhaps inevitably, became the basis for a rather unique collaboration, but in a very important sense, none of this would have been possible had we not first met in 1996 as doctoral students through the auspices of the Spencer Foundation. Our very first conversations about the politics of race, citizenship, and Latinidad between the Mexicans and Puerto Ricans whom we had respectively known in Chicago—and the intuition that comparing our parallel research projects might offer an innovative perspective—owe a great debt of appreciation, in particular, to Catherine Lacey's exceptional vision and concerted efforts as the director at that time of the Spencer Foundation's Dissertation Fellowship program. Without Catherine's determination to cultivate an intellectual community among the cohort of fellowship recipients in the program that year, our acquaintance may have amounted to little more than a chance meeting.

The earliest formulation of our collaborative project took shape in the preliminary drafts of a research paper we prepared for presentation at the 99th Annual Meeting of the American Anthropological Association in San Francisco, for a session that we co-organized entitled "Latino Racial Formations in the United States" (18 November 2000). Shortly thereafter, we were graciously invited by Felix Matos-Rodríguez to present our work to the Center for Puerto Rican Studies at Hunter College of the City University of New York (28 February 2001). We are grateful to all who attended, shared their insights and criticisms, or prodded us with their concerns and questions, at both of these gatherings, especially: Micaela di Leonardo, Juan Flores, Alejandro Lugo, Felix Matos-Rodríguez, Gina Pérez, Joshua Price, Caridad Souza, Carlos Vargas-Ramos, Vilma Santiago-Irizarry, and Pat Zavella.

The essay that we first presented at those two events, and which anticipated some of the central arguments of this book, appeared in the *Journal of Latin American Anthropology* (2003), in a special thematic issue that we guest edited. We are grateful to the journal's editor Mary Weismantel, and her assistant Nancy Randall, as well as Bruce Mannheim in his capacity as president of the Society for Latin American Anthropology, for their exceptional collective efforts to ensure that the project prevailed despite of the vicissitudes of an editorial transition. A particular note of appreciation is likewise due to Micaela di Leonardo and Josiah Heyman in their role as reviewers for the journal. This book has surely benefited from their thoughtful engagements with the argument and the substance of that article.

Dave McBride, our editor at Routledge, exuded tremendous enthusiasm for this project from the very outset, even before all the chapters had been drafted. His persistence and enduring commitment to this book have been a genuine inspiration. In this regard, Neil Brenner deserves a special note of appreciation for his pivotal role in first bringing Nick's work to Dave's attention.

We also would like to acknowledge the academic institutions with which we have been affiliated during the writing of this book. Ana Yolanda would like to thank the faculty and staff of the Departments of Anthropology and Puerto Rican/Hispanic Caribbean Studies at Rutgers University, especially Larry LaFountain-Stokes for his warm and engaging collegiality. We both would like to recognize the congenial interdisciplinary intellectual space and working environment provided by Nick's faculty colleagues, students, and staff in the Center for the Study of Ethnicity and Race at Columbia University, where we most frequently met to work on the book. A particular note of gratitude is due to Nick's research assistants—Ryan Chaney, Danielle diNovelli-Lang, Lulu Meza, and especially Ashley Greene for her remarkable resourcefulness and diligence in compiling the relevant U.S. Census data. Nick would also like to extend his warm regards to colleagues in the Department of Anthropology, especially Steven Gregory and Sherry Ortner who read significant portions of the manuscript. Nick Dirks also provided crucial assistance and Janaki Bakhle offered invaluable advice at a decisive moment in the life of this book.

In addition to the many friends and colleagues already mentioned, still others have supplied crucial intellectual and political sustenance at various junctures during the writing of this book. Susan Coutin, María Lugones, [**Suzanne Oboler?**], Josh Price, Mérida Rúa, and Bonnie Urciuolli have each been important interlocutors, directly or indirectly. Chris Wright pored over the finished manuscript in its entirety with remarkable care and devotion; his rigorous and thoughtful criticisms were indispensable.

Nicholas' research in Chicago was always profoundly intertwined with the comforts of home and the pleasures of family. I am particularly grateful for the love and support of my parents, Donna and Wally, whose hard work and unfaltering generosity have been a permanent inspiration and the ultimate foundation for all of my work. Home and family have also acquired new meanings for me in New York, throughout the writing of this book. The energy that I have invested in this project will always be inseparable from the sweetness of my life with Magdalena and our daughter Silvia. From the very inception of this project through her uncompromisingly critical, incisive, and engaged reading of the finished manuscript, Magdalena has consistently provided just the right combination of reassuring confidence and challenging skepticism, and always with both patience and passion in ample measure.

Ana Yolanda would like to thank her parents, Ana Hilda and Vicente, her aunt and uncle, Yolanda and Manuel, and her "adoptive" brother Oscar. They are more important to me than they could ever realize. I also appreciate the support, love, and crazy ideas of Aixa, Clara, Javi, Julie, and Magali.

Throughout the long conversation entailed by reading and thinking through each other's ethnographic materials, we gained together an even deeper appreciation and admiration for the travails of so many of the Mexican and Puerto Rican men and women whom we each knew in Chicago. In our own struggle throughout this study to responsibly convey their voices and represent their perspectives, we are hopeful that what we have learned from them, as well as in debate with them, may inspire and provoke the kinds of poignant dialogue and fruitful argument that would be the most fitting and well deserved testament to the enduring meaningfulness of their everyday lives and conflicts.

For my father, Al De Genova, who taught me through his quiet but persistent example to explore Chicago and know and love the city, and from whose example I have otherwise learned so much about vulnerability, misunderstanding, and conflict—the central concerns of this book.

—N.D.G.

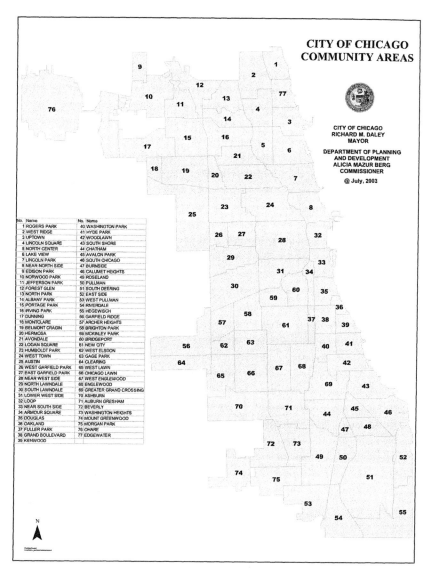

CITY OF CHICAGO
COMMUNITY AREAS

CITY OF CHICAGO
RICHARD M. DALEY
MAYOR

DEPARTMENT OF PLANNING
AND DEVELOPMENT
ALICIA MAZUR BERG
COMMISSIONER

@ July, 2003

No.	Name	No.	Name
1	ROGERS PARK	40	WASHINGTON PARK
2	WEST RIDGE	41	HYDE PARK
3	UPTOWN	42	WOODLAWN
4	LINCOLN SQUARE	43	SOUTH SHORE
5	NORTH CENTER	44	CHATHAM
6	LAKE VIEW	45	AVALON PARK
7	LINCOLN PARK	46	SOUTH CHICAGO
8	NEAR NORTH SIDE	47	BURNSIDE
9	EDISON PARK	48	CALUMET HEIGHTS
10	NORWOOD PARK	49	ROSELAND
11	JEFFERSON PARK	50	PULLMAN
12	FOREST GLEN	51	SOUTH DEERING
13	NORTH PARK	52	EAST SIDE
14	ALBANY PARK	53	WEST PULLMAN
15	PORTAGE PARK	54	RIVERDALE
16	IRVING PARK	55	HEGEWISCH
17	DUNNING	56	GARFIELD RIDGE
18	MONTCLARE	57	ARCHER HEIGHTS
19	BELMONT CRAGIN	58	BRIGHTON PARK
20	HERMOSA	59	MCKINLEY PARK
21	AVONDALE	60	BRIDGEPORT
22	LOGAN SQUARE	61	NEW CITY
23	HUMBOLDT PARK	62	WEST ELSDON
24	WEST TOWN	63	GAGE PARK
25	AUSTIN	64	CLEARING
26	WEST GARFIELD PARK	65	WEST LAWN
27	EAST GARFIELD PARK	66	CHICAGO LAWN
28	NEAR WEST SIDE	67	WEST ENGLEWOOD
29	NORTH LAWNDALE	68	ENGLEWOOD
30	SOUTH LAWNDALE	69	GREATER GRAND CROSSING
31	LOWER WEST SIDE	70	ASHBURN
32	LOOP	71	AUBURN GRESHAM
33	NEAR SOUTH SIDE	72	BEVERLY
34	ARMOUR SQUARE	73	WASHINGTON HEIGHTS
35	DOUGLAS	74	MOUNT GREENWOOD
36	OAKLAND	75	MORGAN PARK
37	FULLER PARK	76	OHARE
38	GRAND BOULEVARD	77	EDGEWATER
39	KENWOOD		

N

Special thanks to Larry Hanson, GIS Manager at the City of Chicago Department of Planning and Development, for graciously supplying this map.

CHAPTER 1

Introduction: Latino Crossings

This book explores the possibilities for and, more importantly, the obstacles to the emergence of a shared sense of "Latino" identity, or *Latinidad,* between two of the largest and most historically significant Latin American groups in the United States. Based upon ethnographic research in Chicago—one of very few major sites where Mexicans and Puerto Ricans have both settled over several decades—this study is concerned with the sociopolitical relations between Mexican migrants and Puerto Ricans within the space of the U.S. nation-state. Through the critical analytic lens enabled by these two experiences and their intersections, this research is focused primarily on the politics of race and citizenship in the U.S. "Racialization" and "the politics of citizenship" are posited as the central categories of our analysis.

The analytic framework of racialization emphasizes the ways that "race," or "racial difference," cannot be presumed to be based upon the "natural" characteristics of identifiable groups or the "biological" effects of ancestry, but rather comes to be actively produced as such, and continually reproduced and transformed as well. To the extent that "racial differences" appear to be self-evident, our point of departure is to inquire into the social struggles over the ways that those apparently stable distinctions between groups have come to be naturalized and fixed. Thus, "race" is always entangled in *social* relations and conflicts, and retains an enduring (seemingly intractable) significance precisely because its forms and substantive meanings are always eminently historical and mutable. The analytic framework of racialization, furthermore, attends to the extension and elaboration of racial meanings to social relations, practices, or groups that have previously been unclassified racially, or differently racially classified (Winant, 1994:58–68; cf. Omi and Winant, 1986:64–66).

"Race," even in its most crudely biological formulations, has always been preeminently construed not simply around what particular groups of people naturally and inherently "are" but also, more importantly, in terms of differences that might otherwise be glossed as "cultural"—what people "do" and how—which serve to distinguish them as distinct groups. Nevertheless, even the most purely "cultural" notions of racial difference always fall back on a presumed concept of the existence of identifiable, enduring, and relatively bounded "groups," and thus, always retain quasi-biological assumptions about shared kinship and common ancestry as the ultimate basis for "community." Indeed, to the extent that the concept of "culture" has been persistently deployed, historically, to account for the differences among "groups" that might otherwise have been depicted in terms of shared "blood," the idea of "culture" has never been coherently or consistently separable from racialized notions of groups defined by their putative "biology."

In light of the predominantly "cultural" focus of contemporary racialization processes, therefore, it is crucial to emphasize that we are *not* interested here to produce an account of the differences between Mexicans and Puerto Ricans in a manner that would contribute to the objectification of these social and political differences in terms of a presumed inventory of supposed "cultural" characteristics. Much less would we attribute these divisions and antagonisms to any kind of inherent conflict purported to arise from some essentialized "cultural" disparity between the two. Rather, we want to examine how the construction of differences—whether "cultural" or "biological"—between Mexicans and Puerto Ricans, *as groups,* operates within a larger social framework of racialized inequalities of power and opportunity. Theodore Allen argues that what is substantive and systemic about racial oppression is precisely oppression, rather than "race" itself (as a phenotypic or phylogenic category of distinction). "By examining racial oppression as a particular system of oppression—like gender oppression or class oppression or national oppression," he explains, it becomes possible to consistently theorize the organic interconnection of these systems of oppression (Allen, 1994:28). Allen's critical intervention is instructive, in that it makes it possible to sustain an analytic distinction between racialization, on the one hand, and racism (or more precisely, racial oppression), on the other. This distinction is critical for our purposes here, where two racially oppressed groups each find themselves ensnared by a larger racist hegemony that is sustained, in part, by the extent to which they come to position themselves socially in racialized opposition to one another.[1]

A crucial difference that Mexican migrants and Puerto Ricans often produced as a *racialized* distinction between one another—as groups—directly or indirectly concerned their respective positions in relation to U.S. citizenship. Mexican migrants ordinarily arrive in the U.S. as noncitizens; by contrast, people born in Puerto Rico, a colony of the U.S., are automatically counted among its citizens. Insofar as the institution of U.S. citizenship is commonly presumed to differentiate subjects in relation to the power of the nation-state, differences, divisions, and inequalities are elaborated in terms of "citizenship" and "immigration": Who is a U.S. citizen? Who is a "foreigner," or an "alien"? Who is eligible for citizenship? Who is deportable? And moreover, who is a "real American"? Furthermore, how do apparently formal or legalistic distinctions of citizenship translate into substantive inequalities of "rights" and entitlements, such as access to various social welfare benefits? This is the spectrum of concerns that comprises what we are calling "the politics of citizenship."

Our account of the differences produced between Mexicans and Puerto Ricans in Chicago is, therefore, concentrated on the centrality of politics in the most everyday senses of the word. Specifically, this study reveals the constitutive way that the unequal politics of citizenship produced by the U.S. nation-state for these two Latino groups, respectively, has entailed radically different relations to the U.S. state on the part of each, and thus, has engendered significant divisions between their two experiences. Likewise, we emphasize the ways that these divergent relations to U.S. citizenship have come to be racialized in distinct and historically specific ways—including in the ways that the two groups are positioned, and position themselves, in relation to one another. Ultimately, then, this ethnographic research enables an interrogation of the institution of U.S. citizenship itself as a mode for producing social inequality and racialized subordination, within the larger framework of U.S. nationalism as a racial formation.

This introductory chapter provides an historical overview of Mexican and Puerto Rican migrations and their distinct relations to the legal economy and racial order of the U.S. nation-state. Furthermore, this chapter provides a discussion of the two research projects that are the source of the ethnographic materials examined in this book, and addresses some of the methodological comparisons relevant to the collaboration that sustains this study. Finally, this chapter also outlines the thematic concerns that will be the focus of the rest of the book.

Mexican Migration and "Illegality"

Mexican migrants are very commonly the implied if not overt focus of mass-mediated, journalistic, as well as scholarly discussions of "illegal aliens" (Chavez, 2001; J. García, 1980; Johnson, 1997). The genesis of their condition of "illegality," however, is seldom examined. The figure of the "illegal alien" itself has emerged as a mass-mediated sociopolitical category that is saturated with racialized difference, and moreover, serves as a constitutive feature of the specific racialized inscription of "Mexicans" in general, regardless of their immigration status in the United States or even U.S. citizenship (De Genova, 1999; in press; Ngai, 1999; in press). Although the Immigration and Naturalization Service (INS) itself has estimated that Mexicans comprise only 54% of the total number of undocumented migrants in the U.S.,[2] the vigilance and enforcement by the INS (and especially the Border Patrol) against so-called "illegal aliens" has consistently been directed overwhelmingly against Mexicans in particular, historically.

There has long been a commonplace recognition of the fact that significant numbers of Mexican migrants came to work without documents in the U.S. (Gamio, 1930; Taylor, 1932; cf. Calavita, 1984; J. García, 1980; Martínez, 1976; Ngai, 1999; Reisler, 1976:24–25; Samora, 1971). The fact of undocumented Mexican migration arose as a consequence of a shared, albeit unequal, history between Mexico and the U.S. At the outset, it is instructive to recall that, in the first instance, it was white U.S. citizens who were the "illegal aliens" whose undocumented incursions into Mexican national territory provided a prelude to the eventual U.S. invasion and war in 1846 (cf. Acuña, 1981:5; Mirandé, 1985:24; Vélez-Ibáñez, 1996:57–62).[3] The U.S. conquest of Mexico's northern frontier imposed a border where there had previously been none, dividing Mexico in half; it also entailed the colonization of the Mexican population on the U.S. side of that new boundary. According to the terms codified by the Treaty of Guadalupe Hidalgo of 1848, approximately 80,000–100,000 Mexicans were summarily disenfranchised of their Mexican nationality the following year and became U.S. subjects, if not quite citizens (Griswold del Castillo, 1990:62). Despite official ("legal") guarantees, therefore, they were despoiled of their land, and their civil rights were regularly violated, often through outright racist terror (Acuña, 1981/1988/2000; Barrera, 1979; De León, 1983; M. García, 1981; Montejano, 1987; Pitt, 1971). As a regional political economy took shape in what came to be called the "American Southwest," mining, railroads, ranching, and agriculture relied extensively upon the active recruitment of Mexican/migrant workers (Acuña, 1981/1988/2000; Barrera, 1979; Gómez-Quiñones, 1994; R. González, 1981). In the following decades, a steadily increasing and effectively permanent importation of Mexican labor by U.S. employers cultivated and sustained a largely unregulated and numerically unrestricted migration between the two countries (Samora, 1971). During and after the years of the Mexican Revolution and World War I, from 1910 to 1930, over a million people—approximately one-tenth of Mexico's total population—relocated north of the border, partly owing to social disruptions and dislocations within Mexico during this period of political upheaval, but principally driven and often directly orchestrated by labor demand in new industries and agriculture in the U.S. (cf. Cardoso, 1980).

After its creation in 1924, the Border Patrol quickly assumed its role as a special police force for the disciplining and repression of Mexican workers in the U.S. (Cockcroft, 1986; Mirandé, 1987; Ngai, 1999). The Border Patrol's selective enforcement of the law—coordinated with seasonal labor demand by U.S. employers (as well as the occasional exigencies of electoral politics)—has long maintained a "revolving door" policy, whereby mass deportations are concurrent with an overall, large-scale importation of Mexican migrant labor (Cockroft, 1986; cf. Samora, 1971). Prior to the enactment of the 1965 amendments to the Immigration and Nationalities Act, however, the regulatory and disciplinary role of deportation operated in a context in which there were no statutory restrictions imposing numerical quotas on "legal" Mexican migration. Although there were no *quantitative* restrictions on their legal migration, Mexican migrants could nonetheless be conveniently denied entry into the U.S. on the basis of a selective enforcement of *qualitative* features of immigration law; in addition to a required $8 immigrant head tax and a $10 fee for the visa itself, entry was typically refused on the grounds of "illiteracy," or a perceived liability to become a "public charge" (due to having no prearranged employment), or, on the other hand, for violation of prohibitions against contracted labor (due to having prearranged employment through labor recruitment). Likewise,

Mexican workers could be deported if they could not verify that they held valid work visas, or if they could be found to have become "public charges," or violated U.S. laws, or engaged in acts that could be construed as "anarchist" or "seditionist"—all of which rendered deportation a crucial mechanism of labor discipline and subjugation, and was intended to counteract union organizing among Mexican/migrant workers (cf. Acuña, 1981/1988/2000; Cockcroft, 1986; Dinwoodie, 1977; Gómez-Quiñones, 1994). During the Great Depression of the 1930s, however, the more plainly racist character of Mexican criminalization and deportation became abundantly manifest, culminating in the systematic exclusion of Mexicans from employment and economic relief, followed by the forcible deportation of at least 415,000 migrants as well as U.S.-citizen Mexicans (born in the U.S. to migrant parents), and the "voluntary" repatriation of 85,000 more (Balderrama and Rodríguez, 1995; Guerin-Gonzáles, 1994; Hoffman, 1974).[4] People were expelled with no regard to legal residence or U.S. citizenship or even birth in the U.S.—simply for being "Mexicans."

In the face of the renewed labor shortages caused by U.S. involvement in World War II, the United States federal government initiated what came to be known as the Bracero Program as an administrative measure to institutionalize and regiment the supply of Mexican migrant labor for U.S. capitalism (principally for agriculture in the Southwest, but also for the railroads).[5] This legalized importation of Mexican labor meant that migrant workers, once contracted, were essentially a captive workforce under the jurisdiction of the state. In this way, the U.S. government provided a federal guarantee to employers of unlimited "cheap" labor. In addition to this protracted legal contract-labor migration, however, the Bracero Program facilitated undocumented migration at levels that far surpassed the numbers of "legal" (contracted) braceros—both through the development of a migration infrastructure and through employers' invitations of braceros to overstay the limited tenure of their contracts. Employers came to prefer the undocumented workers because they could evade the bond and contracting fees, minimum employment periods, fixed wages, and other safeguards required in employing braceros (Galarza, 1964; cf. Calavita, 1992; Samora, 1971). Some have estimated that four undocumented migrants entered the U.S. from Mexico for every documented bracero (Cockcroft, 1986:69).[6] Early in 1954, in an affront to Mexican negotiators' pleas for a fixed minimum wage for braceros, the U.S. Congress authorized the Department of Labor to unilaterally recruit Mexican workers, and the Border Patrol itself opened the border and actively recruited undocumented migrants (Cockcroft, 1986; Galarza, 1964). This period of official "open border" soon culminated, predictably in accord with the "revolving door" strategy, in the 1954–55 expulsion of at least 2.9 million "illegal" Mexican/migrant workers under the militarized dragnet and nativist hysteria of "Operation Wetback" (J. García, 1980; cf. Cockcroft, 1986). Thus, the Bracero years (1943–64) were distinguished not only by expanded legal migration through contract labor, but also the federal facilitation of undocumented migration and the provision of ample opportunities for legalization (what was called the "drying out" of "wetbacks"), simultaneously coupled with considerable repression and mass deportations.

Due to the critical function of deportation in the maintenance of a "revolving door" policy, the tenuous distinction between "legal" and "illegal" migration has been deployed to stigmatize and regulate Mexican/migrant workers for much of the twentieth century. This reflects something of the special character of Mexican migration to the U.S.: it has provided U.S. capitalism with the only "foreign" migrant labor reserve so sufficiently flexible and tractable that it can neither be fully replaced nor completely excluded under any circumstances (cf. Cockcroft, 1986). Since 1965, however, the ongoing history of U.S. immigration law has been central in structuring the inequalities that have shaped Mexican/migrant experiences. The historical specificity of the "migrant" status of Mexicans is inextricable from the fact that all of the prominent changes in U.S. immigration law since 1965 have been restrictive in unprecedented ways, weighing disproportionately upon migrants from Mexico, in particular, through a legal production of Mexican/migrant "illegality" (De Genova, 1999; in press). According to estimates based on the 2000 Census, Mexico has furnished 7.5–8.4 million (so-called "legal" as well as undocumented) migrants who currently reside in the United States, and approximately half of them (49.3%) are estimated to have arrived during the decade of the 1990s.[7] No other country has supplied even comparable numbers; indeed, by 2000, Mexican migrants alone constituted nearly 28% of the total "foreign-born" population in the U.S. (Camarota, 2001:14). The INS projected in October 1996 that 2.7 million of these are undocumented, but by May 2002, based on estimates calculated from the 2000 Census, researchers have suggested that the more accurate figure is 4.7 million, of whom as many as 85% had arrived in the U.S. during the 1990s.[8] Mexicans have continued to migrate, but an increasingly restrictive immigration regime has ensured that ever greater numbers have been relegated to an indefinite condition of "illegality."

The category "illegal alien" has long been a profoundly useful and profitable one that effectively serves to create and sustain a legally vulnerable—and hence, relatively tractable and thus "cheap"—reserve of labor (cf. De Genova, 2002). Undocumented Mexican/migrant labor in particular has been increasingly criminalized, subjected to excessive and extraordinary forms of policing, denied fundamental human rights and many rudimentary social entitlements, and thus is consigned to an uncertain sociopolitical predicament, always subject to deportation, often with little or no recourse to any semblance of protection from the law. The coupling of "Mexican"-ness and migrant "illegality," therefore, has rendered Mexicans in the U.S. as permanent "outsiders," and has ensured that the politics of citizenship is always a thoroughly racialized matter. The total number of Mexicans in the U.S. (including both migrants and those born in the U.S) is approximately 21–23 million, and comprises over 65% of all U.S. Latinos. While the overall majority are, in fact, U.S. citizens, then, approximately 22% of the Mexican population may be currently undocumented, and a considerably greater percentage will have been previously undocumented. Likewise, among those who are U.S. citizens, a significant proportion are the U.S.-born children of Mexican migrants. Thus, it is impossible to underestimate the extent to which the disproportionate and unprecedented legal production of migrant "illegality" for Mexicans in particular has directly or indirectly affected *all* Mexicans in the U.S., regardless of nativity or citizenship, and supplies a defining feature in their racialization as "Mexicans."

Puerto Rican Migration and U.S. Citizenship

Puerto Ricans, along with African Americans, are commonly implicated in journalistic and mass-media representations of welfare "abuse," and are figured as prominent "exceptions" to hegemonic narratives of social mobility in the U.S. Not unlike the stereotype of the African American "welfare queen," the figure of the "welfare dependent" Puerto Rican is a persistent racialized stigma that distinguishes Puerto Ricans from other Latino groups. The fact that, unlike other migrants to the U.S., all Puerto Ricans inherit the seeming advantage of being born into U.S. citizenship further accentuates the insinuation that endemic poverty and "welfare dependency" can ultimately be attributed to Puerto Ricans' own "failings." In this sense, the image of "welfare dependency" marks Puerto Ricans as a culturally "deficient" group who apparently lack the work ethic and concern for family that are celebrated as good "immigrant values." In spite of their U.S. citizenship, then, Puerto Ricans have been largely treated as a public liability, implicitly signaling that they are incorrigibly inassimilable and fundamentally un-"American." Thus, their birthright citizenship tends to be devalued and disqualified. The meanings of citizenship for Puerto Ricans, and the ways in which the divisive politics of citizenship contributes to the racialization of Puerto Ricans by dominant U.S. society and even by other Latino groups, however, have received scant attention (cf. Ramos-Zayas, 2003).

Throughout the twentieth century, the fate of Puerto Rico and its people has been inextricably bound to the U.S. In 1898, the U.S. occupied the island of Puerto Rico (as well as Cuba, the Philippines, and Guam)—until then, Spanish colonial territory—as the spoils of victory in the Spanish-Cuban-American War. By the late nineteenth century, the U.S. had come to perceive the Caribbean region as an important commercial route to Central and South America and a strategic military location for defending both the U.S. mainland as well as U.S. interests in the rest of the Americas, such as access to the Isthmus of Panama. Prior to the U.S. occupation, U.S. capital investments had increased dramatically in the region, especially in Cuba, culminating in the direct control of much of the Caribbean's sugar production and trade (Estades-Font, 1988). Within weeks of acquiring Puerto Rico, the U.S. began an intensive drive to dismantle and replace the state apparatus of Spanish rule with a new colonial regime that would conclusively transform the Island into an enclave of the U.S. economy, principally for the large-scale production and export of sugar (Cabán, 1999; R. Carr, 1984; Dietz, 1986). This involved "Americanization" projects intended to mold the Puerto Rican people into loyal and docile colonial subjects who would supply U.S. capital with a "cheap" and disciplined labor force. In the decades that followed, Puerto Ricans also became the pawns of official labor recruitment campaigns established on the Island under U.S. colonial rule to contract migrant workers to serve the labor demands of Mainland industries.[9] As colonial subjects, and racialized as not-white, Puerto Ricans (along with African Americans from the U.S. South) became an important source of "cheap" labor imported to the Mainland's urban Northeast, especially New York City. Following the U.S. Congress's passage of the Jones Act in 1917, furthermore, Puerto Ricans became U.S. citizens, and so, unlike other "foreign" migrant contract laborers, they could not be deported once their contracts expired.

The Jones Act of 1917 unilaterally conferred U.S. citizenship upon Puerto Ricans collectively, and legally abolished their prior status as citizens of Puerto Rico in an unequivocal affront to Puerto Rican sovereignty aspirations, without their own consent or participation in the change of their juridical status, and in flagrant disregard for any organized expression of their political desires (Cabranes, 1979; cf. Burnett and Marshall, 2001; Cabán, 1999). In effect, the extension of U.S. citizenship to Puerto Ricans irrevocably tied the fate of Puerto Rico to the U.S. (Cabán, 1999; R. Carr, 1984). The law's passage on the eve of the U.S. entry into World War I, furthermore, ensured for many Puerto Ricans that the most palpable significance of their newfound citizenship status was Puerto Rican men's eligibility to be drafted into the U.S. military. Approximately 60,000 Puerto Ricans—more than 12% of the Island's adult male population—served in the U.S. armed forces during World War I (R. Carr, 1984:65). In contrast, when rumors arose suggesting that Mexican migrants would be forcibly conscripted into military service for the U.S. war effort during World War I, Mexican workers began to flee and their employers began to panic; the outcry was so great that both the U.S. secretaries of War and Labor had to intervene and sponsor a campaign to reassure Mexican migrants that they were required only for their "temporary" labor, and that the U.S. government had no intention whatsoever to draft them (Reisler, 1976:25–27). Puerto Ricans' citizenship, while expanding their legal "duties" to the U.S. nation-state, did not even safeguard for them the full protection of the Bill of Rights or other constitutional guarantees of the presumed "rights" of citizens (R. M. Smith, 1997:433; cf. R. M. Smith, 2001). In the 1922 decision of *Balzac* v. *Porto Rico,* the U.S. Supreme Court ruled, for example, that in an officially "unincorporated territory" such as Puerto Rico, the constitutional right to trial by jury did not apply (Cabranes, 1979:49; cf. Burnett and Marshall, 2001; Rivera Ramos, 2001; Thornburgh, 2001). In addition to the extension of U.S. citizenship, the Jones Act established an elected senate for the Island, but established that the Island's governor would continue to be imposed from the Mainland, and thus would be a federally appointed (non–Puerto Rican) U.S. official. Likewise, the U.S. president and the U.S. Congress would retain veto powers over any act of the new Puerto Rican legislature, and thus would never be beholden to any legislative expression of the Puerto Rican people (R. Carr, 1984:54–55). Meanwhile, Puerto Rico would have no representation in the U.S. Congress, and the Island's inhabitants would not be permitted to vote in U.S. national elections. This restriction on Puerto Rican citizenship remains in force today, such that the Mainland-vs.-Island residence distinction sustains an unequal two-tiered structure for Puerto Rican political rights. Inasmuch as they were denied equal rights to political participation, Puerto Ricans were bestowed with a decidedly "passive" or "second-class" citizenship which itself has been the juridical expression of their colonial subordination.

In the post–World War II epoch of decolonization, Puerto Rico's colonial status was revised in order to create the appearance that Puerto Rico was no longer a U.S. territory without any semblance of self-government (Burnett and Marshall, 2001:19–20; Cabán, 1993). In 1948, Puerto Ricans were allowed to elect their own governor for the first time. Beginning in 1950, moreover, through Public Law 600 and the Puerto Rico Federal Relations Act, U.S. president Harry Truman authorized a constitutional convention that led to the approval by referendum in 1952 of a new Constitution of the Commonwealth of Puerto Rico (Trías Monge, 1997, 2001). Whereas Puerto Rico had previously been officially designated an "unincorporated territory" of the U.S., the Island's colonial condition would now be represented euphemistically as a "commonwealth" of the U.S., with the official and disingenuous title of "Free Associated State" (Estado Libre Asociado—ELA). The peculiar language was purposely designed to evade the salient concerns of both independence and statehood (Cabranes, 2001:45; cf. Burnett and Marshall, 2001). The apparent grant of self-government through the establishment of Commonwealth status, however, was rather compromised and provisional. The U.S. Congress reserved its rights to repeal the law that permitted Puerto Rico to draft its own constitution, to annul the Puerto Rican Constitution, to veto any legislations passed by the Island legislature, and otherwise to unilaterally alter any of the terms of the putative "compact" between the U.S. and Puerto Rico (Cabán, 1993:21). Furthermore, the ELA consolidated U.S. territorial prerogatives to establish military training facilities on the Island as well as federal transfers of funds in the form of federal programs for health, education, and housing, and other social welfare and public assistance benefits (Cabán, 1993; Grosfoguel and Georas, 1996:194–95). Nonetheless, claiming that Puerto Ricans had freely chosen through democratic elections to retain their long-standing "association" with the U.S., the U.S. unilaterally removed Puerto Rico from the United Nations' official list of non-self-governing territories, and procured a permanent exemption from the requirement to submit annual reports on the country's socioeconomic conditions to the UN secretary-general (Cabán, 1993:23).

The provisions of P.L. 600 and the 1952 Constitution, while initially purporting to move Puerto Rico closer to sovereignty and autonomy, actually created a framework of social institutions and arrangements that enhanced the prospects for long-term capital investment and profitability for U.S. corporations by strengthening the autonomy and flexibility of local officials to devise planning and social policies necessary to promote a new model of capital accumulation (Cabán, 1993:22). According to this "Commonwealth model," Puerto Rico was favored with duty-free access to the Mainland market, a common currency, a familiar legal framework, and U.S. military force to protect private property from insurrection or expropriation. U.S. companies investing and establishing manufacturing operations on the Island enjoyed broad exemptions from both federal and local taxes on their profits remitted to the Mainland (R. Carr, 1984:204). Furthermore, Puerto Rico was exempted from federal regulations over industrial labor relations, wage rules, health standards, and environmental protections (Cabán, 1993:22). The new Commonwealth status, therefore, promised low-wage labor coupled with political stability and local government compliance. By the late 1950s, Puerto Rico was being showcased as "Profit Island USA," the United States' model of "industrialization by invitation," otherwise known as Operation Bootstrap.[10] This comprehensive program of incentives to lure U.S. capital to the Island, notably, attracted an extensive development of the environmentally hazardous production operations of the pharmaceutical industry. This rapid industrialization, which by the 1960s had moved Puerto Rico from a predominantly agrarian to an industrial society, was later presented to the world as an alternative to the "Soviet model" embodied by the neighboring island nation of Cuba (Grosfoguel, 1999).

In part, Operation Bootstrap's success relied on "cleaning up" the Island of its "surplus" (i.e., poor) population, so that the appearance of a virtually instantaneous improvement in the standard of living of the Puerto Rican middle class on the Island could be achieved. This boiled down to a two-pronged policy of population control (primarily through the mass sterilization of Puerto Rican women) and the inducement of mass labor migration to the U.S. mainland. Puerto Rican women on the Island served as guinea pigs for experimental methods of birth control, before these methods were considered suitable for citizens on the U.S. mainland. Rampant female sterilization, which became popularly known as "*la Operación*," was justified as a "solution" for what the U.S. government termed "the overpopulation problem" (Littlewood, 1977; Ramírez de Arellano, and Scheipp, 1983; Reilly, 1991). Simultaneously, while the Puerto Rican government claimed to "neither encourage nor discourage" migration, the displacement of Puerto Ricans from the Island to the U.S. mainland was always considered an inviting alternative to "unemployment" and "overpopulation" in Puerto Rico. Especially following contract-labor migration initiatives during World War II, migration had already become a well-established and favored means for supplying labor to Mainland industries, and during the Truman-Muñoz negotiations of the late 1940s that led to the ELA and Operation Bootstrap, the U.S. government made deliberate provisions for the reduction of air fares between the Island and the Mainland in order to foster migration (Grosfoguel and Georas, 1996:194–95).[11] However, the model offered no provisions for the livelihood of the mass exodus of more than one million predominantly rural-origin and "unskilled" Puerto Ricans who eventually migrated and created barrios in the U.S.

Puerto Rican migration has few contemporary or historical precedents, since few other countries have exported such a large proportion of their population abroad—more than a quarter of its total population between 1945 and 1965 (Duany, 2000:2). According to Duany's calculations (2000), nearly 44% of all Puerto Ricans were living in the United States in 1990. By 2000, that figure had risen to 48.6%; the U.S. Census reported that over 3.4 million Puerto Ricans resided on the U.S. mainland, compared to 3.6 million on the Island. The social phenomenon of back-and-forth migration between Puerto Rico and the United States is facilitated by U.S citizenship, and thus is one of the defining elements that distinguishes the historically specific transnationalism of Puerto Rican migration and differentiates Puerto Ricans from many other Latino groups, who often cannot avail themselves so readily of the legal preconditions that facilitate such easy back-and-forth migration.[12] While the Puerto Rican migration stream of the 1940s through 1970s was overwhelmingly working-class in composition, a more socioeconomically mixed migration, which included students and professionals, followed in the 1980s and 1990s. Despite this increasing class differentiation among Puerto Ricans in the U.S., however, according to estimates from 1998 and 2000, 30.4% of all Puerto Ricans lived below the official poverty line, with an unemployment rate of 8.3%, and 7.3% receiving some form of public assistance.[13] Thus, Puerto Ricans as a group have persistently remained among the poorest of all Latino groups and among the poorest U.S. citizens as well (Latino Institute, July 1995).

Colonization, Racialization, and the Politics of Citizenship in Comparative Perspective

Taken together, these brief sketches of Mexicans' and Puerto Ricans' respective relations to the institution of U.S. citizenship provide an instructive contrast in the history of relations between the U.S. and Latin America. These distinct relations to the institution of citizenship, moreover, derive their specificities from particular histories of colonization. At the end of the U.S.-Mexico war in 1848, the U.S. nation-state annexed over one million square miles of land, comprising roughly half of Mexico's former national territory. Mexico's vast northern frontier lands were directly incorporated as U.S. territories that would later become the states of the "American Southwest." Thus, one Latin American people—Mexicans—are distinguished by a legacy of colonization by the U.S. nation-state that produced a new distinction between U.S. subjects (the colonized Mexicans, or Chicanos, of the "Southwest") and unauthorized outsiders (Mexicans migrating from Mexico) whose movements across a formerly continuous space were now recast as "illegal" border crossings. On the other hand, another Latin American people—Puerto Ricans—are distinguished by a legacy of colonization by the U.S. nation-state that reduced their land in its entirety to an officially "unincorporated territory" in a condition of indefinitely (permanently?) deferred exception, and that reduced them to subordinate U.S. citizens. Ironically, then, the annexation (direct incorporation) of half of Mexico created the preconditions for Mexican migration to be stigmatized by "illegality," whereas the possession but nonincorporation of Puerto Rico bestowed upon Puerto Rican migration the contradictory inheritance of colonial citizenship. Two analogous legacies of war, invasion, and conquest yielded strikingly contrasting outcomes with regard to the politics of citizenship.

The analogies between these two histories of colonization are even more profound when we consider that the politics of citizenship in both cases were expressly racialized. Indeed, overtly racial preoccupations were decisive in the determination by the U.S. to *not* colonize all of Mexico. In the wake of a military invasion and reign of terror by U.S. troops that ultimately extended as far south as Mexico City, there had been considerable debate around the question of annexing the entirety of Mexico. The debate largely centered on the questions of whether U.S. troops would become quickly embroiled in what would effectively be a protracted guerrilla war, and whether it would be manageable to maintain a colonial administration over the more densely populated Mexican territories. On one side of the debate, the chairman of the Senate Committee on Foreign Relations, Ambrose Sevier, promoted the idea that the majority of Mexicans (those deemed to not be "white") could be removed to reservations as had been done with North American Indians (Hietala, 1985:162n62; Price, 1967:17). In a manner analogous to the racist reasoning that motivated the brutal displacement of Native Americans, whites recurrently insisted that Mexicans were racially incapable of properly developing the land they possessed to its greatest productive capacity, and so would either irresistibly retreat in the face of the purported superiority of white civilization, or would have to be forced to relinquish it in the interests of white expansion (Horsman, 1981; cf. Drinnon, 1980; Takaki, 1979). Reflecting such preoccupations with land, the position that finally prevailed against the proposition to colonize all of Mexico was that articulated by Michigan senator Lewis Cass, who declared, "We do not want the people of Mexico, either as citizens or subjects. All we want is a portion of territory, which they nominally hold, generally uninhabited, or, where inhabited at all, sparsely so, and with a population, which would soon recede [by which he meant Indians], or identify itself with ours [by which he meant those who could be considered whites]" (quoted in Horsman, 1981:241). In other words, to the extent that there was any debate whatsoever, there was no dispute about the virtues of conquering Mexican land. The argument was not about territory but rather about the "racial" character of Mexicans and the advisability of trying to manage the subjugation of such a large and dense population of people deemed to be largely not-white (Horsman, 1981:236). Mexicans were routinely depicted as a "mongrel race"—at best, "half savage, half-civilized"—comprised of a mixture of the worst elements of all its component parts: indigenous American Indians, Spaniards, and to some extent, formerly enslaved Africans. A significant portion of the Mexican people, furthermore, were considered to be simply "savage" or "barbarous" Indians (Hietala, 1985: 152–66; Horsman, 1981:208–48). Hence, the new border between the U.S. and Mexico at the Rio Grande also involved a remapping of the color line, drawn in such a way as to take as much land and as few Mexicans as possible (Hietala, 1985:162–66; cf. Foley, 1997:22).

At the end of the U.S. war with Mexico, the Treaty of Guadalupe Hidalgo of 1848 appeared to provide for the U.S. citizenship of the newly colonized Mexican inhabitants of the conquered territories. Although the colonized inhabitants of the newly annexed Mexican territories were officially eligible for citizenship according to the terms of the treaty, the substantive terms of citizenship were relegated to the explicitly white supremacist determinations of the state constitutions. Thus, in its implementation, that citizenship came to be explicitly racialized as the preserve of "white men," and all but the wealthiest and "whitest" were left with a largely implausible claim to the status of citizens. Citizenship, then, was systematically subverted for the great majority of Mexicans on the U.S. side of the new border (De Genova, 1999; in press; cf. Almaguer, 1994; Griswold del Castillo, 1990; Perea, 2001:147–52).

Fifty years later, at the end of the Spanish-American War of 1898, the Treaty of Paris established the native peoples of all of the occupied territories (not only Puerto Rico but also Cuba, the Philippines, and Guam) as "nationals" of the U.S. but not "citizens," whose political status would be left for the U.S. Congress to determine (Jacobson, 2000:239; Rivera Ramos, 2001:107–8). Soon thereafter, the U.S. Supreme Court case *Downes* v. *Bidwell* of 1901 justified as constitutionally sound the U.S.'s right to "own" its newly colonized territories and legislate over subject peoples that it did not incorporate into the U.S. nation. It declared the inhabitants of these occupied territories—Puerto Ricans, Cubans, Filipinos, and the Chamorro people of Guam—neither citizens nor aliens (Burnett and Marshall, 2001, especially Levinson, 2001; Perea, 2001; Weiner, 2001; Cabán, 1999; R. Smith, 1997:429–39). Thus, like African Americans in the *Dred Scott* decision fourty-five years earlier, these now "domestic" noncitizens would be treated, in effect, as legally unrepresentable nonpersons (Levinson, 2001; Neumann, 2001; Perea, 2001; Torruella, 1985, 2001; cf. Wald, 1993). Even the European-descended native elites in these "unincorporated" colonies would not be considered "citizens."

Like Mexicans earlier, all the conquered subjects of U.S. imperial power following the Spanish-American War were racialized as "alien" peoples utterly "unfit" for U.S citizenship and self-government (Cabán, 1999; cf. Jacobson,

2000:239–41). Puerto Rico, specifically, was widely characterized as being populated by a "hybrid" people produced principally from the racial mixing of Spaniards and Africans, a significant portion of whom, furthermore, were considered to be simply Black (Perea, 2001). Despite the fact that the small island of Puerto Rico was indeed quite densely populated (in marked contrast to the relatively sparsely populated Mexican lands annexed in 1848), U.S. imperial military ambitions made the direct subjugation of all Puerto Ricans seem imperative. During congressional debates about whether or not the U.S. should become a colonial power ruling over an overseas empire, Albert Beveridge, a new senator from Indiana making his first senatorial speech, declared that the colonial question was deeper than any disputes over politics, policy, or constitutionality— it was a matter of racial destiny. He argued, "[God] has made us the master organizers of the world to establish system where chaos reigns. . . . He has made us adepts in government that we may administer government among savage and senile peoples. . . . And of all our race, He has marked the American people as His chosen nation to lead in the regeneration of the world. This is the divine mission of America. . . . " (quoted in R. M. Smith, 1997:430–31; cf. Jacobson, 2000:226). Beveridge's speech established his credentials as a devoted white supremacist committed to an imperialist project that he celebrated in the familiar ideological terms of "Manifest Destiny"; in recognition of these credentials, he was then included on the Special Committee to determine U.S. policy for Puerto Rico and the Philippines. The policy that the committee elaborated was explicit in its understanding of the colonial administration of these newly colonized Latin Americans and Asians to be effectively the same as well-established patterns of U.S. rule over Native American tribes (R. M. Smith, 1997:431; cf. Drinnon, 1980).

The principal objection to granting U.S. citizenship to newly colonized Puerto Ricans, explicitly and vociferously expressed by members of the U.S. Congress in the years following 1898, was their objectionable racial composition and, therefore, their presumed incapacity for self-government. Racism has always played a central role in the ideological formulation of U.S. citizenship (R. M. Smith, 1997). The reluctance in majoritarian institutions to admit to full and equal citizenship the "nonwhite" inhabitants of conquered territories demonstrates the importance of race in defining the "American" national identity that underwrites the institution of citizenship (Perea, 2001:141; cf. Burnett and Marshall, 2001). Although the Jones Act was ultimately enacted in 1917, granting U.S. citizenship to Puerto Ricans, this grant of citizenship was never intended to be a grant of full citizenship as non–Puerto Rican U.S. citizens knew it. As Senator Joseph Foraker had originally recommended in 1900, upon first introducing legislation to extend citizenship to Puerto Ricans: "In adopting the term 'citizens' we did not understand . . . that we are giving to those people any rights that the American people do not want them to have. 'Citizens' is a word that indicates . . . allegiance on the one hand and protection on the other" (quoted in Perea, 2001:162). Congress's ability to unilaterally define the civil and political rights of the people of Puerto Rico, and thus, the quality of their citizenship and political participation, in utter disregard for the democratic aspirations of the Puerto Ricans themselves, allowed colonial racism to shape subordinate citizenship for Puerto Ricans. Race emerged as the determining factor in shaping policies that were ultimately not limited to Puerto Ricans living on the Island, but extended to migrants to the U.S. mainland and subsequent generations as well. When the Jones Act was passed in 1917, finally granting a distinctly subordinate U.S. citizenship to Puerto Ricans only after much explicit debate about the racial character of the Puerto Rican people, its terms also imposed literacy and property requirements for the right to vote in a manner that effectively disenfranchised 70% of the adult male population; thus, in a manner analogous to the implementation of the Treaty of Guadalupe Hidalgo for the original Mexican inhabitants of the "Southwest," the Jones Act predictably secured voting rights in the hands of only the wealthiest and the "whitest" Puerto Ricans (Jacobson, 2000:241).

Given the deeply ingrained prohibitions against racial mixing and intermarriage at the symbolic center of racial segregation in the U.S. social order, the perception of Mexicans and later Puerto Ricans as quintessentially miscegenated peoples condemned them to white racist revulsion and contempt (cf. Perea, 2001). As U.S. senator John Calhoun declared with regard to all of Latin America during the debates over the war against Mexico, "Ours, sir, is the Government of a white race. The greatest misfortunes of Spanish America are to be traced to the fatal error of placing these colored races on an equality with the white race" (quoted in Perea, 2001:146). Thus, an examination of Mexicans' and Puerto Ricans' respective experiences of colonization in comparative perspective enables critical insights into the historical foundations of their analogous racializations in ways that anticipate contemporary "Latino" racial formations. Nevertheless, this same comparative perspective allows for a sharper focus on the historical divergence between each group's specific relation to the U.S. state, and the divisive politics of citizenship that has emerged as a consequence. These contrasting sociopolitical locations within the field of citizenship inequalities, therefore, likewise require a careful scrutiny of distinct and competing racial formations of "Mexican"-ness and "Puerto Rican"-ness that come to be juxtaposed as mutually exclusive.

In concert with this book's emphasis on the inequalities generated through the politics of citizenship in the U.S., then, our interest in this study is likewise to elucidate the active dynamics of racialization in the present—the continuous everyday-life production of differences in terms of "racial" distinctions— between Mexicans and Puerto Ricans in Chicago. Rather than taking at face value differences that might otherwise be glossed as "cultural," "ethnic," or "national" between these two Latino groups, we consider these distinctions as they serve the ends of juxtaposing the two—*as groups*—within a wider social framework that relates them to whiteness and Blackness, as well as to one another in ways that are mutually exclusive and often opposed.[14] Whether Mexican migrants or Puerto Ricans in Chicago construed the differences between one another, variously, in terms of ideologies of deservingness based on work or dignity, civility or modernity, gender and sexuality, or language—all of which will be substantive concerns among the chapters that follow—these disparate themes tended to be orchestrated through the intersecting rubrics of racialization and the inequalities of citizenship.

Mexicans, Puerto Ricans, and Latino Racial Formations

The historicity of social and political differences that distinguish the various relations of particular Latino groups to the U.S. state requires a careful skepticism about claims that too readily make the leap to asserting such groups' presumed "cultural" or "ethnic" commonalities as "Latinos." Nevertheless, the intrinsic incoherence of social categories such as "Latino" or "Hispanic," combined with their persistent meaningfulness, are telltale indicators of the ongoing reconfiguration of "Latinos" as a *racial* formation in the U.S. It is a commonplace among many commentators, not the least of which is the U.S. Bureau of the Census, to assert that Latinos are not a "race" and that Latinos may be, variously, white or Black or "some other race" that presumably entails any number of conceivable "interracial" mixtures. Yet these claims inevitably take refuge in anachronistic, crudely biological notions of "race" and overly simplistic naturalized reifications of "racial" difference understood in terms of phenotype and "color." Similarly, the legacy of Latin American nationalisms that promote ideologies of *mestizaje* does not really supply a viable alternative; while they abide by a contrary logic of racialized distinction and meanings, these official endorsements of the racially "mixed" character of their respective "nations" share the same fundamental premises of discrete originary races whose innumerable combinations have yielded identifiable phenotypic categories. As an effect of these conceptual lacunae, many of the prominent contributions to the Latino Studies scholarship opt instead to rely upon the analytic categories of "culture" or "ethnicity" in order to specify and theorize "Latino" identity and community formations, and thus evade the question of "race" and racialization altogether.[15]

Relying upon biological or phenotypic notions of discrete racial categories, the U.S. Census has explicitly reserved the "Hispanic" category as an officially non-"racial" one. By its treating "Hispanic" as an "ethnic" designation, Latinos in the U.S. are thereby encouraged to identify "racially" as white, Black, or Native American—in short, as anything but Latino. Nevertheless, this hegemonic "ethnic" distinction instituted by the U.S. state has been particularly instrumental for the allocation of affirmative action entitlements, deliberately constructing "Hispanics" as an effectively homogenized "minority" population analogous to African Americans. Thus, the "Hispanic" status of Latinos is widely treated as a racial condition all the same. Many Latinos' responses to the "race" question on the Census confirm precisely this fact of their everyday social experiences: while a significant number, confronting the peculiar and narrowly limited options available on the form, readily identify as "white" (even if many may never do so on virtually any other occasion), what is more revealing is that a comparable number opt instead for the nondescript "none of the above" category of "Some other race." Consequently, social categories such as "Hispanic" or "Latino" are notorious for the ambiguities and incongruities they entail for efforts in the United States to identify and name diverse groups of people with origins in Latin America. Nonetheless, these labels have become pervasive and increasingly salient, both for hegemonic projects that homogenize these groups as a "minority" population, a political constituency, or a market segment, as well as for efforts that seek to produce community and build strategic coalitions for self-representation.

The process by which particular Latin American groups have come to be homogenized as "Hispanics" (or alternatively, as "Latinos") cannot be divorced from the ways in which such pan-Latino labels were first formulated by the U.S. federal government. The "Hispanic" label was devised by the U.S. state as a deliberate strategy of erasure with regard to the more particular histories of Mexicans and Puerto Ricans, precisely at that historical moment of political crisis characterized by the racial militancy of the 1960s and '70s (Oboler, 1995; cf. Omi and Winant, 1986). In 1969, U.S. president Richard Nixon's proclamation of a "National Hispanic Heritage Week" served to conflate the different historical experiences of Mexicans and Puerto Ricans at the precise juncture when Mexicans (especially those born or raised in the U.S. who had increasingly come to assert a specifically nonmigrant identity as "Chicanos")[16] and Puerto Ricans were each engaged in increasingly militant and often nationalist acts of cultural affirmation *as distinct groups* with particular histories of subjugation and resistance, and were emphasizing their specific (and potentially divergent) political demands (Oboler, 1995:81–84).[17] The heightened public awareness in the aftermath of the civil rights era—at both local and national levels—of the existence and increasing political assertiveness of historically disenfranchised groups of Latin American descent, was unprecedented in the history of the United States (Oboler, 1995:83). At an historical juncture when there were still only very small numbers of other Latino nationalities in the U.S., however, the federal government's efforts to submerge the two major Latin American national-origin groups under the unitary and homogenizing "Hispanic" label reveals an insistent effort to undermine the specific demands of Chicanos and Puerto Ricans. Furthermore, the invention of "Hispanic" homogeneity also created an unprecedented opportunity for the numerically small but remarkably influential community of Cuban exiles (who were predominantly from elite or professional middle-class backgrounds, racially white-identified, politically conservative) to mobilize their newfound "Hispanic" identity as a platform (cf. Acuña, 1996:9; Oboler, 1995:82). Thus, against Chicano and Puerto Rican affirmations of indigenous and national identities that often embraced Third World anticolonial nationalism or Marxist theories of national self-determination, anti-Castro Cubans supplied a vociferous "Hispanic" expression of Cold War–era anticommunism that was resolute in its newfound allegiance to U.S. nationalism and capitalism.

The promotion of an Hispanic "ethnic" identity, moreover, could serve to distract Latin American populations within the U.S from mobilizing politically—on the basis of "race" or "nation." Such overtly racialized or nationalist bases of identity formation could more readily identify U.S. military interventions and political and economic domination in Latin America as the colonial or imperialist backdrops for the marginalization, inequality, and racial subordination experienced by migrants from Latin American countries and their U.S- born or-raised children. In contrast, hegemonic representations of "Hispanics" in "ethnic" terms have reduced Latino identity to a collection of "cultural" elements and sustained essentialist constructions of the presumed values, beliefs, and everyday practices purportedly shared by members of all Latin American nationality groups. The Hispanic "ethnic" construct was rapidly institutionalized ideologically in the homogenized categories of liberal multiculturalism, largely produced and disseminated through educational curricula as well as the mass media. Hence, public education institutions have performed a kind of officially mandated "cultural sensitivity" through the implementation of multiculturalist curricula. The recognition of "Hispanic Heritage Month" through a focus on "traditional" foods, music, family values, and folkloric displays, however, facilitates a general neglect of the social, economic, and historical contexts surrounding the racialization of Latinos as "minorities" in the United States.

The proliferation of mass-mediated marketing images of homogenized "Latinos" or "Hispanics," though not exclusively a top-down process, likewise, has been historically inseparable from the state's historical attempts to homogenize the militant particularisms of Latin American nationality groups during the civil rights era. Both the Latino and Hispanic labels, but especially the more aggressively depoliticized Hispanic label, increasingly became hegemonic categories of capital with the production and cultivation of specialized Spanish-speaking market segments. Commercially motivated constructions of "the Hispanic audience" for advertising purposes produced a largely undifferentiated or massified notion of Latinos as a discrete and unitary racialized market, conflating racial nonwhiteness with a presumed dominance of Spanish language that served as a proxy for "low" socioeconomic status (A. Rodríguez, 1998). By focusing on the Spanish language as a paramount basis of Latinidad, furthermore, "Hispanic marketing" and "Hispanic-driven media" have repackaged Latinos through images that are especially "pleasing to corporate clients," effectively fashioning them as "traditional and extremely family-oriented," and, by implication, "stubbornly brand-loyal consumer[s]" (Dávila, 2002, 4). This recasting of Latinos as rigidly tradition-bound embodiments of cultural "authenticity" contributes to Hispanic marketing's role in promoting a simplistic, generic, and depoliticized

Latinidad that is readily disseminated and eminently marketable (cf. Dávila, 2002; Rodríguez, 1998).

The names of social collectivities, and racialized groups in particular, of course, are sites of struggle between hegemonic labeling and efforts at self-representation. The homogenized cultural markers and historical experiences of "the Hispanics"—largely invented and propagated by politicians, uncritical social science, and the mass media and advertising sectors—have certainly inspired some to ambivalently question or frankly repudiate such generic labels as Hispanic or Latino altogether. Others have nonetheless come, to varying extents, to internalize these terms, or at least to strategically appropriate them for various purposes of self-identification and self-organization (Aparicio, 1997; Aparicio and Chávez-Silverman, 1997; Jones-Correa, 1998; Oboler, 1995; F. Padilla, 1985). Upon its introduction, in addition to supplanting specific national/colonial heritages, the term "Hispanic" served as a surrogate for such prior administrative/demographic categories as "Spanish-surname" and "Spanish-speaking," both of which had inevitably failed to adequately encompass the anomalies of U.S.-born English-speaking Latinos, or Latinos with non-Spanish surnames, such as the nonwhite children of "interracial" marriages (especially between Latina women and Anglo men)—all of whom belonged to the fundamentally racialized category for which these other terminological alternatives had been deployed (cf. Jones-Correa and Leal, 1996:217). Although one criticism of the "Hispanic" label is its transparent Eurocentrism and the implication that the people of the Spanish-speaking Americas are best understood to be fundamentally derivatives of their former colonizer (Spain), the term "Latino" (although it arguably allows for the inclusion of Portuguese-speaking Brazilians, for instance) is not strictly any less Eurocentric.[18] *Latinoamericano* (rather than *hispanoamericano*) is, however, the far more frequently used term *within* Latin America. It is precisely for these various reasons that "Latino" has been the widely preferred category among those who embrace a pan–Latin American identification but reject the "Hispanic" label imposed historically by the U.S. state.

The adoption and internalization of a pan-Latino identity among Latin American nationality groups in the United States are often central to processes of middle-class formation and articulations of upward social mobility aspirations among Latinos (Oboler, 1995; cf. Acuña, 2000:386–421; Foley, 1998).[19] Beyond the more parochial maneuvers of privilege and status that may unify middle-class Latin Americans beyond their nationally inflected particularities, however, various formulations of Latinismo, or the strategic deployment of a Latino or Hispanic identity, have also been shown to enable cross-class efforts at political mobilization. In his early study of Latinismo as a mode of coalition-building between "Mexican Americans" and Puerto Ricans in Chicago, for instance, Felix Padilla (1985) calls attention to the potentially effective political mobilization of a strategic and "situational" Latino identity that can serve as an oppositional organizing principle to ensure public visibility, mobilize electoral influence, and thereby cultivate the responsiveness of those who broker political power. In this sense, Latinidad as a principle of racialized (or "ethnic") organization can acquire unprecedented meaning in the production of an oppositional *political* identity aimed at securing substantive citizenship rights, entitlements, and electoral representation. For noncitizen Latino migrants, and especially for transnational Latino migrants systematically relegated to political existences in the interstices between states and citizenships, Latinismo may serve more tentative ends, but may likewise sustain a significant political identity (cf. Jones-Correa, 1998).[20]

Not only have Latinidad and Latinismo been promoted as bases for oppositional organizing in relation to institutionalized politics, but also as viable strategies in the everyday processes of community formation. By developing a wide array of distinctive forms of collective assertion and visibility, including grassroots activism and local community-building, that retain nationally inflected particularities and simultaneously cultivate a shared sense of Latinidad across lines of difference, Latinos have not uncommonly been better situated to claim rights in a manner that expands the boundaries of social inclusion and eventually secures political entitlements (Rosaldo and Flores, 1997).[21] The prospect of community formation among distinct national-origin groups on the basis of a shared sense of Latino identity, however, never ceases to be problematic. Struggles over hegemonic labeling and efforts at self-representation are not only oriented "outward" beyond the group's variously conceptualized boundaries, but also simultaneously operate internally among contending claims among presumed "Latino" subgroups. A politics of inclusion and exclusion, therefore, is at stake in competing productions of who can be counted as "authentic" or "legitimate" Latinos.[22] The Latino label, therefore, is inevitably configured in diverse ways in relation to the particular Latin American groups who vie with one another in specific locations. Furthermore, one of the central conflicts over the constitution of these locally inflected notions of Latinidad ultimately involves the racialized stigma of an abject "minority" status that is unevenly distributed among distinct Latino groups.

The boundaries of inclusion and exclusion for the Latino category, then, are remarkably elastic and contested. Indeed, much of the principal analytical theorizing of Latinidad has relied upon a notion of Latino identity as a kind of "instrumental ethnicity," emphasizing the U.S. state's imposition of the Hispanic label and the deliberate subsequent deployment of symbolic markers and "cultural" commonalities for strategic political goals (cf. Jones-Correa, 1998). An emphasis on the instrumental nature of Latino "ethnicity" may appear to shift the analysis away from primordialist approaches that dominated the social sciences until well into the twentieth century. Nevertheless, by foregrounding instrumental struggles to define and manipulate group boundaries, such approaches continue to either uphold essentialist assumptions about the presumed cultural "content" that is contained by those malleable boundaries or to regard essentialist myths as inexorable and necessary.[23] Thus, the instrumentalist emphasis on the strategic mutability of "ethnic" boundaries tends to naturalize the presumed substantive commonalities and positive coherence of "ethnicity" as a social category based on shared "cultural traits." However, there is no automatic or inevitable necessity to the emergence of a shared sense of Latino identity, as indeed there are never any natural or self-evident positive grounds for *any* identity. Identities must be *produced* through social relations and struggle. In this way, they coalesce rather more negatively than positively, relationally instead of on the basis of essential a priori "truths."

If we dispense with any such culturalist essentialisms about the "content" within the infinitely manipulable boundaries of Latino "group" identity, then, what indeed could supply the meaningful basis for such substantive commonalities between and among distinct Latino groups? This, finally, is one of the organizing questions that unify our work. Broadly speaking, and building upon the insights of the previous section of this chapter, the basis for such commonalities must be located in an analysis of the shared historicity of peoples throughout Latin America in relation to the colonial and imperialist projects of the U.S. nation-state, in concert with the concomitant historical as well as contemporary racializations of both Latin America, as a whole, and Latinos in the U.S. in relation to a sociopolitical order of white supremacy. Such a perspective has the advantage of situating Latino commonalities within a broader transnational perspective that connects U.S. Latinidad to Latin American history and, more specifically, to the historical specificity of the U.S. nation-state's imperial projects in Latin America that have so commonly produced Latino migrations to the U.S. (cf. J. González, 2000). The imperial history of the U.S. nation-state's relations with Latin America has always been a preeminently *political* one, and, moreover, an overtly racialized one. Indeed, any adequate theorization of Latino social formations in the U.S. demands a critical scrutiny of how the homogenizing racialized discourses of U.S. imperialism with respect to Latin America have been implicated in the organizing conceptual frameworks for the incorporation of U.S. Latinos as a generic and unitary "minority" group (Aparicio and Chávez-Silverman, 1997; Burnett and Marshall, 2001; Saldívar, 1991; 1997). This perspective does not presume any guarantees or certainties about a Latinidad grounded relationally in histories of conflict and social inequalities of power and wealth, but it makes possible the more effective formulation of Latino commonalities and coalition across lines of difference rather than on the untenable basis of imagined sameness.

In our research, when Mexicans and Puerto Ricans did posit various formulations of Latinidad, their diverse perspectives on "Latino" commonalities consistently tended to be already framed in terms of the politics of race and citizenship (see chapter 7). If there are indeed commonalities between Mexicans and Puerto Ricans, they are historically specific and actively, purposefully produced. Therefore, such gestures toward "community" are always necessarily contingent. Thus, it is imperative to foreground the *political* character of these productions of both identity and difference between Mexicans and Puerto Ricans, and thereby to situate the ethnography of these divisions as a critical lens through which to interrogate U.S. nationalism itself as a racial formation and the institution of U.S. citizenship as a framework of social inequality and subordination.

Collaborative Ethnography: Research and Methodological Comparisons

The analytic framework of racialization, which emphasizes the historicity of "race" and thus foregrounds the active social processes of "racial" differences in the making, is developed in this study through ethnographic research methods. One of the potential strengths of an ethnographic approach is precisely its capacity to illuminate the dynamic production of distinctions and categories of meaning in the apparently mundane details of everyday life. Racialization is a premier example of such processes of signification. Ethnographic methods, then, have provided us with a research strategy that effectively captures the complexity and fluidity of racialization in everyday life in a textured and nuanced way.

This book combines ethnographic data from two research projects, conducted independently of one another, during the same time period (1993–95), by each of the coauthors (De Genova, 1999; in press; Ramos-Zayas, 1997; 2003). These two studies did not share exactly the same research questions, nor were the ethnographic materials produced by these distinct projects, in any rigorous sense, precisely comparable. What we attempt here is nonetheless to bridge some of the inevitable discontinuities between our respective data. Certainly, this selective conjoining of rather particular aspects of our two studies is informed by a set of shared concerns, both theoretical and political. It is indisputable, however, that the dialogue which we stage here is enabled in a very practical sense by the empirical intersection of our distinct ethnographies. This study, which emerges from the conjuncture of these two projects, genuinely serves to shed new light on each of its two component parts, substantiating a comparativist inquiry that we contend to be not merely validated by the material, but indeed demanded by it.

Nicholas De Genova's materials were primarily produced over the course of two and a half years of ethnographic field research in Chicago (May 1993–December 1995). This primary research was augmented, furthermore, by ongoing communication and frequent visits during a subsequent sixteen-month period (April 1996–August 1997), and then by another year of research (August 1999–August 2000). During the entirety of the primary research period, De Genova was employed in a workplace literacy program as an instructor of English as a Second Language (ESL), as well as basic mathematics (in Spanish), for workers (of whom the great majority were Mexican migrants) in ten industrial workplaces (principally, metal-fabricating factories), located throughout the metropolitan area. He also worked, to a lesser extent, as an ESL teacher in a voluntary job-placement vocational training program, and in community organizations. Likewise, during the same period, he was living in the Mexican neighborhood known as Pilsen (or La Dieciocho), on Chicago's Near Southwest Side (a.k.a. Lower West Side), and again resided in Pilsen during the 1999–2000 research. The research involved extensive participant-observation in daily life activities there as well as several other predominantly Mexican/migrant areas of the city, especially that known as Little Village, or La Villita (a.k.a. South Lawndale). The project also entailed conducting ethnographic interviews in people's homes throughout the metropolitan area.

Ana Y. Ramos-Zayas's materials were produced during a year and a half of field research (April 1994–September 1995) and several weeklong follow-up visits (March 1996, August 1997, May 1998, November 1999, March 2000) among activists and residents of the Humboldt Park barrio, traditionally marked as the symbolic center of Puerto Rican Chicago. From the beginning of Ramos-Zayas's research in Chicago in the spring of 1994, she volunteered as a teacher at four main organizations: a local chapter of a national Latino not-for-profit organization, a parents' institute at the local public high school, a grassroots adult education program, and an alternative high school program for "at-risk" youth that overtly promoted a radical politics of Puerto Rican nationalism (Ramos-Zayas, 1998). The organizations where Ramos-Zayas volunteered reflected a variety of political perspectives—from assimilationist social service in the liberal tradition to militant nationalist activism and Puerto Rican separatism. The staff and clients of these various organizations were mostly second-generation U.S.-born or -raised Puerto Ricans, though there were also Mexicans, Central Americans, Cubans, and whites. Ramos-Zayas also participated in neighborhood activities, such as parades, street festivals, political marches, religious services, local museum exhibits, and trips outside the city with young people, local teachers, and activists. Since Ramos-Zayas was interested in examining the intersection of nationalism and class identities, she also conducted interviews with U.S.- and Island-born Puerto Ricans living in the Chicago suburbs, many of whom were middle-class professionals and had little connection with the poor and working-class barrio residents of Humboldt Park. Overall, her collaboration with barrio residents and grassroots activists was more intensive and consistent than her interaction with middle-class Puerto Ricans living outside the barrio, most of whom Ramos-Zayas knew in predominantly institutional contexts or through organized social events. Nevertheless, structured life history interviews yielded significant insights into the professionals' lives and perspectives.

The "anthropological" aspirations of these two research projects were inextricable from the politics of our respective social locations. As a U.S. citizen by birth and as a Chicago native, De Genova was conducting research on citizenship, immigration law, and the politics of nativism among people who had migrated to the U.S.—not only as noncitizens, but very commonly as undocumented migrants, and in a sociopolitical context of heightened hostility and restriction against them as such. As someone racialized as white, he was investigating processes of racialization in the experiences of people who came to be racialized as not-white. As a credentialed intellectual affiliated to an elite university, and thus, as a relatively privileged and effectively middle-class professional, he was studying class formation and labor subordination among factory workers. As someone employed through the initiative of the factory managements to teach courses in which the workers' participation was often mandatory, his position within the organizational hierarchy of these workplaces was always an intermediate and somewhat ambiguous one between the workers and their bosses. As a native speaker of English, he was teaching English as a Second Language to migrant workers who very seldom had completed much more than primary school in their own native Spanish.[24]

In the case of so-called native anthropologists, conducting research among members of "their own" community, the politics of a researcher's social location becomes even more profoundly conditioned by personal and political commitments, constantly shifting self-positionings, and, in the case of groups characterized by high levels of material scarcity and marginalization, even something akin to "survivor's guilt." As a Puerto Rican born and raised on the Island but who had lived nearly as many years in cities of the northeastern U.S. as in Puerto Rico, Ramos-Zayas was primarily interested in the lives of second-generation youth who were Chicago-born and -raised. As a native Spanish speaker, she was interested in the role of Spanish, Spanglish, and English in competing definitions of "cultural authenticity." An upwardly mobile, light-skinned, and Ivy League–educated professional, she was examining class formation, racialization processes, and educational marginality among residents of some of the most impoverished and neglected census tracts in the U.S. As a young woman who grew up in an ethnically mixed area of Puerto Rico (with a large Dominican population), she was also concerned with issues of gender subordination and inter-Latino relations in organizational contexts and among Chicago-based Puerto Rican political activists who frequently considered themselves "*muy nacionalistas*," and thus, who at times sustained rigid norms about gender roles as well as often essentialist understandings of "Puerto Rican"-ness.[25]

These socially and politically significant inequalities comprise some of the defining contours of the material and practical conditions of possibility of our respective ethnographies. Thus, it is imperative to problematize how these conditions can be seen to inflect the actual dialogics of the research presented here, and also how they can be understood to provide a wider frame through which to conceive of the possible limits of the ethnographic claims so produced. Due to the comparativist ambitions of this study, however, a critical attention to some of these questions will remain relatively understated and, except where necessary, considered beyond the scope of this work.

The distinct ways each of us was located in relation to our respective research subjects, of course, are not the only salient differences between our ethnographic materials. Reflecting an interest in the dramatic acceleration of Mexican migration since 1970 and the consequently increasingly "foreign-born" composition of the overall Mexican population in the U.S., De Genova's research was almost entirely focused on the specific social predicaments of Mexican *migrants*, rather than more broadly including Mexicans (such as many of these migrants' children) who were U.S.-born or -raised. On the other hand, similarly reflecting an overall decline in Puerto Rican migration since 1970 and a consequently dramatic increase in the Mainland-born proportion of Puerto Ricans in the U.S., Ramos-Zayas's research, although it included consideration of both Island-born and Mainland-born Puerto Ricans, was primarily focused on second-generation Chicago-born Puerto Ricans. De Genova's work is also more singularly concerned with working-class Mexican migrants, and especially factory workers, whereas Ramos-Zayas's study, while also significantly interested in poor and working-class Puerto Rican barrio residents, includes extensive materials generated among high school students and community activists, as well as comparative material from middle-class professionals. Likewise, Ramos-Zayas's study makes an explicit object of community-building and community organizing and activism centered in the Humboldt Park barrio, while De Genova's work, although it includes materials from his participant-observation in the Pilsen neighborhood and some community organizational contexts in Pilsen, was located across a variety of sites throughout the metropolitan area and was deliberately conceived in terms that were not confined to any particular neighborhood (cf. De Genova, 1998). These are only the most prominent contrasts that might usefully elucidate the differences to be bridged in this comparativist endeavor. Nevertheless, despite these potential disjunctures between the two bodies of research presented here, we are convinced of both the scholarly validity and the political significance of this enterprise of combining our ethnographic materials about Mexican and Puerto Rican perceptions and constructions of one another.

The value of this study's intellectual project derives *not* from a purported point-for-point comparison of Mexicans and Puerto Ricans *as groups*, but rather primarily from a comparative inquiry into the broader framework of the U.S. nation-state that systematically generates the material and practical parameters of each group's subordination, including the inequalities that tend to differentiate and divide their respective social circumstances and experiences. Despite numerous objective similarities and viable analogies between the two, racialization and the politics of citizenship in the U.S. ultimately supply the crucial conditions of possibility for their sociopolitical subjugation in ways that both groups respectively often understood to be divergent, if not frankly opposed. Thus, there is an urgent and necessary political significance as well that validates this scholarly collaboration and our effort to stage a dialogue between our distinct bodies of research. The apparently academic questions concerning the possibilities for and, much more seriously, the obstacles to a shared sense of Latino identity and community between Mexicans and Puerto Ricans, in short, are also dire concerns for the possibility of effective dialogue, mobilization, and organization. Indeed, it is finally only such exchange and collaboration that could enable any viable form of coalition and concerted action for sociopolitical change on the part of any two racially oppressed groups. In this respect, the difficult challenges posed by this book's research may offer a cautionary guide to the complexities entailed by any such endeavor.

Although our research candidly examines and hopes to honestly interrogate the frequently troubling ways that Mexicans and Puerto Ricans in Chicago understood themselves as having very little in common, the political promise of this collaborative study derives from its capacity to illuminate how and why those perceived differences were sustained. This comparative study was uniquely enabled by the fortuitous conjuncture of shared thematic concerns that framed the two original research projects. Ultimately, however, this book emerges precisely because the ethnographic materials—representing two sides of a single social relation—frankly, demanded such comparative inquiry. This book contributes, therefore, to the development of a comparativist direction for Latino Studies and Ethnic Studies, more generally, that can situate relations between distinct racially oppressed groups in terms of wider processes of racialization and the unequal politics of citizenship in the U.S. Furthermore, this book locates these particular Latino experiences as a standpoint of critique with which American Studies may come to more rigorously examine U.S. citizenship as a mode of inequality and U.S. nationalism itself as a racial formation.

As an ethnography of the everyday-life dynamics of racialization and the politics of citizenship, this study makes a major contribution to the anthropology of the United States. As a collaborative ethnography, moreover, this book provides a methodologically innovative model by which scholars might productively work together against pervasive institutionalized academic pressures toward individualism and isolation. These features of professional academic life are not only detrimental to the political integrity of the researcher, but also undermine the ultimate quality of the scholarship. There is a tendency for the researcher to become trapped by her/his particular preoccupations and concerns in ways that readily curtail the interpretive possibilities of the research and its representation. We have discovered in new and unanticipated ways that our intellectual collaboration has challenged each of us to reassess the familiar content of our own work in the face of perspectives that only became available through the other's study. Thus, we have had to confront the inherent limits of our own analyses of the material, and to explore the radically open-ended possibilities for evaluating the claims of ethnographic knowledge when it is properly resituated in the utterly messy and conflict-ridden restlessness of everyday life, where there are always other perceptions and perspectives and never a "last word."

About This Book

Our interest in the distinct relations that Mexicans and Puerto Ricans have to the racial order of the U.S. nation-state, invariably led us to consider the ways in which Mexicans and Puerto Ricans viewed themselves as racially distinct from one another. These constructions of racialized difference, however, were often revealed upon closer scrutiny to be inseparable from the two groups' respective positions as U.S. citizens or "illegal aliens," and signaled the decisive conjunctures of racialization with the legal economy of the U.S. These intersections between the politics of race and citizenship resurfaced repeatedly in our collaborative ethnography through a variety of themes that we explore in the ensuing chapters.

While this introductory chapter has provided an historical overview of Mexican and Puerto Rican migrations and their divergent relations to the legal economy of the U.S. nation-state, as well as a methodological discussion of the ways in which our collaborative ethnography was produced, chapter 2 focuses on the specificities of the urban landscape of Chicago, a notoriously segregated city, as a powerfully racializing social space. Despite the fact that, by the time of our study, Mexicans living on the North Side of the city had come to conclusively outnumber Puerto Ricans, the contiguous Near Northwest Side neighborhoods of West Town, Humboldt Park, and Logan Square commonly continued to be represented as "the Puerto Rican community," while the South Side neighborhoods of Pilsen and Little Village in particular were widely presumed to stand in for "the Mexican community." Hence, chapter 2 examines the productions of social space that have distinguished Chicago and its political economy, and how spatialized differences have played a formative role historically in enforcing significant divisions between Mexicans and Puerto Ricans. Puerto Ricans and Mexicans inhabiting the pronouncedly racialized social landscape of Chicago, furthermore, also produced and reformulated their distinct identities in terms of their legal relations to the U.S. nation-state, and similarly invested distinct urban spaces with the politics of citizenship.

Like the politics of urban space, the inequalities generated through the politics of citizenship became particularly salient for Mexicans' and Puerto Ricans' understandings of the differences between one another, as groups, in ways that ultimately came to be quite forcefully racialized. In chapter 3, we consider how competing moral economies of work and welfare were reconstructed in racial terms. Many Mexican migrants identified the U.S. citizenship of Puerto Ricans only indirectly, by discerning the unequal politics of citizenship through its substantive entitlements, such as access to various social welfare benefits. By perceiving Puerto Ricans as "welfare dependent," many Mexican migrants were also inclined to characterize Puerto Ricans as a group as inherently "lazy" in contradistinction to a sense of themselves as "hardworking." In contrast, Puerto Ricans racialized Mexicans as a group by recourse to an equation of undocumented immigration status with naturalized allegations of "submissiveness." Whereas Puerto Ricans tended to consider themselves to be politically savvy and skilled at navigating the inequalities of U.S. political institutions, they tended to see Mexicans as effectively "Third World" people, constitutively prone to docility and inured to extreme exploitation. Representations of Puerto Ricans as "lazy" and Mexicans as "submissive" referred not only to each group's ideas of the other's juridical status, therefore, but also affirmed their competing visions of their own inherent competences and capabilities as groups. These notions of distinct group virtues and failings, furthermore, had profoundly racialized implications for each group's presumed "deservingness" for the status of full members in the U.S. polity.

Conflicting notions of deservingness, likewise, provided a basis for still broader constructions of each group's putative "civility" or "modernity." We examine these divisive perspectives in chapter 4, where we analyze how Mexican migrants' perceptions of Puerto Ricans as "rude" or "uncivilized," and Puerto Ricans' inclinations to see Mexicans as "backward" or excessively "traditional," served to further sustain their divergent claims to the entitlements to U.S. citizenship. Moreover, in this chapter we also consider the ways in which both Mexican and Puerto Rican migrants deployed such competing notions of "civility" and "modernity" in relation to their own respective U.S.-born generations. U.S.-born or -raised Mexicans and Puerto Ricans, respectively, not only became representatives of the ways in which the migrants' "culture" was presumed to have been "lost" or to have become less "authentic," but, more importantly, these particular types of "Americanization" became inseparable from a kind of abjection that migrants equated with a criminalized, bad-mannered, and violent masculinity oftentimes associated with street gangs. Thus, migrants upheld these notions of their own "cultural" integrity against what they perceived as the advent among their children's generation of the racialized social status associated with becoming a mere U.S. "minority group," approaching or approximating Blackness.

In chapter 5 we consider the ways in which gendered identities and ideologies of family contributed further to the hierarchical organization of racialized differences between Mexicans and Puerto Ricans in Chicago. Mexicans and Puerto Ricans both tended to assume that the preservation of an "intact" (heteronormative) nuclear family depended upon the maintenance of a properly ordered patriarchy. This familial ideal, however, was widely assumed to require women to relinquish their own autonomy and, in effect, to be self-sacrificing, a quality that Puerto Ricans commonly attributed to Mexican women, and which Puerto Rican women often disavowed in their efforts of project themselves as "liberated." For their part, however, Mexicans seldom experienced their own families in the simplistic and romanticized terms that others projected onto them. Thus,

for both groups, the notion of an "intact" family became a site of ambivalence that revolved around the relative costs and advantages associated with
maintaining "traditional" families and, by implication, an "authentic" culture.
By defining group differences in terms of heteronormative gender relations
and ideologies of family, therefore, Mexicans and Puerto Ricans revisited their
respective assessments of one another's perceived entanglements with the "traditional" and the "modern." In this sense, what took the form of a discourse of
"cultural" differences was never extricable from a hierarchical scale of comparison concerned with each group's relative deservingness for proper membership
within the U.S. national polity.

Another prominent discourse of difference that might appear to be fundamentally concerned with "culture" revolved around assessments of language.
However, many scholars, more inclined to take Spanish language for granted
as a reliable and robust source of Latinidad, have seldom adequately examined
the ideologically charged meanings of language, as it is mobilized for competing claims of cultural authenticity. In chapter 6, we explore how Spanish
language was not a natural or automatic source of mutual recognition or Latino
unity, and frequently became a fertile source of further division. Mexicans and
Puerto Ricans in Chicago produced distinctions between one another based
on presumptions that hierarchically ranked the characteristically accented and
idiomatic Spanish spoken by each group according to evaluations of its overall
"correctness." Moreover, the politics of language was not confined only to varied
notions of "good" ("proper") or "bad" Spanish, but also encompassed disputes
over each group's relative capabilities in English, as well as competing claims
with respect to bilingualism and code-switching. Divisions along linguistic lines,
then, were intensified by allegations of "Spanglish" and "bad English." Notably,
these discourses of language difference between Mexicans and Puerto Ricans, as
well as between migrants and U.S.-born generations within each group, tended
to be hierarchically assessed in explicitly racialized relation to a presumed closeness to African American Blackness. Thus, even language—the one element
commonly presumed to supply a basis for Latino-identified unity between the
two groups—often served instead as a forcefully divisive basis for racializing
their divergent identities as "Mexican" or "Puerto Rican."

Having carefully scrutinized so many ways in which Mexican migrants and
Puerto Ricans deployed racialized discourses to uphold notions of the meaningful differences between one another, we proceed in chapter 7 to a consideration
of the various but often fractured ways in which formulations of shared Latino
identity did indeed emerge in our research. An exploration of the possibilities
and prospects for Latinidad as a viable basis for identity formation and enduring
coalitions has been a central concern of our study. The effective formulation
of Latinidad among Mexicans and Puerto Ricans in Chicago tended to coalesce not around notions of any putative "cultural" sameness or commonality,
but rather as a *racial* formation grounded on a sense of shared sociopolitical

circumstances and interests. However, these rehearsals of Latinidad were often fraught, and it was not uncommon to discern the operations of the divisive politics of race and citizenship, as well as the inequalities of class, as prominent sources of the trouble. Indeed, our examination of these diverse expressions of Latino commonalties of identity and interest in chapter 7 largely serves to reinforce this book's critical attention to the intersections of racialization and the unequal politics of citizenship. In our concluding chapter 8, then, we reconsider the lessons of our study by resituating our research in its particular historical and sociopolitical moment, and suggest some of the enduring significance and relevance of this work for ongoing dilemmas and conflicts for Latinos and all people of color in relation to U.S. nationalism as a racial formation of white supremacy.

CHAPTER 2

"Latino" Locations: The Politics of Space in Chicago

When De Genova first introduced himself in 1995 to an exceptionally mixed group of Latino workers whom he would be teaching English as a Second Language at a factory called Die-Hard Tool and Die—a group that included Mexican, Puerto Rican, Guatemalan, Salvadoran, Panamanian, and Bolivian migrants—it seemed a self-evident question when Beatriz Castro, a woman who had migrated from El Salvador, asked him, "Are you Mexican or Puerto Rican?"[1] Despite the heterogeneous Latinidad manifest in the room, even a Central American was inclined to presume that someone whom she perceived to be Latino in Chicago would inevitably have to be either Mexican or Puerto Rican. Today, Mexicans (including both migrants and those born or raised in the U.S.) constitute 70% of the Latino population within the city of Chicago, and Puerto Ricans comprise another 15%. As of 2000, these two groups together still accounted for 85% of all Latinos in Chicago; trailing far behind, the third largest Latino group (Guatemalans) represented only 3% of the total. Thus, although Chicago is counted among the most diversified areas of Latino settlement in the U.S.[2]—with seventeen Latin American national-origin groups, each represented by a presence of one thousand or more, as of the 2000 Census—the decisive debates and struggles concerning Latino Chicago still tend to be largely conceptualized as something that principally transpires between Mexicans and Puerto Ricans (cf. F. Padilla, 1985). Indeed, by the latter half of the twentieth century, Chicago had emerged not only as a major Latino metropolis, but moreover as the premier site where Mexicans and Puerto Ricans have both settled over the course of several decades and multiple generations. This distinctive history gestures toward the ways that the interrelations of Mexicans and Puerto Ricans in Chicago can inform analogous and increasingly common inter-Latino dynamics in other places, but it also calls our attention to the specificities of Chicago as a particular kind of urban space.

Space has been conventionally presupposed as a naturalized and self-evident "context" for social relations. The elusive appearance of space as a given and fixed precondition to be taken for granted is, however, indicative of precisely how fundamental space is for the broader constitution of social life. Rather than a mere background, space can be usefully understood as a social relation in itself, a social relation that therefore must be produced and reproduced, as well as reformulated and transformed. As Henri Lefebvre points out, with specific regard to the city and the urban sphere, space may be "the setting of struggle," but it is not only this; it is also "the stakes of that struggle" (1991[1974]:386). Indeed, differences in social space come to be produced through practice, through the creative ferments of sociopolitical struggles over domination and insubordination, across a variety of spatial scales—such as the urban, regional, national, and transnational—and give substance to ideologically burdened oppositions, such as those generated around the perceived boundaries of urban neighborhoods, or between "the inner city" and "the suburbs," "urban" and "rural," "center" and "periphery," or "local" and "global." Struggles over social space and the differences they produce, in short, are inseparable from more general conflicts over inequalities of power and wealth.

Space, therefore, is preeminently political, and the politics of space are historically specific. In Chicago, one of the most racially segregated cities in the U.S.,[3] ubiquitous distinctions about "neighborhoods" are virtually inseparable from their overt or submerged racial and also class-inflected meanings, and so have a pronounced importance for struggles over identity formation (cf. Bowden and Kreinberg, 1981). The politics of space, then, is necessarily implicated in racialization processes, and, likewise, the politics of race plays out in remarkably spatialized terms in Chicago. Far from neutral frames of reference for points on the map, the mere mention of "Humboldt Park" signaled to Chicagoans of any racialized group a particularly stigmatized image of "Puerto Rican"-ness, associated with criminality, poverty, and "welfare dependency"—even in spite of the fact that Puerto Ricans had by 2000 become a minority within that geographical area. Similarly, a simple reference to "26th Street" could automatically trigger discourses about Mexican "illegal aliens" or "gangs." The racialized connotations about space in Chicago certainly are projected by hegemonic institutions of white power, but also are simultaneously generated, debated, and contested within these Latino communities. Among Mexicans and Puerto Ricans, the differences of class, status, and citizenship *within* their respective racialized communities, as well as *between* them, similarly became meaningful through the politics of space. Thus, Mexicans who lived in the working-class suburb of Cicero or Puerto Ricans who live in neighborhoods northwest of Humboldt Park, for example, each invested the city's respective "Mexican" or "Puerto Rican" geographies with class and status significances coded in spatial terms. Likewise, Puerto Ricans in Humboldt Park could readily equate the entirety of "the South Side" with Mexicans and therefore "illegal immigrants," and Mexicans acquainted with Humboldt Park could likewise treat "Division Street" as a dangerous place where Puerto Ricans could be expected to routinely accost them.

Recognizing that the city was not merely the setting but also the stakes of these struggles, it is important to emphasize the historical specificity of this collaborative ethnography. The spatialized politics of both racialization and citizenship are historical processes, in a double sense: they are grounded in prior histories, but they are also thoroughly implicated in the making of history in the present. Thus, whereas chapter 1 addressed some of the crucial features of the histories of the relations between the U.S. nation-state and Mexicans and Puerto Ricans, respectively, this chapter will explore the more specific histories of each group's community formation processes and how these migrations have intersected in Chicago. The possibility of documenting the ways that history is always being made in the present—the ways that we are all implicated in the production, reproduction, and transformation of our social world in everyday life—is one of the defining and enduring potential strengths of ethnographic modes of research. The historical sections of this chapter, therefore, are followed by materials from our ethnographic research in the mid-1990s that begin to elucidate how the processes of community formation, and the spaces they produce, are ongoing endeavors and open-ended concerns that never come to be resolved once and for all time.

Historically, the politics of Latino coalition-building in Chicago has been deeply shaped by the remarkable preponderance of Mexicans and Puerto Ricans. When Ramos-Zayas telephoned an organization called the Latino Institute and asked a staff member the simple factual question of where the organization's office was located, for instance, the respondent explained that they were Downtown, immediately adding that this location in Chicago's central business district (a.k.a. "Downtown" or "the Loop") had been chosen in order to preserve their neutrality: "If we were located on the North Side, Mexicans would complain that we are too Puerto Rican. If we were located on the South Side, Puerto Ricans would complain that we are too Mexican. So we are here, Downtown, and that's the end of the problem." Indeed, these strategic calculations of the Latino Institute not only revealed the tremendous extent to which "Latino" politics in Chicago tended to be poised precariously between Mexicans and Puerto Ricans, but, furthermore, how the salient difference between these two groups was symbolically spatialized—broadly mapped onto the distinction between the South Side and the North Side. There were pronouncedly spatialized divisions, in short, that complicated the imagining of any conceivable Latino cartography of the city.

Rather than merely take for granted that such spaces correspond to "ethnic enclaves," we emphasize that the active work of producing these spaces is in itself part of the wider process through which group differences are discursively marked and sustained. Renowned as a "city of neighborhoods," and likewise notorious for its racial segregation, Chicago's distinctive urban conjunctures of race and space necessarily supply this study with a degree of irreducible particularity that should underscore how the broader histories discussed in chapter 1 have been configured and continue to be elaborated in ways that are distinct among Latinos in Chicago. Furthermore, to the extent that the racialized differences between Mexicans and Puerto Ricans have become inscribed in the spatial fabric of the city, so also have the inequalities deriving from the politics of citizenship become mapped onto these distinct urban spaces. Thus, neighborhoods marked as "Mexican" or "Puerto Rican" also became variously stigmatized by multiple and intersecting discourses concerning Mexican "illegal aliens" and Puerto Rican "welfare dependency," as well as the more generic discourses of "crime," "drugs," "violence," and "gangs" readily associated with the poverty of both groups. Furthermore, Mexicans and Puerto Ricans themselves commonly resorted to these discourses of race and citizenship to distance themselves from the stigmas attached to these particular urban spaces. In this way, to varying degrees, they participated in reproducing the very politics of space that served as a rubric for the enforcement of their own and each other's subjugation. The spatial politics of the city, therefore, was thoroughly implicated in sustaining the divide between Mexicans and Puerto Ricans that so often obstructed the possibilities for the emergence of a sense of community or a shared identity as Latinos.

Mexican Migration to Chicago, and Community Formation on the South Side

As the United States' quintessential railroad metropolis during the nineteenth century and the early decades of the twentieth century (Cronon, 1991:83), Chicago quickly became an important (one might say, inevitable) destination for Mexican migrant labor, the early patterns of which corresponded so thoroughly to the expansion of railroads (Año Nuevo Kerr, 1976; Cardoso, 1980; Reisler, 1976; Rosales, 1978; cf. Clark, 1908; Gamio, 1930; A. Jones, 1928; Taylor, 1932). Already by 1890, every railroad in Mexico was connected directly or indirectly to all forty-eight states of the continental U.S. (Cardoso, 1980:14–17). Mexican/migrant workers were employed by the railroads in Chicago at least as early as 1907 (Clark, 1908:477). The Mexican population in Chicago first achieved a notable size, however, in 1916 (Taylor, 1932:27). During World War I and again notably during the strike wave of 1919, Mexicans were enthusiastically recruited on deliberately racial grounds alongside of African Americans from the southern U.S. to migrate, often initially as strikebreakers, as a reserve labor supply for large industry, especially in steel, meat packing, and the railroads (Taylor, 1932:117; cf. Acuña, 1981:130–31; Año Nuevo Kerr, 1976:25–26; Rosales, 1978:92–93; cf. Calavita, 1984: 135–37, 147–51). Mexican migrants were originally enlisted into the service of U.S. industry as "temporary" replacement workers who would alleviate labor shortages caused by the exigencies of war-related production, coupled later, after the U.S. entry into active participation in combat, with the mass transfer of urban workers into military service. Despite the purportedly "temporary" status of Mexican labor, however, already as early as the 1920s, the largest single employer of Mexican migrants anywhere in the U.S. was Inland Steel's mill in East Chicago, Indiana, an industrial suburb southeast of Chicago, and by 1925, thirty-five percent of Inland's workforce was

Mexican (Rosales, 1978:145). By 1928, Mexican/migrant workers accounted for 43% of all railroad track labor and 11% of total employment in the most important steel and meatpacking plants; the disproportionate majority worked in low-wage "unskilled" positions, and two-thirds of Mexican families were found to be living below the poverty level (Taylor, 1932:41, 77–79, 155, 157; cf. Año Nuevo Kerr, 1976:25–26). Twenty years later, little had changed: a 1944 survey of Chicago employers established that Mexican workers continued to be predominantly concentrated in "unskilled" jobs in these same three industries (Año Nuevo Kerr, 1976:143).

From only 1,000 Mexicans in Chicago prior to 1916, the community had grown to over 25,000 in 1930, by which time there were established barrios in the South Chicago neighborhood (in the shadow of steel mills), in the Back of the Yards area (adjacent to the stockyards and meatpacking houses), and in the vicinity of Jane Addams's Hull House in the southern portion of the Near West Side (near rail yards) (A. Jones, 1928; Taylor, 1932). During the economic recession of 1921–22, 65% of the Mexicans in Chicago lost their jobs, registering the highest unemployment levels for any group, and while some opted to return to Mexico, others were forcibly repatriated (Betancur et al., 1993:114; cf. Taylor, 1932:39, 277–78). By the mid-1920s, largely because Mexicans lived in close proximity with whites and were perceived to be competitors for whites' jobs, the arrest rates for Mexicans and levels of police violence against Mexicans in Chicago were higher than for Mexicans in the Southwest, and although they were arrested predominantly for rather minor offenses, Mexicans' arrest rates and the proportion of Mexicans killed by police surpassed those of virtually every other migrant group in Chicago (Rosales, 1999:28, 51–54, 79–80, 84). Community-based organizations emerged with the express purpose of defending Mexicans' legal rights (Rosales, 1999:28). With the advent of the Great Depression, Mexicans were targeted for mass expulsion. In 1930 alone, nearly 22,000 Mexicans (migrants as well as their U.S.-born children) were repatriated or forcibly deported from Illinois; although Mexicans in Illinois only accounted for 2% of the total U.S. Mexican population in 1930, the number expelled from Illinois comprised 5.3% of all Mexicans repatriated. Due to the forced removals of both Mexican migrants and their U.S. citizen children during the 1930s, Chicago's Mexican community was reduced by 36% to 16,000 by the end of the decade (Año Nuevo Kerr, 1976:69–77; d. Weber, 1982:213–69), only then to begin growing anew, especially with the added influx of more than 15,000 braceros contracted to work on the railroads following the advent of World War II (Año Nuevo Kerr, 1976:121). The Chicago district (which included Wisconsin and Iowa, as well as northern Illinois) had accounted for 11% of the total number of braceros contracted nationally between mid-1943 and the autumn of 1945 (Año Nuevo Kerr, 1976:121). Although the provision of braceros to the railroad industry in Chicago was terminated with the end of the war, the renewed migration to Chicago continued unabated, and already by 1947 (ironically, on Mexican Independence Day, September 16), the *Chicago Tribune* made its first report of the apprehension of "illegal Mexican aliens" in the city (Año Nuevo Kerr, 1976:131, 162). Between 1940 and 1960, the Mexican population in the city more than tripled to 55,600. Still, the dramatic acceleration of Mexican migration to Chicago began only in the late 1960s and early '70s. Between 1960 and 1990, the Mexican population residing within the municipal boundaries of the city increased by more than six times—from 55,600 to 352,560—and by nearly ten times—to 550,000—in the Chicago metropolitan area. Today, according to the U.S. Census for the year 2000, Chicago is the second largest urban concentration of Mexican settlement in the country, with numbers over 1.1 million in the metropolitan area, and over 530,000 in the city (comprising over 18% of the population within the city limits).[4] In 1980, Chicago's Mexican population was 48% "foreign-born" (Caruso and Camacho, 1985:9). By 2000, migrants constituted an even greater proportion of Chicago's Mexican community: 55% of the Mexican population in the city, and 52% in the metropolitan area, were "foreign-born."[5] Although Chicago's Mexican community has already reproduced itself over four or five generations, the absolute majority continues to be comprised of those who have themselves migrated from Mexico, and the disproportionate majority are either migrants or their children.[6]

The historic Mexican barrios of Chicago's South Side have endured and dramatically expanded into distinctively Mexican working-class and working poor neighborhoods. The Near West Side (Hull House) neighborhood, where Mexican migrants first settled because of its proximity to railroad yards, was ultimately decimated by "urban renewal" projects associated with the construction of expressways and the University of Illinois's Chicago campus during the 1950s and '60s (Rosen, 1980). Much of its Mexican community, however, was merely displaced to the adjacent Pilsen neighborhood immediately to the south and southwest, and continued to be the anchor of what was long considered to be the most important "port of entry" neighborhood for newly arrived Mexican migrants, eventually extending itself further westward and transforming the South Lawndale neighborhood into what has since come to be known as Little Village. Between 1960 and 1980, the Mexican population of Pilsen and Little Village skyrocketed from slightly under 7,000 to more than 83,000 (Caruso and Camacho, 1985:8). The small Mexican enclave that originally was relegated to the most foul-smelling area immediately adjacent to the Union stockyards and the meatpacking plants ultimately came to encompass all of the neighborhood that continues to be known as the Back of the Yards.[7] Likewise, the barrio on the far Southeast Side of the city, where Mexicans first settled due to employment at U.S. Steel's South Works, over time came to encompass much of the neighborhood known as South Chicago (cf. Kornblum, 1974). Although the stockyards and major meatpacking companies shut down their Chicago operations and had almost completely relocated by the 1950s, and, similarly, the railroads and steel subsequently became virtually moribund industries which no longer hire much newly arrived migrant labor in the city, these same South Side Mexican neighborhoods have continued to be vibrant communities. This seeming paradox underscores the fact that Chicago has been an increasingly prominent destination for Mexican/migrant labor in the United States, even as the total population of the city declined in the wake of a dramatic loss of jobs in manufacturing (Betancur et al., 1993; cf. Squires et al., 1987:23–60; cf. Teaford, 1993).

Despite this long history of Mexican community formation through the greater part of the twentieth century, Mexicans in Chicago (including those raised in the U.S.) have continued to be concentrated in so-called "low-skill" occupations, with roughly half holding jobs as industrial operatives, fabricators, and other types of manual laborers. A very significant proportion of the rest work in low-paid service jobs, such as restaurants. As late as the 1980s, only 6.4% of the Mexican workforce in Chicago held managerial or professional positions of any kind.[8] Beginning in 1970 and continuing consistently through the 1990s, Latinos in Chicago (among whom Mexicans were the disproportionate majority) were more than twice as likely to be factory workers as whites or African Americans, and were likewise employed for the lowest average wages in manufacturing (Betancur et al., 1993:125–32). Indeed, during the 1990s, the proportion of Latinos employed in factory work in Chicago (39.2%) was double the U.S. national rate of Latino employment in manufacturing (19.6%), and also twice the percentage of Chicago residents in general.[9] All of these indices serve to underscore the fact that Mexican migrants, and the undocumented in particular, have come to constitute an ever more important segment of the working class in general in metropolitan Chicago, and occupy an especially central place at the "de-skilled" core of industrial production.

The upsurge of Mexican migration after 1965 quickly became synonymous with "illegality." Concentrated overwhelmingly in the Chicago metropolitan area, the number of INS apprehensions of undocumented migrants in Illinois escalated dramatically during the late 1960s and early '70s. The number of INS apprehensions increased to roughly 800% of its 1965 level by 1971, when a Chicago-based State of Illinois Legislative Investigating Commission, comprised of state senators and congressmen, published an alarmist report on "The Illegal Mexican Alien Problem" (Illinois Legislative Investigating Commission, 1971:1, 9). The Commission presumed that the statistics concerning who was *arrested* as an "illegal alien" transparently provided an accurate depiction of the broader phenomenon of undocumented migration, and seamlessly identified which national-origin groups were really culpable for "the illegal alien problem." Thus, the report was explicit in its choice to racialize migrant "illegality" as a specifically "Mexican problem." Mexican nationals accounted for 85% of the 8,728 INS apprehensions during the 1971 fiscal year. In light of these enforcement patterns, the report's summary declared its simplistic reasoning: "Since the illegal alien situation in Illinois primarily concerns Mexican nationals, this report will be restricted to that facet of the problem" (Illinois Legislative Investigating Commission, 1971:1).[10] The Commission's findings identified by name a variety of firms (predominantly manufacturing companies), located throughout the city as well as several industrial suburbs, which had repeatedly been raided by the INS and been found to chronically hire undocumented migrants. Notably, included among these were very large employers, such as the nationally recognized candy manufacturers Brach's and Tootsie Roll (Illinois Legislative Investigating Commission, 1971:32–33).

With the advent of severe economic recession in the early to mid-1970s, the INS dramatically intensified its campaign of workplace raids and neighborhood roundups and mass apprehensions in Chicago. This period has become notorious not only for raids in factories but also in public parks, movie theaters, and on the streets in front of Mexican grocery stores (Mora, n.d.:30). Prior to a federal injunction prohibiting the practice, the INS could detain people on the street with impunity on the basis of their appearance or language, demand proof of citizenship or legal residency, and take the accused into custody until someone else provided documentation vindicating them. This form of INS harassment inevitably persecuted not only Mexican and other Latino noncitizen migrants, but also Puerto Rican and Mexican U.S. citizens. In response, in 1974 and again in 1976, large protest demonstrations denounced this racial profiling of the Mexican community in particular, and Latinos in general, provoking the INS to establish for the first time in its history a community relations committee in Chicago (Belenchia, 1982:123, 127). The pervasive racialized equation of "Mexican"-ness with migrant "illegality," however, was in no way eradicated. Still in the 1990s, an analysis of INS apprehensions in the Chicago area revealed that INS raids almost exclusively targeted Mexicans. Although the INS estimated in a 1992 study that Mexicans comprised only 44% of Illinois's undocumented migrants, of the 1,562 undocumented workers arrested between January 1996 and June 1997 in metropolitan Chicago, the INS could provide demographic information on 1,433, of whom a staggering 98.9% were Latinos. Still more astounding, however, 96.4% were migrants from Mexico.[11]

Although manufacturing employment in Chicago had peaked in 1947 and already registered a loss of nearly 160,000 jobs by 1963 as the city began to undergo a protracted period of economic restructuring (Betancur et al., 1993:124; cf. Teaford, 1993), much of Chicago's "deindustrialization" was in fact an effect of an aggressive wave of capital disinvestment by industries fleeing from the city, especially in reaction to the explosive political militancy of the civil rights struggles of the late 1960s. Consequently, while large industry effectively evacuated the area altogether, smaller manufacturing firms simply relocated to Chicago's suburbs.[12] Undocumented Mexican/migrant labor rapidly became a racialized solution to an already racialized political crisis of labor subordination (De Genova, 1998). During the 1970s, largely following the factory jobs out of the "inner city," the number of Mexicans in Chicago's suburbs more than quadrupled, from 25,555 to over 113,000 by 1980 (Squires et al., 1987:111).[13] By 2000, that number had quadrupled again, perhaps to as much as 461,000.[14] Thus, there has developed a quite significant Mexican presence throughout much of the metropolitan area that renders anachronistic, at best, any effort to circumscribe Chicago's Mexican communities within the original barrios on the South Side; instead, it is much more appropriate to recognize the emergence of a metropolitan Mexican Chicago (De Genova, 1998; in press).[15]

This dramatic spatial dispersion notwithstanding, however, it is not by chance that the Pilsen neighborhood, in particular, or the combined Pilsen/Little Village area of Chicago's Near Southwest Side, more generally, are very commonly celebrated as, in the words of one observer, "the capital of the Mexican diaspora in the Midwest today" (Davis, 2000:40–41). The mid-1970s were not only a period of mass Mexican migration to Chicago, in the midst of capital flight from the city, economic recession, and intensified policing against undocumented Mexican migrants, but also a period of unprecedented Mexican political mobilization in the city. The symbolic and often practical center of that organizing was the Pilsen neighborhood. Already in 1920 and throughout the 1920s, the Near West Side (Hull House) barrio that ultimately generated the Mexican community in Pilsen had become the largest of Chicago's Mexican neighborhoods (Taylor, 1932:54; cf. Belenchia, in Walton and Salces, 1977:17). The movement of Mexicans, primarily from the Near West Side, into the Pilsen neighborhood immediately to the southwest, began in the 1950s. Pilsen (a.k.a. the Lower West Side) was 0.5% Mexican in 1950, but 14% Mexican within ten years (Belenchia, in Walton and Salces, 1977:21). By 1970, Pilsen had become 55% Mexican, of whom 22% had migrated from Mexico within only the five-year period since 1965 (Año Nuevo Kerr, 1976:194). Furthermore, Pilsen was the only Chicago neighborhood where Latinos constituted an absolute majority.[16] Not only the largest, it was also the poorest Mexican neighborhood in the city and ranked in the bottom fifth among the city's most impoverished areas. By the early 1970s, Pilsen had come to be widely considered by younger Mexicans raised in the U.S. as the center of community-based political activity devoted to the promotion of the interests of Mexicans as a distinct group with specific interests (Mora, n.d.:29). In her 1976 dissertation, Louise Año Nuevo Kerr described Pilsen as "a settlement which would for the foreseeable future become insistently more 'ethnic' rather than less" (1976:205). During that period, Pilsen was home to the creation of a great variety of grassroots community organizations, representing a broad spectrum of political perspectives, which devoted themselves primarily to struggles for better public services, education, and housing. Nevertheless, throughout the period, Pilsen continued to be beleaguered by poverty and neglect. By 1980, nearly one-fourth of all housing units were overcrowded in Pilsen, in contrast to less than 10% of housing in the city as a whole. In 1982, the dropout rate for Pilsen's public high school had reached an astounding 49.4% (Caruso and Camacho, 1985:8).

The most prominent Mexican political figure to emerge from Pilsen's political awakening during the 1970s was Rudy Lozano. Notably, while Lozano would ultimately seek to achieve reforms and advance the interests of Mexicans through electoral politics as an "independent Democrat" working against the Democratic Party machine, his political credibility was built through his efforts to organize undocumented Mexican/migrant workers who were themselves ineligible to vote. After becoming an organizer for the International Ladies' Garment Workers' Union (ILGWU), Lozano determined in 1979 that one of his principal objectives would be to organize the overwhelmingly Mexican/migrant and commonly undocumented workers employed in Chicago tortilla factories, beginning with Tortillería Del Rey. Del Rey was the largest firm in the small but highly exploitative industry, employing over 110 workers between its two plants in the Pilsen barrio (Piña, n.d.:62). Some of the workers were even housed in barrack-like conditions on the shop floor of the Del Rey factory (Piña, n.d.:64). Confronted with the union organizing campaign, Del Rey threatened to notify the INS of the undocumented status of union sympathizers, and then, two weeks before the first union certification elections, evidently invited the INS to conduct its first raid in a Del Rey plant in five years, culminating in the arrest of eighteen workers (Piña, n.d.:62–63). In late 1982, Lozano and other organizers were threatened at gunpoint on the street in front of the Del Rey plant by one of the pro-company workers (Piña, n.d.:64; Rosenfeld, 1993:5). In 1983, although he continued to be actively involved in the Del Rey organizing campaign and consumer boycott, Lozano took an official leave of absence from the union to run for public office for the first time. That year, he was a prominent participant in Harold Washington's ultimately successful campaign to become Chicago's first African American and first nonwhite mayor. Simultaneously, Lozano also put himself forward in a Democratic Party primary bid to become the first Latino alderman of Chicago's 22nd Ward (which encompassed much of the increasingly densely populated Mexican/migrant neighborhood of Little Village, where Lozano lived).[17] Lozano ultimately lost to the machine incumbent, coming within mere handfuls of votes of an electoral runoff.[18]

On June 8 of that same year, Lozano was assassinated in his home. The circumstances surrounding Rudy Lozano's murder have remained obscure and were never satisfactorily investigated (Rosenfeld, 1993). Notably, the investigation was conducted by then–Cook County state's attorney Richard M. Daley, the son of Chicago's deceased mayor and Democratic Party machine boss Richard J. Daley. Richard M. Daley had himself been a competitor for the mayor's office against Washington in the Democratic Party primary election earlier that year. Daley's investigation of the Lozano assassination was eventually denounced by an independent Commission for Justice for Rudy Lozano, not only as "inept, erratic . . . ultimately bungled," and in effect, deliberately negligent, but furthermore as a cynical, politically motivated attempt at character assassination based on implicitly racialized allegations that the Mexican politician's murder may have been entangled with street gangs and narcotics dealing (Report of the Commission for Justice for Rudy Lozano, in Taller de Estudios Comunitarios, n.d.:77; cf. Rosenfeld, 1993:5). Eventually, in 1989, in what has been widely seen as a reconsolidation of the white Democratic Party political machine whose hegemony had been temporarily disrupted and partially displaced by Washington's election, and with the support of a significant portion of the Latino political establishment, the younger Daley succeeded to become Chicago's mayor, and has remained in office throughout the 1990s and up to the present.[19]

The political organization of Mexicans in Chicago, however, has not been the narrow affair of Mexicans born or raised in the U.S. who are predominantly U.S. citizens. The dynamic interconnections between the U.S. and Mexico created and cultivated by transnational migration have also ensured the emergence of a Mexican Chicago that has been increasingly implicated in the ongoing affairs and imagined futures of Mexico itself (De Genova, 1998; in press). As early as 1928, José Vasconcelos, one of Mexico's preeminent public intellectuals and former secretary of education, carried his presidential campaign to Mexicans in Chicago (Skirius, 1976:487). In his first bid for the Mexican presidency in 1988, as part of a landmark campaign challenging decades of one-party rule, Cuauhtémoc Cárdenas, the candidate of Mexico's center-left opposition party, the Partido de la Revolución Democrática (PRD), resumed this transnational tradition of Mexican national politics in the U.S. and vigorously sought support among Mexican migrants in Chicago. During the 1990s, moreover, Mexicans in Chicago played a singularly monumental role in political struggles over Mexican electoral reform, democratization, and the substance of "double nationality," by advancing the demand for the right of migrant Mexican citizens in the U.S. to vote in Mexican elections. In 1994, the Chicago-based Consejo Electoral Ciudadano (Citizens' Electoral Council) organized symbolic elections throughout the Chicago area, as well as in California and Texas, in which thousands of migrants enacted their rights as Mexican citizens to vote in the presidential elections in Mexico (Ross Pineda, 1999). The Chicago-based founder of the Consejo, Raúl Ross Pineda, had originally come to Chicago as an undocumented migrant in 1987 (Gómez, 1999:248). He went on to become the coordinator of the movement called Nuestro Voto en el 2000 (Our Vote in the Year 2000 Coalition of Mexicans Abroad) (Ross Pineda, 1999). During Mexico's national elections in 2000, with the support of the PRD and its three-time presidential candidate Cuauhtémoc Cárdenas (by then, mayor of Mexico City), Ross Pineda, the most prominent advocate for Mexican/migrant voting rights, running his campaign from his base in Chicago, became the first Mexican residing outside of the country to run as a candidate for Mexico's congress, the Chamber of Deputies (Arias Jirasek and Tortolero, 2001; cf. Ross Pineda, 1999). Notably, the cover of Ross Pineda's book *Los mexicanos y el voto sin fronteras* (*Mexicans and the Vote without Borders*) features a mural commemorating the border-crossing travails of undocumented migrants that looms above a Pilsen street corner.

In Pilsen and Little Village, the heritage of Mexican political mobilization has not only left a legacy of well-established community-based organizations, but also educational and cultural institutions and a variety of public symbols that provide a testament to the production of these urban spaces as distinctively "Mexican." Pilsen's public high school, the product of protracted community organizing in the 1970s, is named for Benito Juárez. Half a mile away, situated on a Chicago Park District site, is the Mexican Fine Arts Center Museum. Nearby is the José Clemente Orozco Academy, a public middle school. Pilsen's public library is named for none other than Rudy Lozano. In Little Village, a consolidated Catholic church and parochial school is named "Our Lady of Tepeyac" for Mexico's patron saint, the Virgin of Guadalupe. Along Little Village's Marshall Boulevard, furthermore, one encounters a series of monumental statues of prominent figures in Mexican history, officially named the Paseo de los Grandes Mexicanos—the Plaza of Great Mexicans. More than in any other area of the city, the public monuments, statues, street murals, parades, religious processions, and festivals of Pilsen and Little Village sustain a visible manifesto of the defining "Mexican"-ness of these South Side barrios (cf. Baker, 1995; Davalos, 1993; Stark, 1981). Although Mexican communities are evident throughout much of the Chicago metropolitan area, this abundance of public institutions and spatial practices palpably marks these two contiguous South Side neighborhoods as the symbolic center of gravity for Mexican Chicago. That these same neighborhoods are routinely inscribed as sites of migrant "illegality," youth "delinquency," street "gangs," illicit "drug dealing," and "violence" by hegemonic spatial practices such as INS raids and "zero-tolerance" policing, of course, is likewise testimony to the extent to which the politics of space in Chicago is also thoroughly invested by a contest over the racialized salience of that "Mexican"-ness.

Puerto Rican Migration to Chicago and Community Formation on the North Side

The Puerto Rican community of Chicago, as well as smaller Puerto Rican areas throughout the Midwest, largely arose as a result of efforts on the part of government and private business to meet regional labor needs while simultaneously regulating and constraining the concentration of Puerto Ricans on the U.S. mainland. It was not until the late 1940s that Puerto Rican contract laborers started arriving en masse in Chicago, first recruited in 1946 by an employment agency called Castle, Barton, and Associates to serve as foundry and domestic workers.[20] Labor-contract (and seasonal) migration was vigorously redirected to the Midwest, rather than its prior northeastern destinations, after New York City's Puerto Rican population more than quadrupled from 61,000 to 245,000 during the 1940s, and then more than doubled again to nearly 613,000 by 1960 (F. Padilla, 1987:56). As manufacturing jobs in New York City were quickly disappearing by the late 1950s, the "problem" of a disproportionately high concentration of Puerto Ricans in New York became a primary motivation for steering Puerto Rican migration to Chicago. Indeed, by 1960, there were over 32,000 Puerto Ricans living in Chicago; of these, 59.4% of all Puerto Ricans employed in Chicago worked as "unskilled" operatives and other manual laborers, mainly in manufacturing, and another 11.7% were service workers (although none any longer worked in domestic labor); only 2.8% were employed as managers or professionals of any kind (F. Padilla, 1985:44; 1987:111).[21] Within ten years, the number of Puerto Ricans in Chicago had increased by 144% to 79,000.

New York City's so-called "Puerto Rican problem" became a cautionary tale for agencies charged with the responsibility of "integrating" the newcomers into Chicago neighborhoods (Welfare Council of Metropolitan Chicago, 1954). From the outset, governmental agencies were committed to keeping the newly arrived Puerto Ricans separate from the Mexican community in Chicago. The director of the Commonwealth of Puerto Rico Office in Chicago, in collaboration with the Welfare Council of Metropolitan Chicago, focused on "urging Puerto Ricans not to settle down with any Spanish-speaking people, but to distribute themselves all over the city in Polish, Italian, Czechoslovak and other areas . . . [and] stressing Puerto Ricans' scattering all over the city and warning against the formation of colonies or residence with the Mexicans."[22] Indeed, prior to 1970, the defining feature of Puerto Rican residential patterns was precisely the dispersion of Puerto Ricans into minoritized concentrations located in a variety of predominantly white neighborhoods on the city's North Side, as well as a few similarly small concentrations in neighborhoods on the city's South and West Sides (F. Padilla, 1985:40–42; 1987:117–23).

Despite government efforts to prevent Puerto Ricans from "forming colonies" with the Mexicans, however, Puerto Ricans and Mexicans did indeed share social and physical spaces from the very early stages of Puerto Rican arrival in Chicago in the late 1940s. The Chicago Catholic Archdiocese inadvertently played a critical role in bringing together two traditionally Catholic Spanish-speaking populations in the religious and social activities of local parishes. In the early years of Puerto Rican settlement, the Catholic Church often served as a space of social interactions and networking between Puerto Ricans and Mexicans. Likewise, the predominantly Mexican North Side nightclub "Rancho Grande," identified in Elena Padilla's 1947 study, provided a congenial space where Puerto Rican women, employed as domestic workers, would meet to socialize, eat Mexican food, and dance to various types of Latin American music, and inevitably served as a social mixer where these Puerto Rican women made their first contacts with the Mexican community, and sometimes became involved romantically with Mexican men (E. Padilla, 1947:86, 87–88).[23] Furthermore, Mexican organizations sometimes extended their services and fraternity to Puerto Ricans. The Club Azteca sponsored a dance to raise disaster-relief funds for hurricane victims in Puerto Rico, for instance, and the Mexican Civic Committee assisted dissatisfied Puerto Rican workers by directing them to alternative employment options and housing opportunities in the homes of Mexican families (E. Padilla, 1947:54, 88).[24] Indeed, although she noted that Puerto Ricans disliked being identified as Mexicans and developed "attitudes of dislike towards Mexicans," and that "disputes along nationality lines" were frequently evident (1947:90), in her 1947 study, Padilla even predicted that Puerto Rican migrants would tend to become "Mexicanized," as she detected significant numbers seeking the refuge of residence in extant Spanish-speaking communities (1947:63, 71–72, 93, 98).

Once a far more substantial migration had gathered momentum through the 1950s and into the '60s, however, the majority of Puerto Ricans tended not to move into the Mexican neighborhoods of the South Side and instead could be found primarily in highly racially segregated enclaves within various predominantly white neighborhoods bordering Lake Michigan, to the north of Chicago's Downtown (M. Martínez, 1989; F. Padilla, 1987:78–98). Despite the relatively delayed formation of geographically identifiable Puerto Rican communities in Chicago, however, Puerto Rican *colonias* did nonetheless emerge. In the 1950s, for instance, the Catholic Youth Organization assisted Puerto Rican contract workers to find housing in and around the Hotel Lincoln, in the vicinity of the intersection of Clark Street and North Avenue at the edge of Lincoln Park on Chicago's North Side lakefront (M. Martínez, 1989:97). The fact that these incipient Puerto Rican communities often took shape in areas that would soon become particularly desirable as profitable real estate reinvestment areas due to their proximity to the lake and to Downtown, however, ensured that Puerto Rican Chicago would continue to contend with the disruptions associated with displacement and dispersion. The city's "urban renewal" projects and "integration" efforts contributed to the processes of Puerto Rican displacement throughout the 1950s and '60s (Belenchia, in Walton and Salces, 1977:31–32; Belenchia, 1982:125; M. Martínez, 1989; F. Padilla, 1987:117–23). Notably, in this period, Puerto Ricans were often concentrated in the Near North Side, Lincoln Park, and Lakeview neighborhoods. These same areas later came to be thoroughly gentrified during the 1970s and '80s, and now are showcases for some of the city's highest real estate values (cf. Baker, 1995).

During the 1990s, many Puerto Ricans in Chicago still recalled the era when the North Side's gentrified areas had been home to Puerto Rican communities. "Look at this now . . . all these artsy stores and bourgie restaurants were not here before," commented Melvin Rodríguez, a Puerto Rican who lived in Humboldt Park, next door to Ramos-Zayas during the period of her research. Rodríguez routinely expressed such sentiments whenever he drove through the now fashionable section of Lakeview where he had spent his youth, which by the 1990s had come to be officially recognized and marketed as "Boys Town," Chicago's gay neighborhood. Indeed, prior to his family's residence in Lakeview, when Melvin and his sisters were still children during the 1960s, the Puerto Rican area where he had lived was only a short walk away from the exclusive Gold Coast.[25] "I remember how I used to deliver newspapers to these rich people's buildings . . . I always noticed how even the hallways of those buildings were warmer than any part of my house in the winter. I was about eight years old," Melvin remembered bitterly. Puerto Rican residence in many such areas was ultimately shortlived, as gentrification persistently displaced poor and working-class communities from one North Side neighborhood after another throughout the latter decades of the twentieth century.

By the late 1960s, most Puerto Ricans in Chicago either had been displaced or opted to relocate to the Division Street barrio extending from West Town to Humboldt Park on the city's Near Northwest Side. Only a few subway stops from Downtown Chicago, the intersection of these two adjacent neighborhoods, West Town and Humboldt Park, with a third, Logan Square, farther north along the same mass transit line, came to serve as a point of regroupment and as the principal "port of entry" for recent Puerto Rican migrants. Notably, Puerto Ricans who had been living in the Near West Side area, in the East and West Garfield Park neighborhoods on the city's West Side, and in Woodlawn on the South Side—the latter three of which were areas that were rapidly becoming virtually homogeneous African American neighborhoods—virtually evacuated these communities completely in favor of the newly emerging Puerto Rican barrio (cf. F. Padilla, 1987:83–86).[26] Whereas the decline in Puerto Rican residence from the rapidly gentrifying Near North Side area was a remarkable 58% during the decade of the 1960s, from Woodlawn, and East and West Garfield Park, the relocation of Puerto Ricans was consistently, and astoundingly, over 90% (cf. F. Padilla, 1987:83). The stark white-Black racial segregation of residential patterns in much of the city, therefore, was clearly one of the decisive motivations for Puerto Ricans to finally manifest such a forceful desire to establish their own distinct racialized enclave on the North Side. As early as 1965, police brutality in this growing barrio served as a flashpoint for community organizing, when two Puerto Ricans were arrested after police broke into their Division Street home and then repeatedly subjected them to group beatings in police custody. Then, again in June of 1966, immediately following the first annual Puerto Rican Day Parade, police brutality touched off what has been called "the first Puerto Rican riot in the history of the United States" (F. Padilla, 1985:46–50; 1987:123–25, 144–55).[27] The events, which lasted three days and nights, began when a white police officer shot and wounded a twenty-year-old Puerto Rican man, Aracelis Cruz. This young man was alleged to be a gang member and the police claimed that they suspected him to have been armed. The outrage of the community was inflamed when the police unleashed trained dogs to disperse angry onlookers and a Puerto Rican bystander was bitten. Chicago mayor Richard J. Daley publicly blamed the unrest on "unthinking and irresponsible individuals and gangs . . . seeking a climate of violence and uncertainty" (F. Padilla, 1987:150).

The Puerto Rican "riots" were a local expression of the more general climate of radical politics and racial militancy in Chicago during the 1960s. Chicago was the focus of national attention during the summer of 1966, when the city became the scene of civil rights marches against racial segregation in housing, culminating with the summit meeting of Martin Luther King, Jr., and the Chicago Freedom Movement, and which were met with organized white hostility and violence and subsequent confrontations between African Americans and police in Black neighborhoods (Anderson and Pickering 1986). The Puerto Rican community in West Town and Humboldt Park was still in its formative stages at the time, however, and thus the 1966 events shaped the barrio's destiny in significant ways. The 1966 riots were the first widely publicized collective action attributed to Puerto Ricans in Chicago.[28] Regardless of whether or not most barrio residents had approved of, participated in, or condemned the riots, Humboldt Park immediately became an urban space definitively associated with Puerto Ricans, as both the people and the neighborhood became synonymous with civil rights unrest and conflict, and so were effectively criminalized.

These galvanizing events served as a basis not only for the creation of specifically Puerto Rican–identified organizations but also for the consolidation a geographically based notion of Puerto Rican community that had been deferred for over twenty years by the group's prior history of dispersal throughout the city. By 1970, the West Town neighborhood was already more than 39% Latino, and the largest Puerto Rican community in the city; furthermore, like Pilsen, it was among the poorest fifth of Chicago's neighborhoods (Belenchia, in Walton and Salces, 1977:31–32; Belenchia, 1982:126). By 1980, the Division Street barrio alone accounted for 42% of all Chicago Puerto Ricans (F. Padilla, 1987:90; cf. N. González, 1990:48). Already in the 1970s, within less than a decade, the West Town–Humboldt Park barrio had come to be marked as the distinctively "Puerto Rican" section of Chicago, and boasted the largest Puerto Rican community in the Midwest. The proliferation of Puerto Rican *colmados* (grocery stores), barbershops, restaurants, and ambulatory *fritoleros* (fritter cooks), moreover, pointed to the entrepreneurial possibilities fostered by the demand for Puerto Rican–identified goods and services on the part of the rapidly expanding and increasingly concentrated Puerto Rican population (cf. F. Padilla, 1987:91).

The consolidation of a geographically identifiable Puerto Rican community likewise presented new opportunities for political self-assertion. Many recent migrants and second-generation Puerto Ricans in Chicago were coming of age in the late 1960s and the 1970s, and the nature of grassroots politics was deeply impacted by the rapid social transformations and political militancy of the period (Anderson and Pickering, 1986; Rodríguez-Morazzani, 1998b; An. Torres, 1998). The increasingly bold political radicalism of the time enhanced collective awareness of the plethora of socioeconomic problems affecting Puerto Ricans in both Chicago and Puerto Rico. Among the most prominent issues of concern facing the emerging Puerto Rican community were: high infant mortality rates and incidences of preventable diseases; increasing unemployment

due to industrial restructuring; police brutality; inadequate educational opportunities; high incidences of "arson for profit," residential fires induced to
drive residents out of gentrifying areas; and a dearth of social service workers
who spoke Spanish and were sensitive to cultural differences (Martínez, 1989;
F. Padilla, 1987). "War on Poverty" projects and various community action programs were instituted and dramatically expanded in the community to thwart
more radical political initiatives (F. Padilla, 1987:155–68). Many of these programs were staffed by Puerto Ricans and thus, at least temporarily, began to
mitigate the problems of language and cultural insensitivity that had previously
characterized social services. In general, these newer organizations and programs were less invested in maintaining a cultural nexus with the Island (based
on the preservation of folkloric festivities) than in establishing a comprehensive
political base that would include electoral participation, access to state and federal funding for community-building projects, and the creation of white-collar
employment in the nonprofit sector. In short, they were largely concerned with
the civil rights of Puerto Ricans as U.S. citizens.

One manifestation of political insurgency in Chicago's Puerto Rican community took the form of independent electoral campaigns that challenged the
hegemony of Mayor Richard J. Daley's Democratic Party machine. In 1971,
Graciano López became the first Puerto Rican to run for elected public office in Chicago when he made a bid for alderman of the city's 26th Ward in
the heart of the West Town–Humboldt Park barrio (F. Padilla, 1987:250n3). In
1975, three Puerto Rican independent Democrats ran against the Daley Democratic machine in a concerted campaign for the aldermanic seats for the 26th
and 31st Wards (encompassing most of the Division Street barrio) as well as
the 46th Ward in the Lakeview neighborhood, where the candidate was José
"Cha-Cha" Jiménez. Jiménez had been one of the founders and a former leader
of the Young Lords (F. Padilla, 1987:196), which had begun as a street gang
based in Chicago's Lincoln Park neighborhood and transformed itself in 1967
into a Puerto Rican youth organization (cf. F. Padilla, 1987:120–23). Comprised of second-generation Puerto Ricans who had been inspired by the Black
Panthers, the Young Lords tailored similar community-based social agendas to
the articulation of Puerto Ricanness in the sociopolitical context of the advancing gentrification and "urban renewal" projects aimed at the removal of Puerto
Ricans from their neighborhood.

Chicago's Puerto Rican community is exceptionally distinguished for the
historical prominence of its pro-independence and nationalist political radicalism. The recognition of Puerto Rico's colonial reality and its manifestation in an
incomplete and unequal citizenship whose parameters have been determined
historically by white supremacy, provided the ideological template on which
anticolonial nationalist politics developed in Puerto Rican Chicago. The Young
Lords Organization in the 1960s and 1970s, and the Fuerzas Armadas para la
Liberación Nacional (FALN) in the 1980s—both among the most nationally

renowned and better-documented embodiments of Puerto Rican political militancy in the U.S.—were each first organized and remained centrally based in Chicago, and shaped much of the militant grassroots politics in the Puerto Rican barrio.[29] The salience of this history of political radicalism and concomitant state repression, then, has been a particularly distinctive feature of community formation for Puerto Ricans in Chicago. This was especially true for the West Town–Humboldt Park neighborhood, which came to be criminalized not only with its reputation of "riots" but also with allegations of "terrorism."

Grassroots organizations in the Puerto Rican barrios since the late 1960s frequently articulated a level of political militancy that resulted in the intensive monitoring of Puerto Rican activists in Chicago by FBI, CIA, and Defense Department surveillance units (Anderson and Pickering, 1986; F. Padilla, 1987:168–79). Libertad Negroni, a Puerto Rican woman in her late fifties, was the founder of a grassroots organization that promoted various educational programs in the neighborhood. She arrived in Chicago in the 1970s, in the midst of a frenzy of surveillance activity against barrio activists. Libertad recalled:

> When I arrived in Chicago, there were already some sectors within the Puerto Rican community that were organized. Like the Association of Spanish Speaking People of America [ASSPA], and SACC [Spanish Action Committee of Chicago]. That [Spanish Action Committee of Chicago] was primarily Puerto Rican and with a Puerto Rican leadership. ASSPA was community-based, not of a political ideology. Of course, the *New York Times* had published that the FBI had created ASSPA, as a front to counteract the influence of SACC.... They said that the Red Squad, an FBI front, an intelligence front within the Chicago Police Department, was created to dissolve SACC.

Articulating a familiar narrative among community activists and residents, Libertad's account helps to convey that the late 1960s and the 1970s marked a period of intense counterinsurgency activity in Chicago that sowed confusion and suspicion within the community. Like Black militant organizations and some segments of the predominantly white New Left, many Chicago Puerto Rican activists—particularly those advocating Puerto Rico's independence—have been beleaguered by the harassment and surveillance of federal agents and infiltrators from the 1970s to the present. Police files were maintained to record individual Puerto Rican barrio residents' activism and "communist" or "un-American" tendencies in the most meticulous ways (Fernández, 1994; F. Padilla, 1987:171–73).

The early 1980s found the Chicago Puerto Rican community at the center of political controversy on a national scale in the U.S. as well as in Puerto Rico. The Fuerzas Armadas para la Liberación Nacional (FALN), a clandestine group advocating political independence for Puerto Rico, claimed responsibility for a series of bombings in U.S. military facilities. Fifteen Puerto Rican members of the group, thirteen of whom were Chicago barrio residents, were eventually caught and given lengthy sentences in the mid-1980s on charges of "seditious conspiracy to overthrow the U.S. government." Due to the fact that the FALN political prisoners, prior to their incarceration, had participated in grassroots programs serving the Puerto Rican poor, many barrio residents and activists continued to associate grassroots activism with militant nationalism.[30] At the peak of FALN military actions and FBI persecution (when most group members had already gone "underground"), Puerto Rican residents of Humboldt Park/West Town appeared divided. "Signs of 'FALN Welcomed Here' appeared on people's houses and cars," commented Ileana Díaz, a Puerto Rican woman in her thirties, who is the niece of one of the political prisoners and the ex-girlfriend of another. Other community members had agreed with the FBI and other government agents that the FALN members were "terrorists" that "gave all Puerto Ricans a bad name," as remarked Jaime García, an active Statehood advocate.

Throughout the 1980s and '90s, instances of FBI infiltration and surveillance in Humboldt Park contributed to the criminalization of the area most prominently racialized as "Puerto Rican." During the period of Ramos-Zayas's fieldwork, at least three cases involving FBI intervention were documented in the media and supplied a recurring theme in many of the informal conversations Ramos-Zayas had with Puerto Rican barrio residents. In one of these instances, a teacher at the Puerto Rican alternative high school where Ramos-Zayas volunteered was eventually revealed to be an FBI infiltrator who left the school unexpectedly and later testified against nationalist activists who were alleged to be "terrorists" involved with the local public high school's parents' council (Oclander, 1995a). Likewise, the Humboldt Park Infant-Mortality Reduction Initiative (HIMRI), a community health center, was shut down for several weeks while the FBI investigated the agency's files for no publicly stated reason (Espinosa, 1995). Finally, in the summer of 1995, Roberto Clemente High School was also labeled a hotbed of "terrorist" activity in the mainstream news media, as teachers and administrators were required to hand over their records to FBI investigators (Oclander, 1995a). These instances reveal some of the ways in which Humboldt Park has continued to be targeted by the FBI and other government surveillance units, contributing to its stigmatization not only as a "criminal" space of street gangs and drugs, but also as one of "anti-Americanism" and "terrorist" conspiracies.[31] The social space of Humboldt Park has been continuously produced and reproduced through competing practices: hegemonic efforts to criminalize radical political expressions of Puerto Rican citizenship as "un-American" and "terrorist," on the one hand, and a response to this criminalization through the deployment of anticolonial nationalism as a strategy for advancing civil rights demands and community organizing (Ramos-Zayas, 2003).

Despite this admirable legacy of grassroots community organizing efforts, however, the Puerto Rican barrios of Chicago continued to be plagued by alarmingly high levels of poverty. In 1980, more than a third of Chicago's Puerto Ricans were living below the poverty level, and Puerto Rican unemployment was 25% (N. González, 1990:48). By 1991, Puerto Ricans had the highest poverty rate for individuals of any group in the U.S.: nearly 40% of all Puerto Ricans were living below the poverty level, as compared with 33% for African Americans and 14.2% for the total U.S. population.[32] Similar to national trends during the 1990s, Puerto Ricans in Chicago had the highest poverty rate (33.8%) of all Latino groups—40% higher than the poverty rate for Latinos as a group (24.2%), and even higher than that of African Americans (30%). Puerto Rican median family income in 1995 was 18% lower than the Latino average and also 8% lower than that of African Americans.

Segregation and "Latino" Community Formation in "Puerto Rican" Neighborhoods on the North Side

Despite persistently severe levels of poverty, Puerto Ricans in Chicago have seldom shared housing or neighborhoods with African Americans in Chicago. Unlike in other cities, such as New York most notably, almost no Puerto Ricans (or any other Latinos) in Chicago live in large-scale subsidized public housing. In Chicago, "the projects" are virtually synonymous with high concentrations of poor African Americans. Through very explicit policy prerogatives, public housing in Chicago was developed historically according to a logic of social engineering that has deliberately reinforced and intensified the segregation of Black poverty from whites (Hirsch, 1983; Squires et al., 1987), but has likewise served to exacerbate the separation of African Americans from Latinos. Indeed, according to a 1983 study, there were in fact more whites in Chicago's public housing than Latinos; of the total Chicago Housing Authority resident population, 2% were Latino, 3% were white, and the remaining 95% were African American (Orfield and Tostado, 1983; cited in Squires et al., 1987:110; cf. Ropka, 1980:125–26). Indeed, among the ten cities of highest Puerto Rican concentration studied during the 1980s by Massey and Denton (1989:75), Chicago was the one where Puerto Ricans were the most highly segregated from both whites and Blacks (overall dissimilarity indices surpassing .800).[33] Puerto Ricans in Chicago were dramatically more segregated from African Americans than Puerto Ricans in New York, for example (dissimilarity indices were .890 in Chicago and .581 in New York). Indeed, this index of Puerto Rican segregation from African Americans in Chicago (.890) was even somewhat higher than that for the comparably severe segregation of Chicago's Mexicans from Blacks (.843). Significantly, segregation between Puerto Ricans and Mexicans in Chicago, while moderate, was still the highest of all of the five cities having significant populations of both groups (dissimilarity index of .589). By 2000, these figures had scarcely changed. In comparable research on racial segregation based upon the 2000 Census, whereas both groups' degree of residential segregation from whites was very high, with each showing a dissimilarity index of 62 (or in the terms of the previous study, .620), Mexican segregation from Blacks still measured extreme, with a dissimilarity index of 82 (or .820), Puerto Rican segregation from Blacks was still even higher, at 84 (or .840), and the dissimilarity index between Mexicans and Puerto Ricans remained high, at 51 (or .510).[34] In spite of the extreme *social* distance produced by racial segregation, however, many of Chicago's Latinos have, in fact, long lived in remarkably close physical proximity to African Americans (as measured in mere *geographical* distance). Indeed, the most numerically and historically significant Latino neighborhoods have almost all shared starkly segregated borders with African American neighborhoods, and have served as veritable "buffer zones" between virtually homogeneous Black communities and the receding areas of working-class "white flight" (De Genova, 1998; in press; Squires et al., 1987:111; cf. Kornblum, 1974:30).

Predictably, by the mid-1990s, when the real estate values of historically Puerto Rican neighborhoods on Chicago's Near Northwest Side had begun to skyrocket due to westward-advancing gentrification, proposals to relocate displaced African American residents from housing projects located within a fairly short distance to the east or south of the Humboldt Park area into "Section 8" and "scattered site" subsidized housing in some of the most impoverished and not yet gentrifying sections of Humboldt Park created great consternation among Puerto Rican residents. The activists with whom Ramos-Zayas worked were simultaneously concerned about Puerto Ricans being displaced from neighboring West Town by a burgeoning population of "alternative" white artists in their twenties (to be followed, predictably, by more conclusively middle-class white "yuppies" with a pronounced proclivity for the acquisition of real estate), as well as alarmed about Puerto Ricans being displaced from Humboldt Park's "Section 8" housing by African Americans who were themselves being displaced by gentrification (largely evacuated from the stigmatized public housing projects) (Ramos-Zayas, 2001). Melvin Rodríguez—Ramos-Zayas's Puerto Rican neighbor in Humboldt Park—expressed his discontent about an African American family who had recently moved into a house a few blocks down the street. "They won't take care of this neighborhood, because it's not their neighborhood," Melvin commented, "You see gang-bangers here—even those gang-bangers take better care of the neighborhood!—because they are Puerto Rican and their families have lived here for a long time. That's not the case with Blacks. They throw garbage out in the street and you see the men drinking on the corner." As the area occupied by the infamous Cabrini Green public housing complex came to be increasingly reclaimed as prime real estate through the demolition of high-rise housing project buildings and the development of luxury properties on the site and in its immediate environs, African American residents were often relocated to nearby impoverished Latino neighborhoods. Pitted against each other in this context of dramatically accelerated gentrification and a massive state-initiated liquidation of subsidized public housing, both groups have consequently been compelled to compete for what remains amidst a severe scarcity of affordable housing. Although Puerto Ricans increasingly expressed a heightened vigilance about who was moving into "their" neighborhood, however, the increasing residential proximity between Puerto Ricans and African Americans actually continued to be quite restricted to only a few census tracts.

Puerto Ricans' claims to exclusivity in "their" neighborhoods, however, have been beleaguered almost from the very start. This has been particularly true with respect to Mexicans and other Latinos. By the early 1970s, following the dramatic growth of the Puerto Rican community during the 1960s, migration to Chicago from Puerto Rico had in fact already reached its peak; by 2000, the Puerto Rican population had only increased modestly, from 79,000 in 1970 to 113,000–120,000 in the city, and 152,000–160,000 in the metropolitan area.[35] Despite the extreme residential segregation that is otherwise characteristic of Chicago, it is important to note that, between 1970 and 1980, the Mexican population in the most historically significant neighborhoods of Puerto Rican concentration on Chicago's Near Northwest Side (Humboldt Park, West Town, and Logan Square) nearly quadrupled—escalating from 12,000 to over 47,000. By 1990 (the Census that immediately preceded the period of our research), within these three contiguous communities (which together concentrate more than half of the total Puerto Rican population in the city) there were virtually as many Mexicans (61,429) as Puerto Ricans (63,707). Indeed, in the West Town community area, Mexicans had already bypassed Puerto Ricans in 1990. As of 1990, roughly three-fourths of all the Puerto Ricans in Chicago continued to be concentrated in six contiguous North Side neighborhoods, but Puerto Ricans have long been quite routinely exposed to Mexicans living in the same neighborhoods.[36] By the year 2000, Puerto Ricans no longer comprised the majority of the Latinos in *any* of the historically "Puerto Rican" neighborhoods on the North Side, nor in any of the adjacent areas of more recent Puerto Rican settlement: West Town (50% Mexican; 36% Puerto Rican); Humboldt Park (52% Mexican; 37% Puerto Rican); Logan Square (50% Mexican; 35% Puerto Rican); Hermosa (50% Mexican; 37% Puerto Rican); and Belmont Cragin (59% Mexican; 26% Puerto Rican). Meanwhile, the "Latino" communities on the South Side of the city, which historically had always been overwhelmingly Mexican, have indeed remained so: Pilsen (91.7% Mexican; 1.9% Puerto Rican); Little Village (91.5% Mexican; 1.5% Puerto Rican); Back of the Yards (88.7% Mexican; 2.8% Puerto Rican); and South Chicago (85.8% Mexican; 7.2% Puerto Rican).[37] Thus, much of the material in this study contributed from De Genova's research tends to have emerged precisely from those contexts where his Mexican interlocutors had had much more contact with Puerto Ricans. Discourses about Puerto Ricans were rather uncommon among Mexican migrants who lived and worked in places where they had very little exposure to Puerto Ricans. By contrast, it has become increasingly improbable for Puerto Ricans in Chicago to formulate perspectives about their own Puerto Ricanness without accounting for that identity, to some degree, in relation to Mexicans as well as other Latinos.

In response to the perceived "threat" posed by an increasing Mexican and Central American influx into the Humboldt Park neighborhood—traditionally marked as "Puerto Rican," and indeed, symbolically central as "the" Puerto Rican barrio—grassroots activists launched strenuous campaigns during the 1990s to discourage Puerto Rican residents from moving out of the barrio. Local businesses and ambulatory vendors selling Puerto Rican–identified goods worked alongside of grassroots activists to enforce physical and symbolic "boundaries" that were intended to maintain the "Puerto Rican"-ness of the neighborhood, by deploying nationalist and even separatist Puerto Rican symbols (such as a campaign to install a statue of renowned nationalist leader Pedro Albizu Campos) and by developing alternative popular-education programs for youth and adults.[38] The simultaneous perceived onslaught of "encroachments" by gentrifying whites, displaced poor Blacks, and other poor Latinos, especially Mexican migrants, produced a sense of alarm that Puerto Ricans were being "squeezed out" of the Humboldt Park–West Town–Logan Square area. This sense of an imminent loss of identity tied to what appeared to be a loss of control over their proper space also corresponded to an increase among the Puerto Rican working class who were flocking out of the barrio and moving to Chicago's more proximate working-class suburbs (Latino Institute, May 3, 1993). Flyers encouraging Puerto Ricans to buy property in the Humboldt Park area or to sell exclusively to other Puerto Ricans proliferated during the summer of 1994. Soon thereafter, two gargantuan archways that replicate the Puerto Rican flag—comprised of 56-foot-high arches of crocheted steel—were erected over Division Street, crossing the busy street from sidewalk to sidewalk at each end of the main commercial strip in the heart of Humboldt Park. In January of 1995, the enormous flags were unveiled as part of an urban renewal project coordinated by local activists, Puerto Rican politicians, and the city government. These twin monuments to the Puerto Rican flag represent what was a truly extravagant and quite forcefully racialized effort to reclaim and (re)produce a definitively Puerto Rican space in Chicago, exactly when the area's population was becoming less definitively Puerto Rican than it had been for many years prior.

Imbued with the hegemonic mythology of "a city of neighborhoods," urban space in Chicago has very often been distinctively produced through such performative demonstrations of "ethnic" identities and nationalist sentiment. Despite the ever greater numbers of Mexicans even in the city's North Side Latino neighborhoods, Puerto Ricans continued to emphasize the "Puerto Rican"-ness of Humboldt Park, an urban space that remained symbolically central to notions of Puerto Rican cultural authenticity. Despite the presence of Mexicans throughout the city and their numerical predominance in almost all Latino neighborhoods, likewise, the South Side neighborhoods of Pilsen and Little Village have similarly become emblematic of "the Mexican community" in Chicago.

The problem of conceiving of "Latino" political futures in Chicago inevitably had to encompass these spatial divides. Writing in the early 1980s, for instance,

Joanne Belenchia addressed the issue in revealingly spatialized language: "those holding political power cannot expect to silence Latino demands by negotiating only with one or another group: a token appointment of a southside Mexican will not go far in appeasing a northside Puerto Rican" (Belenchia, 1982:144). Confronting these distinct and forcefully racialized urban spaces, city and ward politics and elected officials in Chicago increasingly came to emphasize the importance of strategically courting both groups in the hope of capitalizing on Latino political coalitions, both real and imagined.

The Formation of "the Latino Community": Political Coalitions between Mexicans and Puerto Ricans

During the 1970s, even as Mexican and Puerto Rican organizational efforts toward community consolidation first began to enjoy unprecedented success, there were new motivations for coalition-building and an increasing pressure to move toward a new "Latino" politics (N. González, 1990).[39] Indeed, one significant manifestation of a shared history between Mexicans and Puerto Ricans in Chicago has been the consolidation of Latino-identified political coalitions. At least until the death of Mayor Richard J. Daley in 1976, Chicago politics, under the exceptionally powerful and unrestrained power of the Democratic Party, was widely considered to be the last stronghold of big-city machine politics in the U.S. (Grimshaw, 1982; Guterbock, 1980; Rakove, 1975). In the mid-1970s, when the Chicago Democratic Party machine still relied extensively on local-level patronage, Latinos' profoundly marginal relation to that apparatus was starkly manifested by the fact that they accounted for only 1.7% of the people employed in any capacity on the city's full-time payroll (Belenchia, 1982:131). Reviewing the enduring stronghold of the Democratic Party machine over wards with large Latino constituencies during the 1970s, one commentator declared, "one must conclude that most Latino voters live either in wards where the machine works or in wards where the machine works *very well*" (Belenchia, 1982:139; emphasis in original). Indeed, as late as the early 1980s, in the face of growing political mobilization by the Mexican community in Pilsen, long-time alderman of the 25th Ward and Democratic Party machine stalwart Vito Marzullo bluntly declared to a *Chicago Tribune* reporter, "If this ward ever elects a Mexican alderman, he's going to be *my* Mexican, not *their* Mexican" (quoted in Grimshaw, 1992:12).

Prior to 1980, there was literally only one Latino elected official in Chicago. As late as 1981, the gerrymandering of electoral districts had ensured that there was not a single Latino on the Chicago City Council.[40] Thereafter, a fiercely racialized campaign led to the election in 1983 of the city's first African American mayor, Harold Washington, with as much as 75% of the Latino electoral count serving as a decisive swing vote in Washington's favor (M. Torres, 1991:173). That same year, the Mexican American Legal Defense and Education Fund (MALDEF) sued for violations of the Voting Rights Act, contending that redistricting had deliberately diminished Latino voting constituencies; they pursued the case in concert with legal suits by other organizations claiming discrimination in the way that the fifty aldermanic wards were structured, and they won. Chicago underwent a ward restructuring that resulted in special elections held in seven newly formed wards with Latino or African American majorities. By 1986, four predominantly Latino wards had been reconstituted and saw the election of all four of Chicago's first Latino aldermen. Over several embattled years of internecine struggle within the city's Democratic Party machine, the Washington Reform Coalition, for a time, successfully achieved a partial coordination of the previously balkanized Puerto Rican, Mexican, and Black electoral constituencies in Chicago.[41] It was not until 1992, however, that a mixed-Latino majority of the electorate in Illinois's Fourth Congressional District (in Chicago) succeeded for the first time in electing a Latino to the U.S. House of Representatives—the first Latino congressman not only from Chicago or Illinois, but indeed, from anywhere in the entire Midwest. Much of this Latino political ascendancy during the 1980s was inseparable from a larger-scale renovation of the notoriously corrupt machinery of the Democratic Party in Chicago.

It would be overly sanguine to infer from these genuinely monumental electoral transformations anything resembling a comparably monumental and profound mass-based political movement among Latinos during that period of reform in Chicago politics. Nonetheless, these Latino electoral gains indubitably became possible only on the basis of an unprecedented coordination of efforts between Mexicans (mainly those raised in the U.S.) and Puerto Ricans, which relied significantly upon the strategic deployment of Latinismo (cf. F. Padilla, 1985). However, such politically calculated expressions of Latinismo on the part of a relatively small number of political organizations and their activists provides very little confirmation of the viability of Latinidad in everyday life, which is a major concern of our book. Indeed, in a bitterly ironic turn of fortunes, by 1995, some Mexican and Puerto Rican organizations had even begun to demand the dismantling of the congressional district that encompassed parts of both of their spatially distinct communities, which their predecessors had struggled to create. Both sides concurred that these two "Latino" groups were "racially different and had little in common beyond their language" (Oclander, 1995b).

In light of such reversals, then, and despite the clear historical evidence of some meaningful expressions of Latino identification and collaboration between Mexicans and Puerto Ricans in Chicago, it is a central concern of our book to examine what is likewise a robust evidence of significant divisions between the two, and to consider that this has tended to be especially so precisely in some of the predicaments where they found themselves in greatest proximity. The manifestations of these divisions can be traced historically, but more importantly, they are very much contemporary concerns, as will be evidenced by many of our respective ethnographic findings analyzed in the ensuing chapters of this book.

In the everyday life of workplaces and Latino neighborhoods, beyond the electoral projects that have institutionalized certain Latino-identified political formations, there have indeed been some important anticipations of community and collaboration between Mexicans and Puerto Ricans in Chicago. Predictably, one significant indicator is the evidence of intermarriage between the two groups (cf. Rúa, 2001). Especially during the decades prior to the 1970s, given a disproportionately high ratio of single Mexican/migrant men who were either unmarried or whose families remained in Mexico, consensual relationships were not uncommon between Mexican men and Puerto Rican women. Within the Puerto Rican community (especially among men), however, these unions were often suspected to be "legal arrangements," marriages of convenience through which undocumented Mexican/migrant men were merely taking advantage of Puerto Rican women's citizenship as an opportunity to adjust their immigration status [*casados por buscar papeles*]. Thus, rather than a decisive occasion for communion between the two groups, even intermarriages were often considered dubious and inherently unstable, if not immoral, and also were sometimes viewed as an incipient threat to the sustenance of Puerto Ricanness. What is therefore perhaps most noteworthy here is precisely the salience of the unequal politics of U.S. citizenship and immigration law in constituting a critical fault line between the two groups, even as men and women from each group developed intimate relations.

To the extent that the racialization of urban space in Chicago has so forcefully designated particular areas as "Mexican" or "Puerto Rican," distinctions between Puerto Ricans' U.S. citizenship status and Mexican migrants' "illegality" were likewise inscribed spatially in Chicago. The spatial order of Chicago and the politics of citizenship became forcefully racialized dimensions in the relationships between the two groups, as well as constitutive dimensions of each group's relationship to the larger social order of the U.S. nation-state. As we will consider in the next chapter, Mexicans and Puerto Ricans constructed meaningful differences between one another as groups around their particular relations to U.S. citizenship and its presumed antithesis, "illegality," in ways that often became increasingly conflated with their respective racialized characters and group identities.

CHAPTER 3

Economies of Dignity: Ideologies of Work and Worth

"Mexicans see Puerto Ricans as U.S. citizens who come to this country with a lot of privileges and we don't take advantage of those privileges," explained Adriana Cruz, an eighteen-year-old Puerto Rican high school student. "That we are lazy. That we like living off welfare, that we have this welfare mentality." Discourses of "welfare," which signal differential relations to the substantive entitlements of U.S. citizenship, were variously elaborated in terms of competing ideologies of work and competence, as well as respectability and dignity. Through a stigmatization of "welfare dependency," the U.S. citizenship of Puerto Ricans invariably came to be conflated with their racialized denigration as "lazy," lacking a good "work ethic," and, in effect, being the kind of "undeserving" poor who were ultimately a liability to the U.S. nation. In this sense, many Mexican migrants commonly constructed themselves in contradistinction to precisely these images—as being "hardworking," and capable of making do without having to ask for "handouts"—and so, implicitly subscribed to hegemonic stereotypes about the virtues of "good immigrant values." These same postures, however, were intended to deflect the pervasive and likewise racialized allegations that Mexicans were merely opportunistic "illegal aliens" subverting the "rule of law" and thus corroding the moral fabric of U.S. society.

The presumption of "welfare dependency" as a self-evident indicator of "laziness" was embedded in notions of "respectability" constituted through "hard work" that enabled Mexican migrants to racialize Puerto Ricans in ways that approached or approximated the racial Blackness of African Americans. By contrast, without celebrating the stigma of "welfare," Puerto Ricans nevertheless posited their own political sophistication and their capabilities in maneuvering through the social inequalities orchestrated by U.S. political institutions, in ways that constructed Mexicans as "illegal," helpless, and submissive newcomers from a "Third World" (and by implication, premodern) social background, lacking a sense of dignity and allowing themselves to be easily subjected to exploitation. Thus, around elementary but substantial differences founded upon the unequal politics of citizenship, Mexicans and Puerto Ricans elaborated competing moral economies through which to render meaningful their own locations in the social order of the U.S. nation-state. In so doing, they also commonly produced the grounds for producing and upholding differences that could demarcate a more or less durable divide between their distinct groups—a defining division that tended to be readily racialized.

Citizenship and "Illegality"

Puerto Ricans often explicitly problematized their U.S. citizenship. They deployed their identity as U.S. citizens as the distinguishing feature that demarcated their difference from other Latinos, but also recognized it critically as a unique inheritance of Puerto Rico's colonial condition. Because of their open support for the independence of Puerto Rico, some of the activists at one of the organizations where Ramos-Zayas volunteered were readily identified as "the nationalists" by barrio residents as well as officials of the city and state governments. These controversial but quite influential community organizers had developed popular-education programs premised on a critical pedagogy that promotes Puerto Rican nationalism as an oppositional mode of identity formation among the most disenfranchised barrio youth (Ramos-Zayas, 1998). Barrio residents—many of whom were unemployed, underemployed, or working poor—in turn reformulated the popular nationalism that these grassroots activists promoted by embracing and boldly affirming their distinctive status as citizens of the United States. This "citizenship identity" was constructed in opposition to the "illegal immigrant" status attributed to the Mexicans, Central Americans, and other Latinos living in "the Puerto Rican neighborhood," regardless of their actual juridical statuses within the regime of U.S. immigration and naturalization law. Thus, in the effort to distinguish themselves from "foreign" Latinos, many Puerto Ricans tended to celebrate the U.S. citizenship which was an effect of their colonized condition.

Anticolonial nationalist projects aimed at a consolidation of Puerto Rican national identity in Chicago are presented with an interesting paradox by Puerto Rican views of U.S. citizenship. On the one hand, Puerto Ricans activists grounded successful community-building projects and generated a discourse of anticolonialism by rejecting the premises and questioning the promises of their U.S. citizenship; on the other, Puerto Rican residents of the Humboldt Park barrio oftentimes deployed a citizenship identity to enforce boundaries vis-à-vis other Latino groups, broadly perceived as even more marginalized "illegal" outsiders (Ramos-Zayas, 2003). In this sense, U.S. citizenship served to distinguish and substantiate Puerto Ricanness in the context of an increasingly diverse but largely "Mexicanized" Latinidad identified with migration. Puerto Ricans often countered mass-media and journalistic depictions of Latinos as "immigrants" by deflecting "foreignness" and "illegality" onto "Mexicans," while also advancing claims of legitimacy for their own entitlement to welfare benefits and other rights by emphasizing the political relationship between Puerto Rico and the U.S. nation-state, bilingualism, military service, and other evidences of having "paid their dues" and established their proper membership in "the American nation."

Most Puerto Ricans, both on the Island and the U.S. mainland alike, do not tend to see a contradiction between being U.S. citizens and belonging to the Puerto Rican nation (Duany, 2000; Morris, 1995). Rather than expressing nationalism at the level of electoral politics by demanding Puerto Rico's national sovereignty, Puerto Ricans on the Island commonly negotiate the contradictory demands of nationalism in the realm of popular culture (Díaz-Quiñones, 1993; Duany, 2000). Hence, while Puerto Ricans on the Island have consistently voted against both independence from the U.S. and permanent annexation as the fifty-first state of the union, neither these political options nor the prolongation of the status quo are perceived as in any way negating the existence and vitality of a Puerto Rican "nation" defined in cultural and linguistic terms on the Island.

Among Puerto Ricans in the U.S., a U.S. citizenship identity has become not only compatible with nationalist activism, but actually plays a critical (and largely neglected) role in the creation of a Puerto Rican national identity within broader racialization processes concerning Latinidad. Alma Juncos, a Puerto Rican parent-volunteer at Roberto Clemente High School, articulated this emphasis on a citizenship identity. When asked to describe the area where she was living, Alma replied:

> Where I live, some Puerto Ricans and some Mexicans moved in. There's a building that is mostly Mexican, Guatemalan. Puerto Ricans don't live there. Where I live I feel fne. As Puerto Ricans, we help each other, we motivate each other. And I've also helped Mexican people, a guy who is mute, who lives on the ground floor of my building. I took him here to the West Town clinic and they gave him good attention, they recommended a school to him. I think that many of them are jealous of Puerto Ricans. My [Puerto Rican] neighbor told me: "The thing with Mexicans is that they know they are wetbacks." And, since we [Puerto Ricans] are [U.S.] citizens, they hate us because of that.

During an historical period when anti-immigrant nativism and broader racialization discourses around Latinidad persistently located groups of Latin American and Caribbean ancestry outside of the juridical and ideological borders of the United States, Puerto Ricans found themselves having to straddle the fraught divide between the increasingly counterposed categories of "Latino" and "Puerto Rican" by embracing and reaffirming their (non-immigrant) citizenship identity.

A U.S. citizenship identity allowed even the most vulnerable Puerto Rican barrio residents to articulate their legal rights and make claims for entitlements and resources while simultaneously endorsing community-building projects grounded on popular nationalist discourses. The emphasis on a citizenship identity in relation to other Latinos repeatedly emerged in Ramos-Zayas's life history interviews and informal conversations with a group of Puerto Rican parent-volunteers at the barrio high school where Alma Juncos volunteered, among individuals who routinely interacted with Mexican parents, students, and administrators. This discourse of citizenship identity tended to automatically assume that Mexicans and other Latinos were not U.S. citizens. Nevertheless, Puerto Ricans still upheld the critical distinction between their status as colonial subjects and what they perceived to be "real" "American"-ness, which most associated with racial whiteness.

While a U.S. citizenship identity was evoked to emphasize a specifically Puerto Rican nationality in contradistinction to a more diffuse Latino identification, therefore, theirs was a citizenship identity that remained indelibly marked by its nonwhiteness and subordinate (or "second-class") character. The invocation of a citizenship identity among Puerto Ricans was, in general, unequivocally *not* an assertion of their "American"-ness. For their part, Mexican migrants tended to have little or no historical knowledge about the colonial condition of Puerto Rico. Most commonly, they knew only that here was another Latino group, but one who enjoyed what appeared to them to be a privileged relationship to the U.S. state. Although Mexican migrants did not tend to comment explicitly upon Puerto Ricans' U.S. citizenship, they commonly identified some of the substantive features of that citizenship (such as eligibility for various social welfare programs), which they could conceive of only as a tremendous advantage. Especially during the mid-1990s, with a dominant political climate of distrust and disdain of both "immigrants" and "welfare" in all its forms, the discourse surrounding "welfare" was one that skillfully manipulated the intrinsic ambiguities embedded in the category. Precisely when the aim has been to insinuate that undocumented migrants represent an overall drain on public revenues, the stigmatized charge of the term "welfare" has been deployed very broadly, if also crudely, by fiscal conservative nativists to refer even to such public entitlements as access to emergency medical care or public schooling (cf. Calavita, 1996). Nevertheless, the frontal assault against "welfare" as such during the 1990s, which culminated in the so-called "Welfare Reform" legislation of 1996, was primarily directed against programs such as Aid to Families with Dependent Children (AFDC), Supplemental Security Income (SSI), General Assistance, or the Special Supplemental Food Program for Women, Infants and Children (WIC), more conventionally known as "food stamps." The typical beneficiaries of these programs were the U.S.-citizen poor, with racialized "minorities" such as African Americans and Puerto Ricans very prominently targeted as "undeserving" abusers of the state's presumed beneficence.

Mexican migrants, especially the undocumented as well as many who had been previously undocumented, were most often legally ineligible, or even when they may have been eligible, most often presumed themselves to be forbidden from these entitlements. Thus, it is crucial to identify the way that discourses of "welfare" among Mexican migrants were always inherently concerned with the unequal politics of citizenship, and that such substantive entitlements of U.S. citizenship as access to these "welfare" programs were a preeminent material manifestation of the palpable difference between what it meant to be an "immigrant" and what it meant for Puerto Ricans to be U.S. citizens. In 1990, Mexican migrants who had arrived in the U.S. between 1980 and 1990, and were not U.S. citizens, had a labor-force participation rate (87.5%) that was 17.6% higher than that of the total U.S. population (74.4%). A preeminent exemplar of the working poor, however, their poverty rate (36.6%) was almost three times that of the total U.S. population (13.1%), and roughly comparable to that of Puerto Ricans as a group.[1] Nevertheless, this Mexican/migrant population in poverty received 82.1% less in public assistance payments per capita than the U.S. total poverty population.[2] These dramatic disparities reflect several decisive determinants: the exclusion of undocumented migrants from welfare programs (Supplemental Security Income [SSI], Aid to Families with Dependent Children [AFDC], and General Assistance), the five-year prohibition on receipt of welfare for most migrants whose immigration statuses were adjusted (or "legalized") through the "Amnesty" of the Immigration Reform and Control Act (IRCA) of 1986, as well as standard Immigration and Naturalization restrictions against applicants or their relatives becoming "a public charge." Although Mexican migrants' poverty had been deployed against them by recourse to the allegation of their "liability to become a public charge" throughout much of the twentieth century, it was seldom substantiated.[3]

Whereas Puerto Rican poverty in the U.S. has been abundantly documented, considerably less research has focused upon Puerto Rican labor-force participation. The percentage of Puerto Ricans in "managerial/professional" occupations, though low (15.5% for men and 18.5% for women), is almost twice as large as the percentage of Mexicans in such occupations and comparable to percentages for other Latino groups, which of course continues to be significantly lower than that of whites (IPRP, 1993). In 1993, Puerto Ricans had higher median earnings than Mexicans, and Puerto Rican female median earnings were almost equal to those of non-Latino white females. Nevertheless, as we have already discussed, the poverty rate for Puerto Ricans was simultaneously the highest among all Latino groups. Furthermore, as a characteristic and implicitly pathologizing indicator of "welfare dependency," twice as many Puerto Ricans as Mexicans were likely to be "females heading households." Based on data from the 1990 Census, an Urban Institute study prepared for the U.S. Department of Health and Human Services determined that 23.9% of Mainland-born Puerto Rican teen mothers, 34.5% of Island-born Puerto Rican teen mothers, 30.9% of Mainland-born Puerto Rican young mothers (ages 20–24), and 35.3% of Island-born Puerto Rican young mothers received transfer income from Aid to Families with Dependent Children (AFDC), Supplemental Security Income (SSI), or other forms of public assistance. In contrast, only 3.7% of "foreign-born" Mexican/migrant teen mothers and 6.4% of "foreign-born" Mexican/migrant young mothers received any of these forms of welfare benefits (Kahn and Berkowitz, 1995:Tables A.6, B.5).[4] One of the inferences that we can draw from these admittedly oversimplified statistical portraits is that there is a starkly pronounced bifurcation among

Puerto Ricans in the U.S. labor market; at one end are those Puerto Ricans who are in the labor force and doing reasonably well, and at the other end are Puerto Ricans who are unemployed or are among the working poor. Both of these significant differences between Puerto Ricans and Mexican migrants, however, had everything to do with the inequalities systematically generated and sustained by the politics of citizenship.

When their U.S. citizenship identity comes to be conflated with claims about Puerto Rican "culture," however, or, worse, more plainly racializing claims about the inherent traits of Puerto Ricans as a group, discourses of Puerto Rican "welfare dependency" predictably and almost invariably invoke various insinuations about a "culture of poverty" soon thereafter (e.g., Lewis, 1970).[5] An important and bitter irony of Puerto Ricans' U.S. citizenship, therefore, is that it extended welfare benefits to them and thereby apparently corroborated the racist equation of Puerto Ricanness with laziness, "underclass" pathologies, and anything considered "un-American." These stereotypes effectively conceal the fact that, historically, the predominant labor-market trajectory of Puerto Rican migrants to the Mainland, as colonial subjects, was largely restricted to serving U.S. industries that soon thereafter closed down or were relocated abroad before the Puerto Rican newcomers had had any chance to make any substantial occupational gains that might have supplied a foothold for subsequent U.S.-born generations (History Task Force, 1979). As unionized manufacturing jobs came increasingly to be substituted with low-wage and widely ridiculed low-status service sector employment with few or no benefits, many Puerto Ricans entered the growing ranks of the permanently poor for whom welfare frequently became little more than an insufficient complement to other odd jobs for subsistence (cf. Newman, 1999).

Ramos-Zayas met Carmen Rivera through her son Juan, who was a student at the local high school and member of a youth salsa band that played at neighborhood festivities. The widowed mother of three sons, Carmen had lived in Chicago for ten years. Like most of the parents of the high school students with whom Ramos-Zayas worked, Carmen had experienced frequent and recurrent cycles of underemployment in which she combined part-time "off the books" employment and one or another form of public assistance. Although she could have easily qualified for maximum public aid benefits, Carmen tenaciously held on to her tenuous labor-force connections and drew great pride from the work she did. When asked to describe how she managed to raise three sons on such a tight budget, Carmen did not mention receiving public assistance, but rather focused instead on the clever and skillful ways in which she was able to make ends meet. She emphasized her hard work and budgeting skills, how she had learned to make do with the little that she earned from odd jobs as a part-time caterer, and how her sons helped her with the little they made in after-school jobs (which for Carmen was a meaningful proof of the "good work ethic" she had instilled in them). Although Carmen was receiving welfare in the

form of Medicaid and food stamps, she considered herself "hardworking"—
she excelled at her part-time job as a caterer—and, furthermore, a kind of role
model of civic responsibility, as she sometimes served as a parent-volunteer at
Roberto Clemente High School, where many students regularly came to her for
advice.

In contrast to her self-image as, in effect, a "good citizen," despite her poverty,
Carmen recognized that Mexicans often worked multiple low-wage jobs simultaneously for inordinately long hours, but perceived the jobs that Mexicans were
presumably "willing to take" as clear examples of an extraordinary exploitation
that was degrading. In these respects, Carmen focused on what she perceived
to be the desperation that was rooted in Mexicans' poverty, rather than on their
"hard work." Referring explicitly to the spatialized underpinnings of the racialized distinction between Puerto Ricans and Mexicans, she compared the North
Side and the South Side of Chicago:

> The South Side is much poorer, lots of vacant buildings. The Mexican part is
> like a bit of Central America in the city. The Mexicans try to live as if they
> were in Mexico. All you see is their culture, people in the streets, selling on the
> streets. They work very hard. Yes, they do any kind of work. You see them on
> the bus going to work, from here to there—they're always on their way to work
> or from work. You can tell because you hear them talking among themselves.
> Many of them are very poor, because they come here with nothing. And their
> relatives . . . Let me tell you something, one thing I've noticed is that they are a
> little into themselves, they don't help each other very much . . . not all of them,
> but some of them. Where I live there's a lot of problems among the Mexicans.
> They bicker with each other [*se tiran unos a otros*]. At least where I live there's
> a lot of Mexicans, a lot! The ground floor is always packed with Mexican fam-
> ilies, packed, packed! Mexicans live their own lives. One thing I've noticed is
> that they are rude [*groseros*]—they don't help each other out, not even among
> themselves.

Carmen associated "the South Side" with Mexico, as epitomized by Mexican/
migrant street vendors who reenacted a kind of impoverished "Third World"
informal economy. Carmen seemed to suggest, furthermore, that as a consequence of the desperate scramble to accept any job, under any circumstance,
Mexicans tended to live in competition with one another. The direct contrast
that she drew between Mexicans and Puerto Ricans was underscored on one occasion in November of 1994, when Ramos-Zayas visited Rivera to talk about her
son's college plans. Carmen was concerned because her son wanted to become
a chef and she did not know how much culinary school would cost. Carmen
praised her son's cooking:

> Sonia, you know her, right? [Ramos-Zayas nodded] She lives right here, in the
> building right here. Well, Sonia is always on the lookout to see when Juan is
> going to cook. She tells me: "Let me know when he cooks, so that I can come
> over!" [laughed] Because Juan has always been a good cook. Since he was little.

He'd tell me, "Mami, how do you prepare this [food]? What [ingredients] do you put in?" Always. So when he cooks, I send Sonia a plate. And also when she cooks, she sends me a plate. That's a custom that we keep as Puerto Ricans. We always care for each other and we're there for each other.

Carmen Rivera claimed a higher moral ground for Puerto Ricans by constructing Mexicans' eagerness to "work at anything" as an ultimate shortcoming that undermined their solidarity as compatriots.

Like many other Puerto Rican barrio residents, Carmen also believed that Mexicans saw Puerto Ricans as U.S. citizens who had enjoyed legal privileges for many generations yet had not had the wherewithal to achieve the "American Dream." Citizenship, along with all that it implies in the U.S. nationalist imaginary (e.g., extended residence, high levels of English-language proficiency, institutional access, and ultimately, "assimilation"), could be presumed to be an automatic predictor of Puerto Ricans' upward social mobility. When Puerto Ricans' citizenship was instead associated with poverty, "welfare dependency," social stagnation, and marginality, therefore, the perceived failure appeared to be that of the Puerto Ricans themselves. As a consequence, those who have glorified their own U.S. citizenship but still live in poverty come to be suspect as culturally "deficient" and culpable as socially "deviant."

On one occasion in the fall of 1993, when De Genova was teaching an ESL course at a factory called Imperial Enterprises, he initiated a discussion concerning what types of work people had done prior to their jobs at Imperial. With the exception of three Puerto Rican workers, the remaining group was comprised entirely of Mexican migrants. When the question about his prior work experiences was posed to Héctor, one of the Puerto Rican course participants, he replied, "I was on welfare; I never worked before." Héctor had already been working at this factory for nine years, but prior to this job he had never been employed either in Puerto Rico or Chicago. Héctor had come to Chicago from the Island when he was in his teens, and had been living in Chicago for sixteen years. For the Mexican migrants, such a trajectory would simply have not been an available option. More typically than not, Mexican migrants in Chicago had not only worked continuously since their arrival as young adults in the U.S., but also had already commonly worked in Mexico prior to migration. Regardless of how young they had been when they came, many could recount several forms of employment as children in Mexico. This is not to suggest, of course, that Héctor's attitudes about work were different than those of his Mexican coworkers. To the contrary. What might be called his "work ethic" was strikingly similar to theirs. Indeed, shortly thereafter, when asked what kind of job he would find preferable, Héctor affirmed quite earnestly: "I'll work any job as long as it's honest money; an honest job is a good job—I'll do anything." Like many other Puerto Ricans whom we each knew, Héctor (like Adriana, whose comment opened this chapter) was aware of the "welfare-dependent" stigma that seemed to be inevitably associated with the U.S. citizenship of Puerto Ricans.

The Moral Economy of "Welfare"

Puerto Ricans, regardless of social class, overwhelmingly endorsed a "work ethic" that was indeed very conventional, and largely recapitulated the hegemonic litanies of U.S. society concerning the moral value of "hard work" and economic "independence." "Welfare" tended to be stigmatized not only by those who did not receive these benefits, but also by those who had relatives who were receiving or had previously received public assistance, and even those who themselves were collecting one or another form of welfare payment (cf. Newman, 1999). However, most Puerto Ricans recognized meaningful distinctions among various kinds of "welfare," and deployed diverse contextual considerations alternately to condemn or sanction welfare use. The differentiation of welfare into distinct components—such as disability, Aid to Families with Dependent Children (AFDC), Medicaid, food stamps, Section 8—served to categorize specific types of welfare as "good" or "bad." Popular discourses of "welfare abuse," "cheating," "taking advantage," and "laziness"—which resonated with hegemonic scripts—abounded among Puerto Ricans in Chicago.

For many barrio residents, however, there were also particular circumstances demanding that welfare use be scrutinized in light of the recipients' specific predicaments, employment patterns, and even parenting skills or community involvement. Given the complexities of public assistance, as a social institution, and the particularities of any given person's conceivably multiple social identities, not all forms or instances of welfare use were perceived to be incompatible with being a productive member of society. Among Puerto Ricans in the Humboldt Park barrio, popular perceptions and judgment concerning welfare often depended on a textured understanding of a particular individual's entire life history and public identity, not merely her generic status as a welfare recipient. Hence, those who admitted to being "on welfare" also were commonly inclined to accentuate their own alternative "productive" citizenship identities; some familiar examples included serving as a part-time volunteer at a community organization, former military service, or even gainful "off-the-books" employment on the part of workers for whom public aid was a necessary supplement to low wages and limited opportunities. Sometimes "going on welfare" was perceived to be a rather noble public act of humility, signally a personal recognition of the limited possibilities or inability of any given individual to pull him- or herself up "by the bootstraps," single-handedly support his/her family, and secure basic needs. In contrast, collecting welfare for "no good reason"—for instance, when an individual had a not-so-obvious disability but received workers' compensation—was roundly derided. The recognition of welfare's complexity, therefore, still did not preclude the moral dilemmas entangled in the perceived contradiction between being a properly "productive" U.S. citizen and the commonplace construction of receiving public assistance as being a public liability. The case of Adriana Cruz was illustrative of these tensions.

In August of 1994, Ramos-Zayas was teaching at a Puerto Rican–identified alternative high school in West Town when she met Adriana Cruz, a young Puerto Rican woman who was enrolled as a student there. Adriana had grown up in predominantly Mexican neighborhood on the South Side, but she, her mother, and her brother had decided to relocate to the Humboldt Park area on the North Side to be closer to Adriana's maternal aunt and cousins. Adriana participated in Ramos-Zayas's "Latino Literature" class, and was one of the students most interested in receiving college counseling and pursuing her higher education. Most of the journal entries Adriana wrote for the class stressed her efforts to get into college; one typical entry read: "Today I started filling out my college applications. I thought it was going to be easy, but it was not and I got mad after a while. I got confused with some of the parts. I got so frustrated I started crying" (10/2/94).

The long college and financial aid application process led Ramos-Zayas to spend many hours with Adriana, as well as some of Adriana's friends. The one theme that continuously came up during those conversations, as well as in the journal entries that Cruz shared with Ramos-Zayas, involved Adriana's frustrations with and low opinion of women her age who were getting pregnant. Interestingly, Adriana repeatedly emphasized that her friends who wanted to get pregnant lived on the South Side:

> Today a friend from the South Side [. . .] was telling me about one of our close friends. Her name is Delana and she is Mexican. She is going to take a pregnancy test over the weekend. I think Delana is stupid because she wants to get pregnant. She has her whole life ahead of her and she is throwing it down the drain. Well, one thing is for sure, her mother will be happy because she always told me she wanted Delana to get pregnant at the age of eighteen. I guess her wish is becoming true (9/27/94).

Much of Adriana's frustration with her Mexican friends' pregnancies was certainly inspired by her own educational and career goals and her sense that she and all of her peers confronted formidable obstacles in their shared plight as working-class Latinas. However, the marking of the space of the South Side as "Mexican" became entangled in Adriana's negative appraisal of teen pregnancy. Notably, since Adriana's Mexican friends were largely born in the U.S. and thus U.S. citizens like herself, Adriana's criticisms were implicitly directed against the presumed "backwardness" of a "cultural" environment that she identified as "Mexican," which seemed to subvert higher educational and career ambitions and life goals for the young women she knew. On another occasion, she wrote:

> Maria is one of my friends from the South Side. She is two months pregnant. She told her parents and her father doesn't want her to live at home anymore.

Her mother wants her to drop out of school. Lizette was telling me about all the girls we went to school with on the South Side; half are pregnant and the other half dropped out (10/4/94).

This distinction between Adriana's aspirations and the tragic example of her South Side (Mexican) friends, largely inseparable from the equation of teen pregnancy and hopelessness, was a recurrent theme. Teen pregnancy seemed synonymous with dropping out of school, and thus symbolized an abrupt "dead end" for a young woman's life trajectory.

Adriana's concern with pregnancy and dropping out of school, moreover, always also implied a certain probability of becoming a welfare recipient. Like many other young Puerto Ricans in Humboldt Park, Adriana remembered the humiliation she had felt as a child when she would accompany her mother to welfare offices or to grocery stores where they had to use food stamps. Not uncommonly these personal experiences with welfare translated for young Puerto Ricans like Adriana into insensitive criticisms of neighbors and relatives receiving public aid. Thus, teen pregnancy was not stigmatized on moralistic grounds or developmental concerns related to the immaturity of the mother-to-be. Rather, the figure of unwed teen mothers signaled a young woman's inability to provide financially for her baby and the seeming inevitability of becoming trapped in a cycle of poverty with no prospects for escape. Rather than because of considerations of age, in other words, Puerto Ricans like Adriana stigmatized teen pregnancy because of its presumed connection to welfare.

Significantly, Adriana Cruz took great pride in her job. On one occasion in November of 1994, Ramos-Zayas noticed that Cruz (and other young women in the class) looked extremely tired. She teasingly asked them if they had been out late, partying, but was not surprised by their replies. They were simply juggling very strenuous, thirty-hour ("part-time") work schedules in addition to being full-time students. Adriana also wrote about these strains in her journal: "As you know, I got the job at Target. I was hired to fix up the department. I work in the Green World. Target goes by worlds, not departments. I started at $5.00 per hour and I just got a raise of 50 cents. In a month and a half I will get another raise. I work during the week right after school and on the weekends I work from 10 A.M. through 6:30 P.M." (11/30/94). Although Adriana valued school and had a clearly defined identity as a student (e.g., participating in school-sponsored activities, getting good grades), this school identity was integrated into a more complex sense of herself as a worker as well, with significant responsibilities at her job.

By the end of her senior year, Adriana had been accepted into some quite competitive colleges in the Midwest, with very good financial aid packages. She started at one of the schools, but dropped out after a semester. Even with financial aid, the college expenses were beyond Adriana's reach, and the academic demands limited her ability to work full-time, as she had done during high

school. The rural location of the college was also an unwelcome change for
Adriana, who was used to living in the city and close to her family. Adriana
returned to Chicago and went back to working in retail, this time at a shoe store
in the middle-class Lakeview neighborhood. There she met Ricardo, a Mexican
raised in the U.S. who had moved from Los Angeles to Chicago a few years prior,
and worked as a manager. After a year, Adriana and Ricardo moved in together,
and a few months later, in November of 1997, Adriana became pregnant. The
unexpected pregnancy put a great deal of strain on the relationship, despite
the fact that Ricardo was financially and emotionally supportive of Adriana's
decision to have the baby. Eventually, Adriana's family became enthusiastic about
the pregnancy and her mother began buying various things for the baby. Adriana
continued working at the shoe store, even though she found herself enduring a
difficult pregnancy and Ricardo was urging her to stay home. Finally, at Ricardo's
insistence, Adriana quit her job during her seventh month.

At this point, Adriana decided to seek public assistance. A highly motivated
young woman, who had worked an average of thirty hours a week throughout
all of her high school education, and who had always associated welfare with
laziness, Adriana agonized during the weeks prior to deciding to seek public
assistance. She called Ramos-Zayas several times and Ramos-Zayas tried to
assure her that, contrary to her own perceptions, receiving public assistance
would not make her a lazy or bad person, as she seemed to imply.

In March of 1999, Ramos-Zayas went to visit Adriana and her then seven-
month-old baby girl. Adriana was living close to O'Hare Airport, a twenty- to
thirty-minute subway ride outside of "the Puerto Rican neighborhood." Adriana
called David and Mike, two former classmates whom she had not seen since college, to tell them that Ramos-Zayas was in town and to invite them for lunch.
When Adriana met the two former high school classmates, she explained to them
that she had had to stop working because of the pregnancy. She quickly added,
however, that she planned to go back as soon as the baby got older. Whenever
Adriana mentioned being "on welfare," she quickly explained that she had decided to pursue Medicaid because of her "bad pregnancy" [*mala barriga*] and,
once the baby was born, to cover regular medical checkups. Adriana's insistence
on specifying that she was receiving "Medicaid," a less stigmatized form of public
assistance, was revealing of her concern that other components of welfare, such
as disability and food stamps, tended to be more highly criticized and perceived
as more frequently subject to "cheating" and "abuse." Furthermore, although
Ricardo and Adriana had intended to marry, their plans had been postponed in
order that Adriana could continue to receive public assistance, since Ricardo's
salary was not enough to make ends meet for the struggling young family.

As a first-time mother, Adriana could be "on welfare" in a manner that others,
such as her former classmates David and Mike, could perceive as unequivocally
related to the well-being of her child, and thus as more socially acceptable. David
and Mike, who themselves had previously been harsh critics of people receiving

welfare, were supportive of Adriana because they were well acquainted with her work history and because she was a first-time mother in a "stable" relationship. Implicit in such justifications, however, was the recognition that Adriana did not fit the pathologized stereotype of a woman "abusing" welfare by "having a bunch of kids by different fathers"—something that would be morally chastised. Rather, in spite of her financial difficulties, she remained within the purview of a presumed moral "mainstream." Welfare was perceived to be a minimal and temporary condition in Adriana's life, and thus its stigma was mitigated. At the same time, such affirmations of the fine line between "good" and "bad" welfare served nonetheless to rationalize the more diffuse forms of patriarchal control that monitored and regulated poor women's sexuality and general autonomy.

The Moral Economy of "Work"

In April of 1995, on the occasion of visiting the home of Angélica Sandoval (who had participated in a math course he had taught at the Imperial Enterprises factory) and her husband, Leobardo (whom he was meeting for the first time), with the purpose of tutoring their daughter in math, De Genova conducted an informal interview during which Angélica spoke minimally while her husband presided. Leobardo Sandoval was immediately curious to know where De Genova was from, and upon discovering that he had been born in the U.S. and was not of Latino parentage, Leobardo was even more intrigued at how it happened that De Genova spoke Spanish and lived in the Pilsen barrio. When De Genova explained a bit about his research and mentioned the subject of discrimination against Mexicans as a concern of his study, Sandoval immediately replied:

> You know why? It's because we're taking over, and they're afraid of what we can do—not like the Blacks, they don't want to work—the Americans don't want to work, neither the Blacks [*negros*] nor the whites [*blancos*]—even my own kids! I tell my daughter, who is sixteen, "You have to work hard and make something of yourself." But the Americans don't understand this, they don't understand that you can't just sit around and expect something to come to you—you have to take advantage of your situation and make something out of life. But that's why they're afraid, because we're going to control everything! I'm not saying in five years, but in twenty years, or fifty years—from Canada to the Panama Canal— just like the Aztecs who were a very good people and knew how to dominate other people and places, the Mexicans are going to take over. I was reading that this new House Speaker Newt Gingrich, he wants to help Mexico with a lot of money—not to help the people, but he's afraid there are going to be 50 million Mexicans coming to the U.S.! They think that they can control Mexico that way, but they'll see—we're going to turn it back on them. Because where would the U.S. be without the Spanish-speaking countries? Nobody else in the world wants the U.S., so where would they be if we turned our back on them?!? And Mexico is the head of all of Latin America—if we turn our back on the U.S., everyone else will follow us, and then they will have nobody.
>
> But I have to admit—I have never been discriminated against; everyone has always treated me nice, with respect. I never had any problem. The only ones

that have a lot of problems are the ones who get into trouble, and drink a lot, and make a mess of things, like over there on 26th Street [Little Village] and 18th Street [Pilsen]. I go over there and I feel embarrassed. I say to the people, "Why do you throw garbage on the street? You should make it so people come here and say, 'Wow, they keep it nice over here!'" But me, I never drank a lot or got into trouble, like a lot of the ones that come over nowadays. And why do they stay there, living that way? Why don't they work to change their situation and move out of those neighborhoods? I bought this house when I was illegal, because I worked hard and wanted to have something in this. My dream now is to get a single-family home in the suburbs, but also keep this apartment building. [...] I have always lived around here, since I was a boy. In the '80s, it was becoming almost all Mexican, but now it's mainly doctors and lawyers and other people with money. My daughter has had many friends who had to move out because the rents went up, but I own this building. Most of the people who live here now don't have children [...] they're buying it as an investment, and that means that they want to maintain it in good condition and keep it clean.

But I bought this building and fixed it up when I was still illegal. And nobody gave me any problem; I was never discriminated against. But it's because I work—not like the Puerto Ricans or the Blacks who just go on welfare and don't do anything for themselves. They're very conformist, very resigned, but Mexicans are not. Mexicans work two jobs, sometimes three. I would work for $400 a month if I had to, just to make something for myself. I would sleep only two or three hours a night, if I had to. And that's why we're going to take over everything.

During the course of the interview, Leobardo also emphasized that when he had first come, "there were almost no Mexicans in Chicago—the only place was Pilsen, and you had to go there to buy Mexican foods or find services in Spanish, but they used to say that Immigration would sit outside of Casa del Pueblo [a grocery store] and grab people when they came out." He criticized Mexicans, however, for not learning English, and complained, "Everywhere you go, everything is in Spanish—look at me, I never finished fifth grade, but I picked up little bits of English everywhere I went, all the time."

In this context, but also cognizant of the fact that De Genova's grandparents had migrated from Italy, Sandoval went on to declare that his greatest admiration was for "Polish and Italians, because they come to work and make something for themselves and don't waste time, don't go on welfare, learn English." At this juncture, Sandoval asked De Genova's opinion of whether or not he and his wife looked like "typical Mexicans," adding that many people took him to be Italian. With recourse to a somewhat tentative whiteness (modified as "Italian"), Leobardo seemed to be making a rather direct appeal (albeit implicit) to the white anthropologist to confirm and thus, in some sense, validate his own desire for the racialized status of whiteness. At this moment, Angélica, who was indeed quite light-skinned (and much lighter than her husband), complicated the already complexly racialized scenario by adding that people usually tended to think that she was Puerto Rican. Expected to supply a response, however, De Genova evaded a direct reply to the question and suggested, "Many whites have a stereotype of what Mexicans look like, but it's harder for me to say because I already know the great variety that exists among Mexican people—but there is a common stereotype of what Mexicans look like because they are always put between white and Black in this country." Leobardo replied, "That's right," and Angélica added, "There are lots of white people in Mexico." Leobardo went on to affirm, "You see people with blonde hair and green eyes and blue eyes," and Angélica continued, "You could mistake them for Polish." Interested in complicating this turn in the conversation, De Genova added, "There are Black people in Mexico, too." Angélica quickly agreed, "Yes, Blacks too." De Genova then suggested, "But it seems to me that all of those differences are understood differently there, in Mexico." With this, however, Leobardo was able to resume some of the momentum of his earlier remarks, "Yes," he declared, "because in reality there is no racism in Mexico—it's not like here. If they don't like Americans, it's not because of the color of their skin, it's because of the place that they're from. Because all of this land was ours, and the English came and took it all away from us. So now we're taking it back. You go to Miami, it's all Cubans. Texas, it's all Mexicans; California, all Mexicans; Chicago, all Mexicans."

Despite some of his more favorable pronouncements with regard to Mexico, such as its purported leadership of Latin America and the denial of any racism, and his elision of the virtues of Mexico and Mexicans notwithstanding, Leobardo also was fairly critical of Mexico. Due to the undocumented status of both Leobardo and Angélica until they became eligible for the "Amnesty" after the 1986 legislation (IRCA), the Sandoval family had not visited Mexico until 1987. Leobardo had not returned in twenty years. He recounted driving into Mexico with their two young daughters. He said it was shocking to him to be in Mexico again, once he had stopped at the restaurants on the road, seen the conditions, used the bathrooms. At first, he explained, he had been excited when he drove across the border and saw the countryside open up in front of him, but then he was shocked and had a hard time getting used to it, because he had gotten so used to life in the U.S. Leobardo also declared that he never once dreamed of going back to live in Mexico ever since he came, explaining, "because in Mexico they have everything we have here, except it's all on the top shelf and only the tall [high] people [*la gente alta*] can have it, but in the U.S. all you have to do is work hard and you can have whatever you want—the rich people might have five VCRs, but so can you if that's what you want."

Leobardo Sandoval's faith in the ideology that, in the U.S., "all you have to do is work hard and you can have whatever you want" was in striking contrast to most Mexican migrants' experiences of exploitation and the critical perspectives often elaborated by many concerning how thoroughly disillusioning their work experiences had been. Indeed, Leobardo's account of his own work history was rather less sanguine. Leobardo had previously been employed at Imperial Enterprises, where his wife was still working, but as he explained, "they didn't want to pay very much." At the time of the interview, he worked in a foundry. He added meaningfully that this workplace had previously employed 120 people, but now had only 35 workers remaining. When asked why, Leobardo stated plainly, "New machines." When asked, "Are you working harder now than before?" Sandoval replied unequivocally, "Yes, much harder." "So the new machines only meant that each person who's still working is doing two or three people's jobs," De Genova posited. "You can say that, yes," he agreed soberly.

Leobardo had migrated from the Mexican city of San Luis Potosí with his father at the age of twelve, in 1967, and immediately went to work, first as a busboy in a Chicago restaurant. He had never attended school in the U.S. In these ways, while his overall experience was not at all exceptional, Leobardo had nonetheless begun his working life as a Mexican migrant in Chicago at an exceptionally young age.[6] The overwhelming majority of Mexicans who had migrated to Chicago had done so as young adults, even if still in their teens, had immediately gone to work, and had never attended school in the U.S. Even if a considerable proportion might have already been working to help support their families in Mexico at the age of twelve, few had actually migrated to begin working at that age; most tended to have been in the range of at least fifteen to seventeen years of age, or older. (Indeed, Angélica herself, who had migrated at the age of eighteen, in 1973, from a small town in the Mexican state of Zacatecas, had a migration trajectory that was more typical, and confided later that she disagreed with her husband about many issues). When De Genova suggested that Leobardo Sandoval's lack of interest in returning to Mexico probably had to do with how young he was when he came to the U.S., that this seemed to be quite unlike most people who come from Mexico, who typically migrate with the intention of returning, Leobardo said, "That's true, almost all of them, but 90% probably never do, because they also get used to what they can have here and the conveniences of life here; like me, they have their home and their kids here, and eventually they decide to stay." Notably, it is relevant to add that there was a small U.S. flag displayed at the top of a decorative china cabinet in the Sandoval dining room where the interview took place—something not at all common in most Mexican/migrant homes in Chicago, where it would be infinitely more likely to see a Mexican flag instead.

This extended discussion of Leobardo Sandoval is not at all intended to be "representative" of Mexican migrants in Chicago; neither the defining aspects of his experience nor many of his most forceful opinions are typical. Indeed, he is truly exceptional, precisely inasmuch as he more readily resembles the iconic figure of "the immigrant" whose devotion to an ideal of leaving behind his native country and remaking himself through hard work in a chosen land of opportunity is central to the sustenance of U.S. nationalism (De Genova, 1999:19–104; in press; cf. Chock, 1991; 1996; Honig, 1998). There are, however, quite remarkable ambivalences evident in Leobardo's discourse. Although he acknowledged the fact of racism in the U.S. while extolling Mexico's virtues, he nonetheless more than once disavowed the significance of racist oppression and racialized exploitation in the U.S. by, in effect, blaming the victims. In the case of Blacks and Puerto Ricans—"they don't want to work," "just go on welfare and don't do anything for themselves," "they're very conformist, very resigned"— the predominant allegation was laziness and an aversion to work. In the case of Mexicans—"the only ones that have a lot of problems are the ones who get into trouble, and drink a lot, and make a mess of things"—the apparent failure to take advantage of opportunities in the U.S. was cast in terms of the moral deficiencies of individuals (cf. R. T. Smith, 1996). Although he was triumphalist about the prospect of Mexican industriousness poised to "take over" and "control everything" and expressed a certain suspicion about U.S. political machinations toward Mexico, he also produced a critique of Mexican social inequalities and celebrated the U.S. as a bastion of opportunity, such that migration to the U.S. emerged tacitly as a necessary precondition for Mexican "hard work" to prevail. Although he embraced crucial dimensions of U.S. nationalism, he nevertheless characterized himself always as Mexican and was critical of all "Americans"— whites and Blacks, and even his own U.S.-born children. And yet, despite this inclusive construction of who exactly might be "Americans," he also referred to Mexican attitudes toward "Americans" as having to do not with "the color of their skin" but rather with a history of conquest by "the English"—implicitly treating "American"-ness as a name for racialized whiteness in much the same manner as other Mexican migrants (as well as Puerto Ricans). Despite this pronouncedly Mexican self-identification, he revealed a considerable investment in whether he appeared (phenotypically) to be Mexican or Italian, and was eager to recuperate a certain fact of whiteness within Mexicanness. Coupled with his praise for the Polish and Italians (migrant groups who have come to be racialized as white in the U.S.) and his frank derision toward African Americans and Puerto Ricans, his generationally inflected and moralistic ambivalence about barrio Mexicans—specifically, "a lot of the ones who come over nowadays"—revealed the tormenting question that seemed to be Leobardo's central dilemma: What will Mexicans prove themselves to be?

This quandary of Leobardo's helps to situate the more general social predicament of Mexican migrants in the U.S.—that of a group racialized as neither white nor Black within the hegemonic bipolarity of white supremacy within the space of U.S. nation-state. In these respects, Leobardo's discourse did indeed exhibit certain key features in common with perspectives that were rather ubiquitous among Mexican migrants in Chicago: the identification of "American"-ness with racialized whiteness; the denigration of racialized Blackness; the reformulation of Mexicanness as a transnationality, racialized in relation to both whiteness and Blackness within the U.S. but simultaneously posited in relation to Mexico as well; the unequivocal equation of welfare with laziness and an aversion to work; and the demotion of Puerto Ricans to a degraded racialized status, approaching or approximating Blackness (De Genova, 1999: 287–356; in press). Indeed, all of these characteristics of the historically specific racialization of

Mexican migrants, we would propose, reveal something definitive, not really so much about "Mexicans" as such, but rather about the racialized character of citizenship within the U.S. nation-state and, likewise, about U.S. nationalism as a racial formation.

The Racial Economy of Welfare and Work

Although Puerto Ricans upheld a moral economy of "welfare" that generally sought to deflect pervasive allegations of "laziness" of the sort that many Mexican migrants commonly directed toward the U.S.-citizen poor, Puerto Ricans would nevertheless occasionally deflect the degraded racialized status of "laziness" and "welfare dependency" by joking about abusing the system and discussing various strategies for "getting a free ride," including men ironically celebrating the idea of being supported by their wives. Notably, humor along these lines became a strategy in everyday social interactions precisely to circumvent potential conflicts between Mexicans and Puerto Ricans. Racialized joking and teasing in contexts of differential social power certainly reinforce racist stereotypes even as they mobilize a playful ambiguity to obfuscate intent (De Genova, 1999; Lancaster, 1997; Urciuoli, 1996:151–55). Puerto Ricans in Chicago often resorted to the ironic performance of the very same racial stereotypes that they presumed others attributed to them. In the face of these racializing characterizations, such humor among Puerto Ricans also served to reclaim a certain degree of power to control their own representation.

On one occasion involving a group of graduating seniors at the Puerto Rican–identified alternative high school where Ramos-Zayas taught, when they were asked about their post-graduation plans by a group of adults visiting the school, for example, William, an outgoing and charismatic student leader in the class, playfully responded, "We all plan to go on welfare." The visitors eventually caught on to the joke, but only after the other students had begun speaking in earnest about the colleges they hoped to attend and their more conventional aspirations. William's reply was suggestive of a more general Puerto Rican response to the demoted and degraded racialized status to which Puerto Ricans were often assigned by other Latinos, abundantly manifest among Mexican migrants. First, William's joke acknowledged that outsiders perceived collecting welfare almost as if it were an arbitrary and frivolous decision, available to and more or less automatically utilized by anyone who can "exploit the system." Secondly, his response challenged the visitors' normative expectations that quality education should invariably culminate in upward social mobility. Finally, in the face of the racially mixed group of white, African American, and Latino professionals, William was implicitly letting the visitors know that he was aware of the presumptions they very likely made about him, as a young dark-skinned Puerto Rican in a stigmatized "inner-city" neighborhood. In this sense, William deployed irony and humor to skillfully perform, expose, and subvert the very stereotype harbored by those engaged in racializing him. Moreover, in doing so,

William implicitly questioned more fundamental assumptions about the U.S. as a meritocracy in which sincere "hard work" invariably produces "success." This is not to suggest that William and his classmates did not believe in schooling as a route to "making it." On the contrary. The "American Dream" and its various postulates of meritocracy and "hard work" were continuously rehearsed in the Humboldt Park barrio, and were evidenced by the "success stories" of relatives or neighbors who were presumed to have "made it," yet remained close enough to epitomize the process. Nevertheless, by strategically performing the degraded racialized identity foisted upon his kind, William appropriated the power to represent himself in ways that created a moment of discomfort and defamiliarization for the visitors who might indeed have suspected that young Puerto Ricans like William had grown up in a presumably "pathological" milieu—a "culture of poverty," as it were—in which "laziness" was rewarded with ample opportunities to "exploit the system," and "work" could be evaded by "welfare dependency."

Most Mexican migrants in the U.S., unlike Leobardo Sandoval, would not endorse the view that "all you have to do is work hard and you can have whatever you want"—knowing very well that they have never done anything in the U.S. if not work hard, but without any spectacular rewards. But they were virtually unanimous in their sense that Mexicans as a group are extraordinarily distinguished for "wanting to work," for "knowing how to work," for "not being afraid to work," and for "being ready to work hard" (De Genova, 1999:261–65). It was hardly surprising, then, when one of the countless industrial day-labor services in Chicago, which specialize in extracting a profit from the recruitment and placement of undocumented workers for local factories, circulated flyers in Pilsen in the summer of 2000 that read: "Seeking people who truly want to work and are not afraid of work! [*¡Se busca gente que en verdad quiera trabajar y no le tenga miedo al trabajo!*]." These specific qualifications, of course, are the ubiquitous conditions of possibility for undocumented workers in particular to serve as an exceptionally vulnerable workforce, presumed by employers to be "cheap" and tractable, and thus, honored as a labor pool of choice. These same virtues, likewise, were commonly marshaled by Mexican migrants as the qualities that rendered as competitive and prized the commodity that was their labor-power, in opposition to that of their most proximate competitors in the labor market, who could be denigrated as "lazy."

The topic of welfare was inseparable, among Mexican migrant workers, from allegations of "laziness." At a factory called Czarnina and Sons, in March of 1994, a worker named Evangelina put it concisely: "Mexicans don't go on welfare; welfare is for Blacks, Americans, and Puerto Ricans, because they're lazy; a Mexican might have ten kids, but the kids go to work; ten years, twelve years old, the kids help pay, no problem . . . " She chuckled, but then after a moment's pause, added somewhat more seriously, "Well, it depends on the father, because the mother doesn't want to make the kids work." Evangelina's endorsement of this severe and laborious ideal of "Mexican"-ness was first enthusiastic and then more ambivalent, and overtly gendered. There was certainly an element of hyperbole in this defense of the pronouncedly working-class status honor of Mexicans against "Blacks, Americans, and Puerto Ricans," and Evangelina's mirth acknowledged her own exaggeration. But then, perhaps because she was embarrassed to have depicted her community to a white "American" in terms that could make Mexicans seem extreme and even heartless, she abruptly began to qualify her own claim and convey her own reservations about the harsh image she had just portrayed. Clearly, it is significant that Evangelina did so in gendered terms that suggested a critique of men's patriarchal authority within the family, thereby also implying a direct link between male power and this quite masculinist construction of "Mexican"-ness in terms of "hard work."[7]

It is illuminating here to consider a joke that was circulating among Mexican migrants in Chicago in the spring of 1997. Jokes, of course, operate within a certain moral economy of pervasive assumptions, at the same time as they are really interventions in their own right that reaffirm and help to reproduce those same assumptions. Reduced to its basic elements, the joke can be summarized as follows: It is the time of the Mexican Revolution, and Pancho Villa's army has just captured an invading U.S. regiment; addressing his lieutenants, Pancho Villa gives the order: "Take all the Americans [*americanos*]—shoot them, kill them; the Blacks [*morenos*] and Puerto Ricans—just let them go." The lieutenants are confused and dismayed: "What?! What are you saying?!? But why??" Coolly, Pancho Villa replies, "Don't waste the bullets—they'll all just die of hunger—because here, there's no welfare." Clearly, in order to be apprehended as "funny," a punch line such as this—which imputes that Black people and Puerto Ricans would be literally incapable of sustaining themselves without welfare, indeed that their laziness is so intractable that they would starve to death—must correspond to the presumed assumptions of an intended audience. Indeed, this joke reiterates the hegemonic racial script that has already been seen to have infused many Mexican migrants' commonplace production of their difference from both African Americans and Puerto Ricans. The joke is clearly reminiscent of both Leobardo's and Evangelina's remarks.[8] The expected reception of the joke's irony resides in a collective sentiment that counterpoises the industriousness (and also thrift) of Mexican workers to the "laziness" of their most proximate competitors in the U.S./Chicago labor market—so that what at first appears to be startlingly counterintuitive, even nonsensical, in Pancho Villa's order, is revealed as shrewd wisdom that flatters the commonsense.[9]

The racialized categories of social differentiation to be discerned in the joke's language, moreover, deserve further examination. The joke produces a reductive representation of the U.S. racial economy—one that is specifically resonant for Mexicans in Chicago—but reterritorialized onto Mexican terrain. Within the joke's refracted space, Mexican migrants contend with the U.S. racial economy as Pancho Villa's soldiers (which is to say, as "Mexicans") battling the arrayed forces of the U.S., which in no simple sense comprise only "Americans," but rather, include "Americans" as well as "Blacks" and "Puerto Ricans." Notably, Evangelina had used precisely the same categories, and the opposition in both instances implicitly posited "Mexicans" (as migrants) against an array of U.S. citizens. Three of these four operative categories could be mistaken for "nationality," but what is decisive is precisely the remaining term—"Blacks"—which reveals that it would be erroneous to simply read the other categories according to their explicit "national" surface. That these categories all stand alongside of one another as formal equivalences in the structure of the joke, requires that the apparently "national" skins of three of these terms ("Mexican," "American," and "Puerto Rican") be brought into alignment with the purely and plainly racialized identity of the fourth ("Black"). The lines of adversity are drawn around the axis of citizenship, but this division becomes apprehensible only when it is further fractured by racialized distinctions.

Notably, African Americans are perceived to be separate, distinct, and, indeed, excluded from the category "Americans"—exposing the fact that "American" comes to connote whiteness.[10] As such, "American"-ness is unavailable to Blacks *or* Latinos (whether they be noncitizen Mexican migrants or Puerto Ricans who are born into U.S. citizenship). Neither for African Americans nor for Puerto Ricans does birthright U.S. citizenship secure the status of "American"-ness, which constitutes a national identity that is understood, in itself, to be intrinsically racialized—as white. The nationally or "culturally" inflected differences between Mexicans and Puerto Ricans, furthermore, do not suffice to account for the racialized distinctions introduced by the joke, because the differences between Mexicans and Puerto Ricans are posited in the joke as analogous to those between Mexicans and whites and Blacks. Both Mexicans and Puerto Ricans—together as Latinos—occupy racialized locations in an intermediate space between white and Black, but the more palpable form of their respective differences here is most likely that, rather than being racialized together more generically as "Hispanics" or "Latinos," Mexicans tend to be racialized simply as "Mexicans" (cf. Barrera, 1979; D. Gutiérrez, 1995:24; Mirandé, 1985:76; 1987: 3–9; Montejano, 1987:5, 82–85; Paredes, 1978[1993:38]; Vélez-Ibáñez, 1996:19, 70–87), and Puerto Ricans, likewise, tend to be racialized simply as "Puerto Ricans" (Grosfoguel and Georas, 1996:195; Urciuoli, 1996:41–72).

Puerto Ricans, moreover, are specifically coupled here with Blacks. Within the terms of the joke, "Mexican"-ness is doubly constituted. First, there is a frank recognition of "American" power as a distinctly white power. Against the invasive (colonizing) power of "Americans"—that is, whites—the joke, in a way reminiscent of Leobardo's remarks, constitutes an heroic "Mexican"-ness as a physical and moreover intellectual force to be reckoned with, truly capable of vanquishing the genuine threat of this opponent which is so thoroughly fearsome and resilient that it must be completely obliterated ("shoot them, kill them"). Simultaneously, "Mexican"-ness—as a muscular, masculinist, indeed militaristic kind of diligence and self-sufficiency—is constituted not only against African Americans but also Puerto Ricans, both of whom are constructed to be so lazy as to be helpless, and ultimately negligible. Their mutual fate is formulated in relation to "welfare," an institution of the U.S. state to which both groups have access as a substantive entitlement of their shared citizenship status. The allegation of welfare dependency becomes inseparable, however, from the racialized insinuation of laziness (otherwise equated with Blackness). Within the terms of the joke, then, Mexicans must relegate Puerto Ricans to a racialized status that approximates (or at least approaches) Blackness. Such acts of demotion serve the purposes of a kind of racialized self-promotion among those who are corralled in that agonistic and contradictory space between white and Black and must vie with one another for position. What is revealed about that space, moreover, is that these intermediate racialized conditions— those racialized as neither white nor Black—consistently seem to be already entrenched in the hegemonic denigration of Blackness.

The Racial Economy of Dignity and Respectability

Latinos have often observed that the very reason why Latinismo engenders prejudicial reactions is because of its likely association with Puerto Ricans and Mexicans/Chicanos (Oboler, 1995). Recent migrants appear more vulnerable and thus less threatening to the life of dominant U.S. society—in fact, in very significant material and practical senses, it is possible to contend that they actually facilitate and sustain it. Specialized spaces of exploitation develop, as undocumented migrants in particular fulfill the everyday social needs not only of elites but rather of a vast cross-section of the relatively privileged citizenry through their services as maids, handymen, dishwashers, nannies, etc. In many instances, Latino migrants, especially the undocumented, are preferred for these types of labor over "difficult" or "troublesome" U.S.-citizen "minorities," because the quiet and routine exploitation of seemingly docile "immigrants" can be conveniently reinterpreted by employers—as "hard work," the stuff that perpetually animates the "American Dream."

The meaning of "starting at the bottom" and "working your way up," which relies upon the assumption that the occupational structure of the U.S. is an unhindered ascending ladder which everyone climbs in order to "make it," was deployed in divergent ways by Puerto Ricans in Chicago, according to class differences. The Puerto Rican professional middle class and even the working-class employees at not-for-profit organizations frequently spoke disparagingly of the "lack of drive" [el desgano] of poorer Puerto Rican barrio residents. To various degrees, many middle-class Puerto Ricans subscribed to dominant "underclass" arguments when referring to their compatriots in the stigmatized space of el barrio. A resident of Logan Square whom Ramos-Zayas met through the Office of the Puerto Rican Parade, Haydée Colón, commented, "When we lived on Division and Rockwell [in Humboldt Park], there were more people on welfare. But around here, where we live now [Logan Square], houses are more expensive. Here people work." The implication in Haydée's remark seemed to be that, unlike in Humboldt Park, which is the most pathologized neighborhood of the Puerto Rican community, welfare was not as common in Logan Square *because* people worked instead, and, by implication, because they chose to work, because they preferred it.

Oftentimes, middle-class Puerto Ricans and other Latinos deployed dominant U.S. discourses of meritocracy and "opportunity" to valorize their own upward social mobility as individual achievement. Puerto Rican professionals perceived the apparent willingness of Mexican and Central American migrants to "start at the bottom" (and presumably wait their rightful turn to gradually move up the putative mobility ladder) as commendable evidence of a "work ethic" that they alleged to be lacking among the Puerto Rican poor. "Mexicans sell their flags and foods on every corner. A few years ago, it was the Puerto Ricans who were doing that," commented Brenda Ramírez, a healthcare activist in her twenties, as she walked past an ambulatory Mexican kiosk in Humboldt Park. Elsa Ayala, a parent liaison at the local high school, mentioned, "Mexicans are hardworking. They start at the bottom and work at anything, even [despite being] illegal! You see them being more humble than Puerto Ricans," While Mexicans were perceived as "hardworking," however, the fact that they remained for the most part poor was taken in these Puerto Rican accounts to be indicative of "not knowing how the system works." Ester García, the owner of a beauty school and salon in Logan Square, further explained this perceived lack of social and political savvy. When Ramos-Zayas first met Ester García, Ester was complaining about a Mexican/migrant student who had returned to Mexico only a few weeks prior to completing the year-long course of study at the beauty school. When Ramos-Zayas asked García about this student, she remarked:

> She didn't get used to it [*No se acostumbró*]. Mexicans don't get used to being here. They may have left their children back there or they have problems with English, but they end up going back. It happens all the time. This girl...I don't know. She always had a problem. She always had to be at her other job. I told her, "But why don't you just wait a few more weeks? Complete the course, then you can go back [to Mexico] with the certificate." But she still left before finishing. Sometimes Mexicans don't have a vision of progress...not all, but...That's also because in Mexico they don't even ask for a certificate to practice hairstyling. In Puerto Rico, yes, you need one. But not in Mexico.

In addition to implying that Mexico was provincial and unsophisticated in contrast to the "modernity" that Puerto Rico shared with the U.S. (see chapter 4), Ester's comment suggested that Mexicans in general, while "hardworking," nonetheless were too "traditional" or rigidly "stuck in their ways" to adapt to the dynamic demands and challenges of life in the U.S.—"Mexicans don't get used to being here"—and returning to Mexico was virtually synonymous with presumed "failure." In Ester's account, if Mexicans lacked an appreciation of the importance of credentials as a means of attaining a better social position in the long run, it was indicative of a more profound deficit—the putative lack of a "vision of progress" necessary for "success" in the U.S. (see comparable discussion in chapter 5).

Puerto Ricans across class lines, as we have already suggested, tended to perceive being on welfare, and particularly welfare not counterbalanced by one's mitigating life circumstances, as shameful. However, for Puerto Rican barrio residents, "working for nothing" or being exploited in a dead-end job (which were often perceived as the only other available options for the poor) also raised concerns about dignity. Alma and Elda, two Puerto Rican women who attended parenting workshops at the public high school in Humboldt Park, expressed indignation as they explained that Teresa, a Mexican participant in the program, would have to miss that day's workshop. In this instance, as on other previous occasions, Teresa's Cuban boss did not permit her to leave work a half hour early, even though the program coordinator had informed employers that the City was sponsoring these workshops and had requested that they adjust work schedules to allow their employees to attend twice a month. When Alma and Elda commented that Teresa should have given her boss hell, so that he would let her come to the workshop, another Puerto Rican parent explained: "There's not much [Teresa] can do. And they [Mexicans, other migrants] accept it because they don't have choices. They can't go complain to anybody. No, no. You have to bow down [*tiene que ser eñangotao*] and accept that you are less than your boss. You just have to accept it." Similarly, Carmen, a working-class resident of Logan Square, commented, "The *mexicanitos* are very humble. If you talk to them, they right away tell you, '*Mande...?*' Very obliging [*serviciales*].[11] We, Puerto Ricans, are arrogant and we don't help each other. Mexicans do." In Carmen's view, the very "humility" and "obligingness" exhibited by Mexicans derived from the migrants' perceived existence in tightly knit groups with a predominantly communitarian orientation, a quality juxtaposed to the implicitly more "modern" and "individualistic" character that Carmen ambivalently projected onto Puerto Ricans in Chicago. Many Puerto Rican barrio residents attributed the job patterns exhibited by Mexicans and Central Americans not only to the vulnerability caused by their "illegality," but also to a lack of knowledge about "how this country works" and "being used to exploitation" (originating in their "backward" countries of origin). On the one hand, then, Puerto Ricans identified how substantive rights and entitlements to which they could avail themselves— as U.S. citizens—seemed to be simply foreclosed for many Mexican migrants. On the other hand, Puerto Ricans also often celebrated their citizenship as a distinctive group identity that could be counterpoised to Mexican and other Latino migrants (especially the undocumented) whose legal status and consequent social conditions could furthermore be presumed to derive from defining traits, such as humility and obligingness, alleged to characterize them as a group.

Thus, the difference of citizenship provided Puerto Ricans with the means to demote Mexicans, as a group, to an effectively premodern condition of passivity and subservience. Rather than exuding the virtue of being "hardworking" then, Mexican migrants from this perspective seemed to be merely submissive. Nevertheless, while such concerns with dignity were evoked by the Puerto Rican poor and working poor, middle-class Puerto Ricans tended to evade these issues in their persistent characterizations of the Puerto Rican barrio poor in ways inseparable from allegations of "laziness" and the lack of a "work ethic," deploying discourses analogous to those of Mexican migrants with regard to Puerto Ricans in general.

In late October 1994, at a factory called Liberty Carton located in a South Side Mexican/migrant neighborhood, where there were only a handful of Puerto Ricans working among over one hundred Mexicans, a twenty-three-year old Puerto Rican worker named Ricky López offered a very different account of his own "laziness" than the sort of discourses typical among his Mexican coworkers. Although Ricky had only migrated from Puerto Rico five years earlier, he spoke extraordinarily fluent English in comparison to his largely Mexican/migrant coworkers. When asked how he had learned the language so well, Ricky replied enthusiastically, " I'm *presentao.*" This was a specifically Puerto Rican colloquialism with which De Genova was unfamiliar, and he needed for López to explain what he meant. Ricky replied, "*Presentao*—I want to know everything, I'm lazy—lazy people know everything." Still perplexed by how López was accounting for his exceptional command of English by celebrating his own "laziness," De Genova continued asking for further clarification. Ricky provided examples of learning things simply by watching, without requiring instruction—punctuating each example, emphatically, with "*presentao, presentao!*" As it turned out, Ricky had come to the mainland and immediately began collecting welfare for two months until he found work; during those two months, he had studied English intensively. But this is not what Ricky was characterizing as his admirable "laziness." Instead, his use of the term "*presentao,*" which describes someone who is "nosy" or meddlesome, an outgoing "busybody" who is therefore always hanging around and curious about everybody else's affairs and everything happening around him, created a continuity between this kind of avid curiosity and the "laziness" that, for him, made it possible to learn new things and take advantage of opportunities for advancement. This rather particular Puerto Rican self-construction as "lazy" was perhaps a bit eccentric, but it stood in stark contrast to the widespread denigration of "laziness" as construed by Mexican migrants.

Mexican/migrant discourses about Puerto Rican "laziness" tended to be always coupled with the opposition between work and welfare, but they were embedded in broader concerns with a distinctly working-class sense of status honor or "respectability." Thus, on one occasion during a math class at the Imperial Enterprises factory, when a Puerto Rican worker named Oscar teased his Mexican classmate Rosa that she was cheating by copying her answers from her friend Angélica's work, Rosa's immediate and quite aggressive response was, "What do you think—that I'm Puerto Rican?!" Not merely aggravated by Oscar's needling, Rosa was visibly insulted that he would have insinuated that she wasn't doing her own work—to which the self-evident retort seemed for her to be that it was really Puerto Ricans like Oscar who cheated and did not take responsibility for their work.

Mexican migrants likewise presumed a continuity between the "laziness" they ascribed to Puerto Ricans and a concomitant inclination on the part of Puerto Ricans to cheat, trick, or swindle them, to take advantage and exploit them. In April of 1994 at a factory called DuraPress, two Mexican/migrant workers, Adelberto and Benito, both reported having been connived over the telephone into one-year contracts with health clubs, tricked by swindler sales representatives who were bilingual but only provided partial explanations in Spanish. It was seemingly self-evident and preemptive of any further discussion of the topic when they summarily characterized these dishonest salesmen as, simply, "Puerto Ricans."

In conclusion, the respective ideological contrasts of "hard work" as opposed to "laziness," or "submissiveness" in contradistinction to notions of "savviness" and "sophistication," revealed the ways in which substantive differences rooted in the unequal politics of citizenship generated and sustained distinct moral economies. Furthermore, they signaled how these divergent relations to the U.S. state also supplied the meaningful differences of value and virtue that could be used to uphold opposed ideas of each group's character *as a group*. Once formulated in "moral" or "cultural" terms, such differences ascribed to one another's group identity, therefore, readily lent themselves, on the one hand, to rather explicitly racialized understandings of these divergences, and on the other, to implicit discourses of deservingness or competence for U.S. citizenship. The repercussions of such dichotomies produced between Mexican migrants and Puerto Ricans, furthermore, opened onto an expansive terrain of related discourses that similarly appeared to corroborate an increasingly durable basis for division. The result of these competing notions of competence and capacity for productive work, then, were similarly contested visions of each group's more generally "civilized" or "modern" qualities, juxtaposed to the other's putative "backwardness" or "rudeness." It is to these themes that we now turn, for a more thorough examination in chapter 4.

CHAPTER 4

Performing Deservingness: "Civility" and "Modernity" in Conflict

The respective ideological contrasts of Mexican migrants' and Puerto Ricans' constructions of their competing competencies, as seen in the previous chapter, had important ramifications beyond the racial economy of welfare and work. What emerge are competing visions of each group's "civilized" or "modern" qualities in juxtaposition to the other's purported "rudeness" or "backward-ness." This chapter explores how Mexican migrants often generalized from the allegation that Puerto Ricans were "lazy" to posit variously that they were like-wise untrustworthy, deceptive, willing to cheat, disagreeable, nervous, rude, aggressive, violent, dangerous, and criminal. In constructing these racialized images of the character of Puerto Ricans as a group, Mexicans were implicitly or explicitly celebrating a sense of themselves as educated, well-mannered, and civilized. In contrast, Puerto Ricans frequently elaborated further upon their perceptions of Mexicans as uninitiated into the workings of the sociopolitical system in the U.S. and inclined to sacrifice their dignity in a desperate quest for work. Puerto Ricans commonly coupled these judgments with allegations that Mexicans, as a group, were submissive, obliging, gullible, naïve, rustic, out-moded, folksy, backward, and predominantly "cultural," in contrast to a vision of themselves as political, principled, sophisticated, stylish, dynamic, urban, and modern. Remarkably, these parallel discourses on the parts of both groups served to sustain their own divergent claims of civility or modernity, in ways that implied their differential worthiness for the entitlements of citizenship.

Discreet "Civility," Assertive "Modernity"

The long history of Spanish conquest and colonization in Mexico, and virtually all of Latin America, predictably invested the ideological category of "civiliza-tion" with a range of profoundly racialized meanings that were inseparable from the subjugation and denigration of indigenous people and their ways of life as "savage" or "barbaric." While the "Indians" were equated with nature and wild-ness, "civilization" necessarily implied cultivation, moral community, social order, and subjection to the political authority of the state. Thus, the "civiliz-ing" mission of the colonizers (as well as that of the post-Independence Mexican nation-state with respect to its own sociopolitical peripheries) was conceived significantly as one analogous to the domestication of animals, which would transform wild nature into a properly ordered conformity to "cultured" norms and the dictates of "reason." Notably, therefore, civility was inextricably bound to political power and social order, and had implications not only for those considered presocial "savages" but equally importantly for the fully developed, mature, rational, refined personhood of every "civilized" subject. "Civilization" did not only refer to the domestication of the external nature of the wilderness and the frontier, but also the subordination of every individual's "natural" being through a rational control of the brutish instincts and passions and the diligent cultivation of a well-governed and orderly self (Alonso, 1995; cf. R. Gutiérrez, 1991).

A prominent enduring legacy of such notions of "civilization" is epitomized by one of the central tenets of Mexican racism—the equation of being an "Indian" [*indio*] with rudeness (Alonso, 1995; Friedlander, 1975; R. Gutiérrez, 1991; Lomnitz-Adler, 1992; 2001; Nagengast and Kearney, 1990; cf. Domínguez, 1994; Klor de Alva, 1995; C. Smith, 1997; Wade, 1997). In an intriguing but revealing way, the deep connections between the racialization of "Indians" and the broader discourse of "civility" emerged on one unlikely occasion in November of 1995, during an ESL course at an industrial container-cleaning and waste-disposal plant called Caustic Scrub. In this workplace, where the Mexican/migrant workforce routinely handled extremely dangerous chemicals, a worker named Reynaldo Zaragoza mentioned that a coworker had fallen into a vat of highly acidic soap and literally "burnt his ass." This remark provided the occasion for another participant in the all-male ESL group, Manuel González, to ask for a clarification of the different meanings of the words "ass" and "asshole." Although this particular workplace was a remarkably masculinist space where, for example, workers spoke with no inhibition of such topics as weekend carousing in nightclubs that featured strippers, Manuel's sincere question about English-language vocabulary nevertheless inspired some nervous laughter and embarrassment. Manuel, a Mexican migrant who was forty years old and had migrated to the U.S. thirteen years prior, from a small town in the state of Jalisco, who was living with a Mexican woman born in the U.S. and her children from a prior relationship, frankly criticized his coworkers' inhibitions about this subject. Although he was indeed a man rather particularly prone to sexual humor and innuendo, Manuel demanded reasonably and sincerely why adults should be uncomfortable discussing these body parts as opposed to any others, such as the eyes or nose, arms or legs. Reynaldo chastised him in return, explaining, "Those are personal things, intimate things." In response, Manuel insisted that these words were part of the everyday language to which all of these men were exposed routinely, and therefore that they ought to be able to understand clearly.

Now directing himself to De Genova, González continued, "That's how it is here with the *gabachos* [(white) "Americans"]. In Mexico, people are very embarrassed to talk about these things—they're more civilized [*más civilizados*]—but here, people are very open. There [in Mexico], if you go to some remote villages, where they still speak indigenous languages [*dialectos*], they go hide when you enter their homes!" Nodding, another coworker, Mateo, concurred, "Yes, they're more refined [*más refinados*]." Manuel continued, "Here [in the U.S.], people will say anything out in the open, they'll talk about all these things without any shame." In their various remarks, these Mexican men reestablished a shared sense that "civilization" was distinguished by refinement and discretion, and being "civilized" involved being "reserved" in direct and explicit contradistinction to the brazen "openness" of the "American" *gabachos.* Rather than a sign of modernity and sophistication, such "openness" revealed shamelessness.

An appropriate sense of "shame" was also necessary for the kinds of "civility" that the heritage of Spanish colonialism has inculcated in much of Latin America. Indeed, the Spanish colonial rhetoric of "civilization" reserved a particular place for Catholic discourses of "shame" as part of a wider aristocratic concern with masculine "honor" and feminine "virtue" (R. Gutiérrez, 1991). In the Americas, such notions of "shame" were deeply rooted in the Christian missionizing project that accompanied and, in some respects, anticipated the more brutal and overtly racist "civilizing mission" of Spanish colonialism. Notably, in this exchange among the Mexican/migrant workers at Caustic Scrub, there were remarkable revisions and inversions of that colonial legacy. Rather than the Eurocentric and Hispanophile whiteness of elite Mexico that might be associated more directly with the enduring legacies of the Spanish colonial "civilizing mission," it was instead those Mexicans associated with the most "remote" villages, racialized as indigenous by the claim that these were spaces "where they still speak *dialectos,*" who came to be represented as "more civilized" and "more refined." In this conversation, the deep font of Mexican "civilization," then, was actually to be found in its indigenous roots. This racialized sensibility about the "authentic" foundations of the workers' own Mexican "civility" marked a striking contrast with the exaggerated openness and shamelessness of white "Americans" and all things associated with their vulgar modernity.

The charged and conflicting meanings associated with the palpably racialized notions of "civilization" and "modernity" similarly came to inflect the interrelations of Mexicans and Puerto Ricans. During an ESL class at Imperial Enterprises in November of 1993, one of the Mexican workers, Ramiro, casually mentioned that he and his family had gone to eat at a well-known taquería over the weekend. One of his Puerto Rican classmates, Ramón, responded, "That place!? That's where they cook dogs!" Everyone immediately reacted to Ramón's scandalous charge, with the Puerto Rican workers in the group bursting into good-humored laughter, while several of the Mexican workers began to quarrel with what seemed to them to be a preposterous allegation. Various course participants acknowledged that there had indeed been a controversy in the news about an incident in which the severed head of a dog had purportedly been discovered in the trash behind the taquería in question, leading to its temporary closure by the Board of Health. Ramiro defended his favorite restaurant, insisting that because of their delicious food and bustling business, one of their competitors had planted the dog's head in their garbage and cynically stirred up the scandal. In the face of this fairly plausible defense, Ramón resiliently opted to shift course, still grinning mischievously and now asserting, "Well, in Mexico, they *do* cook dogs in some restaurants." Now, however, a few of the Mexicans—Jorge, Fernando, Carlos—actually began to laugh along and admitted, "Now, that's true." Another Mexican worker, Victoria, on the other hand, became visibly offended and angry that Ramón seemed to be slandering Mexico, adamantly protesting, "No, they don't! That's not true!" Beneath the surface of this playful dispute was the insinuation by a Puerto Rican coworker that Mexico was "backward," and even perhaps somewhat uncivilized.

Puerto Ricans, especially the U.S.-born, commonly resorted to implicit distinctions between an image of themselves as "modern" and one of Mexican migrants, if not as plainly "backward," then certainly as parochial. Puerto Ricans often identified this perceived parochialism among Mexicans by characterizing them as overly "cultural," manifesting an excessive attachment to their provincial traditions and folksy ways. This perception was candidly articulated by Hilda Ayala, a Puerto Rican woman in her sixties, who had spent half of her life in Chicago and was contemplating the possibility of moving back to the Island. Ayala sold her bridal shop a few days after Ramos-Zayas met her. When asked about her bridal shop, she explained that she was selling it because, as she saw it, Puerto Ricans were "losing their culture," an unfortunate consequence of which was that they no longer conducted *quinceañeros,* elaborate and festive coming-of-age celebrations for girls on the occasion of their fifteenth birthdays, as Mexicans continued to do. Hilda attributed her business's decline partly to an increasing disregard for these ceremonial parties among younger Puerto Ricans, emphasizing that most of her customers now were actually Mexican: "Mexicans care about culture. They spend whatever is needed on weddings and *quinceañeros* without protesting—regardless of how poor they are. Puerto Ricans don't even want to participate as godparents!" While driving Ramos-Zayas around Humbold Park, Ayala commented, somewhat nostalgically:

> [Mexicans] know how to demonstrate their culture. Have you seen Pilsen or La Villita? It's like being in Mexico! There it gets so crowded, people can't even walk! All culture—street vendors, festivals...Mexicans, they are...they co-operate more with each other. We Puerto Ricans are not like that. We are not like that, because...we celebrate, but we are also always divided around politics [*la política*]. There's too much personalism over politics. The Cubans have gotten ahead of us...and the Mexicans, too!

In Hilda's account, while the Mexican/migrant neighborhoods of Pilsen and Little Village were so "cultural" that there was effectively no difference between them and Mexico itself, Puerto Ricans were too involved with "modern" concerns like politics, which was divisive and individualizing and tended to undermine the prospect of a holistic sense of the group's "cultural" integrity. Furthermore, this perceived "loss of culture" ironically seemed for Hilda to be the cause of Puerto Rican "failure" as other presumably more "culturally intact" groups were actually bypassing Puerto Ricans in a kind of intra-Latino competition for "success" in U.S. society.

Hilda's sense that Mexicans cooperated with each other more than Puerto Ricans—that they were more "cultural" in the sense of being group-oriented and communal—was echoed when Imelda, a U.S.-born Puerto Rican who had grown up in the Mexican community of Pilsen, related a stereotype about Mexicans held by her parents. As the landlords of an apartment building in Pilsen, they frequently complained that it was a problem having to always rent to Mexicans, because Mexican tenants were always bringing in more and more people to share their cramped living space—"first, they say it's just two [tenants]—then, it's nine!" While Imelda's Puerto Rican parents identified this kind of group-oriented ethos as a problem with Mexicans, and Hilda, in contrast, regarded it more ambivalently as a strength that counteracted the excessive individualism and invidiousness she detected among Puerto Ricans, both shared a more basic notion that Mexicans were fundamentally "intact" as a "community." These perceptions of the Mexican household—as overcrowded with extended family and other needy friends and acquaintances—or the Mexican neighborhoods—as teeming with crowds, street vendors, festivals, and "culture"—simultaneously evoked images of the type of "self-help" communitarianism that is paradigmatic of "ethnic" success sagas in U.S. "immigration" discourse (cf. Honig, 1998), and a stereotypical kind of premodern collectivism associated with overpopulated "Third World" conditions.

Such images of Mexicans as exceedingly "traditional," and generally "more cultural" than Puerto Ricans, exacerbated a more general anxiety among Puerto Ricans, particularly among U.S.-born Puerto Rican youth, of their own "loss of tradition." Puerto Ricans' perceived loss of tradition, however, was ambivalently entangled with a conception of themselves as "modern" and culturally dynamic in ways that, it seemed to them, Mexicans were not. One prominent source of this perception was commonly attached to notions of group differences as manifested in musical preferences. The *ranchera* and *norteña* musics (as well as their progeny, electronically enhanced dance musics, such as *banda*) that were exceedingly popular among Mexican migrants in Chicago, especially the majority who hailed from rural origins, were celebrated as culturally distinctive and defining of a certain Mexicanness. Likewise, it was not at all inconceivable for the U.S.-raised children of Mexican migrants, in addition to whatever variety of other musical genres they enjoyed, to be fairly well acquainted with the lyrics to *ranchera* and *norteña* songs, to know the proper dance steps, and even to exude great enthusiasm for dancing to the same music enjoyed by their parents' generation. In February of 1995, at a party comprised predominantly of young

Mexicans raised in the U.S., when the soundtrack shifted from English-language disco and techno dance musics to *norteñas,* the host of the party, Ray Obregón, a Chicago-born Mexican in his late thirties, declared to De Genova (who, he knew, was teaching Mexican/migrant factory workers), "Hey, if you're workin' in the factories, this is their music—they love this stuff, it's what they live for! Those are good people, hardworkin' people who bust their asses and do an honest day's work, and this music is their only escape—this is what they live for, because it's their escape from reality." Thus, in Ray's assessment, a music identified as characteristically "Mexican" was also reinscribed in Chicago in class-specific ways that equated factory labor with Mexican migrants, and celebrated the centrality of "hard work" in the production of this migrant Mexicanness. At the same party, the only Puerto Rican in attendance entertained himself by playing along during the Mexican music on a set of bongo drums, and, consciously mediating a certain incommensurability between the prevailing musical sensibility of the gathering and his own Puerto Rican difference, joked that others would ask, "Hey, what's that guy's problem?" and that someone else would then explain, "Oh, he's just Puerto Rican." Indeed, in sharp contrast to the rural inflections of Mexican *rancheras* and *norteñas,* any mention of salsa music tended, among the vast majority of Mexican migrants in Chicago, to elicit an immediate and singular response—"Puerto Rican music."

For their part, most Puerto Ricans tended to be unanimous in their agreement with the Mexican appraisal of salsa as something to be unequivocally equated with Puerto Ricans.[1] Indeed, the global popularity of salsa was a particular point of pride for many Puerto Ricans. Despite a concern over the loss of their "traditional culture," therefore, Puerto Ricans often celebrated a sense of "modernness" that was premised nonetheless on a notion that they had demonstrated the creative vitality as a group to impact the popular cultural markets of the U.S. and, to some extent, the entire world with media celebrities like Ricky Martin and Jennifer López, and cultural forms such as salsa music and dancing, Latin rap and hip-hop styles. Ramos-Zayas met Clara Pérez, an ESL teacher who lived in Logan Square, a few months after moving to Chicago in March of 1994. A very sociable and energetic woman in her mid-thirties, Clara offered her insights into the opportunities for salsa dancing in Chicago's nightclub scene:

> Here you have Tania's and you have Excalibur . . . on Thursdays they have "Latin night" . . . You have Hank's. There are a few places where you can go salsa dancing. Depending on the place you go to, you'll find different kinds of crowds.

"You mean," asked Ramos-Zayas for clarification, "that not all the crowds are Puerto Rican?"

> No, no. *Of course they're all Puerto Rican!* Puerto Ricans are the ones that really like salsa music. But Tania's is a more casual, not really professional crowd. Excalibur is more elegant. You see the men in suits . . .

While Clara noted the class or occupational distinctions among the specific Puerto Rican crowds that attended the various salsa clubs, for her, salsa was a decidedly Puerto Rican music. From Clara's emphatic statement, it seemed almost inconceivable that non–Puerto Ricans would be an identifiable clientele regularly attending the salsa clubs. Nevertheless, Clara herself later admitted to having a good friend who was a great salsa dancer, "despite being Guatemalan."

The appreciation of salsa and the ability to dance to its rhythms were often related to a primordial, quasi-biological quality unique to Puerto Ricans. In this sense, the ability to dance to salsa music was not perceived as a product of socialization, much less as something that could be learned, but rather as something Puerto Ricans had "in the blood." The idea that rhythm was "in the blood" and the primordial association between Puerto Ricanness and salsa dancing was recurrent among the barrio residents and community activists with whom Ramos-Zayas worked in Chicago. Sandra Marrero, a parent-volunteer at Roberto Clemente High School, for instance, was describing her house-cleaning ritual of getting the appropriate detergents ready and dancing to blaring salsa while mopping and scrubbing her home, when she initiated a broader discussion of music and the difference between Puerto Ricans and Mexicans. As Marrero told Ramos-Zayas and a few of her coworkers in an informal conversation during their lunch break:

> You know, people can say that Puerto Ricans this, or Puerto Ricans that. And I'm not saying we're perfect—no! But one thing I have to say is that we have changed the world of music like no other group. The *rancheras,* that kind of music, sure they like their music. It's like American country music. But in terms of music that has really changed this country in recent times—Puerto Rican music, salsa music! Anyone can dance to *rancheras* or *norteña*—I'm not sure about the distinctions, but I know they make distinctions in that kind of music—still, you don't have to really know how to dance. You just jump around! [she remarked, now laughing] But not everyone can dance to salsa music. You have to have the rhythm. It's in the blood.

While Sandra's claim that a responsiveness to salsa's distinctive rhythms was locatable in the body and even "in the blood" was not strictly literal, to the extent that this music was so completely embedded for her in any conceivable assessment of the identity of Puerto Ricans as a group, her celebration of salsa's Puerto Ricanness implied racialized notions of Puerto Ricans' intrinsic cultural vitality. Like Sandra, many Puerto Ricans took great pride in salsa music and oftentimes elaborated the superiority of this music in comparison with musical genres associated with Mexicans, such as *rancheras* or *norteñas*. By suggesting that these characteristically Mexican musical categories were akin to "American country music," furthermore, Sandra implied a backward-looking provincialism about Mexican cultural forms in contradistinction to the forward-moving cosmopolitanism and dynamism of a Puerto Rican–identified music and dance style that had proven itself capable of "really" transforming U.S. popular culture, and revealed that "we"—Puerto Ricans—"have changed the world of music like no other group." Ironically, whereas transnational Mexican migration, and its defining labor relation to global capitalism, had brought in its wake the dramatic proliferation of Mexican "country" music throughout the U.S., the globalization of mass-media and entertainment-industry commodities had simultaneously catapulted Puerto Rican music from its own more parochial sociohistorical location in poor barrios in the U.S. into an unprecedented transnational publicity.[2]

If salsa music was widely viewed as something unquestionably "Puerto Rican" and also as a positive symbol of the globalization of "Puerto Rican culture," live music events featuring salsa entertainers served as racialized markers of social space in Chicago's Puerto Rican neighborhoods by affirming clear associations between Puerto Ricanness, creative vitality, cultural pride, and urban territoriality. Margarita Arroyo was one of the organizers of a street festival in Humboldt Park. In her late forties and a Chicago resident for twenty years, Margarita had lived in New York during her adolescence. When Ramos-Zayas asked her about the festival she was organizing, Arroyo immediately conflated the festival as a whole with the particular salsa bands she was thinking of inviting, and with salsa music in general:

> One of the things about New York is that it is very Puerto Rican. Puerto Ricans predominate over other groups and you can tell right away. You hear salsa music on all the [radio] stations. Here in Chicago you only have salsa music on the Puerto Rican stations...though that's also changing. That's why these street festivals are important. We bring singers, performers—all Puerto Rican! And people love that. You see people dancing right away. Because if there is one thing that Puerto Ricans are proud of, it's their music. Some people say that we should have *bomba, plena, jíbaro* music—[Puerto Rican] folkloric music. Some other Latinos do that. We should, but salsa music has gotten farther, all over the world. There are even Chinese that play and dance to salsa music!

Implicit in Margarita's comment was the sense that salsa music had to be deliberately promoted, since Puerto Ricans did not dominate Chicago's Latino social landscape. Even in Puerto Rican neighborhoods, residents were aware that Puerto Ricans were a minority among Latinos in Chicago and that Mexicans dominated the city's Latino cultural scene. Nevertheless, Margarita also emphasized the "universal" quality of salsa music, in contradistinction to less renowned genres of Puerto Rican "folkloric" music and, by implication, the distinctive musical expressions of all other Latino groups. Salsa's global appeal was taken to symbolically affirm that there was something so vibrant about Puerto Ricans that it was irresistibly recognized by the whole world.

The "universal" appeal of salsa music became a sign of the apparently "transcendent" particularity of Puerto Ricanness itself. The "universality" associated with the global appeal of salsa as an entertainment industry commodity, moreover, was apparently mirrored by the mass-mediated popular cultural global successes of Puerto Rican celebrities. When the Hollywood producers of a film about the popular U.S.-born Mexican singer Selena officially announced that Jennifer López would be playing the part of Selena, Puerto Ricans widely perceived the decision to cast a Puerto Rican actress in the role of the Mexican teen idol as a defining sign of the inexorable ascendancy of Puerto Ricans in U.S. popular culture. "They look all over for people to audition to play Selena and they end up getting a Puerto Rican girl from the Bronx," marveled Ramón Martínez, a Puerto Rican teacher from Humboldt Park, with an evident sense of triumph, during a phone conversation with Ramos-Zayas. Notably, during the auditions and the casting for the *Selena* movie and then when the film was first screened in theaters, Jennifer López's Puerto Ricanness was immeasurably more marked than it has ever been since, as the actress has pursued her own career as a musical performer and has come to be marketed as a more generic Latina popular culture icon. Hence, ironically, Jennifer López's racialized status as a specifically *Puerto Rican* celebrity was never so pronounced as when she was cast in the role of a Mexican.

In the context of the *Selena* film, the racialized and gendered differences between Mexicans' and Puerto Ricans' bodies were further accentuated. Popular culture Latina icons, such as a Mexican singer like Selena, upon being reanimated on screen by a Puerto Rican actress, might have signaled a potential convergence of Mexican and Puerto Rican femininities into a more generic image of Latina female beauty and sexuality (e.g., Negrón-Muntaner, 1997). Instead, examples such as Selena were largely treated instead in these Puerto Rican discussions as exceptions who proved the putative rule of the superiority of Puerto Rican female beauty and sensuousness. Many Puerto Ricans enthusiastically endorsed the particular body type embodied by the media-enhanced spectacle of Jennifer López as an emblem of Puerto Rican womanhood. For many Puerto Rican viewers of López's cinematic representation of Selena, Selena's Mexicanness was effectively trumped and thus erased by López's Puerto Rican womanhood.

Salsa and the successes of Puerto Rican performers like Jennifer López served for Puerto Ricans as marker of a certain presumed capacity that they possessed, as a group, which other Latino groups appeared to lack: the means to influence U.S. popular culture and global media. To the extent that such group differences between Puerto Ricans and other Latinos, especially Mexicans, whom they perceived to be more provincial or outdated, were elaborated in terms of distinct cultural forms such as salsa music and dance, nevertheless, these divergent musical preferences were not a source of conflict in and of themselves; rather, they were mobilized for the purposes of Puerto Rican discourses of their own purported "modernity" in contrast to cultural forms that appeared to be irreducibly particular and hence parochial. Many of the adolescents whom Ramos-Zayas met in Chicago listened and danced to salsa music regularly. Salsa thus provided many Puerto Ricans with an intergenerational middle ground where the tastes of both parents and children often converged, unlike other types of music popular among Puerto Rican youth—such as techno, rap, and hip-hop—that were generally perceived by their parents' generation as evidence of cultural "loss." It is revealing, therefore, that Puerto Rican youth showed genuine enthusiasm for and took great pride in Son del Barrio, a salsa band comprised of students at a Humboldt Park high school, whereas the attempt to create a Puerto Rican folkloric music and dance group had been notably unsuccessful with teens at the school. Similarly, while watching a Spanish-language television variety program that happened to be showcasing a Mexican folkloric dance performance, Alicia Morales, a Puerto Rican peer counselor at a Latino youth organization, remarked that one could tell if someone was Mexican by whether or not they were wearing shiny black shoes. She then added, "Mexicans are also into these folkloric groups and like dressing up in that traditional way. But, at Clemente High School, if you tell any Puerto Rican kid to wear a *jíbaro* [rural Puerto Rican] hat or join a traditional dance group, they'll look at you like you're crazy!" Still, conceptions of themselves as "hip," and related perceptions of Mexicans as "dated" or "out of style," were also a source of anxiety among many Puerto Ricans who felt that contemporary expressions of Puerto Rican–identified rap and "crossover" pop music in general had supplanted more culturally "authentic" and traditional folklore and expressive forms. Thus, young Puerto Ricans also retained for themselves an image of the Island as an imagined space of "purity" and "rurality," in ways that revealed deeper ambivalences about constructions of Mexicans as "rural"/"traditional" in contrast to Puerto Ricans as "urban"/"modern."

By imagining the Island—the foundation of "real" Puerto Ricanness—as an idyllic paradise, U.S.-born Puerto Rican youth reserved for themselves a little of the folksy-ness that they otherwise projected disparagingly onto Mexicans. Many U.S.-born Puerto Ricans depicted Puerto Rico as an ancestral homeland—fundamentally rural and "traditional"—in sharp contrast to Chicago, which they characterized in exclusively urban and "modern" terms. The rural images and narratives that many Puerto Ricans in Chicago evoked were also coded interpretations (and concrete referents) of the reality of poverty and marginalization that their own poor and working-class relatives experienced on the Island, expressed in the terms of nostalgia for an idyllic rural landscape. Focusing on their own U.S.-based communities' *urban* poverty rather than that of rural Island populations, second-generation Mainlanders tended to "jibarize" the Island's rural poverty, and so obstructed the possibility of more accurate insights into the analogies between the two experiences. Even Puerto Rico's urban dwellers often remained folklorized as rural *jíbaros* in the imaginations of their U.S.-based relatives. Such presumably "urban" concerns as crime and street violence, therefore, were reserved as the attributes of Puerto Ricans' lives in U.S. cities like Chicago. For instance, Mike Santana, a second-generation Puerto Rican who lived a few buildings away from Ramos-Zayas's apartment in Humboldt Park, once advised her to close the gate that led to her building's front door, paternalistically reminding her, "You're not in Puerto Rico. This is

Chicago, and you can get robbed." In contradistinction to Puerto Rico, Chicago was constructed as crime-ridden and dangerous. Ironically, everyday public discourse on the Island at the time was dominated by talk about "crime" and sprawling "gated communities." When Ramos-Zayas replied that she would in fact be more reluctant to leave her door open in Puerto Rico than in Chicago, Santana was visibly troubled. Here, a Puerto Rican from the Island was threatening his romanticized vision of life there as crime-free, peaceful, and harmonious. Claims of cultural "authenticity" in Puerto Rican barrios in the U.S. commonly involve such selectively folklorized ideals of rural Island life and strategic understandings of Puerto Rico's past. (Ramos-Zayas, 2003) Manifested through the deployment of iconic representations of "the *jíbaro*" (peasant smallholder) or the Taínos (the Island's original indigenous inhabitants), or Afro–Puerto Ricanness, symbols of a more provincial Puerto Rican identity were abundantly mobilized in various public performances such as the construction of rural-style *casitas* (used as community centers), festivals, artistic events, and local political campaigns.[3] In spite of this Puerto Rican emphasis on folkloric symbols, however, when such cultural displays were mobilized by Mexicans—and particularly Mexican migrants—Puerto Ricans tended to condescendingly view them as an excessive attachment to a "backward" or "Third World" culture that was fundamentally out of touch with the dynamic forward march of a "modern" way of life.

Puerto Ricans often perceived Mexican migrants as unworldly country bumpkins and neophytes, and so could see themselves as sophisticated and "modern" by comparison. Despite the occasional concern, as epitomized in Hilda Ayala's remarks (above), that Puerto Ricans were somewhat obsessed with politics and that too much politics had been divisive for Puerto Ricans as a community, Puerto Ricans frequently valorized the image of themselves as "more political" than Mexicans, recurrently viewing Mexicans as generally vulnerable, and thus more passive and politically submissive. Thus, Puerto Ricans understood themselves to be insider "experts" on how the U.S. works, while Mexicans were seen as naïve and "foreign" to the U.S. system of dispensing benefits and penalties. This perception was grounded largely on the more general feeling that Puerto Ricans were more "Americanized." A second-generation U.S.-born Puerto Rican in his late twenties, Bobby Rosa described the relationship between Mexicans and Puerto Ricans:

> Puerto Ricans and Mexicans do not always click. When I was growing up there was a lot of friction. The Mexicans think a lot of shit about Puerto Ricans. I think they view Puerto Ricans within the realm of Black, as similar to Blacks. Puerto Ricans think that Mexicans are docile . . . or idiots . . . or they're out of style. They're late. From my experience, I know that Mexican women were quieter—unless they've grown up around Puerto Rican neighbors! [Ramos-Zayas laughed] Because the Mexican area . . . although the Mexican area has become more different. They've grown up here in the U.S. too, but . . . They have become a little more aggressive after a while of . . . of being here. I think Puerto Ricans have set the tone a lot.

Bobby initially identified the view that Mexicans commonly held of Puerto Ricans as being "similar to Blacks," and, similarly, noted that Puerto Ricans—himself included—largely considered Mexicans to be submissive, behind the times, or simply ridiculous. However, Bobby's comments also suggested areas of confluence between Puerto Ricans and Mexicans: Mexicans who, like Puerto Ricans of his own generation, had grown up in the U.S. diverged from the image that Puerto Ricans had of Mexican migrants as "docile" and "quiet." Thus, Mexicans who had grown up in the U.S.—largely as a result, in Bobby's account, of having been racialized as "minorities," like Puerto Ricans or African Americans—but especially those Mexicans who had lived in greater proximity to Puerto Ricans, were positively evaluated as having become "a little more aggressive."

For their part, Mexican migrants took a certain pride in the sense that they were in fact the more civilized of the two groups, and often valorized their own presumed humility and civility against that same "aggressiveness" exuded by Puerto Ricans that Bobby Rosa had celebrated—what Mexican migrants perceived in Puerto Ricans to be a distinctive contentiousness, if not outright hostility. During the spring of 1995, De Genova was employed to teach the ESL component for a voluntary job-training and -placement program, through which course participants were otherwise being trained to work as line cooks for hotel kitchens. Moisés, the cooking instructor—himself a Mexican migrant who had been trained through the same program—complained repeatedly about Timoteo, the only Puerto Rican in the class. Moisés considered Timoteo a "troublemaker," and characterized him as very much equivalent to a Black trainee with whom he had worked previously—"always criticizing others, not cooperative, confrontational," concluding that "with people like that, it's better to just get them out." When De Genova conducted an interview with Felipe Beltrán, a Mexican/migrant participant in the same course, similar issues arose, but with regard to Puerto Ricans as a group. When asked what groups of people he had come to know in Chicago, and what experiences he had had with them, Felipe mentioned that, in addition to Mexicans, he had known one or two Salvadorans and also a Guatemalan, and felt that there was something about their way of thinking that was similar to that of Mexicans: "more than anything, human feeling, or rather, the total essence, right . . . the human feeling as persons—it's almost always alike." Then, however, Beltrán abruptly shifted his focus:

> I think that, uhm, I'm going to give an opinion, right—and it's not that I'm against, uh . . . uh, people from Puerto Rico—in that they're a little more aggressive, in that they're a little bit more nervous among the people that I've had the chance to meet . . . out of Puerto Rico, and of all Latinos, I think they're the ones who are a little bit more, uhm, how would you say—I'm not trying to offend them, a little bit more, uhm, a little bit violent. Uh-huh.

"Well, violent how?" De Genova asked.

"Or rather, that they try a little more to make themselves stand out."

"Have you known many people from Puerto Rico?"

"No, not many—I think, well...about six, I think, right, but almost all of them are the same, in their way of being, I think that it's maybe [coming from] the same environment over there in their homeland, right, that it might be that; that heat of theirs, or rather...their way of being raised since childhood, I think that that's it, natural for them also..."

"The heat?"

"Or rather, their climate, their environment, in that it's a little more, uh, aggressive."

Felipe's discernment of a fundamental continuity of "human feeling" between Mexican migrants like himself and Central American migrants contrasted dramatically with his sense of Puerto Ricans as a group. Alternating between "cultural" explanations of what had apparently become "natural" for Puerto Ricans based on their presumed "way of being raised since childhood," on the one hand, and climatological and environmental determinisms for making sense of how the actual physical setting of Puerto Rico had invested its people with its "heat" and conveyed to them, as a people, a kind of "natural" aggressiveness, Felipe posited explanations for what he deemed to be an inherent and essential difference between Mexicans and Puerto Ricans. Careful to choose his words with a certain delicacy (especially in this context of a tape-recorded, formal interview with a white "American" whom he knew to be interested in writing a book about Mexican/migrant experiences and perspectives) and concerned not to seem offensive in his characterization, Felipe nevertheless opted for fairly strong language—depicting Puerto Ricans as "nervous," self-promoting," "a little more aggressive," and even "a little violent."

The Racialization and Spatialization of Criminality and Violence

The perceptions among Mexican migrants that Puerto Ricans variously tended to be lazy, untrustworthy, uncooperative, disagreeable, confrontational, aggressive, and even violent—all contributed to their sense that Puerto Ricans were also dangerous. In March of 1994, during an ESL course at the DuraPress factory, the workers' discussion turned to sharing stories that were unified by allegations of Puerto Rican criminality. Homero was the only Ecuadorian employed at the factory, and the only non-Mexican in this ESL group; moreover, he was married to a Mexican woman, and lived in a disproportionately majority-Mexican working-class suburb. Homero recounted, "When I first came here [to the U.S.], two Puerto Rican guys came up behind me when I was entering my front door on pay day, and they robbed me." A Mexican coworker, Ricardo, then proceeded to relate a similar experience: "When I first came, a couple Puerto Ricans tried to hold me up when I was waiting for the bus, right there at the bus stop...but I ran!" And now with a sparkle in his eye, Ricardo began to chuckle: "I got away, too—although I was wearing platform shoes at the time!" If the Puerto

Rican perpetrators could not catch him running in high heels, Ricardo seemed also to imply, then not only were they thieves but apparently also lazy ones. Other related narratives of Puerto Rican criminality followed. Not only did this exchange of experiences seem to confirm that, as a group, Puerto Ricans were generally unsympathetic and could not be trusted; it insinuated furthermore that they were largely dangerous and, at least potentially, criminals.

For their part, young Puerto Ricans from the Humboldt Park barrio were often quite sensitive to the idea that Mexicans (and other Latinos), like whites, saw them as "aggressive" and "violent." Some Puerto Rican youth—particularly those attending alternative educational programs based on critical pedagogy and sponsored by grassroots Puerto Rican nationalist organizations—redeployed these criminalized images of their reputed "aggressiveness" as evidence of their political militancy and radical conscientization. In so doing, however, they also reproduced more generalized attitudes common among Puerto Ricans that constructed Mexicans as passive and vulnerable. In one instance, a group of students at the alternative high school in Humboldt Park where Ramos-Zayas volunteered began to joke about the television series *COPS*. (On this program, cameramen are routinely sent to film on-duty police officers and present close-up portrayals of people getting apprehended and arrested; predictably, most of the cops are white and a large portion of the people arrested are African American or Latino, and particularly Mexicans and Central Americans). The group of predominantly Puerto Rican students laughed that the television show was "about police beating up Mexicans in L.A." Then, William, one of the Puerto Rican students, teasingly alerted his friend David (who considered himself "three-fourths Mexican, one-fourth Puerto Rican") that David therefore needed to be very careful of the police, and, contributing to the general mirth, followed by breaking into a chorus of the television series's theme song—"Whatcha gonna do, whatcha gonna do when they come for you?" Irritated by the insinuation that he was especially vulnerable because of his "Mexican"-ness, David retorted that if they were to film *COPS* in Chicago, they would do so in Humboldt Park and "confuse William for a nigger."[4] The exchange between William and David initially suggested a glimpse into the formation of a potential notion of shared Latino identity since these two young men produced an analogy between the vulnerability of "Mexicans" (implicitly based on migrant "illegality") with a vulnerability that Puerto Ricans shared, based on "skin color" and racialization. While William tried to emphasize David's vulnerability as a "Mexican," David quickly equated William's Puerto Ricanness with Blackness, and reminded William that—as a dark-skinned Puerto Rican, and particularly in the distinctively racialized space of the Humboldt Park neighborhood—he was even more vulnerable to police brutality in the specific context of Chicago's racial economy. Thus, both William and David (each in his own way) expressed a general recognition that Latinos are invariably implicated in representations and public discourses of violence and criminality in the U.S. Yet rather than providing a moment of communion, these insights into the racialization of Latinos as "criminal" and subject to police suspicion and abuse instead served the divisive ends of counterpoising Mexicans and Puerto Ricans. The fact that David and William were close friends, and that the exchange largely involved friendly teasing, further emphasizes the fugitive quality of this instance in which a potential Latinidad— one that could envision Mexicans and Puerto Ricans together against the police as a racist U.S. institution—was nevertheless subverted, or at least curtailed.

The conjunctures of race and space in Chicago, as we have seen in chapter 2, are notoriously stark, and even further exaggerated by the distorted perceptions that come with severe racial segregation. Inevitably, then, discourses about crime and street violence tend to overlap remarkably with racialized discourses about urban space. The racialized stigma of crime and violence attached to the Humboldt Park neighborhood where William and David lived, however, was also routinely endorsed by many Puerto Ricans living in the Chicago suburbs and even the "better areas" of Logan Square. Not only did such Puerto Rican discourses participate in the criminalization of the space of the barrio, but also its U.S.-born Puerto Rican residents. These middle-class Puerto Ricans, especially the suburbanites, were largely Island-born and -raised professionals, for whom such allegations of criminality were profoundly entangled with notions of cultural inauthenticity. Puerto Ricans living in the most solidly working-class or increasingly gentrified middle-class areas of Logan Square, themselves often U.S.-born and -raised, likewise viewed Humboldt Park with various degrees of embarrassment or disdain and disassociated themselves from it. This was especially the case among Logan Square residents who had actually lived in Humboldt Park previously in their lives, and commonly still had relatives living in the barrio.

The image of the "Nuyorican"emerged historically to confirm significant differences between Puerto Rican migrants and U.S.-born populations (originally associated singularly with New York City).[5] The figure of the Nuyorican became a way of categorizing poor Puerto Ricans in U.S. barrios (or "ghettos") that distanced their impoverished and racially subordinated status from notions of Puerto Rican cultural "authenticity," proper behavior, implicit social knowledge of contemporary lifestyles in Puerto Rico, and romanticized constructions of the "purity" of the Puerto Rican homeland. The repudiation of the so-called Nuyoricans was inseparable from a rejection of the association of Puerto Ricanness with the degraded racialized status of African American Blackness.[6] When Chicago's middle-class Puerto Ricans sought to distance themselves from the stigmatized Puerto Ricanness of the Humboldt Park barrio, they often projected similar notions of the barrio poor as U.S. "minorities" whose status approximated Blackness.

Deploying stereotypes of U.S.-born Puerto Ricans as a conclusively stigmatized U.S. "minority" group, and intent to retain the presumed prestige and "purity" of being "from the Island," many Island-raised professionals often rejected altogether the idea that they were themselves "migrants," and disassociated themselves from long-term Puerto Rican (working-class or poor) migrants in the U.S., generally. Carmen Pérez, a community activist involved in organizing the Puerto Rican Day Parade, was in her sixties and had lived in Chicago for about thirty years when Ramos-Zayas first visited her in her Logan Square home. Ramos-Zayas was first introduced to Pérez by a college friend whose father knew the mayor of the Puerto Rican town of Vega Baja. Carmen was an active member of Chicago's Club Vegabajeño, a social club comprised of barrio residents who traced their ancestry to the town. When Ramos-Zayas described her research to Pérez and commented that most of the studies on Puerto Ricans had focused on New York, Carmen became visibly uncomfortable and commented:

> That [the Nuyorican] is an image that they [Puerto Ricans in Puerto Rico] have, but I don't see it like that. Because I didn't arrive here to migrate. I didn't arrive here poor and starving. On the contrary. There [in Puerto Rico], I was better off than here. I've never lived off welfare. And like me, there are many more. But there's a bad image that all Puerto Ricans who come to live here come to live off welfare. And that's an image that has damaged us here. I'd like to know where that image comes from. Because there are Puerto Ricans here who live proud of themselves. They live well. They have good houses. They're not all professionals, but people who have businesses and like to live well.

While Carmen had integrated herself thoroughly into the life of the Chicago barrio through her participation in neighborhood organizations, when it came to describing her position as a Puerto Rican woman living in the U.S., Carmen emphasized that she "didn't come here to migrate." Seemingly a contradiction in terms, since she had in fact lived in Chicago for thirty years, Carmen was still deeply affected by the stigma sustained on the Island that characterized "migrants" as impoverished, maladjusted, and, by implication, an embarrassment to the Puerto Rican nation. The early Puerto Rican migration, motivated by poverty, industrialization, and contract labor, continued to be perceived as the "real" migration, which working-class migrants like Carmen felt compelled to distinguish from their own presumably more autonomous decisions to move to the U.S.[7]

The criminalization of U.S.-born Puerto Ricans (and even long-term working-class migrants on the Mainland) was not only based on intergenerational differences, therefore, but on the general assumption that those who migrated were the "undesirables" of the nation. They were clearly inflected by various "culture of poverty" themes in the official public discourse on the Island that rendered being a U.S.-born Puerto Rican as inseparable from a social location identified with "ghetto" life. Many barrio residents shared the view that even if Humboldt Park, the neighborhood most economically marginalized and more definitively racialized as "Puerto Rican" in Chicago, were to undergo "urban renewal," the stigma attached to the area would still prevail. In the words of Pedro Figueroa, a former resident of Humboldt Park who had moved to a solidly working-class section of the Logan Square neighborhood, and then later relocated to Orlando, Florida: "It's good that there are efforts to improve the area, but I don't see any Puerto Rican professionals moving there. They want to move to the suburbs. If you mention Humboldt Park to them, they are disgusted, they immediately think gangs, crime, welfare."

The equation of the space of Humboldt Park with U.S.-born Puerto Rican youth gangs, and the disavowal by Island Puerto Ricans of those gangs as an "inauthentic" product of Chicago's urban pathologies, and thus, as fundamentally un–Puerto Rican, were themes well illustrated in Ana Castro's narrative. Castro, a woman in her thirties who had migrated from Puerto Rico as an adolescent, and a student at an adult education program where Ramos-Zayas volunteered, vividly described how members of her family, who had come from Puerto Rico to attend her nephew's funeral, could not comprehend or accept the seeming pervasiveness in Chicago of youth gang involvement. Ana wrote in her journal:

> One thing I remember very vividly is when they killed my nephew last summer . . . When they told us that they had killed Kevin we did not believe it. When they shot him the ambulance took him to Norwegian Hospital, but they said that he was already dead when he got there. [At the funeral home] . . . Kevin's friends started coming and there were so many of them and some of the family members from Puerto Rico started getting upset because Kevin was in a gang and all the friends were Cobras and the family that came from Puerto Rico did not understand what was going on and when they saw that they were putting colors and snakes in the coffins, there were problems with a lot of the family and some started saying to other members of the family not to go the next day to the cemetery . . . No one knows what you feel until they have experienced something that bad . . . I see Kevin's name on the sidewalk in front of the house and there are memories of him everywhere.

As implied in Ana's narrative, Puerto Ricans on the Island were simply not able to relate to youth involvement in gang activity in Chicago because the Island was presumably a more "peaceful" and "gang-free" place. Like many Humboldt Park Puerto Ricans, Ana sought to contextualize the involvement of her nephew and other young men in street gangs in the barrio by understanding their complex identities and multiple roles in their families and community. Consciously problematizing the ways that Humboldt Park had been racialized with allegations of criminality, barrio residents commonly challenged the ways that other Puerto Ricans unsympathetically disavowed their poverty as "culturally" inauthentic or merely the aberrant symptom of a circumscribed "pathological" urban space.

As we have already seen, the starkly racialized segregation of many of Chicago's neighborhoods exacerbated the possibilities for spatially locating "crime" and "violence" in racialized terms. This was abundantly evident in Mexican/migrant discourses about African American or Puerto Rican neighborhoods. For instance, on one occasion, on a street corner of the commercial strip along 18th Street in Pilsen, a male Mexican migrant randomly accosted a male African American who had been minding his own business, attempting to engage him in a line of inquiry that was not overtly aggressive but was very clearly charged with a racial motivation: "Now you see a lot of Blacks around here on 18th Street. It's because we [Mexicans] have become more intelligent and more stable. There used to be gangs always shooting here, guys on every corner ready to rob you—but now it's not so bad, so Blacks come here and they don't have no problem. But we can't go over there in their neighborhoods—why??" Alone and without any other African Americans in sight in this virtually homogeneously Mexican area, the Black man visibly dismissed and ignored the provocation, and very deliberately went on his way. This poor Mexican shopping district was only two blocks from the elevated railroad tracks along 16th Street that, with the exception of relatively few viaducts through which intermittent streets passed from one side to the other, literally walled Pilsen off from the even more impoverished Black neighborhood immediately to the north. This was the kind of blunt material barrier that typically served to sustain the quite pervasive and comprehensive type of racial segregation that has long been a hallmark of Chicago's spatial fabric. Obviously, the implication was that, whereas Mexicans had become "more intelligent and more stable," and in effect were more "civilized," Blacks had not, and for this reason, their neighborhoods remained dangerous and violent. A further possible implication was that, even if African Americans had no need to be fearful of Mexican crime or violence against them, Black people were still not welcome in the Mexican neighborhood. Similarly, in another instance, when De Genova was misunderstood to have said that his apartment was located at the corner of "Damen and Fullerton" (rather than "Damen and Cullerton," where he was actually living, in Pilsen), his interlocutor, Faustino Galarza, immediately demanded incredulously, "Why do you live *there?!* They're all Puerto Ricans over there!" The presumed undesirability of living in a Puerto Rican neighborhood, for Faustino, was self-evident. The racialized theme that framed Black and Puerto Rican neighborhoods as fundamentally inhospitable spaces was fairly ubiquitous. However, in ways analogous to the internal differentiations within the Puerto Rican community that enabled Humboldt Park to be stigmatized even by other Puerto Ricans, similar allegations of crime and violence also pervaded the distinctions Mexican migrants deployed to maintain familiar status hierarchies among their own Mexican neighborhoods, especially with regard to the poorest, most dilapidated, most densely populated Mexican barrios, such as Pilsen or Little Village (as we have already seen in previous chapters). Thus, it was equally likely that Mexican migrants would find it surprising, or even inconceivable, that one such as De Genova—evidently a highly educated, effectively middle-class, white "American" professional—would want to live in so notorious an area as Pilsen if he could afford to reside elsewhere. Indeed, if this was especially true of those who did not live in Pilsen or Little Village, it was nonetheless also a sentiment commonly expressed by many who—with their various desires for access to better housing, social services, or schools—were regrettably still living there.

The absolute aversion and candid disdain many Mexican migrants commonly articulated about the crime and violence they attributed to Black or Puerto Rican neighborhoods was clearly an effect of the more decisively racialized divisions that separated them from these other groups. The ambivalence they expressed toward the most degraded of their own neighborhoods, on the other hand, often tended to reveal a rather more profound ambivalence toward U.S.-born or U.S.-raised Mexicans, which often involved subsuming them into a discourse that revolved around street gangs, crime, and violence. Notably, Mexican migrants were subjected to the same barrage of racialized mass-media images that routinely provide a relatively permanent stock of criminalized stereotypes of both Blacks and Latinos. In April of 1994 at the DuraPress factory, a few weeks after the exchange of stories about Puerto Rican criminality discussed above, Ricardo mentioned that he had just seen a film, entitled *Blood In, Blood Out*. When asked what the movie was about, another Mexican migrant, Benito, asserted plainly, "It's about Mexican people." This remark provoked general disagreement and disapproval from Ricardo, Federico, Adelberto, and David (all of whom were Mexican migrants). Ricardo, Adelberto, and David simultaneously began to dispute the claim, demanding, "What are you saying, dumb-ass [*güey*]?!? It's about gang-bangers [*cholos, gangueros*], not *mexicanos!*"[8] Clearly, street gang members and "Mexicans" were posited as mutually exclusive sets, and Benito's sloppy elision of that stark separation was fairly anathema to everyone else in the group.

At one point, the conversation turned to a comparison of Chicago to other places in the U.S. that some of them had known, such as Texas and California. Miguel began this ensuing exchange when he remarked, "Well, there are *cholos* in Texas, too...." Ricardo responded, "All along the border!—they [*cholos*] rob us, they fuck up [rape] the women...." There was general assent in the group about the perils and tragedies of the U.S.-Mexico border region for migrants. David, however, wanted to introduce a different comparative perspective, based upon his having lived several years in Los Angeles: "But in California, they don't rob you like they do here [in Chicago]—here you can't walk down the street with a nice gold chain, they rob you! There, they [gang members] just fight between themselves; they ask you, 'hey *ese*, where you from?'—you don't say *nothing* to that question!" David's coworkers grinned and chuckled at his performative imitation of the distinctive forms of expression that are widely associated with California *cholos*, as well as the characteristic question, "where you from?"—meaning, "which neighborhood do you live in?"—through which gang members, in Chicago much like in Los Angeles, seek to locate strangers in relation to other gangs' territories, and thus implicitly challenge them to identify with a rival gang. For his part, Benito, who had also lived in Los Angeles, was likewise eager to demonstrate his competence at imitating the distinctive slang of California *cholos*. The theme of danger was again lightheartedly defused, how-ever, when Benito resumed the topic of comparative criminological geography. Speaking of California *cholos* again, he added, "And they look first for a good stereo, using a flashlight, and then they don't break your car window—they open the door . . . or just take the whole car!" With everyone laughing now, Ricardo added a note of ironic admiration, declaring, "They do good work!" Of course, much of this commentary was ironic, humorous, and playful, but the overall effect of these various examples and comparisons was, nonetheless, to reaffirm these Mexican migrants' collective sense that gangs in Chicago, as elsewhere, were a genuine menace.

Yet, in the course of the conversation, there surfaced a series of quite inti-mate connections between these Mexican migrants and the gang-bangers whom they disavowed. David revealed that his brother-in-law's brother was actually serving time in La Pinta (in prison) in California. Ricardo announced that a new gang had made its appearance in La Selva ("The Jungle"), the ghettoized Mexican/migrant enclave near the factory (in a predominantly white, working-class suburb) where many of them and their coworkers either still lived or had lived previously, and that this new gang was called "Los Vatos Locos," appearing to have adopted their name from the same movie the group had been discussing. Ricardo knew this latter detail to be true, furthermore, because his own nephew was involved with that gang. Nevertheless, despite the group's remarkable famil-iarity with street gangs and this array of quite intimate connections with "gang-bangers," David proceeded to clarify, "They're Chicanos, not real Mexicans." De Genova pursued the issue, turning David's comment into a question: "Are Chicanos not real Mexicans?" Ricardo explained, "They're born here, they're not from Mexico, they just have Mexican parents . . . they're called *pochos*."[9] "But their parents are from Mexico," De Genova continued, ". . . that means somebody will call *your* kids *pochos*." Confronted with this dilemma, Adelberto reworked the formula for inclusion and exclusion, specifying, "If both parents are from Mexico, then they're 100% Mexican, not Chicano." Ricardo's wife, how-ever, was not from Mexico—she was a "Chicana"; this meant that Adelberto's solution would not serve to recuperate Ricardo's children. Ricardo went on to explain that "some [Mexicans raised in the U.S.] will tell you, 'I'm not Mexican, I'm American,' but others will say they're more Mexican than the Mexicans, the ones from Mexico . . . they wave the Mexican flag, wear it on their shirts and pants . . . but it's different for us, because it's against the law in Mexico to wear the flag on your clothes or wave it around, except on September 16." Thus, even when Mexicans raised in the U.S. tried to perform their "Mexican"-ness, Ricardo implied, they merely exposed all the more just how un-Mexican they really were. Concerning the ostentatious display of very large Mexican flags that was very popular in Chicago during Mexican Independence celebrations during the month of September, David likewise mentioned a criticism he had heard on one of the Spanish-language radio stations: "They say people shouldn't do that—that it's not patriotic, it's patriot-ist [*no es patriota, es patriotista*]." If this was not enough of a reason to refrain from a lot of demonstrative flag-waving, however, David then added, "Also, when Puerto Ricans see you wave the flag like that, you get into fights." Then, Benito and David, both of whom had lived in Los Angeles (where there are much larger Central American communities), asserted that, "Chicano means they're born here, but the parents can be from anywhere, they might be Mexicans, but they can be from Guatemala and El Salvador, too." Now, confronted with yet another reformulation, De Genova asked, "So what about those who are born here but have Puerto Rican parents?" David replied adamantly, "No, they're Americans."[10]

In this discussion, a Mexican/migrant discourse on the abject criminality of *cholos* was more or less seamlessly coupled with the still more contradictory one on the inauthenticity of Mexicans raised in the U.S. (whose difference and distance could be further marked with the term "Chicanos").[11] Ultimately, the relations between Mexican migrants and those raised in the U.S. are always more or less intimate ones. Thus, any attempt to produce a stable or coherent opposition between the two inevitably founders in spite of what are sometimes very palpable sociocultural incongruities. It is remarkable, furthermore, that while these men grappled with various formulations of how to sustain the divide between "Mexicans" and "Chicanos," there was a measure of fluidity that could accommodate an analogy between themselves and some other Latino groups. Nevertheless, in this instance at least, any analogy between Mexicans and Puerto Ricans seemed wholly impermissible. Moreover, a sociospatial practice of identification as "Mexican" (namely, waving the Mexican national flag on Chicago streets)—here attributed primarily to Mexicans raised in the U.S., and thus (implicitly) a practice of non-Mexicanness—was in part disavowed precisely because it threatened to incur the violence of Puerto Ricans. Significantly, then, these thoroughly ambivalent Mexican/migrant discourses can be seen to figure Mexicans raised in the U.S.—in effect, Mexican migrants' own children—as a pivotal link in the fraught nexus between Mexicans and the Puerto Ricans whom they often perceived as threatening and antagonistic.

Ultimately, Mexican migrants' disavowals of the criminality and violence associated with youth gangs became a condition of possibility for the disavowal of Mexicans raised in the U.S. as such, and supplied a precondition for figuring "Chicanos" in general as a deracinated group that approached or approximated the debased condition frequently attributed to Puerto Ricans and African Americans. On some occasions, this process became very sadly explicit. In June of 1994, for instance, in front of the apartment building where he rented, De Genova encountered his landlord, Franciszek Czuba, an elderly Polish migrant who had settled in Pilsen when it was a predominantly Polish and Polish American community, and had remained there for forty years. Czuba had recently become increasingly obsessed with the lifestyle of some young U.S.-raised Mexicans who had moved into an apartment in the adjacent building. The new neighbors were visibly involved with the local gang, and frequently held gang meetings as well as loud parties that both involved a fairly frequent traffic of large numbers of young people into the apartment as well as occasionally raucous gatherings on its front porch, where they tended to casually congregate, drink beer, sometimes smoke marijuana, and not uncommonly leave a lot of trash in their wake. On this occasion, Czuba related to De Genova that, in one of his recent confrontations with the "problem" neighbors, one of the group had bluntly told him, "Go back to where you belong." As Czuba told the story, insulted and incensed, he asserted, "*This* is where I belong, because I'm a U.S. citizen! I been in this country forty years, and I live in this house already for thirty-five years! I never had a problem here until these animals came here!" And now performing his indignant retort, Czuba responded in outrage, "...so you go back where *you* came from!" Probably due in part to the limits of his comprehension of the English language, Czuba had elided the possible distinction between "go back to where you belong" (which very conceivably could have meant simply "go home and mind your own business") and "go back to where you came from" (which, as someone who had migrated to the U.S., he knew to be a nativist affront). Nevertheless, as a migrant racialized as white and as a naturalized U.S. citizen, Czuba did not hesitate to question the legitimate claim to belonging within the space and polity of the U.S. nation-state on the part of these very probably U.S.-born (nonwhite) Mexicans. Although these Mexicans were really from the U.S. and not Mexico, his racial whiteness authorized this Polish migrant to charge that these Mexicans raised in the U.S. should go back, by implication, to Mexico, denouncing them as effectively undeserving of the benefits of U.S. citizenship. As Czuba continued his infuriated narrative, a few Mexican migrants, who lived in the same adjacent building as the young Mexicans whom Czuba was disparaging, were quietly passing the afternoon on the porch just a short distance away. One of the Mexican/migrant neighbors soon approached and greeted the two. Eventually, in response to Czuba's protracted denigration of the young Mexican neighbors as being "like animals," the Mexican/migrant neighbor replied, "Yeah, they're also Hispanics, but they live just like Blacks—like animals." Then, apparently content that he had affirmed the difference between migrant Mexicans and those raised in the U.S., and had seemingly achieved some mutual understanding and accord with his Polish neighbor, the Mexican parted with good wishes, smiles, and a handshake, and returned to his friends on the porch. De Genova was acutely aware on this occasion that his racist landlord did not make the same distinction between Mexican migrants and those raised in the U.S. that the Mexican/migrant neighbor had sought to establish. As a Mexican, he repudiated the U.S.-born Mexicans as being "just like Blacks—like animals," in a manner that apparently presumed that this in no way reflected badly upon himself or his own group. Indeed, his will to distance his own kind (Mexicans) from that kind (Mexicans raised in the U.S.)—"they're also Hispanics, but..."—seemed specifically intent to deflect any possible association that his white neighbor might have been inclined to make between the two, and led him to an awkward gesture of fraternity with the white man's racism.

An analogous exchange transpired in September of 1995, at Caustic Scrub, a workplace with a disproportionately Mexican/migrant workforce, where De Genova was employed as an ESL instructor. The company had just hired two young Latinos—one Mexican, one Puerto Rican, both clearly raised in the U.S. and very probably U.S.-born—who were both fluent in English, since a requirement of English fluency was now being mandated as part of the management's new hiring policy. "The company is only hiring people who speak English now," a Mexican/migrant worker named Mateo explained, noting that job applicants who did not speak English fluently were being turned away, even if they had previously worked in the plant and already knew the job well. His Mexican/migrant coworker Manuel added, "They're hiring whites [*güeros*], or Blacks [*prietos*], or little gang-bangers [*gangueritos*]—and they all quit the job after three days because they don't want to get their hands dirty!"[12] Here, U.S.-born Mexicans and Puerto Ricans together came to be equated with "gangs" in a manner that entailed an overtly racialized disavowal, juxtaposed explicitly to both whites and Blacks. If, as we saw earlier in this chapter, the criminalization of Puerto Ricans led Mexican migrants into a more ambivalent terrain of discourse concerning "gangs," where their principal object was Mexicans raised in the U.S., here it became more manifest that the category "gang-bangers" also could serve to comprise both the U.S.-raised children of Mexican migrants, as well as U.S.-raised Puerto Ricans. Much as in the example above (formulated as "they're also Hispanics, but . . ."), Mexican migrants like Manuel could posit a shared (racialized) Latino identity among Mexicans and Puerto Ricans who could be spatially marked as U.S.-born or -raised—a kind of Latinidad which was reducible to the abjection condensed in the stigma of the category "gang-bangers," a Latinidad, in other words, that was to be disparaged and disavowed as criminal and violent.

In conclusion, then, Mexicans and Puerto Ricans deployed competing visions of their own group's "civility" or "modernity" in reference to various constructions of the other's comparative "backwardness" or "rudeness." These competing discourses not only sustained their divergent claims, explicit or implicit, concerning their own respective "deservingness" of the full benefits of citizenship, but also configured notions of racialized difference between Mexican and Puerto Rican migrants (and their respective U.S.-born or -raised counterparts)—as groups. These same constructions of difference, however, had corresponding meanings *internal* to each group across the divides of generation and class. Mexican and Puerto Rican migrants tended to consider U.S.-born or -raised Mexicans and Puerto Ricans as less culturally "authentic" than migrants who had been raised in their respective countries of origin. While these intergenerational differences were certainly entangled with notions of cultural "authenticity," however, they likewise always involved a spatialized distinction grounded on substantive connections to the U.S. and defining connections to Chicago itself. The city, after all, was a thoroughly racialized and racializing space in which criminality and violence were routinely attributed to particular Latino or African American neighborhoods. Thus, Mexican and Puerto Rican migrants sometimes articulated a view of these U.S.-born generations as sharing a kind of abject Latinidad, ultimately based not on being truly "Mexican" or "Puerto Rican" but rather on being merely U.S. "minorities," approximating Blackness. In this sense, notions of "Americanization" often became inseparable from a kind of abjection, as the migrants connected the U.S.-born generations to constructions of a criminalized, bad-mannered, and violent masculinity oftentimes associated with "gangs." Thus, Mexicans' and Puerto Ricans' competing racialized constructions of what was or was not "civilized" or "modern," and also the way that these distinctions similarly differentiated Mexican and Puerto Rican migrants from their own respective U.S.-born generations, were decidedly gendered. In chapter 5, we examine in greater detail the contradictory ideologies of gender that served to uphold the perceived differences between Mexicans and Puerto Ricans.

CHAPTER 5

Familiar Apparitions: Gender and Ideologies of the Family

When Ramos-Zayas asked a group of Puerto Rican women in a parent-volunteer program at a public high school in Humboldt Park why they believed that domestic violence was more pervasive among Mexicans than among Puerto Ricans, as the women had claimed, Maritza Jiménez's narrative about a young Mexican woman best epitomized what the other women in the group similarly expressed:

> She used to come to my cousin's store crying about her husband. That he would beat her up if she didn't have his food ready. That he would never give her money for her kids' food and clothes. He was spending his money on other women. Now, if he found her out with her friends, uuff! All Hell would break loose! He is also Mexican, very *machista*. But, you know what? Good or bad, she wanted the man in the house. She didn't want to get divorced, because they had gotten married—really married, not like those people that say they are married, but they are just living together. She wanted to say, "We've been married for this or that many years." Just to say, "Look at us, we have a perfect family." It doesn't matter if he's beating you up—at least you still have the man in the house. I also think that many of them don't want to raise their children alone. That's looked down upon in their community. That's very different from us. Puerto Rican women are more independent in that way. You know that you can give your children a decent life on your own. They think we are like that because we want to get welfare, that we don't care about the family.

The rest of the group concurred with Maritza in their perceptions that Mexican men were abusive of their spouses, and that the Mexican women they knew routinely tolerated domestic violence in the name of having an "intact" family, out of a sense of reverence for what it symbolized. They likewise upheld the image of Puerto Rican women as fundamentally "more independent" and were confident that they could always resourcefully devise alternative strategies to provide for their children without having to depend on the father.

Most of the Puerto Rican women involved in the popular-education program were welfare recipients. Nevertheless, although they were not gainfully employed according to official definitions, all of them were usually employed "off the books" to supplement the meager incomes they received in public aid benefits. Maritza herself, prior to migrating to Chicago in the late 1980s from the town of Jayuya, Puerto Rico, had worked alongside the father of her children running a small grocery store. Once she arrived in Chicago as a single mother of three young sons, however, Maritza had found it difficult to find regular employment, and opted to assist her cousin with an informal daycare business that she operated in her West Town apartment. Once Maritza's children started school, she found work as a bank teller, where she was employed for nearly two years before she was laid off. By the spring of 1995 when Ramos-Zayas met her, Maritza Jiménez had been working as a part-time parent-aide for nearly a year, while receiving public assistance in addition to the modest additional income that came from her adolescent sons' part-time employment. Notably, Maritza both alluded to the stigmas of welfare "dependency" and "abuse" that commonly discredited Puerto Rican women's admirable efforts to provide for their families, and also recast such women's recourse to welfare as a proof of their greater "independence" and their determination to secure opportunities for their children. Indeed, narratives of Puerto Rican single mothers who had successfully raised "straight-A" or college-bound students on their own despite the severe challenges of poverty were commonly deployed as the vindication of their alleged "dependency."

What none of the Puerto Rican women in this group acknowledged, however, was that their own access to various public assistance benefits came as a sub-stantive feature of their U.S. citizenship, whereas most of the Mexican women they encountered were largely ineligible, as migrants, to avail themselves of these same alternative sources of income. Instead, this material inequality between the two groups was figured in terms of presumably inherent "cultural" differences of gender relations, family ideologies, and community sanctions. Thus, allegations of Mexican machismo and Mexican women's martyrdom frequently served the ends of a gendered racialization of the differences between the two groups.

The conflicting and equivocal meanings attached to "tradition" and "moder-nity," and the related discourses of "deservingness," which we considered in chapter 4, emerged once again as racialized distinctions between Mexicans and Puerto Ricans, but as group differences understood in terms of gender and fam-ily. If notions of "tradition" and even "culture" itself could often serve the ends for many Puerto Ricans of affirming their own "modern" dynamism in contrast to constructions of Mexican "backwardness," there were nonetheless important ambivalences surrounding such discourses of "tradition." As we consider in this chapter, contradictory feelings about "tradition" became even more pronounced when they were invested in sustaining ideologies of well-ordered patriarchal relations between men and women. "Traditional" families regularly emerged as a positive sign of cultural integrity, even alongside a partial "feminist" critique of the price of such "traditions" for women. Thus, the two groups' competing claims of "civility" and "modernity" were persistently reassessed with regard to the relative degrees of women's autonomy and "liberation" from male dom-ination and masculine violence. "Violence," therefore, which emerged in the previous chapter as a figure of racialized abjection, associated with criminality, reappears in these gendered discourses as a defining attribute of masculinity, in general.

Violence and Masculinity

If, as we saw in the previous chapter, Mexican migrants sometimes made allegations against Puerto Ricans that equated a perceived proclivity for violence with a more generic inclination to criminality, discourses of violence among men tended, nevertheless, to operate ambivalently, in a manner that was widely inclined to reserve the ideological resource of "proper" or "legitimate" violence as a central pillar of masculinity itself. During the ESL class at the DuraPress factory, discussed above (see chapter 4), when the Mexican/migrant workers' discussion turned to allegations of Puerto Rican criminality, the example of how Ricardo had narrowly escaped an assault by Puerto Rican thieves inspired his coworker David Villanueva to share a still more dramatic story. He declared, "One time, eight Puerto Ricans tried to take my brother's wife." Although this claim appeared rather preposterous, what David meant became more clear as he continued. David explained that a group of men had surrounded the woman and were talking to her in a flagrant and provocative affront to her husband's masculinist prerogative, which he had interpreted to indicate that the men were intent on literally "taking" his wife. David continued the narrative, admiringly: "So my brother said, 'Alright then, let's see, who's first?'—one came forward, my brother put a gun to his head—the guy started begging, 'Don't kill me! I got three kids...' So my brother told him, 'Next time, I'll kill you.'" In addition to the masculinist heroics celebrated in this tale, however, David indicated that it had been for him a cautionary tale: "When I first came here, he told me not to go out after 7 p.m.—because there are so many gangs around Armitage." At the time that he related this story, David still lived in his older brother's home near Armitage Avenue, to the west of Humboldt Park, in the mixed Mexican and Puerto Rican neighborhood called Belmont Cragin. Implicitly, his own continued presence in that neighborhood signaled that David himself had to be understood to embody some of his brother's bravery, merely by having managed to survive in that racially charged and contested space. Thus, these narratives of Puerto Rican criminality among Mexican migrants served to create a gendered ordering of these racialized urban spaces.[1] Furthermore, this exchange of stories involved a recuperation of the masculinist honor of these Mexican/migrant men as "valor" in spite of the racially debased menace of Puerto Rican men's "criminality." David's narration of his brother's audacious feat was certainly romanticized. What is especially salient is that the Mexican protagonist accomplishes this by subordinating their potential violence with his own threat of violence. Thus, he not only proves capable of defending "his" woman but also verifies his own masculinity as one *superior* to that of his Puerto Rican tormentors.

The distinction between "criminality" and "valor" that Mexicans evoked in their contrasting characterizations of Puerto Rican and Mexican masculinity was paralleled when Puerto Rican men racialized what they, in some instances, perceived to be the debased character of Mexican men's violence in contrast to their own honorable capacity for violence. A Puerto Rican masculinity that could be celebrated as superior to Mexican manhood, on the basis of Puerto Rican men's capacity for violence, was also frequently coupled with the affirmation that Mexican (heterosexual) men were indeed violent, but primarily against women. Pablo García revisited this allegation in revealing ways. Pablo, a Puerto Rican man in his late twenties, was married to Carla, a hairstylist at a beauty salon in Logan Square. On this occasion, Pablo related the story to his wife and the other women at the beauty salon of an incident that transpired when he and his cousin had been driving down California Avenue toward Logan Square, and he witnessed a man beating up a woman on the street. He narrated:

> I stopped the car and got out. My cousin was with me in the car and he was like, "Wait, what are you doing?" But I had to get out and stop the situation. She was screaming and he kept beating her up. Mexicans beat up their wives. That's common in Mexico, and they do it here too. But I was always taught that you never—*never*—hit a woman. No-o-o-o! A woman, you have to treat her like the petal of a rose. Because hitting a woman is cowardly. So I told him: "What?!? You wanna hit somebody? You think you're a real *machote* [a big macho]? Let's see if you want to hit me!" And he was shitting in his pants!

Pablo's performance of this tale of masculinist heroics to a group of women, including his wife, notably celebrated his own chivalry. Pablo juxtaposed two competing models of masculinity—one distinguished by brute force deployed to dominate a woman, the other characterized by the will to challenge another man's violence with the threat of a morally superior violence committed to the paternalistic protection of a woman, as an intrinsically delicate being who ought to be treated "like the petal of a rose." Thus, Pablo's account redeemed not only his own moral integrity but also his male honor as a distinctly Puerto Rican masculinity, against the degraded, empty masculinity of a Mexican man whose capacity to overpower a woman was denounced as mere cowardice. Pablo insinuated that the violence of Mexican men manifested an implicitly "barbaric" or "uncivilized" masculinity, best understood as the routine behavior of deficiently modern, "Third World" men, an atavistic behavior that had merely been transplanted through migration to the U.S. and was fundamentally out of place. Pablo's Puerto Rican masculine violence was informed by absolute moral strictures that demanded self-control and demonstrated self-discipline. In contrast, Mexican/migrant wife-beaters' bombastic "*machote*" masculinity was disqualified as essentially abject and "backward." Notably, this narrative's allegation of Mexican cowardice is achieved with the concluding image of a most incriminating kind of lack of self-control—"And he was shitting in his pants!"

If Pablo García's conclusive repudiation of Mexican men's distinctly hetero-sexual masculinity, and its undisciplined violence, marked one kind of Puerto Rican disqualification of Mexican manhood, some Puerto Ricans conducted a similar operation by indicting what they perceived to be the sexual ambiguity of Mexican men. Ricardo Vélez was seventeen years old when Ramos-Zayas met him during the summer of 1994 at the Puerto Rican–identified alternative high school in Humboldt Park where she was teaching. Ricardo's mother was Mexican and his father was Puerto Rican. Despite having seen his father only sporadically throughout his life, Ricardo was very close to a paternal uncle, lived in a predominantly Puerto Rican area, and his peers were mostly Puerto Rican. Although Ricardo considered himself Puerto Rican, he was selectively racialized as "Mexican" by some of his classmates. A very sensitive and artistic young man, Ricardo rarely participated in team sports or other activities popular among the other male students at the school. During the time that Ramos-Zayas was a teacher at Ricardo's school, she recurrently heard of how some students would bully Ricardo in ways that conflated Ricardo's "Mexican"-ness with speculations about his sexual orientation. One incident was particularly telling.

One afternoon a group of the boys discovered that Ricardo's mother had come to the school to talk to a counselor. Ricardo's mother was very active in the school's cultural and political activities, something that the other students interpreted as further evidence that Ricardo was a "Mama's boy." In the aftermath of Ricardo's mother's visit to the school, Tony, one of the students who teased Ricardo constantly, asked, "So your mother was here this morning . . . Why? Was she upset that you're a fag?" David, one of the other Puerto Rican students, quickly added, "He's been hanging out with the Mexicans at the orchata place too much!" Ricardo got visibly enraged at the others' harassment and pushed his way out of the group of taunting students, forcefully banging a desk against a wall in the process, and then broke into tears.

David, Tony, and the other boys had a running joke about the owners of a trendy taquería that had recently opened in the area. The boys perceived the restaurant's owners to be flamboyantly gay, and Tony and David had been insinuating that Ricardo was associating with the taquería owners. (Notably, one of the owners was not even Mexican—he was Salvadoran). Living in an overwhelmingly Puerto Rican section of Humboldt Park, with a small minority of African American residents, Tony and David's primary views of Mexican men were rather narrowly based on the owners of the taquería. In addition, the boys had come to view Mexican men as effeminate, and thus less masculine than Puerto Rican men, because they believed that Mexicans could not hold their liquor. "When they get drunk, their feathers fly all over the place. It's all that orchata they drink!" Tony continued the joke as his friends laughed. Here, it became evident that orchata, the Mexican sweetened rice-water drink commonly sold in taquerías, not only signaled the particular restaurant and its owners who were the objects of the boys' homophobic jokes, but also that they seemed to associate the milky white beverage with semen, and thus by implication, the sexuality of all Mexican men was compromised by drinking it.

These Puerto Rican adolescent men's allegations of Mexican effeminacy might seem anecdotal or tangential, amidst pervasive mass-mediated representations of Mexican men's "machismo" suggesting a more commonplace hypermasculinization. However, this homophobic depiction of Mexican men as effeminate drew its force from the insinuation that Mexican masculinity could be called into question for its undignified lack of restraint—"When they get drunk, their feathers fly all over the place." This image marked a striking analogy with Pablo García's indictment of the Mexican wife-beater's intimidation, in the face of a "manly" opponent, as a metaphorical loss of bodily self-control—"And he was shitting in his pants!" Thus, both images involve a more elementary lack of self-control projected onto Mexican masculinity. This theme recapitulates a more general history of subordination whereby people of color or colonized nations, like women or sexual "minorities," are excessively identified with their bodies, emotions, and passions and are equated with a deficiency of rationality and an incompetence for self-government that has repeatedly served historically to legitimate conquest and subjugation (cf. Bederman, 1995; Nelson, 1998; Takaki, 1979). Thus, much as Pablo had disparaged Mexican machismo for its cowardly, undisciplined violence, the Puerto Rican adolescents strained to affirm their own heterosexual masculinity in racialized terms that demoted Mexican manhood according to this well-established association of masculine power with self-control.

A few weeks later, Ramos-Zayas mentioned the incident to Tony and David. Tending to trivialize Ricardo's hurt feelings, they explained that they only teased Ricardo because he never wanted to admit that he is Mexican. When Ramos-Zayas pointed out that Ricardo's father is Puerto Rican, Tony responded, "Yeah, but his mother is the one that's always solving his problems, giving him money, kissing up to the teachers, making life easier for him." To some extent, then, Ricardo's peers resented him for what they perceived to be the advantages he enjoyed due to his mother's active engagement with the school administration on his behalf, and for the material privileges associated with having a mother who was somewhat better off than the parents of most of the other students at the school, most of whom had incomes below the poverty level and often had fewer opportunities to get involved in the school's activities. Ricardo's mother's visibility at the school and his relative financial privilege encouraged the view that Ricardo was more dependent and less street-savvy than his peers, and was relatively protected from all forms of adversity, especially the experience of street violence that these adolescent males tended to view as a requirement that one had to endure to become a "real man."

Viewing Mexican men, more generally, as somehow less tough or "street" than Puerto Rican men, Tony, David, and the other Puerto Rican boys readily equated Ricardo's support system and his sensitivity with "being Mexican." Tony and David implicitly equated Ricardo's perceived dependency on his Mexican mother (as manifested by the fact she came to school to talk to the counselor, and so on) with the effeminate "Mexican"-ness attributed to the gay owners of the nearby taquería. Furthermore, Tony and David explicitly insisted that Ricardo himself must acknowledge his Mexicanness. Thus, despite the fact that Ricardo's father was Puerto Rican, Ricardo was selectively racialized as "Mexican" and his masculinity and sexuality came to be defined through his Mexican mother. The fact that Ricardo was generally accepted as "Puerto Rican" in most school-related contexts, further accentuates that his racialization as "Mexican" became specifically salient in relation to incidents in which his sexuality was considered to be ambiguous and his masculinity appeared to be undermined. Ricardo's Puerto Rican peers racialized him as "Mexican" in a manner that was specifically gendered and sexualized.

The class-inflected debate over discrepant ideals of masculinity and their relation to street violence in poor communities like Humboldt Park was not confined to Puerto Rican discourses about the deficiencies of Mexican manhood, however. These same gendered and sexualized distinctions were manifest in struggles over masculinity that raged internally, within the Puerto Rican community. Daniel Santiago was a Puerto Rican man in his late twenties who had just started attending classes in computer science at a vocational technical college. Ramos-Zayas met Santiago at a Puerto Rican bakery in Humboldt Park in the fall of 1994. The grandson of the bakery's owner, Daniel frequented the bakery often, and on this particular day he was also helping out, serving the customers. On this occasion, he was also complaining about the rudeness of the local teens. Soon thereafter, a group of four Latino boys wearing oversized and color-coordinated clothes came into the bakery to buy soda. It was evident that the boys were eager to generate some controversy, speaking loudly in order to command everyone's attention and making offensive references to various aspects of the bakery. "What kind of fucking music is that [playing in the background]?!?" one of them exclaimed, not really expecting a response. With regard to a photograph on the wall of a baseball team sponsored by the bakery, another commented that they looked "fucking ridiculous." Deliberately trying to ignore the young men, Santiago directed a meaningful glance toward Ramos-Zayas and another volunteer teacher with whom she was having lunch, as if to reaffirm what he had been telling them about disrespectful adolescents. After making their purchases, as they were leaving, the young men yelled back into the bakery, referring to Daniel, "What a fag!" The boys laughed boisterously, impressed with their own audacity. Daniel immediately began to complain to his grandmother that this was the reason why they should just close the bakery and move out of the area—it was becoming "too ghetto." Ramos-Zayas asked Santiago and his grandmother Elvira Fuentes if they knew the young men. Daniel responded that he had seen them around, while Elvira remarked that she was not even able to "tell these kids apart." She explained, "They all dress the same. I don't know why they like those clothes, so big like that. The other day I even asked one kid that came here why did he have to wear clothes that show his underwear. I just don't understand that fashion." Daniel immediately interjected, "You know why, because they're in gangs. They don't want to do anything to improve themselves. They want to carry knives or even guns, and fight each other to death—so they can be the great machos." This ideal of a "re-spectable" manhood, and Daniel's insinuation that such displays of masculinity were "ghetto," reveal the competing status distinctions inherent in formations of Puerto Rican masculinity, and the class-inflected and gendered identities that ordered the urban spaces of Puerto Rican Chicago. When Ramos-Zayas asked Daniel if he was certain that these young men were in gangs, he remarked that it did not matter, because one could tell, simply by their "look," that they were "trouble." The way they dressed and their general demeanor was sufficient for Daniel to believe these young men to be gang-bangers, and encouraged him to affirm his own difference from them. "Even when I was that age, I knew how to be polite, how to be well-mannered. I was respectful of adults. But here, if you don't pull a knife on someone, you're not a real man. They don't realize how ghetto they are. In high school, I would get a lot of crap from other kids. There was a group of guys—Boricua and Mexican, too—that would mess with me. But you know where they are now? They're in jail, or dead."

The connections between rudeness, violence, and a class-specific degraded "ghetto" masculinity appeared in Daniel's narrative to apply indiscriminately to Puerto Ricans and Mexicans. Nevertheless, in a life history interview that Ramos-Zayas conducted with Santiago a few months after the bakery incident, Daniel recuperated the association of physical force and the capacity for violence as positively valued attributes of a proper masculinity as well. Furthermore, it became more evident that Daniel viewed the male Puerto Ricans as fundamentally more powerful (and thus, potentially menacing) than Mexican men. Daniel recalled his high school experiences:

> I hung out with the guys that did well in school and I was in the wrestling team. Going to wrestling matches on the South Side . . . well, the South Side teams were mostly Mexican, so they were small . . . smaller guys, compared to our team. Now, when we would go to the West Side high schools—ha! that was scary because those *morenos* [Blacks, on the rival wrestling team] were big! We would always get in trouble with them, because you still had to prove you were tough, a real man. There was a lot of pressure to take it [endure pain]. A few times we won matches with the *morenos* too. Our team was Puerto Rican, but also we had a Mexican kid—José Luis Vélez. He was Mexican, but lived on the North Side in Humboldt Park. He was skinny, but that guy was strong! He could wrestle and also did boxing. He'd grown up fighting, in a rough area.

While Daniel had viewed the young men that walked into the bakery as gang members who used their potential for violence to project an exaggerated and bombastic hyper-masculinity, he also located another masculinity in the racialized space of city-wide high school athletic competitions. In Daniel's narrative, Puerto Ricans occupied a middle position between the "smaller [Mexican] guys" and the "big *morenos*" who were members of wrestling teams identified spatially with the South Side and West Side of the city, respectively. The relative size of the Mexicans and African Americans was generally presumed to be indicative of their athletic prowess and physical strength, and implicitly, their masculinity. A revealing exception in Daniel's account of the Puerto Rican wrestlers' general pattern of triumph over their Mexican opponents was José Luis Vélez. Although, like the other Mexicans on the South Side teams, José Luis was also physically small, Daniel considered his teammate to have been a formidable wrestler. Most significantly, Daniel directly attributed José Luis's strength to the fact that he had grown up in a very "rough"—and symbolically Puerto Rican—neighborhood. Daniel seemed to attribute José Luis's physical strength, and by implication, his admirable masculinity, to the young man's formative association with Puerto Ricans in Humboldt Park ("He was Mexican, but . . ."). In this sense, José Luis's masculinity could be valorized precisely because it was rendered an exception, implicitly de-Mexicanized through the spatially inflected Puerto Ricanization of his Mexicanness.

Various conceptions of a masculine capacity for violence, therefore, were constitutive and symbolically central to both Mexican and Puerto Rican men's notions of personal and collective honor, even as allegations of one or another kind of debased violence sometimes allowed them to respectively construct one another's manhood as dubious or frankly illegitimate. Certainly, although violence occupied a profound and inextricable place of prominence in these competing racialized visions of masculinity, the symbolic power associated with these capacities for violence was merely one dimension of much more complex formulations of masculinity with respect to heterosexual gender relations and the particular ideologies and practices that upheld various configurations of the patriarchal family.

Masculinity and Ideologies of the "Traditional" Family

If dominant constructions of masculinity tend to be ubiquitously produced in relation to violence and various capacities for violence—and, as we have seen, this was true for both Mexican and Puerto Rican men—it is also true that hegemonic ideals of masculinity are inseparable from ideologies of properly patriarchal and well-ordered (heterosexual) families. In narratives about family life, Puerto Ricans often had quite conventional views of what "being a man" was supposed to entail, revolving around the central themes of fidelity, parental responsibility, and wholesome living. At the seventy-fifth birthday of Esteban Cruz, a Puerto Rican man well-known in his neighborhood and a member of various church-sponsored groups, Alicia Torres, a teacher at the Puerto Rican alternative school and a longtime friend of Esteban's, told Ramos-Zayas, "Esteban is like the other men of his generation in Puerto Rico, in the countryside. The kind of men that were so respected in their communities that they would just walk into a room, and their presence . . . you could feel their presence. Because these are the men that care about their children, wives, their communities. They even take care of children that are not their own. They don't drink. They don't have vices. They never even have to raise their voice [to command respect]." The men that Alicia described were understood to occupy a higher moral ground; their masculinity had a quasi-spiritual quality based on their personal integrity, self-restraint, and orientation to family and home. At the same time, Alicia's depiction of these men seemed to consign them to a remote and increasingly irretrievable past. Not only did they belong to another generation, they were associated with another space—Puerto Rico, and especially the island's rural areas.

Ironically, these views of an old-time and honorable Puerto Rican masculinity that was presumed to be rather anachronistic, if not already extinct, paralleled the views that some Puerto Ricans had of Mexican men, as distinguished by intact families and churchgoing. As we have seen, Puerto Ricans were sometimes ambivalent about their sense that Mexicans were more "cultural" or "traditional," and this feeling resurfaced when they reflected upon how Puerto Ricans seemed to have neglected or lost their own religious customs. Estela Alvarez worked as a parent-volunteer at the local public high school in Humboldt Park when Ramos-Zayas met her in November of 1994. An energetic woman in her late twenties, Estela was renowned among her neighbors for her *pastelillitos de guayaba* (guava puffs), which she occasionally sold to local bakeries, grocery stores, and friends who would place orders for special occasions. Estela and her son, Mario, lived with her parents. A few months later, Estela invited Ramos-Zayas to Mario's First Communion at a Catholic church in Logan Square. About fifty children who had attended catechism classes together were about to receive their First Communion, and their relatives and friends filled most of the noisy church. A group of Estela's friends from the parent-volunteer program and her extended family occupied an entire bench of the church, and were commenting on the outfit that each of the children was wearing. Maritza, one of Estela's closest friends, remarked that many of the boys were wearing "Mexican outfits," as she referred to their white mariachi-style *charro* outfits with matching jacket and pants. When Ramos-Zayas mentioned that some of the boys were also wearing *guayaberas*—a type of traditional shirt popular among Puerto Rican men—another woman in the group remarked that she was surprised by how many Puerto Ricans were even receiving their First Communion. "You'd never know there are so many Puerto Ricans here—let alone Puerto Ricans that would go to church!" She laughed, and the rest of the group agreed. This inspired some of Estela's cousins to express their surprise at seeing Estela's father in church, teasing, "Francisco! I can't believe *you're* here. The church is going to start shaking!"

After the ceremony, the group reconvened in Estela Alvarez's home for lunch. When asked if she knew the other children's parents, Estela commented that some of them, specifically a Mexican and a Guatemalan family whom she had greeted, were regular churchgoers. Ramos-Zayas asked her if she knew any of the Puerto Rican families. Estela immediately responded, "Those are the people that go to church for First Communion and then never show up again." She added:

> Puerto Ricans don't even go to church . . . not like the Mexicans [. . .] and the other groups from Central America, Guatemalans. They are more religious than us. The whole family comes to church—the grandparents, the father, mother, children. And you know how they celebrate processions and all that in their countries! Crowds and crowds of people! They carry the Virgin, and that's a big deal. In Puerto Rico, nobody does processions anymore. . . . A friend of mine told me that she went to a church on the South Side for a *Virgen de Guadalupe* celebration, I think it was, and the church was threatening to fall down [from being overcrowded]! People had to stand. They [Mexicans, Guatemalans] care more about the family, the church. But if you see Puerto Ricans, you never see the father going to church. The woman goes alone or takes the younger children. That's also because there are a lot of divorced Puerto Rican women or the father is just not in the picture. But even when it's a regular family . . . the man still doesn't go. My father never set foot in church. It's a miracle he's here! If you see Puerto Rican families going to Church, they're Pentecostals, not Catholics.

Puerto Ricans commonly perceived the image of the intact, churchgoing family as a standard feature of community life for Mexicans (and also Central Americans), and perhaps as a lifestyle that Puerto Ricans had once shared in a seemingly distant past. The Virgin of Guadalupe celebrations and other religious processions among Mexicans both in their country of origin and on Chicago's South Side were perceived in contrast not only to Puerto Ricans in Chicago, but also in contradistinction to an image of Puerto Rico as a more secular society.

Furthermore, the perceived demise of religious observances among Puerto Ricans as a community, in Estela's remarks, was attributed to Puerto Rican gender relations characterized by "divorced Puerto Rican women" and absent fathers. By implication, in Estela's account, the perceived crisis of the Puerto Rican community, its literal "fall from grace," was rooted in a crisis of the Puerto Rican family and the troubled relations between men and women. Like Estela, many Puerto Ricans agreed that Mexicans (in this regard, almost invariably coupled with Central Americans) "filled up their churches," and that such religious devotion was rooted in their countries of origin, their faithfulness to old-world customs, and a "traditional" family structure. Unlike the absentee Puerto Rican fathers to whom Estela referred, Mexican men were viewed as responsible to their duties as husbands and fathers. Whereas Alicia Torres eulogized the loss of the moral integrity ascribed to the honorable masculinity of past generations of Puerto Rican men, particularly those identified with a revered and romanticized image of rural Island life, Estela Alvarez projected analogous virtues onto the Mexican men in her church. While both of these Puerto Rican women expressed regret for the demise of such qualities among the men of their own community, their belief that such an idealized masculinity was properly understood as "traditional" and belonging to the past nonetheless implicitly posited a contemporary Puerto Rican masculinity that was apprehensible as fundamentally more "modern" and "Americanized."

The nostalgia for more "traditional" and "stable" (heterosexual) gender relations that inspired these Puerto Rican accounts of Mexican masculinity, which necessarily entailed assumptions about being "modern," could also be projected onto the Mexican community as a whole. In August of 1994, Jaime Flores was working for a Pilsen-based, Latino-identified social service agency. Jaime had grown up in Chicago since the age of five, in a Costa Rican family comprised of a widowed mother with ten children; as Jaime liked to put it, "We weren't working-class, we were welfare-class." Indeed, Jaime had grown up in predominantly Puerto Rican communities on Chicago's North Side, and mainly in Humboldt Park. Upon first hearing of De Genova's research, Flores immediately volunteered his analysis of the differences between his experience growing up among Puerto Ricans and that which he observed as a social worker among Mexicans in Pilsen. Jaime perceived a greater tendency toward residential mobility and "household instability" among Puerto Ricans (with whom he included himself), which required that children had to frequently change schools, and thus, as he saw it, tended to undermine their chances of developing or maintaining long-lasting friendships. He contrasted this scenario with Pilsen or Little Village, where he perceived Mexican families as staying in one community for a long time, and thus allowing for people to become very attached to each other and develop lasting and meaningful bonds. This broader framework provided a context, in Jaime's account, for his transposition of a model of the idealized nuclear family onto Mexicans, in juxtaposition with his sense that "Puerto Rican" families (including his own Costa Rican "welfare-class" family) were endemically headed by single mothers. Jaime's higher education and his social service training had already supplied him with a certain sociological theoretical apparatus that served to pathologize single mothers (in terms of "female-headed households") and insinuated a causal relation between absent fathers and welfare dependency; indeed, he juxtaposed this repertoire for explaining his own family's experience of poverty, and persistent poverty among Puerto Ricans in general, with the notion that Mexican families and also communities were more "traditional" and "stable." Several months later, in March of 1995, Imelda— a Puerto Rican woman who had grown up in Pilsen almost entirely among Mexicans and knew very few Puerto Ricans—related how she never understood why everyone had always expected or presumed that her parents would have been "divorced," and that she would have been growing up with a single mother. This only came to make sense to Imelda much later, she explained, when she got to know Jaime and he explained to her that "single-mother households" were the norm in Puerto Rican neighborhoods, especially the poorest of them, such as Humboldt Park (where he had grown up), and that "almost all" Puerto Rican parents are "divorced." These stereotypes are, of course, quite pervasive, and, much worse, are relentlessly propagated by hegemonic social science, but it is important to emphasize that they command the complementary stereotype of "the Mexican family" as a "traditional" and at least implicitly more wholesome, properly ordered patriarchy.[2]

There were, in fact, a broad range of circumstances and arrangements in the Mexican community by which the ideologically valorized presence of fathers in Mexican families was revealed to be rather more complicated. While Mexican men did indeed usually provide income for their families' sustenance, which was hardly negligible, their "presence" or active involvement in family life was otherwise often largely symbolic. During an extended discussion about heterosexual gender relations, the family, and the politics of community—on the same occasion as Imelda's reflections on how dominant ideologies about the family had colored her Puerto Ricanness—two young Mexicans, Luis and Maribel (both U.S.-born and -raised children of Mexican migrants), emphasized their sense that, even though Mexicans seemed to uphold a family ideology that appeared to keep divorce rates relatively low, Mexican/migrant fathers commonly worked so much, and were generally so uninvolved in their families' everyday affairs, that they tended to be symbolically present largely through their literal absence. A month or two later, María Gaitán, a single mother in her late twenties who had grown up in both Mexico and the U.S. as a result of her family shuttling back and forth every year or two, reported a similar experience of her father: "He's always had two jobs. . . . He also worked for a long time at a kind of, like, retirement home for, like, rich white people where they have their golf course and swimming pools and stuff. He worked there for a long time, just doing janitor stuff. He was there, but he always had two jobs. So, I rarely saw my dad. *Rarely.*" When the family repeatedly moved back to Mexico, furthermore, María's father generally stayed in California. She explained:

> The reason that we were told we were staying in Mexico was for financial reasons. You know, send the dollars to Mexico. But later on [many years later], my mother told me that the reason we went to Mexico was because she couldn't stand my father. Which was probably true. Or a little bit of both, but probably more that, because she and my father had a lot of problems and she's heavily into the thing where you don't get divorced.[. . .] A year or two ago, she was, like, so fed up that she just wanted everyone to know what a big piece of shit he was, ya know? So, she started telling everybody, "Remember when we used to go to Mexico? [. . .] It was because of your father." . . . During that time, we were all, like, "Why don't you divorce him? Before it was the children, now we're all grown. Why don't you divorce him and start your life over?" And you know, [she responded] "I've talked to a lawyer and I know if I get a divorce I'll be fine financially." That's always the biggest concern, but . . . "The church says you're married for life."

These observations from Mexican migrants' children are indicative of the heterogeneous experiences that are obscured and the subtleties concealed by sociological reifications of heteronormative nuclear family patterns as a predictor of the kinds of community "stability" that Jaime Flores had praised. As in the case of María's family, the fact of transnational migration, likewise, could necessitate long-distance separations that facilitated marital separations that were, nonetheless, not required to appear as such.

Not uncommonly, some Mexican men had migrated to the U.S. individually and maintained their families in Mexico with regular monetary remittances and commonly with periodic visits, but had eventually come to cohabitate with second wives and even start new families in the U.S., sometimes following formal separations or divorces from their first wives, and in other instances, without ever having even explicitly informed, let alone officially divorced, the women they had left in Mexico. In some cases, their support of the first family in Mexico might diminish and ultimately cease, but in other instances, they remained materially and practically devoted to their responsibilities as migrant fathers, even as they might or might not honor their responsibilities as migrant husbands. During an interview conducted in his home in the summer of 1995, with his second wife, Matilde, seated quietly at his side, Alfredo Reynosa reflected on the breakup of families and issues of paternal responsibility as they had evolved in his own life's trajectory:

> Consecutively, I was going and coming to the United States, each year, every two years, there I go, there I come, just like that, until ... here I come to the point at which families sometimes break up ... uhmm, for many reasons—it will be due to the woman's loneliness, or that of the man, that one comes to separate. One separates by leaving [to come to the U.S.], but with the thought that in any event, "I'm going to return, and I'm going to return," but the day comes when there's a separation in which you might say, "I'm sorry, woman, enough already, I'm not coming back anymore," or the woman can say, "I'm not waiting for you anymore," and it's finished. In my case—it doesn't shame me to say it—I'm a man like any other, but I personally have been a responsible man up to this date. I was responsible with my wife until we ended the cycle that God had prepared for us, until it was truly over, but with the family I haven't finished because I still support them, still. And ... I got married again, for which I give thanks to God that I have a wife here at my side, who is good, I believe, who is a good woman, and knows me, understands me, right. And that's how life has been, the life we've led, I as an immigrant, up and down, right, pursuing life and the well-being of, of the family. But it always comes to the point of the family, there is nothing else.

Notably, for Alfredo, it was a point of honor and a matter of great importance that he could claim to have honored his first marriage until it came to its proper end, and that he continued to honor his responsibility to support the children of his first marriage in Mexico, while he nonetheless had affirmed (earlier in the interview) that he also loved his second wife's children as his own. Life itself, in Alfredo's narrative, was inseparable from and synonymous with providing for the family, even if circumstances might ultimately saddle a man with the responsibility for two families.

Spectres of Machismo Haunting the "Traditional" Family

The affirmations of the theme of paternal responsibility in Alfredo Reynosa's life history narrative drew their inspiration from a recognition that many Mexican/ migrant men did not in fact abide by such virtuous moral strictures. On one occasion in October of 1995, during an ESL course De Genova was teaching at Caustic Scrub, a group of male Mexican/migrant workers were unexpectedly (and reluctantly) challenged to explore the moral and emotional complexities of these conflicts between sexual infidelity and paternal responsibility. The topic arose, initially, when Mateo responded, somewhat evasively, to an apparently mundane question about why he had come to the U.S. Mateo's initial reply was "intellectual improvement . . . in order to know/learn [*para conocer*]—I like to go to different places to get to know them." Unconvinced by this rather peculiar explanation, his coworker Manuel immediately presented Mateo with a good-humored challenge: "I don't think you came for vacation!" Mateo persisted in his claim that his real reason for migrating was not, as he suspected Manuel to be implying, to try to make a better life for himself in the U.S., contending, "Life is not so different here—the way we live here is equal to how we live there, because of so many expenses." He explained that the cost of living in the U.S. was much greater than in Mexico, and that whatever one could earn here had inevitably to be spent, such that a migrant could never really save much money and thereby do better than provide for his basic subsistence and so create any appreciable difference in his basic standard of living. In response, another of Mateo's coworkers, Reynaldo, who was twenty-eight years old, had been in the U.S. for seven years, and came from a small town in the Mexican state of Durango, disagreed passionately: "No! It's fucked up over there! I couldn't have any of what I have over here if I had stayed [in Mexico]." Manuel, who was forty years old and had migrated to the U.S. thirteen years prior, from a small town in the state of Jalisco, also interjected his own blunt realism, directing his comment to Mateo: "Accept it, it's better [in the U.S.]—just accept it already [*ya acéptalo*]." At this point, however, Mateo, who was thirty-eight years old but had only been in the U.S. for two and a half years and had migrated not from an agrarian small town, but rather from Mexico City, opted not to dispute any further with his coworkers the respective points of this familiar argument among fellow migrants about the relative merits of returning to Mexico versus permanent settlement in the U.S. Instead, Mateo proceeded to explain more frankly his reasons for migrating: "Well, I also came because of sentimental problems [*problemas de los sentimientos*]—you see, I have two wives in Mexico . . ." Reynaldo immediately demanded a further clarification of the precise circumstances to which Mateo was referring when he said "two wives." Implying that the two women could only truly be considered "wives" if Mateo had children with each of them, Reynaldo asked, "Do you have family with both of them [*tienes familia con las dos*]?" Indeed, Mateo had three children with his first wife, and then another child with the second woman.

Mateo continued, now speaking more softly and with visible emotion, "I came [to the U.S.] in order to decide between the two, because I couldn't go on like that, split down the middle. For six years, I've lived a double life. The second always knows, but the first has no idea. So I send money to both, and I spend more on the phone bill than on rent. And it was the same there. So I figured, better if I just get out of here and go to the U.S. I need to make up my mind, but it's hard." For Reynaldo, the answer to Mateo's dilemma seemed obvious, and he did not hesitate to sympathetically but firmly chastise Mateo: "Well, you have a responsibility to the one with three kids." But Mateo objected, "It's not so easy, it's sentimental, it's a matter of the feelings one has." The other men were visibly frustrated by Mateo's recourse to sentimentality in defense of his moral equivocations, even as they might have empathized with the more banal practical quandary that had arisen from Mateo's sexual infidelity. Losing his patience a little, Manuel, who frequently enjoyed making sexual innuendos and was always extraordinarily uninhibited about making explicit references to his own sexual appetite, sighed and chided, "That's why you learn to use a condom." De Genova commented that he had known many men who had one wife in Mexico and another here. Manuel, who lived with a Mexican woman raised in Texas and her children from a prior relationship, and who never spoke of having any family in Mexico, simply shrugged his shoulders, and, seeming to consider that an altogether different problem, replied in a manner that might have revealed a passing glimpse of regret, but was nonetheless matter-of-fact, "It's *necessity* . . . it's necessity." Mateo concurred, rationalizing, "They already know when their husbands leave for the U.S. that they'll find a woman here, and they more or less accept it," but here, Mateo needed to underscore exactly how much more difficult his situation truly was, adding with emphasis, ". . . but to have two women *there*—they won't stand for it, it's intolerable." In response to this claim, however, as if to qualify Mateo's characterization of the state of heterosexual gender relations in Mexico, Reynaldo contended, "But in the small rural villages, sometimes men even keep two wives in the same house!" This comment provided Manuel with the cue that made it possible to inject some levity into this discussion and to disrupt the rather somber mood it had generated. The image of a man with two wives under one roof inspired Manuel to comically perform a man having to turn back and forth in bed between two women, kissing each of them in turn, a joke that he then augmented by performing the man making another turn back from the second woman to the first, only to have her chop his penis off. The men's bawdy laughter served to defuse the rather serious and somewhat charged atmosphere created by Mateo's confession, and, probably to their mutual relief, no further discussion of such moral and sentimental dilemmas ensued thereafter.

For as long as Mateo's marital problems remained unresolved, however, neither of Mateo's two wives, nor the children that he had left with each of them in Mexico, could be described as truly "abandoned" in the conventional sense. He had certainly betrayed one woman and seemed to have completely forsaken her emotionally, but he sustained the charade of a marriage with her from afar, and, materially, remained actively involved in her and their children's lives through his continued remittances. Similarly, although his second wife knew about Mateo's continuing entanglements with the first, she was also a regular recipient of the money he earned as a migrant in the U.S. In these rather narrowly circumscribed but not insignificant senses, both of these two women, left alone with their children, could have been regarded, much like any other women in Mexico whose husbands had migrated to the U.S., as having a spouse who consistently provided for his family. In such instances, the stigma for women of having been "abandoned" always looms as a prospective disgrace, but they may often elude any public reckoning with that prospect, sometimes indefinitely.

Even in cases when Mexican men had indeed abandoned their families completely, what deserves to be emphasized is that some men's "abandonment" of their wives and families was not always a once-and-for-all-time, conclusive act. Paco Uribe, a Mexican in his mid-twenties raised in the U.S., related the history of his parents' relationship with a memorable opening comment: "My father has always been kinda unpredictable." Paco's father was originally from the Mexican city of León, Guanajuato, and had first met the woman who would become Paco's mother in the Mexican state of Puebla. The couple met and went out on a date once, but then didn't see each other for a while; when they met again, they resumed their romance, and now continued dating for three or four months, by the end of which they were married. "That's the way it was in those days," Paco declared. "It was different back then." The couple had three sons in Mexico (Paco was the third), and then migrated to Chicago when Paco was still a baby, little more than one year old. Within a year or so after the family's arrival in Chicago, Paco's father left his wife and children. In time, the woman's closest brother came to stay with her and the three young boys for about six months, during which he made a great impression on the young boys, but he had a family of his own in Mexico and had to return. After three and a half years, Paco's father returned. During his father's long absence, Paco maintained, his mother had "remained faithful" to her husband, "and always put us first." Shortly after the husband's return, Paco's mother became pregnant again, and the couple had another son. Following the couple's reunion and the birth of their fourth child, there were family visits to Mexico, after which they relocated to Pilsen. Then Paco's father vanished again, this time for a year or so. When the husband resurfaced, Paco's mother had moved her family to a different apartment, but he had managed to locate their whereabouts. As Paco remembered, "He came in winter, knocking on the window, 'Hey, it's me.' My mother asked, 'So what brings you around?' . . . but she let him in, and that was it, he came back." On this second occasion, Paco claimed, "She took him back just because he was our father, but she didn't have any feelings for him anymore." Nevertheless, not long thereafter, the couple had another child, a girl, and then eleven years later, another girl (who was only five years old when Paco related this story). "Now they're together and they talk like friends, but not like husband and wife," Paco reflected:

> During those times he was gone, we don't know anything about where he was, or what he did . . . except one time when he was mad at my mother, he said he had another woman, but we don't really know anything . . . Maybe I have another brother somewhere . . . Sometimes I wonder how I would be if he didn't come back—I still remember a lot of bad things he did to my mom, but I try to leave that in the past and just look forward. We still don't get along, though. I'm not close to him at all, but I love him as my father. My father never cared what we did, and just said, "Do whatever you want." My mother was always the one who made sure we didn't do bad stuff. She's more conservative, my father is more wild, I guess you would say, more adventurous . . . I guess he felt isolated by having a family and staying at home. When he was young, his father was an alcoholic and used to be really hard on him since he was the oldest, so now we see him repeating it and we all understand why he's the way he is . . . my father is very *machista*.

Paco's comments revealed the deep strains of ambivalence he felt about his father's presence in the family, sentiments that were the price of his Mexican/migrant parents' apparently "intact" marriage. Even in his effort to love the man out of a sense of filial duty, and, likewise, despite his best efforts to produce a balanced assessment of the sources of his father's restlessness, his "wild" desire to break out of the confinements of domestic life, and his machismo, Paco was profoundly estranged from his father, and pondered how it might have been different, and perhaps better, had his father never returned to the family.

In some instances, of course, the men never did return. Ray Obregón, a Mexican in his late thirties, born and raised in Chicago, told De Genova on several occasions that his mother had always instructed him, meaningfully, "not to go around making babies and then leaving them alone, 'because you know what it's like to grow up without a dad.'" However, Paco Uribe's narrative was not particularly exceptional. Many Mexican women's experiences, both in Mexico and the U.S., have been decisively shaped by men who leave them with children to raise alone for years on end, sometimes repeatedly, only then to return and be accepted back into the family's home as husband and father. In cases such as that of Paco's parents, a marriage that may have appeared ruptured by a man's abandonment of his wife and children could be resumed and ultimately produce the semblance of a long-term, "stable," and "intact" family.

The narrative of Ricky Chávez's family provides an interesting analogy to that of Paco Uribe. Ricky was a twenty-three-year-old Mexican raised in the U.S. who lived in a single-family home with his parents and all of his siblings when De Genova interviewed him in 1994. In this example, rather than being abandoned by her husband, Ricky's mother had concluded while still in Mexico that, due to marital problems, it was necessary to get away from her husband as urgently as possible. Recounting the family's history in Chicago, Chávez explained how, after the first several months, his mother had found an affordable apartment in Pilsen: "She had just got here, didn't speak any English, and umm, three children on her back." Seeking to clarify the details, De Genova asked, "At that point, she was with your dad? Or . . . ?" Chávez continued, "At that point, they had broken up. After I was born, they separated for . . . many years, and uh, my dad stayed in Mexico and my mom came up here with us, and uhm, that was about eight or nine years that passed, and then my mother and my father got back together again."

Because Ricky's maternal grandfather had migrated to Chicago many years prior, and had been legally authorized to work in the U.S., Ricky's mother found herself in the position of being able to apply to migrate legally to the U.S., accompanied by her young children. Because Ricky was still unborn when she had submitted her immigration application, she had succeeded to arrange for legal passage for herself and her two older children, but not for Ricky, who had only been born shortly before her desperate and hurried departure. Thus, when the time came for the family to cross the border, Ricky's mother had managed to borrow a green card that belonged to a baby girl which would serve as fraudulent documentation for Ricky, and so had dressed her infant son in girl's clothes and thus secured his passage. Although Ricky had grown up entirely in the U.S., he was the only member of his family who was undocumented. "I was a *mojado* [wetback] when I was one year old," Ricky declared with a certain delight.

Resuming his narrative of how his parents had gotten reunited, Ricky related, "Yeah . . . I went with her back to California one time when she went to visit her brother, and uhm, I met my dad for the first time. Ya know, and I was like, uh, eight or nine years old. After that, he came to Chicago, and he saw how we were doin' . . . he moved back with us. [. . .] For a few years, they struggled with their relationship; then he came and went for a while, and uh, finally, he decided he's gonna stay here, so . . ." De Genova asked Chávez to clarify how his father had ended up in California at the time that his mother and he had made their visit. Ricky explained, "Right, right . . . well, he lived in Mexico for a while, and then he worked in California. Ya see, what a lot of people do . . . in Michoacán, is uh, since they're migrant workers—they work in the fields and stuff, you know, they have harvest season over there, when it's cold over here, and so they'll stay there in the wintertime, and . . . and during the summertime, they'll come up here to the States, like to Chicago to work, or . . . most of 'em went to California [. . .] but uh, my dad at that point was traveling from California to Mexico to California to Mexico, and [. . .] they worked in the strawberry fields; one time I think he worked in the grape . . . uhm, the grape industry out there in California; I had a cousin that used to . . . drive all the way to Oregon, to pick roses or somethin' like that . . ."

Thus, in the remarkable case of Ricky Chávez's family history, his mother's decision to escape her troubled marriage and migrate to Chicago with her three young children as a single mother, and his father's participation in a seasonal transnational farm labor migration to California, culminated in the intersection of their two Mexican/migrant trajectories many years later, and the resumption of their married life. Not surprisingly, his parents' example had hardly inspired Ricky or his siblings with much faith in the virtues of marriage:

> None of us has gotten married yet. All my cousins are getting married at eighteen, nineteen . . . and my sister's twenty-eight, no she's like twenty-nine! and she still hasn't gotten married; my brother's twenty-six . . . bachelor!" [Ricky chuckled light-heartedly as he pronounced the fateful word] I'm twenty-three and still a bachelor. Yeah, I'm not ready for marriage yet, I don't know what's the big rush with all these people getting married real young; you know, especially seeing the way my parents' relationship went, you know, where they had a family, and my mom *had to* stick—she's a wonderful person, ya know—sticking with us all these years, you know [. . .] she really sacrificed everything for us while my father was living out in California, so . . . my mother pretty much supported us, raised us, fed us, and taught us. [. . .] You know, she taught us . . . everything, pretty much; she was real strict.

Later in the interview, Ricky reflected further on his father's role in the family once his parents had reunited:

> My dad always . . . he never really participated much in the family affairs . . . he had his own way of thinking, and . . . uhm, he always had problems communicating. [. . .] He'd been in between jobs, and really couldn't hold on to a job for too long . . . for a while there, he was an extreme alcoholic; he couldn't hold down a job, much less responsibilities, you know . . . so that's why he was comin' and going for a long time.

By all appearances in 1994, theirs seemed to be a fairly "stable" and "intact" nuclear family, but Ricky's father's "presence" in the family belied a rather circuitous history of greater or lesser absences. Ricky Chávez's parents' Mexican/migrant marital history, much like that of Paco Uribe's parents as well as the others we have examined, reveals a tremendous heterogeneity. Thus, a much wider array of complications distinguishes actual Mexican/migrant practices and household arrangements from the kinship and family ideologies that they themselves may often have been found to cherish and endorse, and which are easily fetishized as "stable" and "intact" by a sociology of poverty intent on pathologizing families sustained by independent women. Furthermore, if the prevalence of "divorce" and families distinguished by single mothers is indeed a ubiquitous stereotype of

Puerto Ricans as a group, what is remarkable for our purposes is to note that Mexicans very seldom stigmatized Puerto Ricans along these lines. One rather sensible hypothesis to explain many Mexicans' disinclination to produce the difference between themselves and Puerto Ricans in terms of an opposition between "good" or "traditional" families and "dysfunctional" or "broken" ones, therefore, would very probably posit that such a stark contrast was most often simply untenable on the part of those who appreciated the complexities and contradictions of Mexican families from within.

The pervasive image of "traditional," duty-bound Mexican families was commonly haunted by the specters of heavy-handed patriarchy, domestic violence, and the unbridled and reckless power of men who coupled the enforcement of their dominance over their wives and families with their own masculine freedom to pursue their every lecherous desire and to satisfy any rapacious appetite. Caricatured and hyperbolic stereotypes of the machismo of Latino men abound, as is well known, and this stereotype is especially pronounced for Mexicans, as we have already seen in commentaries made by Puerto Ricans as well as Mexicans (Franco, 1989; Gutmann, 1996; cf. Lancaster, 1992). Indeed, and not surprisingly, caricatured images of Mexican machismo were sometimes celebrated and promoted by Mexican men themselves. On one Monday in November of 1995 at Caustic Scrub, among the same group that had been challenged by Mateo's confession, at the start of an ESL class that the workers attended prior to starting their day's work, all of the course participants seemed very sleepy and none showed much eagerness for the day's lesson. Manuel immediately explained their collective condition in relation to the routine festivities of the weekend: "Anywhere you go where Mexicans are working, you'll see the same thing on Mondays—everybody sleep-deprived, hungover [*desvelados, crudos*]—because we like to drink on the weekends! A lot of drinking, a lot of dancing, and a lot of..." At this moment, with a sly grin, Manuel began to repeatedly slap his one open palm with his clenched fist, using one of his favorite gestures to complete the sentence with the missing third term, signifying "a lot of fucking." Now, with everyone laughing, Manuel continued, boasting, "That's how we Mexicans are—*¡unos muy machos, unas muy muchas!*" [roughly: A few good machos, and plenty of willing women to go around]. Of course, Manuel was playfully and knowingly performing the stereotype of his own racialized masculinity, but even if there was a tacit acknowledgment among all of the men in the room of Manuel's blustering exaggeration, Manuel also seemed to take an indubitable pleasure in his affirmation of this masculinist ideal. Nevertheless, while Manuel could indulge his *machista* excesses among his Mexican/migrant male coworkers, and, moreover, fashioning himself as their collective spokesman, could affirm for De Genova, the white "American" English teacher, that these hedonistic traits were the distinctive pedigree of Mexican manhood, it was clearly a performance that conveniently took place with no women present. Indeed, the impulses toward debauchery and lasciviousness that Manuel celebrated as the hallmarks of his

Mexican machismo were also precisely the most characteristic issues of contention on the contested terrain of Mexican heterosexual gender relations, as variously exemplified by the troubled marriages that we have examined above.

The Subjugated (Mexican) Woman beneath Puerto Rican Women's Liberation

There was clearly no shortage of "evidence" that appeared to support the impressions that Mexican families were indeed very often extraordinarily "intact," and seemed to exhibit an astounding durability in their capacities to withstand much trial and tribulation. For related reasons, nonetheless, the semblance of greater devotion and attachment to family that Puerto Rican women sometimes perceived among Mexican men, which could be valorized, as we have seen earlier in our discussion, was also often viewed with a certain suspicion.[3] Mercedes Padró, a Puerto Rican–identified woman in her late teens, and René, a Mexican in his twenties raised in the U.S., had been living together for two years when Mercedes became pregnant. In order to save money, René suggested that they move in with his grandparents for a few months. Mercedes, René, and Mary, their two-year-old baby, had lived with René's grandparents for over two years when Mercedes eventually decided to move out with the baby and find her own place. When Ramos-Zayas talked to Mercedes Padró on a visit to Chicago in the fall of 1998, Mercedes was feeling exhausted from her on-again, off-again relationship with René. Mercedes commented:

> I thought that we were trying to save money, but René still goes out with his friends every weekend and spends a lot of money. I just hate living at his grandparents' house. They like me, but I just feel that I have to eat what they cook or they get offended. I can't cook in their kitchen and I don't always like the way they cook the rice or the condiments they use … They cook Mexican rice, and I have to go to my mom's house if I want to eat Puerto Rican food. I've been looking at apartments, but they're very expensive. I'm thinking of moving with Mary. René will probably stay with his family. I think that's something about Mexican men. Maybe Puerto Rican men are like that too, but I haven't seen that case. When Puerto Rican men grow up, they move out of their relatives' house, and that's it. No ifs, ands, or buts.

Mercedes, who had recently been promoted to the position of assistant manager at a shoe store where she had been working for two years, was obviously frustrated by René's socializing with his friends and squandering the money that they, as a couple, were supposed to be saving to rent an apartment for themselves. She suspected that René's insistence on staying in his family's home was somehow related to his Mexican upbringing, and viewed this masculinity in contradistinction to what she considered to be Puerto Rican men's absolute desire for independence. In this case, Mercedes viewed Puerto Rican men as more ready to take on the responsibilities of adulthood and independent living. Realistically, it would have been difficult to imagine how Mercedes, René, and their baby could have sustained a comparable lifestyle on their own, since René's grandparents provided a home and frequent childcare free of charge, and also subsidized many other basic household expenses. Nevertheless, Mercedes seemed to perceive their living situation under the auspices of René's grandparents as a tremendous compromise if not a trap, and had begun not only to resent René's weekend carousing but also to distrust his attachment to and dependence upon his family, as related shortcomings typical of "Mexican" men.

Mercedes had grown up in Humboldt Park and had always self-identified as "Puerto Rican," although her mother was half Mexican and half Puerto Rican. Moreover, Mercedes's father had been entirely absent from her life until a few months before her visit with Ramos-Zayas in November of 1998. Mercedes had always believed that her father was, like her mother, also half Mexican, half Puerto Rican, but when she finally met her father, Mercedes discovered that he was "just Mexican." "I'm three-quarters Mexican, and only one-quarter Puerto Rican," Mercedes commented, visibly saddened by this new revelation. Ramos-Zayas asked Mercedes what this meant to her, and she replied, "Well, I guess I'm not who I thought I was, but I also know that that doesn't mean that I'm all of a sudden Mexican, since I didn't grow up in that culture. So I will always be Puerto Rican, you know, even if I have Mexican blood in me. I grew up in the Puerto Rican culture." The powerful tension between an essentialist view of identity and belonging, based upon a biologically determined notion of "who I am" as derived from what's "in the blood," and the importance of growing up in "the Puerto Rican culture," was quite stark in Mercedes's analysis.[4] Mercedes was interpreting her father's "Mexicanness" from the standpoint of her own identity as a woman who had grown up thinking of herself as "Puerto Rican," in a neighborhood and social milieu where "Puerto Ricanness" was an asset. When Ramos-Zayas asked Mercedes if she was trying to maintain contact with her newly found father, Mercedes was very skeptical and candid about her doubts:

I didn't like how he handled meeting me. All of a sudden he wants to be my father, and treat me like he can tell me what to do—after eighteen years?!? Hell no! And also, there was a situation . . . He told me that he'd put new tires on my car, since he works at a garage. But, after he offered, he wanted to charge me for them! And I told him, "You know what? I don't need this kind of shit in my life." For me, he's like a stranger that I just met. He grew up Mexican and I can't relate to his macho thing. And he lives with his sister and mother on the South Side, and they don't even recognize that I'm his daughter.

Mercedes had found her Mexican father's orientation to family to be both too much and too little, as he seemed overly inclined to abuse his patriarchal authority over her, but still insufficiently devoted to her to help her as he had promised, and very probably too susceptible to the opinions of his Mexican family, who were apparently unwilling to accept that she was indeed his child. Based on her experiences with René and his family, and her brief encounter with her father, Mercedes had concluded that Mexican men had a "macho" inclination to be domineering, and, simultaneously, betrayed an excessive and unhealthy dependency on their families.

Puerto Rican women who had more indirect experience with Mexican families also expressed their reservations and doubts about what they supposed to be the costs of these "traditional" marriages for Mexican women. A Puerto Rican ESL teacher who lived in a Chicago suburb, Ingrid González, described her neighbors:

> The area where I live is very mixed. There are Orientals, a Black family, a Mexican couple. The [Mexican] woman—all she does is stay at home. I'm always telling her that she should get a job, but there's also the element of machismo. She doesn't even speak English. I see that among Mexicans a lot, that the woman is more like a maid and is supposed to stay at home.

In Ingrid's account, Mexican women were figured as submissive to their husbands and beholden to the cultural standards of machismo. By apparently not taking an active interest in learning English and pursuing a career, the Mexican woman in Ingrid's narrative was reduced to the status of a servant, effectively subordinated to her domestic role. By implication, Puerto Rican women were considered to be more strong-willed, independent, and thus, relatively liberated.

Discussing the changing demographics of Logan Square, Claribel Laboy and Sofía Acevedo, two Puerto Rican women in their late thirties, who worked as clerical assistants at a health clinic in West Town, told Ramos-Zayas about a new couple who had moved into their building. "Let me tell you, I don't know what's going on there. Because she cannot be older than sixteen, eighteen at most, and he is at least forty! We thought she was his daughter, but no-o-o-o!," Laboy remarked. "Well, you know how some young girls are these days. They see an older guy, and they assume that he has money, that he'll be getting them things. And especially if they are illegal, you know," added Acevedo, insinuating that the woman was an undocumented migrant. "So you think she's here illegally?" Ramos-Zayas asked. Speculated Sofía, "Well, it's not that they have told me she is or anything . . . of course, they wouldn't go around saying that . . . but there are certain things that make you wonder. Because why would such a young girl want to be with an old man like that??" Claribel pondered the enigma further: "We can't know if they are together because of that reason, because it can also be that that's a custom in their country. You know that in some of those countries, in the countryside, people give their young daughters away or set up their marriage with older guys." "What countries are those?" Ramos-Zayas asked. Laboy replied:

> I couldn't tell you of all the countries, but Mexico—I know for a fact that in Mexico they do that. Because there was a teacher in my sons' school where that was the case. Her parents wanted her to marry this older guy in their town in

Mexico, because he was a pharmacist and made good money. They are like that.
Me? I would only marry someone younger. Why would I want an older guy? To
be worried about his prostate problems?!?

As the women laughed at Claribel's joke, Sofía continued with the admission that
there was an age gap of twelve years between her grandparents, to which Claribel
responded, "Yes, that used to happen in Puerto Rico too, but not anymore,
because Puerto Rican women even date younger guys now!"

Reflecting momentarily on her own preferences among men, Claribel added,
laughing, "My mother was a cab driver in New York and she would always say
that Jewish men made the best husbands—but I'm hard-headed and keep getting
involved with Boricuas!" Having previously lived in New York City, Claribel's
mother, Irene, would not have considered the prospect of a romantic union
between a Jewish man and a Puerto Rican woman to be as implausible as it
probably seemed to her daughter who had grown up in Chicago, where the
Jewish community was dramatically smaller and the two groups rarely had
much occasion for social intercourse. Especially in the context of having made
her living by driving a cab in New York City, Irene would surely have interacted
with passengers from diverse backgrounds. Likewise, Irene would have been
better acquainted than her daughter with stereotypes about Jewish people, such
as the notion that Jewish men are universally industrious, frugal, and prosperous.
Such images could easily have served to figure Jewish men in Irene's imagination
as viable approximations of the hegemonic ideal by which men can only be
"good husbands" if they are "good providers." Notably, Irene's suggestion that
her Puerto Rican daughter seek a *Jewish* husband, rather than simply a white
man, also seemed to acknowledge the ways that Jewish claims to the privileged
racial status of whiteness had long been quite tentative and relegated to the
outer margins of racial acceptability in the U.S., even as she perceived Jewish
people as a group to have been able to partake in the economic benefits that are
largely the preserve of white social dominance. The suggestion that a working-
class Puerto Rican woman might find a Jewish husband in a city as racially
segregated as Chicago probably seemed fairly preposterous to Claribel, in any
case, but she also celebrated her "hard-headedness" in favor of Puerto Rican men
as evidence of the depth of her intimate emotional commitment to sustaining
her own "Puerto Rican"-ness even in defiance of conventional social imperatives
for gendered strategies of upward mobility.

In reference to the Mexican couple they were discussing, Claribel and Sofía
both hypothesized opportunistic scenarios of social climbing that might have explained what seemed to them to be a dubious relationship between a very young
woman and a considerably older man. Nevertheless, insofar as they presumed
that the couple were Mexican, their gender relations were also readily taken to
be apprehensible either in terms of premodern social norms typical of "some
of those countries, in the countryside," or of compromising considerations

of practical and financial vulnerability attributed to migrant "illegality" in the U.S. In either case, the Mexican woman was distinguished by her subjection and her dependency. In contrast, these Puerto Rican women characterized their own sexual relations with men in terms of their own fundamental autonomy, and celebrated their own and other Puerto Rican women's willingness to defy social conventions—by seeking younger men, or rejecting the social mandate to desire a white man with money over men of her own racial and social status. Whereas she alleged that Mexican women could still be bartered through arranged marriages—simply because "that's a custom in their country"—Claribel furthermore celebrated the independence of much older Puerto Rican women, such as her mother who had made a living in a big city in an occupation ordinarily gendered as the strict domain of men. While Irene had also worked various more conventionally female-identified jobs, including as a hotel housekeeper and a homecare worker, tending to the elderly in private homes, Claribel proudly cited her mother's job as a cab driver as evidence of strength, resilience, and self-confidence, as well as the distinctly urban and ordinarily masculine brand of savviness known as "street smarts." Claribel did not seem to appreciate the irony, however, that employment in the taxi industry in New York is generally racialized as the thankless work of "Third World" migrants who are presumed to be easily exploitable, in a manner very much akin to the vulnerable predicament that she and Sofía projected onto the "illegal" Mexican/migrant neighbors. Instead, Claribel and Sofía affirmed a sense of Puerto Rican women's implicitly "modern" identities as sexually autonomous subjects, but only in contrast to the foil of a Mexican "illegal" migrant woman who was trapped not only by legal vulnerability, but also by "backward" customs and dependency—purportedly, because "they are like that."

The racialized differences of citizenship between Mexicans and Puerto Ricans that came to be constructed in terms of their respective heterosexual gender relations also had ramifications for how Puerto Rican women perceived themselves as mothers vis-à-vis their status as legal rights–bearing subjects. For example, Puerto Rican women often viewed themselves as more capable than Mexican women to guarantee their children's well-being in the absence of a responsible father. This became evident in a conversation between Vivian Colón and Adela Figueroa, two of the Puerto Rican mothers who participated in a GED program sponsored by a cultural center in West Town. The program was an early example of a "welfare-to-work" initiative, which paid participants to attend so-called "personal improvement" workshops, including various forms of job training, résumé preparation, and GED certification, among others. Colón was explaining to Figueroa and Ramos-Zayas that her sister, Marta, was getting a divorce because her husband had cheated on her. Vivian explained that Marta and her husband had three sons under the age of ten. A divorced mother herself, Adela promptly intervened: "Well, you should tell Marta to go see a lawyer right away, so that she's not in the same situation as that Mexican girl that used to come here. Her husband left her and she had nowhere to go. Tell Marta to make sure her kids get what's theirs. Does he [the husband] work?" Responded Vivian, "Yes, he has a good job with [the telephone company] and he's always been very responsible as a father. He gives money to the kids," Adela continued, "But you see, he may do that now, but you can't depend on the kindness of his heart, you know. Marta needs to guarantee that she'll be getting child support. She is responsible for having the kids be taken care of." Adela further elaborated the contrasting example of the Mexican woman who had previously attended the parenting workshop, as a cautionary tale of what could happen if a woman did not secure child support for her children. As Adela explained, "She got nothing. They take a little off his paycheck, but he makes all the money off the books. So he has all this money, but the kids only get like 4 percent of his check, and she's taken three jobs now. But nobody ever advised her. I think her being Mexican has a lot to do with that, because you know that Puerto Rican women fight for their kids and make sure the bastard gives what he must to support their children!" Puerto Rican men might be bastards, in Adela's account, but Puerto Rican women know how to defend themselves and fight for their children's best interests. Although the Mexican woman to whom Adela referred might have been better advised about her legal options or might have consulted a lawyer, as Adela was recommending that Vivian's sister should do, Adela nevertheless explained the other woman's incapacitation in terms of her "Mexican"-ness—"I think her being Mexican has a lot to do with that"—and affirmed Puerto Rican women's strength only in juxtaposition to the figure of a Mexican woman who would not or could not exude the same fighting spirit on behalf of her rights and her children's needs. Furthermore, Adela's characterization of Mexican women as submissive endured despite immediate and intimate contact with some very self-assured, professional Mexican women employed in local social service agencies or engaged as activists in community politics.

A kind of Puerto Rican feminist sensibility thus recurrently emerged in connection with the gendered racialization of Mexicans. Such partial feminist narratives disputed uncritical views of Mexican men as family-oriented and Mexican families as more stable, by emphasizing the costs for women of upholding patriarchal gender and family ideologies, but tended to do so at the expense of Mexican women's dignity in favor of a self-congratulatory celebration of Puerto Rican women's will to defend themselves and demand their rightful due. Many Puerto Rican women likewise maintained that subscribing to patriarchal family ideologies, which they invariably associated with Mexicans, not only had implications for a woman's opportunities for socializing with her friends or resisting domestic violence, but also for a woman's prospects of ever escaping a condition of dependency by securing the skills that might allow her to better support herself. A youngish-looking woman in her late fifties, Ester García was the owner of a beauty salon and a beauty school in Logan Square. On one occasion when Ramos-Zayas visited García at her salon in 1995, one of Ester's Mexican beauty school students, Lorena Hernández, was weeping and still visibly distraught from having broken up with her boyfriend. Lorena was explaining that she suspected that her boyfriend of five years had been cheating on her with another woman whom she knew. Apparently, Lorena had helped to get this woman into the U.S., and had even allowed her to stay in her home for a few months, so she felt exceptionally betrayed.

Ester and the four other women listening to Lorena's story commiserated with her, and Ester suggested that Lorena take the day off and go home. Once Lorena left, however, the other women discussed how Lorena should never have allowed another woman to stay in her house, implying that this would have inevitably supplied the boyfriend with the opportunity to make advances toward the other woman. Very matter-of-factly, Ester declared to the other Puerto Rican women at the salon:

> Let me tell you something. Men are not worth a single tear. I've been married for over thirty years and even my husband is not worth one tear. You know why I have this business? Because it allows me not to depend on any man. And that's what I always tell my students, even Lorena. I tell them to get their school degrees, and save money for your own business, so you don't have to depend on a man. Some of them pay attention, but others say "yes, yes, yes, yes," and then don't follow through. I just see too many women like that, always in some drama, always messing up their lives because of some man. I see that *a lot* among my Mexican students. Most of my students are Mexican, except for one Puerto Rican. The other day, one of my best students, a Mexican girl, came to tell me that she would have to drop the courses. Imagine! She had almost all the credits she needed and was almost ready to take the certification test. And I asked her, "But why?!?" But I knew why before she even told me. She was with a loser. He didn't want her to work. He saw that she was moving ahead and he didn't like that. And I see that over and over again. They end up letting men control their lives, get them pregnant, and they end up with two, four, five kids. This one wanted to go back to Mexico to leave her other kids with her parents. And I told her, "Why don't you just get your certification, since you're so close to finishing, and then you can leave with a degree in hand?" I haven't heard from her and it's been almost a month now.

Ester's commentary began as a general cautionary tale about the need to strive for financial self-sufficiency and avoid emotional drama or manipulation in relationships with men. Nevertheless, as she continued, the narrative moved toward a racialization of the gender ideologies and practices that Ester specifically attributed to Mexican women. In particular, Ester characterized Mexican women as invariably ready to sabotage their own future prospects for greater independence by disregarding their own career aspirations in order to satisfy the "loser" men in their lives, or in favor of negatively valued and stereotypical gendered options (such as getting pregnant). Furthermore, the fact that the particular woman in Ester's narrative had presumably returned to Mexico prior to completing her studies was presented as conclusive evidence that the woman had willingly forfeited her personal independence in favor of a presumed move backwards.

Indeed, returning to Mexico was figured in Ester's remarks as effectively synonymous with a kind of "failure," in effect, a renunciation of more challenging "modern" options. In fact, in a subsequent conversation with Ramos-Zayas, García added, "In Mexico, unlike in Puerto Rico, they don't require any certification to have a beauty salon or be a hairstylist. So these Mexican girls don't understand the value of these credentials. The Puerto Rican students I've had through the years understand that. They know that whether they stay or go [back to Puerto Rico], they'll need to pass the test and get certified." Thus, what Ester perceived to be Mexico's more informal and implicitly more "backward" way of life seemed to undermine the Mexican women's capacity to comprehend the value of educational certificates and credentials for their future employment opportunities and prospects for advancement, whereas Puerto Rico had already adopted the more "modern" requirements of U.S. society. Ester's praise for Puerto Rico's "modernity," however, indirectly celebrated the "Americanization" that was historically inseparable from the Island's quite compromised condition and strikingly dependent status as a U.S. colony. Ironically, then, these colonialist conflations of "modernity," "Americanization," and "progressive" gender politics altogether impeded Ester and the other Puerto Rican women from appreciating Mexico's autonomous status as a formally sovereign, independent, and self-governing nation-state—arguably a more politically "advanced" condition than Puerto Rico's dependent status vis-à-vis the U.S.

If many Puerto Rican women were inclined to celebrate their own rejection of conventional (heterosexual) gender roles, however, many Puerto Rican men seemed to believe that this circumvention of "traditional" gender roles necessarily generated much of the conflict that led to the volatile relationships between Puerto Rican men and women, which were so often juxtaposed to the presumably more "stable" unions between Mexican men and women. Tony Santiago, a Puerto Rican man in his early twenties, was teaching at a middle school in the West Town neighborhood. Although Tony was born and raised in Chicago, he recalled that when he was in high school, his parents had considered moving to Puerto Rico with the hope of solving their marital problems. Tony commented:

> The whole family moved back to Puerto Rico. Come to think about it, it was naïve of my parents to try to solve their problems by running away to another place. But back then, my father really wanted to move back to the Island. But my mother never really wanted to go back to Puerto Rico. She wanted to stay in Chicago. We were all fine with going back to Puerto Rico, except my mother. She had more freedom in Chicago to spend time with her friends, have her own beauty shop, go out. In Puerto Rico, my aunts and cousins were more traditional. My mother was more Americanized in that sense. I think that most Puerto Rican

women are . . . at least here in Chicago. That's probably part of why my father wanted to go back to the Island. They went there to save their marriage, but what it did was speed up their divorce. And, as soon as the divorce process was in place, my mother came back to Chicago again.

Tony's recollections of his mother's independence and the turmoil it produced for his parents' marriage left a lasting impression on his own endorsement of "traditional" gender ideals. In fact, a few years later, Santiago called Ramos-Zayas to let her know that he was getting married and moving to California. Tony's fiancée was Mexican. He remarked, jokingly, "I never thought I'd end up with a Mexican." As he laughed, he continued, "But I know that I'm very traditional, and so is she. It would be more difficult to find that in a Puerto Rican woman. I'm not putting down my race or anything, but that's just my experience." Indeed, the depiction of Puerto Rican women, in general, as "more Americanized" (or less "traditional") than other Latinas was oftentimes associated with narratives of high divorce rates, single-headed households, and beleaguered gender relationships between Puerto Rican men and women.

There were instances in which a type of Puerto Rican feminist sensibility emerged among women who affirmed the distinction between a more "traditional" Puerto Rico and the more "modern" or "liberated" way of life attributed to their experiences in Chicago. Elda Aponte, a Puerto Rican woman in her forties and the single mother of three teenage sons, was a participant in a popular-education program in Humboldt Park. An upbeat and resourceful woman, Elda lived in one of the most depressed areas of Humboldt Park. She supported herself and her sons by combining public assistance, in the form of food stamps and Medicaid, with her part-time employment as a parent-aide responsible for monitoring the hallways of the public high school, for which she received $20 per workday. Through her involvement at the popular-education program, Elda had met a group of Latina women who became very close friends. Most of Elda's friends were Puerto Rican women, although the group included a mix of various Latino nationalities. With the exception of herself and another Puerto Rican woman, Elda perceived the other women in the group to be more subordinate to the men in their lives. As Elda explained, "Well, Lourdes is crazy! I like her! Because she's great—she's always inviting me to go out, go dancing, stuff like that. Since she moved to Chicago from Puerto Rico, Lourdes told her husband, 'Here things are not like there. Here men have to cook and clean just like women do.' And she went off and continued school, and goes out, and all that." When Ramos-Zayas asked Elda how other women perceived Lourdes's independence, she laughed and commented, "Some think she's crazy—even loose!—but she's not. She loves her husband and her husband knows it. But other women can't understand that, because of the culture. They still have the culture from their parents in Puerto Rico, or they come from other countries where men are the ones who give the orders, like the Mexicans." Whereas Puerto Rican heterosexual gender relations existed in historical time and were subject to change, and Puerto Rican women, moreover, were figured as actively making their own history, other women, "like the Mexicans," simply came from countries where patriarchal male dominance appeared to be an immutable fixture.

Although the Puerto Rican women at the various popular-education and parent-volunteer programs, in which Ramos-Zayas participated, often befriended Mexican women, they still viewed these friendships as constrained and context-bound. Puerto Rican program participants explained that they knew that their Mexican counterparts would not be able to socialize after the programs finished, because they had to "report to their husbands" [*reportarse a su marido*]. Elda Aponte was empathetic with the plight of the Mexican women, and identified with the demands of "reporting to the husband," which she associated with her prior marriages, during her first few years in Chicago. She commented:

> Some Mexican women are still more conservative about what they wear. You don't see Mexican women wearing slinky dresses, jewelry, or wearing makeup that much, unless it's for a wedding or something like that. They don't fix themselves up as much as we Puerto Rican women do. When they go out, they ask for their husband's permission, and they have to report to them. [. . .] Puerto Rican women who are raised here go to dances, to parties. Alone. Without their husbands. That's a difference between how you grow up in Puerto Rico and here. My husband wouldn't even let me go from here to the corner alone when we first arrived in Chicago. I had to train him. Puerto Rican men think that Puerto Rican women living here are too aggressive! [she laughed] Not like the ones in Puerto Rico! They are *machistas,* and we are aggressive.

Elda's empathetic perspective explicitly sought connections between Mexican women's experiences and behaviors and those of Puerto Rican migrant women, such as herself. Nevertheless, she suggested that the "more conservative" dress styles, as well as the more "traditional" gender norms that these fashions were presumed to signal, were related to how attached these women were to their country of origin—whether Mexico or Puerto Rico. Despite the similarities she identified between the two groups, Elda nevertheless judged Mexican women to be, in effect, lagging behind "aggressive" Puerto Rican women on a presumably unilinear scale of migrant adaptation to the "modern" way of life in the U.S.

Many Puerto Rican women's presumptions of their own independence relied consistently upon the figure of a subjugated—and submissive—Mexican woman, who was not only suffering under a husband's tyrannical domestic regime, but was also most commonly perceived to be resigned to her suffering plight and accepting of her own inferior status. The life history narrative of Luisa Zambrano—a Mexican/migrant woman who was thirty-nine years old, and had been in the Chicago area for eighteen years in 1995, when De Genova interviewed her in her home—in some ways could appear to substantiate many of these Puerto Rican women's perceptions of the long-suffering Mexican victim of a violently abusive husband. However, Luisa's story provided a complex series of contrasts that profoundly disrupt and challenge any simplistic caricatures of her putative "submission" or accommodation to her subjugation.

Zambrano was a worker at the DuraPress factory and had participated in two of De Genova's ESL courses. Luisa was often quite jovial with her coworkers in the factory. Her general demeanor was a testament to the resilience and strength that she had marshaled during a life of many hardships and struggles. Luisa was raised in a small agrarian village in the Mexican state of Guerrero, where she had lived since her infancy with a maternal uncle, his wife, and her grandmother. Her mother lived in the neighboring village with a second husband, after having been abandoned by Luisa's father, but the uncle refused to permit Luisa's mother to take her daughter back to live in her home, because he needed the girl to work in his field and tend to his goats. "My uncle," Luisa explained, "is one of those men who says, 'Here, it has to be this way,' and that's just the way it is." On one occasion when Luisa's mother had tried to take her daughter back, the uncle beat the woman. Her uncle was also in the habit of beating his wife, who resented Luisa and, in turn, routinely beat her throughout her childhood and adolescence. De Genova asked if she ever thought of running away; Zambrano replied:

> Uuhm, I never thought of running away; I always thought of getting married, and then, I got married [. . .] I got married, I went off with him. I was thinking that this way my life was going to be different, that it was going to change. [. . .] When I got married [. . .] we went to Veracruz, because there many people go to cut sugar cane. Well, from there we returned, and then we were going to Acapulco and Mexico City. In Acapulco, our first daughter was born, and then we went back to the village again. [. . .] I married my husband, but I didn't love him. I got married just because I wanted to get out of the house . . . well, I thought it was going to be different, and I was thinking that with time, I was going to love him, and well, I didn't love him much, we might say, not much, right, because he too was always treating me really badly, and he was beating me, and running around with other women.

Later in the interview, Luisa returned to this subject and explained further how her husband mistreated her while they were still in Mexico:

> [In Mexico City], that's when my husband was going to dances, and there he was leaving me behind in the house. [. . .] We lived in Acapulco [. . .] like a year and a half, right, but it was also the same way, like I'm telling you, there's always me in the house and him working, he'd get home and change his clothes, eat, and then take off with his friends. Over there, he was already coming home drunk at dawn; sometimes he didn't even come home, and it was just like that, like that . . .

After the birth of their first child, the couple returned to the village, and it was then that Luisa determined that she would try to escape her abusive marriage by migrating to the U.S. as a single mother with her newborn daughter; she continued:

> And me, I decided to go to the United States—I told my dad that he was treating me badly, and that I wanted to come to be with him [in the U.S.]—my dad was already here [in the U.S.], and he sent me a letter to say that I could come right away, and I was going to come, me alone, with the girl [her daughter] only, but then he also wanted to come and said that he was going to change, and that it was going to be different over here [in the U.S.], and so we came. We arrived here one twenty-…fifth of December, in '77, and time passed and…he didn't change, nothing changed, and here we had five children total, and he never changed. Always a womanizer and a drunk and a good-for-nothing, and…he didn't like having any obligations in his home—he'd come and it was all the same to him if the kids were alright or not well—yes, that was him.
>
> And I put up with it like that for a long time, I put up with it for ten years because I didn't want my children to suf— [didn't want] for them to grow up without their dad, and I wanted another life, a different life, for them, because it's really hard when one doesn't have a dad. And for that, I put up with it, but then later…the day came when no more—to the point […] that it disgusted me for him to come home, and…he would want to touch me or something, and I no longer wanted to be with him. And I decided, I decided to leave him, and he was thinking that I was never going to do it […] he was telling me that he had me very secure. […] He was thinking that I wasn't going anywhere with so many kids. And, well, yes, it made it very hard for me, taking that decision…the smallest girl was only two years old. And, well, there were times that I didn't even have money for a gallon of milk for my children, but I came out ahead with the help of God and an older woman who helped me too. I came out ahead and my kids are already big.

Explaining that she had divorced her husband seven or eight years prior, Luisa continued:

> Two or three years passed, I got together with a guy, but as things turned out, he left us too. […] I, yes, I loved him, right, but he took off to Mexico, and he took another woman with him, and that was that, there it all ended.
>
> My kids are with my mom [in Mexico], because I had a lot of problems with the younger boy […] they wanted to do what the older girl was doing, and I didn't agree […] so then I decided to send them to my mom. The older girl, the oldest one, well, she went with a guy and now she's not living very well, right, she already has a daughter. And now […] I'm thinking that I'll go to Mexico and I'm thinking that I'll bring my oldest daughter too, and then later—next year, I'm thinking that I'll bring all my kids back with me, if God gives me license.

Luisa's story was one replete with domestic violence, beginning from her earliest childhood memories, and she had been trapped in an abusive marriage with five children for twelve years or more. What is all the more remarkable, therefore, in the face of such tremendous adversity, was Luisa's determination to change her situation. Like Ricky Chávez's mother, discussed earlier, the initial decision to migrate to the U.S. was Luisa's, in a deliberate effort to escape her oppressive marriage. Although Luisa fell prey to her abusive husband's insincere promises to change, and thus migrated with him, she eventually managed to make a permanent break with her children's father, despite the tremendous hardships that she assumed in order to provide for her five children as a single mother.

Like many Puerto Rican women who perceived that women enjoyed greater liberties in the U.S. than in Puerto Rico and who, moreover, readily presumed that women's plight in Mexico was indisputably even more treacherous, Luisa also juxtaposed her experiences in Mexico with what ensued in Chicago, and explicitly addressed the theme of women's "liberation" in the U.S. With much justification and without reservations, Luisa drew severe conclusions about Mexican husbands. She explained:

> Well, Mexican husbands are always the sort that go out to a dance and the woman stays at home, they roam the streets and we have to be waiting for them until they get back, and well, there are more problems, because there isn't much liberation like here [in the U.S.]. One always has to be sub— submissive toward the husband, and here, well, it's not like that, it's more different.

When De Genova asked Zambrano to further elucidate what she had in mind when she spoke of "liberation," Luisa continued:

> The difference is that over there [in Mexico], one just has to be in the house doing the wash, ironing the clothes, doing the cooking, and the man goes off to dances, or he goes to drink a few beers, or to fool around with his friends, whatever, and one can never go out, one always has to be in the house. And here, well sometimes, well, even here they want to do the same thing, right, but sometimes they already see the difference, and so [...] from time to time take one out to a dance, or out to eat in a restaurant. And over there, well, one can't afford to do that, right, because the income is very little, and it makes it more convenient for them to just go by themselves than to take you along, because if they take you along, well, they spend more. And here, well, it's more different . . . because if the husband wants to beat his wife, now no, now he can't beat her because now one can defend herself a little, because you call the police and right away the police are coming and they do something. In turn, over there, no, there if the husband leaves her for dead, well, good and dead she stays, because nobody, nobody gets involved in anybody else's business.

"It doesn't happen here?" asked De Genova; Zambrano continued:

> Well yes it happens, but the woman can defend herself more [...] or there are these . . . shelters where the woman can seek help, hide out or something, and there, no. [...] In Mexico, they don't help the woman, and here, yes, they help her.

Although Luisa was incontrovertibly emphatic, even adamant, about her certitude that women had far more recourse in the U.S. to escape domestic violence and abusive situations, when she described her own experience of coming to the

U.S., the stark contrast she drew between the U.S. and Mexico seemed rather more complicated.

The Zambrano family's circumstances upon their arrival in 1977 in the U.S. had almost immediately required Luisa to seek gainful employment, and, for the first time in her married life, she began to work outside of the house. While her husband had found work in a restaurant making $90 a week, Luisa began working in a clock factory where she made $120 a week. The fact that Luisa was now employed outside of the home and making even more money than her husband, however, did not automatically translate into an empowering "liberation" from her subjugation as a housewife, or even a modest improvement of her domestic circumstances. To the contrary, it meant that she merely became encumbered by the double demands of a full-time job in addition to the full burden of the household labor. De Genova asked directly, "When you started working, did your life change a little bit? Were you feeling more independent or—?" Interrupting him, Zambrano replied flatly, "Uhm . . . No. I never felt independent." She explained further:

> How could I tell you?—I felt free only when I left him, because in the meanwhile I did not, I was not feeling that I was free. I always was there with the housework, checking on the little girl, changing her, I had to do the cooking, like that, but I never felt independent, and neither did we ever go out, because he was never interested in me for anything.

Following her divorce, while her five children were still young, Luisa had received unemployment and then some form of public aid for several years.[5] Later, she returned to work, at restaurants, an industrial bakery, and eventually the DuraPress factory, where she was a punch press operator. During the period when De Genova knew her, Luisa Zambrano was frequently required to work routine mandatory daily overtime as well as full days on Saturdays. As we have seen, furthermore, by 1995, she had sent her younger children to live in Mexico with her mother.

Despite her grim judgments about the plight of women in Mexico, Luisa in no simple sense equated her Mexican/migrant factory worker's life in the U.S. with any unproblematic notion of "liberation," and had not at all relinquished the dream of returning to Mexico. When De Genova asked Zambrano how her plans had changed from when she had first migrated to the U.S., she responded:

> How have my plans changed? Well, I've worked very hard and yes, yes I was able to build a house in Mexico . . . not just me, with my siblings too, with their help, among the three of us, we built the house, and well, sometimes the plans are to leave and go to Mexico, but I still don't know, because as she [her eldest daughter] is already married here and I wouldn't like to leave her, and also, her husband, I don't think that he'd want to go off to Mexico—he's Puerto Rican—and so I'm, uhm . . . to share . . . I don't know what to do [*estoy um . . . compartir . . . no sé qué hacer*].

When De Genova responded to Zambrano's incomplete thought, unsure of what she meant to suggest by the word "to share," and suggested, "[You're] shared ... [*Compartida*...]," Luisa continued, "Yes, shared/split [*compartida*], because I want to be here and I want to be over there, and not be in the two places at the same time." Luisa was quite explicitly ambivalent about her competing impulses—her aspiration to return to Mexico to live in the house that she had helped to build there, on the one hand, and her desire to remain close to her eldest daughter who had begun a family in the U.S., on the other. Earlier, Luisa had expressed her intention to be reunited with her younger children in Mexico and her desire to be able to also bring her oldest daughter (and presumably, her granddaughter as well), but had also contemplated the prospect of later returning to the U.S. as a family. Of course, this latter scenario would most likely depend on what might become of Luisa's nineteen-year-old daughter's relationship with her Puerto Rican boyfriend, the father of her child; here, Luisa frankly acknowledged that it was not likely that she could bring her daughter and granddaughter back to Mexico as long as the young woman was still involved with someone who was not himself Mexican. Although Luisa's options could lead in divergent directions and were still clearly unresolved, she had certainly achieved a hard-won independence and was deliberating over her family's future as a confident single mother. Even after eighteen years in Chicago, Luisa's transnational migrant commitments remained quite substantial, and in very practical and material ways, she was sustaining a transnational family shared between a remote village in Mexico and an industrial suburb of Chicago. Furthermore, after having spent the greater part of her life enduring domestic violence and spousal abuse, Luisa, like many other Mexican/migrant women, had deep insights into the price of her liberation as a woman.

The production and performance of competing understandings of the "traditional" and the "modern," in conclusion, was most abundantly manifested in constructions of "Mexican" and "Puerto Rican" as overtly gendered identities. These specifically gendered productions of Mexican and Puerto Rican group differences further enhanced the ideological elaboration of hierarchical "racial" distinctions between Mexicans and Puerto Ricans in Chicago. Both Mexicans and Puerto Ricans tended to assume that the preservation of a "good" (intact) family depended on the maintenance of a properly ordered patriarchy, even when this required women to be self-sacrificing. Although the "presence" of fathers in many apparently "intact" Mexican families was often more symbolic than not, gendered constructions of a racialized difference between Mexicans and Puerto Ricans largely relied upon each group's putative identification with or distance from the "traditional," and the perceived costs or advantages associated with notions of cultural "authenticity." By projecting images of victimization, self-abnegation, and "weakness" onto Mexican women, Puerto Rican women upheld an image of themselves as assertive, independent, and, by implication, more "modern," and devised a gendered Puerto Rican group identity grounded on a quasi-feminist ideological template, even as they frequently considered these same characteristics to be basically incompatible with sustaining a long-term "traditional" family life.

Distinctly gendered constructions of the differences between Mexicans and Puerto Ricans were readily articulated in terms that might appear to be "cultural," but as we have seen, these discourses of the differences between the two—as groups—tended to rely upon universalistic notions of greater and lesser degrees of "tradition" and "modernity." By locating these apparently "cultural" differences along an ascending scale of greater of lesser "modernness," however, such differences were readily recast as inherent group inequalities and, at least implicitly, as racialized distinctions. Such imaginings of the relative "authenticity" of Mexicans and Puerto Ricans, respectively—whether competing or complementary—were certainly premised upon notions of "culture," but as we have already seen in chapter 4, even the depiction of Mexicans as "more cultural" served to consign them to a condition that was, by implication, "traditional," static, and insufficiently "modern." Thus, distinctions that apparently concerned "culture" often served to differentiate the two groups' respective and distinct locations along the kind of presumed unilinear scale of "progress" and civilizational "development" that has historically served to insinuate "cultural" differences into the hierarchical assessment of racialized inferiority and superiority. The presumptuous claim "that's how they are," finally, underscores the ways that the demarcation of seemingly "cultural" differences can become virtually impossible to distinguish from more plainly racialized characterizations of differences or inequalities purported to be intrinsic to a group as such. As we will explore further in chapter 6, language was another prominent and ideologically charged "cultural" attribute that was recurrently exploited for the purposes of producing and ranking the divergences between Mexicans and Puerto Ricans in ways that differentiated them as distinct racialized groups.

CHAPTER 6

Latino Languages, Mixed Signals

In a discussion of holiday foods in December of 1993, during an ESL class at the DuraPress factory, one of several Mexican women, Carmen, teased Yadira, the only Puerto Rican worker in the group, joking that "in Puerto Rico, all they eat is the 'r' [*na'más comen la 'r'*]." This exchange may have been innocuous banter among Latina coworkers, but it was nonetheless embedded in a much more widespread discourse among Mexican migrants about how Puerto Ricans' habits of pronunciation indicated that they did not know how to speak proper or "good" Spanish. While racialized constructions of the difference between Mexicans and Puerto Ricans tended *not* to focus narrowly on notions of biology or physical differences between their respective bodies, there emerged nonetheless very pronounced productions of the difference between the two groups' respective "tongues," which is to say, their language. Whereas it is precisely the apparent commonality of Spanish language that so frequently is presupposed as a basis for unification among Latino groups, this chapter reveals that Mexican migrants' and Puerto Ricans' shared language was instead an especially salient object around which to produce their difference, and often a source of significant division. This chapter examines hierarchical judgments that the two groups deployed with regard to each other's distinctive Spanish language, as well as bilingualism and English language. Notably, all of these discourses of language difference come to be quite explicitly ranked in terms of class—through competing notions of civility or urbanity, or cultivation and proper upbringing—and are also forcefully racialized in explicit relation to Blackness.

Throughout the preceding chapters of this book, we have emphasized the diverse, divergent, and inherently contradictory ways in which Mexicans and Puerto Ricans, very frequently, come to be marked within the U.S. racial order as "Mexicans" and "Puerto Ricans," respectively. These racialization processes are perpetrated by dominant social institutions as well as the members of privileged social groups, as individuals and collectivities, but also by the more or less deliberate and active participation of other working-class and poor people who are, to varying degrees, analogously exploited and oppressed, in terms of the systemic inequalities of class, race, and citizenship. Furthermore, as has been one of our central concerns, these racialization processes are likewise perpetrated through the active collaboration of Mexicans and Puerto Ricans themselves, as social actors very much invested in the production, reproduction, reformulation, and transformation of the differences through which they respectively constitute their collective identities as well as elaborate the distinctions and enforce some of the divisions between one another. In short, while the hegemonic racism of the U.S. nation-state subjugated and oppressed both groups, Mexicans and Puerto Ricans in Chicago nonetheless also racialized themselves and one another—as "Mexicans" and "Puerto Ricans." In addition to the pervasive racialization of their distinct national-origin identities, however, both Mexicans and Puerto Ricans were also grouped together within the hegemonic racial order of the U.S. Although Mexicans and Puerto Ricans may have been more typically inclined to foreground the differences between their groups, and often racialized those differences, as we have seen, they nevertheless commonly found themselves homogenized—as "Hispanics," or Latinos. That is to say, they were racialized *together* as members of a generic category of nonwhiteness, comprised of Latin American speakers of the Spanish language. Yet, as we examine in this chapter, the ubiquitous racialization of the Spanish language that Mexicans and Puerto Ricans shared, which sometimes served as a basis for recognizing their commonalities of interest and for formulating visions of a shared Latino identity (see chapter 7), was no less fertile ground for the cultivation of the forcefully pronounced differences between them.

The Racialization of Language

It was quite commonplace for both Mexicans and Puerto Ricans in Chicago to identify their language—both speaking Spanish as well as speaking a stigmatized accented English, or the presumed inability to speak or comprehend English at all—as an object of routine discrimination and racial contempt.[1] Alfredo Reynosa, a Mexican migrant in his fifties who had been in the U.S. eighteen years when De Genova interviewed him in 1995, spoke both as a Latino and specifically as a Mexican when he related a very characteristic narrative of his experience of discrimination in connection with his language:

> I tell you one thing: that . . . as a Latino, Nico—I don't know about others, ohh [. . .] such as those from Central America or from other such places—we as Mexicans, I as a Mexican, yes I have felt some discrimination—in workplaces, on buses, in government offices, in hospitals, in, you know, Nico, so many things. [. . .] Sometimes including your own people, one's own people. I at times have even felt that . . . they have even made fun of you right there to your face, because of not understanding the language. Many times, it's true, many people [when asked], "Do you speak English?" they say, "No, nothing, I don't understand anything." Then if one does understand a little, they turn around and say, "No, he doesn't understand." [. . .] There at work, they don't want you to make any noise [complain] because, no, there they want to have you a little isolated [*relegado*], you see, but I think that is all because of being Latino. [. . .] The American throws the blame on you, [saying], "he doesn't study because he doesn't want to, because he's lazy . . .

Later in the interview, De Genova returned to the subject of discrimination and asked Reynosa for some examples of his own experiences; he continued:

> Okay, look, I was in the hospital [...] they had just operated on my stomach, and there we were—a Mexican (because that was me), and an American. [*un americano;* i.e., a U.S. white] [...] Okay, so then I say something—and look, I've been in really bad shape, really sick—I was telling them to help me, right [...] and then they tended to the other person first, and even after an hour, an hour struggling to get them to attend to me. [...] So then there I was in that hospital, I felt that I was dying, and I felt that they weren't attending to me, and that it had to be because [...] one feels that, that perhaps, it's because of being Latino—that other person, they took care of him first, and I was saying "but why is it like that?" But then, I tell you, one simply goes and makes a complaint to the administration there—"Listen, I want to talk to someone about this..."—aah, forget about it, just forget about that already. They still do attend to you, but yes, one feels the discrimination [...] yes, you feel that one has to fight for that, and not only in the hospitals, you go looking for work, or right there at your own workplace [...] one feels that... that it's not equal, it's not equal—yes, one feels the discrimination. And it will be because of... everything—because of the language, because of race or color, as we say, but... it's difficult, Nico, difficult.

Alfredo expressed his certainty about having often been the object of discrimination, and explicitly identified the ways in which he had been mistreated as a *racial* matter, but the inability (or presumed inability) to speak English was designated a central importance within this particular racism.

The frequent conflation in Chicago of one's racialization—either specifically as Mexican, for example, or generically as "Hispanic" or Latino—with the incapacity to speak English, was evident in the following incident. During the summer of 1994, the workplace literacy program where De Genova was employed was conducting what it called a "Literacy Audit" for a new corporate client, at the Die-Hard Tool and Die factory. This involved administering written tests of mathematics and English-language reading comprehension to the entire workforce, as well as oral tests of English-language aural comprehension and fluency for those workers who spoke English as a second language. Juan Villa was a Mexican in his twenties who had been raised (and probably born) in Chicago. The only U.S.-raised Mexican employed at Die-Hard, whose workforce was comprised mainly of migrant Latinos and Appalachian whites, Villa listened to heavy-metal rock music and associated mainly with his white coworkers. Thus, it was a rather revealing albeit bizarre oversight when the company management included Juan for the spoken English test. One of De Genova's coworkers, another ESL instructor named Evelyn O'Brian, later remarked, "I don't know why he was sent for testing—he speaks better English than me!" Later, in preparation for the presentation of the testing results to the factory management, when this scheduling mishap was brought to the attention of Elaine Yablonski, the director of the workplace literacy program, she remarked candidly that the oversight had only occurred "because he's called Juan, instead of John." Nevertheless, although Evelyn had been befuddled by the absurdity of having to test the spoken English of someone who was perfectly fluent and for whom English was in fact his primary and dominant language, the middle-aged white woman did not, however, refrain from administering the unnecessary exam to the young Mexican. Furthermore, although O'Brian could joke that Villa spoke English even better than she herself did, De Genova noted that she had nevertheless penalized his imperfect grammar and had opted not to give him a perfect score on the rudimentary test.

The elision of a Spanish surname—and, most likely, also brown skin—with Spanish language, and, furthermore, the presumptuous equation of Spanish language with a *lack* (or deficiency) of English language, were commonplace manifestations of the racialization of U.S.-born or U.S.-raised Latinos. The racialized assumptions that operated in order to presume that a U.S.-raised Mexican such as Juan Villa needed to have the adequacy of his English-language capabilities scrutinized by an "expert," however, were also mirrored in the practices of many Mexican migrants who automatically expected that someone who "looked Mexican" ought to be able to speak Spanish. On one occasion when De Genova had just begun teaching an ESL course at a Pilsen community organization called Casa del Pueblo in 1995, during break-time, a casual conversation transpired. Faustino Galarza, a factory worker in his fifties who had migrated to the U.S. twenty years prior from the Mexican state of San Luis Potosí, inquired as to whether De Genova was Mexican. This initiated a very familiar round of questions by which Galarza learned that De Genova's family was Italian, but that he himself did not speak Italian. Faustino replied, " But you don't speak Italian?! That reminds me of a family I know—Mexicans—eleven children, and none can speak Spanish!" Now, directing his remark to another course participant, Luis, a teenaged migrant from the Mexican state of Jalisco, who had only been in the U.S. for a year and also worked in a factory, Faustino continued, chuckling at the marvel of it: "Brown like you, like me [*morenos como tú, como yo*] but not a one can speak a word of Spanish! Incredible!" A month later, Faustino once again had occasion to mention this family of U.S.-raised Mexicans who could not speak Spanish, this time revealing that this was actually his son-in-law's family. He explained, "I used to dream of my kids marrying people from my town—from the same town in San Luis that I came from—that was my dream in those days, but that's not how life goes . . . but all three of my kids married Mexicans." Referring to his son-in-law, Faustino continued: "He's more Mexican than me, more brown than me [*más mexicano que yo, más moreno que yo*]—but not a word of Spanish!" Referring to others among the eleven children, Faustino also noted that one brother had a girlfriend who was "a white girl [*una güerita*], she calls and it's all English, and he has another brother who married a Black woman [*una morena*]," and then to immediately clarify the potential ambiguity in his equivocal use of the same racialized skin-color category to identify the

African American woman as he had previously used to characterize his own color, Faustino added emphatically, "—a *Black* girl! [*una negrita!*]." Faustino then shrugged his shoulders in good-hearted perplexity at such marvels, and concluded, "Well, that's just how it is [*pues, así es*] . . ." In a manner that was initially uncharacteristic among most Mexican migrants in Chicago but very much characteristic of most Mexicans in Mexico, Faustino retained the racialized color category "*moreno*" (or "brown") to refer to himself and generically to a kind of racialized template of "the" typical Mexican, and then later resorted to the use of "*moreno*" as the distinct and exclusive racialized category for African Americans that was more conventional among Mexican migrants in Chicago (cf. De Genova, 1999:287–356; in press). What was most remarkable for our purposes here, however, was not simply the invocation of "Mexican"-ness as an already racialized category equated with the skin-color term that roughly translates as "brown" (i.e., neither white nor Black), but the sheer wonder for Faustino that these peculiar Mexicans could be so visibly, indeed transparently, identifiable as "Mexicans," but not speak any Spanish.

The expectation that anyone who was evidently "Mexican," or was otherwise able to be racialized as Latino (or, simply put, "brown"), should also speak Spanish, which Faustino expressed with such a sense of marvel, was also very commonly articulated with a sense of frustration or even suspicion. A year earlier, when De Genova first arrived at the home of an elderly Mexican/migrant woman named Juana Quiroz, who had lived in Chicago for many years, meeting her for the first time, as the guest of her nephew Patricio Zaragoza who had recently arrived from the state of Zacatecas, she soon declared that De Genova spoke better Spanish than her grandchildren, and complained that often when they spoke to her, she could not understand what they were trying to say. Juana went on to bemoan how "they grow up here and speak only English; you meet them all over, and can see in their face and their hair that they're Mexicans, but they tell you, 'I no espeak espanich.'" Sarcastically and comically ridiculing the sound of the English words, Juana laughed heartily with her nephew and their guest, but also conveyed her own aggravation that these young U.S.-raised Mexicans' faces and hair ought to be accompanied by a properly Mexican tongue that did not produce such clumsy and foreign sounds.

Indirectly, Juana was identifying the consequences of a less evident system of racialized class inequalities routinely reproduced through U.S. educational institutions. In marked contrast to the relatively privileged educational opportunities that De Genova had enjoyed, enabling his acquisition of a second language in addition to thoroughly ensuring his professional competence in English, the overwhelming majority of Latino children tend to have access only to underfunded public schools. Thus, the children of Mexican migrants, such as those to whom Juana had referred, are commonly "mainstreamed" at the earliest possible time into an effectively English-only curriculum and are seldom educated in a manner that would support the maintenance and advanced development of their native language, while they are simultaneously deprived of the opportunity to acquire a professional-level competence in English. In its service to the reproduction of class inequalities in the U.S., public education tends to systematically undermine Latino children's native Spanish, while also inculcating them with the social dominance of English but often equipping them only with a limited or stigmatized competence in their second language.

Several months later, when De Genova met the Mexican/migrant mother of a friend, Luis Aragón, she described the meatpacking factory where she and her husband worked, in the neighborhood where De Genova had spent his childhood. In her discussion of the racial composition of the workforce at the plant—where the union representatives were African Americans, the great majority of the workers were Polish migrants, and only a small minority were Mexicans—Mrs. Aragón mentioned that there was also one young U.S.-raised Mexican employed there. Whereas she would have expected him to serve as a bilingual intermediary between Mexican migrants like herself and their non-Latino coworkers, Mrs. Aragón was not only frustrated but also stated plainly that she did not believe him: "He says he can't speak any Spanish, not a word, nothing! Can you imagine?!? We ask him, 'What, you never spoke to your parents?!'" A Latino who claimed to be unable to speak Spanish seemed to her to be dubious and frankly suspicious. The racialized expectation that a Latino face should come equipped with a Spanish-speaking mouth, when thwarted, frequently inspired distrust, if not a sense of betrayal.

The implicit Mexican/migrant demand that Mexicans raised in the U.S. should know Spanish, as a matter of racial integrity and allegiance to their racial community, revealed important presuppositions about the necessary multigenerational adhesion of Spanish language within the U.S. nation-state for Mexican/migrant transnationalism. Rather than endorsing the assimilationist notion that their children would no longer have any substantial relationship with Mexico and should single-mindedly embrace the English language as a vehicle for advancement in the U.S. labor market, most Mexican migrants articulated a transnational vision in which their families' trajectories would inevitably produce inextricable linkages between the U.S. and Mexico, for which both English and Spanish would be requirements. Between the two languages, however, there was always a primary (and essentialized) connection presumed between a racialized Mexican identity and fluency in Spanish. Mexicans raised in the U.S. who could not speak Spanish, of course, often experienced these demands with predictable anxiety and not uncommonly with great bitterness. In other cases, when such demands were directed at Native Americans or the Spanish-surnamed children of Mexican fathers and Native American mothers, the racialized character of these assumptions about language were exposed for all their absurdity. On one occasion during the fall of 1994, at an elementary school in the Back of the Yards neighborhood, a U.S.-raised Mexican teacher in her early twenties, Chela Guerrero, related a story of how that same absurd presumption could have cruelly unthinking consequences. She explained how one of the students in her school was a "full-blood" Native American girl, who was being compelled by an overzealous Mexican bilingual teacher to learn Spanish on the assumption that she too was Mexican. The child had approached Chela in distress, explaining, "I told him I don't speak Spanish, but he just said, 'I know you don't, but I'm gonna make sure that you learn it, because you should know Spanish and be proud of your culture.' Miss Guerrero, please tell him I'm not that!" In such remarkable instances, the experiences of those presumed to be transparently Latino, and thus mandated to know how to speak Spanish, help to demonstrate the extent to which Spanish language was racialized as "brown."

The extent to which these same racialized assumptions about language operated across the lines of particular Latino national-origin subgroups became manifest when Ramos-Zayas was teaching at a Puerto Rican–identified alternative high school in Humboldt Park in the fall of 1994. Eddy Matos, a Puerto Rican high school senior, began speaking in Spanish to Sandra Herrera, a Mexican student raised in the U.S. who was starting her second year. Carlos, a classmate of Eddy's and Sandra's, intervened, informing Eddy, "She doesn't understand Spanish!" Herrera then turned to Ramos-Zayas, explaining, "Everybody thinks I speak Spanish!" Eddy interrupted, insisting, "Because you should! You're not white!" In reply, Sandra proceeded to very calmly but deliberately explain, "Some Mexicans don't speak Spanish. My mom doesn't speak Spanish either. She only speaks a little, when she talks to her mother." Eddy's insinuation that Sandra had been choosing to not speak Spanish, out of a purported sense of Latino self-contempt, and in an alleged effort to "act white," was particularly ironic, since Eddy's own mother frequently complained that when her children had been younger she would speak to them in Spanish and they would only want to respond in English. Once Eddy was enrolled at the Puerto Rican–identified high school, however, where Spanish classes were required of all students and speaking Spanish was treated as virtually inseparable from notions of cultural authenticity, Eddy had become more invested in speaking the language. Eddy's reaction also suggested that he found it unacceptable that a Latina peer like Sandra should be resistant to speaking a language (Spanish) that she did not know, equating her English language with a presumed evasion of her "real" identity as "Mexican" or "Latina," and therefore as necessarily Spanish-speaking. Eddy's presumptuous allegation also implied that Sandra was deliberately repudiating the potential commonality between herself and the Puerto Rican students based on their putative shared connection to the Spanish language. Policing her language was intended to serve as a guarantor of her inter-Latino racial allegiance to a pan-Latino identity and community.

Good Spanish/Bad Spanish

If Spanish-language competence was widely presumed to be an attribute that might be expected of anyone racialized as Latino, and so sometimes could supply a basis for recognizing commonalities and forging a shared Latino identity between Mexicans and Puerto Ricans, it was nevertheless quite commonplace that something so constitutive of these Latinos' notions of their respective particular identities—as Mexicans, or as Puerto Ricans—became a basis for distinction and division rather than community. The differences between Mexican and Puerto Rican Spanish were a common topic for both groups, however. When De Genova first met Luisa Cabán—a Puerto Rican migrant in her fifties who had been in Chicago for about thirty years, who was the neighbor of his Puerto Rican friend, Sandra Santander—Luisa asked if he understood everything that she and Sandra were saying in their conversation in Spanish. De Genova explained, "My difficulty is mainly with the Puerto Rican accent—because I learned Spanish with Mexicans, and the accents are very different." To this, Cabán replied, "Well, yes, Puerto Ricans don't sing when they talk, you know—like, '¡ó-o-or-a-le-e-e!' and all that!" Delighted with her imitation of Mexican Spanish, Luisa not only imitated a Mexican accent, but also chose an idiomatic expression that was distinctively Mexican and would never be heard from a Puerto Rican; laughing, she turned to Sandra; "You know how they talk!" But then, to De Genova's surprise, Cabán proceeded to give a brief but nuanced discourse on the variety of characteristic habits of pronunciation among Puerto Ricans, that very much resembled remarks that Mexicans had typically made, albeit judgmentally, with respect to Puerto Rican Spanish: "The Puerto Ricans don't like to pronounce their r's—they make it an 'l,' especially in the middle of a word, they just swallow it up . . . and they drop the 's' at the end of a word, like 'arro(z)' . . . oh, and Puerto Ricans speak *fast!* . . . but the Mexicans talk pretty fast, too." Whereas Luisa demonstrated a remarkably self-reflexive sensibility about her own Puerto Rican linguistic habits even as she joked about Mexicans' seemingly singsong inflections, however, Mexican migrants simply tended to comprehend the differences between Puerto Rican Spanish and their own in terms of a hierarchy. For them, Puerto Ricans spoke a debased Spanish, while their own language—however much inflected by their own usually rural origins and relatively low levels of formal schooling in Mexico, and thus degraded in class terms on some grander scale of value—was assumed to come out as superior.

Most U.S.-born Puerto Ricans, in particular, were acutely aware that many recent Puerto Rican migrants as well as Mexicans criticized them for not speaking "proper" or "good" Spanish. Comments concerning the fact that Mexicans disliked Puerto Rican Spanish, or even questioned Puerto Rican's "Latinidad" based on the English-dominance of most U.S.-born Puerto Ricans, frequently surfaced in informal conversations. In October of 1994, Ramos-Zayas met Raquel Colón, a Puerto Rican woman who had moved to Chicago with her husband and eldest son in the 1970s. Raquel was a student at a beauty school in Logan Square. When she had first arrived in Chicago from the town of Ponce, Puerto Rico, however, Raquel had lived on the South Side. Ramos-Zayas commented that not many Puerto Ricans lived on the South Side, compared to Mexicans. Raquel agreed and added that there was always a lot of friction between the two groups. "Did you like living there?" Ramos-Zayas asked. Colón replied, "I like it much better on the North Side. I don't like to say bad things about anyone, you know. But sometimes Mexicans are a little . . . I don't know—they're not very friendly. There were some Mexican guys that would always be saying '*ajoz*' and '*veldad*' when my sister and I walked by—making fun of us! They made fun of Puerto Rican Spanish. Like we Puerto Ricans can't say '*arroz*' . . . they make fun of that." "So," Ramos-Zayas responded, "they made fun of the accent?" "Yes, yes," Colón continued, "but we were like, 'big deal, at least we can speak English! They resented that! And you could tell that they *really* wanted to know English." Raquel identified Spanish language, in particular—while supposedly a commonality between Mexicans and Puerto Ricans—as in fact supplying the premier cause of friction between her family and their Mexican neighbors on the South Side. Indeed, one of Raquel's most salient recollections of her very early years in the U.S. involved a questioning of something that she had always taken for granted: her ability to speak her own native language, Spanish. Even this fundamental competence was put to the test, as Mexicans treated her "Puerto Rican Spanish" as an object of ridicule. Nevertheless, to a certain extent, Raquel seemed to accept that such ridicule might indeed be applicable to some Puerto Ricans other than herself, as she performatively emphasized that she in fact did know that the "correct" pronunciation of the word for rice is "*arroz*" rather than "*ajoz.*"

Raquel, like many other Puerto Ricans, including more recently arrived Puerto Rican migrants, took great pride in the fact that, in contradistinction with Mexicans, most Puerto Ricans knew English. Indeed, she emphasized that even Puerto Ricans who had only recently migrated from the Island tended to have greater knowledge of English than many Mexican migrants. Given the frequent back-and-forth migration between Puerto Rico and various Puerto Rican communities in the U.S., as well as the U.S. colonial dominance over Puerto Rico's public education, mass media, and market systems (Cabán, 1999), it is hardly surprising that English is more widely spoken in Puerto Rico than perhaps in any other Latin American country. For Raquel, knowledge of English was a valuable possession that, rather than undermining her Puerto Ricanness, actually distinguished and reinforced it; it was a precious skill that other Puerto Ricans, on the Island and in the U.S. alike, were presumed to share, and one that Raquel perceived many Mexicans to lack and envy. Hence, the ability to speak English, rather than suggesting an unequivocal "Americanization" or deracination among Puerto Ricans in the U.S., actually tended to sustain a sense of Puerto Rican national singularity in contradistinction to other national-origin groups racialized as "Latinos."

Nevertheless, knowledge of English—and a view of the English language as perfectly compatible with a Puerto Rican national identity—rarely compensated for the notions of cultural authenticity that Puerto Ricans attributed to a knowledge of "proper" Spanish. As both Luisa and Raquel exemplified, Puerto Ricans (especially those who had spent a long time, or were born, in the U.S.) commonly sought various ways of performing their mastery of Spanish, including the informed, self-reflexive demonstration of the very "linguistic deficiencies" attributed to them. In another instance, Martín Figueroa, a musician and teacher volunteer at a cultural center in West Town, came into the room where a meeting of the cultural center's staff was in session, unable to contain his laughter. When the staff asked him why he was laughing, Martín explained that a woman from the Board of Education had called and he had referred to her as "sir" instead of "ma'am." Martín exclaimed, "She sounded like a man!—*Estoy embarazado!*" A U.S.-born and -raised Puerto Rican, Martín deliberately and performatively called attention his own excellent Spanish proficiency by playfully deploying the nonsensical term "*embarazado*" (the masculine form of the Spanish word for "pregnant") as a false cognate of the English word "embarrassed." Through his joke, Martín implied that using English-derived false cognates in Spanish—particularly, those that significantly and ridiculously distort the speaker's intended meaning—was expected of U.S.-born Puerto Ricans, an identity he was performing. Nevertheless, while demonstrating that these stereotypes were not universally true, Martín was simultaneously fashioning himself as a U.S.-born Puerto Rican who had a clear understanding of and command over these linguistic mistakes.

Alberto Ruíz, a teacher at a popular-education project for youth in West Town, asked Ramos-Zayas if she would meet with him so that he could read aloud to her from a book written in Spanish. Ruíz wanted Ramos-Zayas to help him with the pronunciation of various words. After several reading sessions, in which Alberto insisted on repeatedly pronouncing words until his Spanish was "flawless," he recalled:

> Until very recently, I didn't know that the right word is "*toalla*" [for "towel"]; I used to say "*toballa*" . . . I also used to say "*carpeta*" [for "carpet"], instead of "*alfombra*." Because nobody would correct me when I was growing up. My parents never took the time. And it's very hurtful not to know these things. Back then, other kids, kids who spoke more Spanish, would make fun of me in school. Even now—sometimes I need to talk to the parents of students, parents who speak fluent Spanish, and I'm embarrassed. When I go to Puerto Rico, I can see how people look at me—like, "he's not from here." Even my children, they live in Cayey [a town in Puerto Rico] with their mother, and they speak great Spanish, and English!—both languages—really well. And they tell me, "*Papi, tú no sabes hablar español!*" ["Daddy, you don't know how to speak Spanish!"] They make fun of me for that. That's why I try to read in Spanish as much as I can.

Alberto's young sons had spent the first five years of their lives in Chicago, but then had relocated to Puerto Rico with their mother, when Alberto and his ex-wife divorced. The boys were fully bilingual because they attended a school with other children of returned migrants on the Island, so they continued to practice English at school, while speaking Spanish at home. For Alberto, language was as much a distance from his kids as was geography, even though he understood and spoke Spanish. Alberto was not striving to simply "understand" or "get by," but to achieve a mastery of what he considered "proper" Spanish. In Alberto's case, knowing Spanish had profound emotional as well as professional repercussions. A very committed teacher, Alberto considered his own limited Spanish as a "lack of respect" for his students' parents. Indeed, Alberto was very hesitant to address the parents in Spanish at public events, unless he had practiced the speech intensively. Likewise, a devoted father, Alberto felt that his limited Spanish was an indignity that clearly functioned as an obstacle to getting closer to his children on the Island, even though the children were perfectly bilingual and thus capable of communicating with him in English.

Notably, however, Alberto's conception of "proper" Spanish also excluded Mexican Spanish, as became clear a few months later, when Alberto's program was in the process of hiring a replacement for a Puerto Rican Spanish teacher. There were two possible candidates for the position: a Puerto Rican woman who only spoke Spanish and did not understand any English, and a fluently bilingual Mexican woman. Since most of the students enrolled in the popular-education program were English-dominant, one of the teachers, a white woman, recommended that the Mexican woman be hired. Alberto immediately disagreed, arguing that the Mexican woman would only be able to teach a Spanish that was unfamiliar to Puerto Rican students. Further, Alberto contended, "These students have too much trouble speaking Spanish, as it is, to add to their confusion by bringing in someone who speaks with a different accent." Half-jokingly, Elena, another Puerto Rican teacher, then added that hiring the Mexican teacher would generate "a bunch of students saying '*Ay, manito-o-o!*'" Like Luisa Cabán's mimicking of the distinctively Mexican expression "*órale,*" discussed above, phrases like "*Ay, manito!*" and "*¿Mande?*" were unequivocally viewed as Mexican expressions and were often used by Puerto Ricans to similarly mimic Mexican Spanish, inflected with a "Mexican" accent whenever a Puerto Rican performed them. Not only was Alberto emphasizing that Mexicans and Puerto Ricans spoke identifiably distinct versions of the Spanish language, however, but also that Mexican Spanish would fundamentally corrupt the larger vision of this particular popular-education program, which was centered on "teaching Puerto Rican youth about their culture." Ultimately, the monolingual Puerto Rican woman was hired for the job, but many English-dominant students predictably complained that the new teacher was not able to explain difficult grammar concepts in English. As it turned out, the Mexican teacher was also hired—but to teach art classes. Her Mexican Spanish was determined to be inadequate to the task of teaching English-dominant Puerto Rican youth the particular Spanish language that was properly "theirs."

Bilingualism

If Mexicans and Puerto Ricans in Chicago frequently marked the contrast between their respectively distinctive Spanish languages, an even more pronounced difference between the two groups was the comparatively high level of bilingualism among Puerto Ricans. In an effort to encourage a critical relation to English-as-a-Second-Language learning among the participants in the courses he taught, De Genova would regularly ask people to discuss what might be the negative aspects of the workplace-based "vocational ESL" classes that they were often being obliged to attend by their employers. When De Genova initiated such a conversation at the Imperial Enterprises factory in 1993, a Mexican/migrant worker named Victoria Carrasco commented, "We're at different levels; in Puerto Rico, they learned English in school—but not us [Mexicans]; they speak more, but it's harder for us." Although the workers in her class had all been administered a test of spoken English in order to constitute a group who would be at roughly comparable levels, Victoria seemed to feel intimidated by the presence of the three Puerto Ricans in the predominantly Mexican group, if not distrustful of them and suspicious that they might ridicule the Mexican workers' efforts. In any case, she was fairly clear in her contention that her Puerto Rican coworkers had an unfair advantage and, all told, should probably have been kept separate. During a similar discussion at the DuraPress factory, a Mexican migrant named Fidencio related, "My brother said it's dumb to learn English, but I told him, 'Then you would always get cheated in the store.' You know, I used to work at a job where there were Puerto Ricans who spoke a lot of English, and they would say bad things about Mexican people in English; I told them, 'Hey, I speak English too, so watch what you say!'—so that's why it's very important to learn English." Thus, the sense that Puerto Ricans were not trustworthy and were prone to cheating and taking advantage of Mexicans became coupled with a certain resentment of the perceived advantage of their greater degree of bilingualism. At Liberty Carton, where there were only a few Puerto Ricans employed among over a hundred Mexican/migrant workers, Lino Pacheco—a thirty-two-year-old Mexican worker who had come to the U.S. when he was only fourteen, was exceptionally fluent in English, and very enthusiastic about the ESL classes that were being initiated—declared, "Just don't put me in a class with the Puerto Ricans!" When De Genova inquired, "You have a problem with Puerto Ricans?" Pacheco explained, "It's because they laugh at you! Since they grew up here since they were very young, they think they know everything—but I know they make mistakes with their English, too—I hear it!" Although Lino clearly expressed his resentment for Puerto Ricans' advantage of bilingualism, he also insinuated that, in fact, their English was itself deficient, and might even contaminate his own sincere efforts to master the language.

For their part, most of the Puerto Ricans whom Ramos-Zayas met in popular-education programs where she taught on the Northwest Side of the city recognized their bilingualism as an advantage. This was particularly so when they compared their bilingualism to Mexicans, whom they frequently presumed to be largely monolingual Spanish speakers. The main advantage that many Puerto Ricans attributed to being bilingual concerned the ability to avoid having others take advantage of them, expressing the same preoccupation that Mexican

migrants like Fidencio had articulated in favor of learning English, but in opposition to (English-speaking) Puerto Ricans. Puerto Ricans in Humboldt Park
conclusively considered the English language to be a skill helpful in understanding and navigating "the system," and in counteracting the ways in which whites
could try to take advantage of them. Nevertheless, they also perceived Spanish as
a skill needed if one was to avoid being mistreated by other (Spanish-speaking)
Latinos. For instance, Marcos Santana, a part-time cook at a local bakery, whom
Ramos-Zayas met in March of 1995, related:

> I was on the bus with these Mexicans guys. They were making fun of me. I was
> reading a book. We were on Division Street, near California [in Humboldt Park].
> And they were talking badly about Puerto Ricans, about Humboldt Park, about
> how you couldn't tell if someone was Puerto Rican or *moreno* [Black], or what. I
> guess they thought I was white. They didn't know that I understood Spanish—so
> I cut them off when I started speaking Spanish. They were very surprised!

When Ramos-Zayas asked Santana about what specific comments the Mexican
men were making about Humboldt Park, he clarified that they were saying
that the neighborhood was dirty, dangerous, and gang-infested. The Mexican
men on the bus apparently viewed Humboldt Park, and especially the Division
Street area through which the bus was passing, not only as a space racialized as
"Puerto Rican," but also as an area whose residents approximated the status of
racial Blackness. In Marcos's comment, Spanish was viewed as a necessary skill
that allowed Puerto Ricans to defend themselves against the insults of other
Latinos, and equipped them to dispute the images that Mexicans (and other
Latinos) had of them as a degraded Latino group, hardly distinguishable from
African Americans. Moreover, by showing these men that he too could speak
Spanish, Marcos put himself in the advantageous position of moving effort-
lessly between both Spanish and English. Marcos also seemed to discern an
analogous advantage in his own phenotypic ambiguity, which had provided
him with the possibility of camouflaging his Latino racial identity, such that the
Mexicans had not assumed that he could understand their Spanish. The phenotypic heterogeneity that Marcos implicitly indexed among Puerto Ricans, more
generally, thus seemed to endow Puerto Ricanness with an elusive capacity for
racial "passing," much as their bilingualism enabled a kind of linguistic mobility
that seemed to destabilize racialized identities. Remarkably, Marcos, a relatively
dark-skinned Puerto Rican, assumed that the reason that the Mexicans had felt
at ease speaking in Spanish in his presence was that they had thought that he was
white, rather than that they had presumed him to be Black. It appeared from his
narrative that Santana was unwilling to admit the possibility—either to himself
or perhaps to Ramos-Zayas, whose complexion was lighter—that the Mexicans
could actually have perceived him to be African American. In either case, however, Spanish language was critical in Marcos's account for distinguishing Puerto
Ricanness both from whiteness and, most importantly, also from Blackness.[2]

Yet, in the interaction that Marcos described, even when Puerto Ricans' ability to speak Spanish would presumably secure a space for them, with Mexicans, apparently outside of the white-Black racial binary,[3] the Spanish language in no way automatically provided a shared space for the creation of a mutual Latinidad between Mexicans and Puerto Ricans.

Most bilingual Puerto Ricans speculated that prospective employers would favor knowledge of both English and Spanish, but in general, they could not recall any instance in which their bilingualism had actually helped them get a job. Indeed, while Marcos Rivera had asserted that the principal advantage of bilingualism for U.S.-born Puerto Ricans was that it equipped them, not with English, but rather with Spanish against the affronts of other Latinos, another Puerto Rican raised in the U.S., Freddy García, also suspected that the bilingualism that equipped Puerto Ricans with English-language skills actually disadvantaged them with prospective employers who would favor other Latinos' Spanish monolingualism for low-wage jobs in the low-skill labor market. When García, a Puerto Rican man in his twenties who had grown up in Chicago, returned to Humboldt Park after living in Puerto Rico for two years, he visited one of the popular-education programs where Ramos-Zayas taught. García was seeking help in finding a job. Freddy expressed his interest in finding work as an auto mechanic, but had also applied to two large retail chain stores—one a discount department store, and the other a hardware and construction supplies store. In an effort to be encouraging about his job prospects, Ramos-Zayas mentioned that the fact that he was bilingual would most likely be an advantage that Freddy would have over other applicants. García replied, "Quite frankly, I don't think that they will even care that I'm bilingual. They don't even need you to speak at any of these jobs, because they just want someone to stack boxes. They probably would favor someone who can't speak [English] but just follows orders!" Although at some level Freddy deemed his bilingualism to be a positive skill, he was so discouraged by his employment prospects that he had become convinced that his bilingualism was degraded and virtually irrelevant to his competitiveness on the low-wage job market. In fact, he seemed to feel that his bilingualism, and by implication, perhaps also his Puerto Ricanness— in contradistinction to those who were unable to speak English and would simply "follow orders" (such as monolingual and presumably more vulnerable migrants, such as Mexicans)—were actually obstacles to getting hired for such unskilled positions.

Like many other Puerto Ricans, Freddy García did not see bilingualism as an advantage that would help him get hired, but rather as an attribute that gave him an advantage in understanding the U.S. social system and enabled a sharper critical insight into the inequalities of the social order. Freddy's reflections about his mother, Lydia, sustained his views of bilingualism as a skill useful in navigating the U.S. social and legal system, but not always a clear advantage when it came to finding jobs. In an interview with Ramos-Zayas, García recalled Lydia's work history:

> When we arrived here for the second time it was in 1977 or '78 . . . I was about six or so . . . My mom's sister found her work at a factory. I think it had to do with paint, creating paint or mixing it or maybe it was [filling] the cans of paint. I can't remember well, because I was very young. But I remember that my mom didn't last very long in that job. Maybe she lasted two or three years . . . not even. My aunt ended up leaving even sooner. The work conditions were awful and my mom was getting sick a lot, you know. But there was little incentive to make the working conditions better, because at that time a lot of the people working there were illegal [*ilegales*], you know, and they had them by the balls, as we say . . . My mom said that they [the undocumented workers] were suspicious of her, because she was legal and they had bad experiences with other Hispanics born here . . . although my mom was not born here—she was born in Puerto Rico, in [the town of] Ceiba . . . but still. They didn't know the language or how things work here, you know. After that experience, my mom tried a few more times to find a job . . . But her health was getting worse, from the chemicals that she had already absorbed . . . She had to get disability. I remember having to go with her to apply for it. Back then I didn't understand what disability was, but there were all these bums and cripples, stinky people—literally stinky from not taking showers—at the office, and I was kind of embarrassed to be there. I was already in school and back then most of my friends' parents had jobs—bad jobs, but they had jobs. So, having to go with my mom to get disability . . . I was like, they're going to think that she's on aid—welfare, whatever! I was really young, so I didn't understand too well. I just knew that people at that office were nasty, everyone there was, even the workers.

Freddy's recollection of his mother's work experience alongside of undocumented migrant workers at the factory where she had been employed in the late 1970s colored his views of bilingualism as not being a particularly useful skill in the jobs available to Puerto Rican migrants. In his narrative, Freddy emphasized further that his mother's "legality" generated suspicion among her undocumented migrant Latino coworkers, to whom he attributed the endemic deplorable working conditions at the factory. The migrants' vulnerability as "illegals," he presumed, had ensured their docility as workers and, by implication, had also imposed profound limits on the prospects for better working conditions for U.S.-citizen workers such as his mother. While Freddy did not see Lydia's bilingualism—or her juridical status as a citizen, more generally—as sufficient qualifications to secure a Puerto Rican a decent job, he did nevertheless recognize that her English proficiency and U.S. citizenship had enabled his mother to leave a hazardous work environment and seek disability and medical benefits. Freddy's poignant images of the disability office also suggested his overall dismal appraisal of "welfare" and his having had to accompany his mother to government offices that serviced the poor. In retrospect, he attributed his negative views of public assistance to his own inability, as a young child, to distinguish between "good welfare" and "bad welfare" (see chapter 3).

While Marcos Rivera's and Freddy García's respective views weighed the relative merits of their bilingualism, most Puerto Ricans on the Near Northwest Side did not feel that Puerto Ricans were "really" bilingual. Rather, parents commented on how their own children did not want to speak Spanish to them. Ramos-Zayas met Maribel Arroyo at an adult education program in West Town that focused on developing literacy and computer skills. The program participants consisted mostly of Puerto Rican women in their thirties and forties, but three of the twenty participants were Mexican. Roughly half of Maribel's classmates, including Maribel herself, were Spanish-dominant. Although one of Maribel's main reasons for joining the program was to learn English, she jokingly admitted that she found herself speaking more and more Spanish, since her three Mexican classmates and two other Puerto Rican women spoke only Spanish. Maribel recognized the need to learn English, and that had motivated her initial involvement in the program, but she felt that it was equally important for her to retain her Spanish and even insist on speaking Spanish with her adolescent children. She commented:

> Here [in the U.S.] the one that dominates is English. The race [*la raza*] that dominates is the American and . . . it's good that kids get involved with one's culture, but they spend more time out of the house, in the streets, in the school. School [in the U.S.] doesn't teach them as much about their culture as they do in Puerto Rico. My sons talk to me in English. But at home they don't speak English, because if they don't speak to me in Spanish, I don't talk to them! [laughed]

Notably, her children's prospects of learning about their own Puerto Rican culture were inseparable, for Maribel, from their fluency in Spanish. Young Puerto Rican migrant parents commonly expressed the fear that their children born or raised in the U.S. would "lose their culture" through extended contact with institutions in which English would be the dominant language. Especially among the most recently arrived Puerto Rican migrants, the perception prevailed that English-language acquisition often occurred to the detriment of retaining or learning Spanish; indeed, many were inclined to view the younger generations' bilingualism as insufficient at best, a kind of English-dominance that was tantamount to linguistic degeneration.

While Maribel Arroyo's concerns about her children's retention of their Spanish language were widely shared among many other migrant Puerto Ricans, many mentioned that their children had refused to learn Spanish in early childhood, but later regained an interest in learning the language as adolescents. Maribel's older son, Rafael, had become more interested in learning Spanish when he joined a youth salsa band. Although Rafael was becoming increasingly involved with Puerto Rican activist groups, was interested in Puerto Rican history, and had generally become quite visibly self-identified as Puerto Rican,

Maribel nonetheless viewed Rafael's English-dominance as evidence of his fundamental detachment from his own "Puerto Rican culture." When Rafael had first expressed his interest in learning Spanish, Maribel related, laughing, that she had advised him: "Well, you better start dating a *jibarita* [country girl] from Puerto Rico, or a Mexican girl, so you can get to practice!" When Ramos-Zayas asked Arroyo if her son had followed her advice, she commented, "No, he went to Puerto Rico last summer to stay with my sister, and he hated it. Yauco [their hometown] is very different from Chicago, and his friends were here . . . He said he was bored and came home after a week, but my sister told me that he met a girl there, and that the girl always asked about him, even now [laughed]. But he dated a Mexican girl for a while too . . . I don't know what happened with that either! He's just a ladies' man [*picaflor*]." Maribel seemed to take a considerable degree of maternal pride in her son's masculine charms, and attached her interest in her son learning Spanish to his apparently erratic romantic involvements, in the hope that speaking Spanish might be best facilitated by girlfriends who were either Puerto Rican country girls or Mexicans. Thus, not only did Maribel presume that a U.S.-born, "urban" Puerto Rican woman would be English-dominant and thus an inadequate Spanish "tutor" for her son, but also that a "*jibarita*"—a woman from the most remote rural areas of Puerto Rico—would only be matched in Chicago by a Mexican woman. Thus, the inclination among Puerto Ricans to view Mexicans, and Mexican women in particular, as more "traditional," and thus more "cultural" (see chapters 4 and 5), in ways only analogous to Puerto Rico's countryside—for better or for worse—was reaffirmed with respect to language as well. Having posited that in the U.S., "the [language] that dominates is English," and "the race that dominates is the American [white]," Maribel relegated Spanish to a subordinate social status and, with the language, also those racialized groups (Puerto Rican country folk, and Mexicans) who epitomized Spanish monolingualism. By implication, urbanized bilingual Puerto Ricans such as her sons had merely demonstrated the greater wherewithal to successfully adapt to the social order of white supremacy and Anglo hegemony in the U.S. Yet, Maribel's judgments were hardly celebratory; it was only with evident regret that she depicted English-speaking U.S. Puerto Ricans as having effectively accommodated themselves to racial and linguistic domination.

Extraordinary insights into the connections between English-dominance among U.S.-born Puerto Ricans and U.S. colonialism were articulated as part of the nationalist vision of activists such as Alicia Rodríguez, a Puerto Rican political prisoner in her early forties at the time when Ramos-Zayas met her in 1994. The first time that Ramos-Zayas visited her in jail, Rodríguez showed immediate interest in the fact that Ramos-Zayas could speak Spanish, asking, "You grew up in Puerto Rico, right?" When Ramos-Zayas explained that she had indeed been raised on the Island and that her parents still lived there, Rodríguez remarked, "I can tell, because of how you speak Spanish. You see, I was born here, so I've had to teach myself Spanish. It takes me so long to read Spanish! This is one of the ways in which I feel I've been stripped of my culture by colonialism." Of course, as Alicia was inclined to posit definitive associations between her personal loss of the Spanish language and the violence of U.S. colonialism, her nationalist analysis was not "typical" of other Puerto Ricans, like her, from poor or working-class backgrounds in Chicago. Nonetheless, Alicia's analysis of the U.S. nation-state's colonization of Puerto Rico was fundamentally transposed onto her own experience of that colonialism, as someone who had grown up in the U.S. and not in Puerto Rico. Thus, when she spoke of colonialism, she referred primarily to racial subjugation as a Puerto Rican in Chicago, and her own English-dominance as having been "stripped of [her] culture." In explicit contrast, the Island (which, after all, was the primary object of colonization) was figured in her account as more culturally intact and resilient, as manifested by the enduring vitality of the Spanish language. The gravest depredations of colonialism, on the other hand, were inflicted on those Puerto Ricans like herself who had been physically displaced and estranged from their nation.

Some Puerto Ricans, however, rejected such anti-assimilationist inclinations as the resistance to learning English as the source of Puerto Ricans' supposed failure to succeed in the U.S. in contrast to other Latino groups' putative achievements. Awilda Oquendo, a Humboldt Park resident in her late forties and the owner of a convenience store, expressed this fairly exceptional perspective:

> The Puerto Rican is not sure of what he is. The Puerto Rican doesn't stand on the same ground as the *Hispanos* in Los Angeles and the Cubans in Miami. They [*Hispanos*, Cubans] feel American. They think, "We are Cuban Americans." The Mexican that lives here in Chicago says, "I am American." And the first thing they do is go to school and learn English. That's a shame for us [Puerto Ricans]. I am a person with little academic preparation, but I hold my own [*me defiendo*], when it comes to speaking English.

Although Awilda spoke enough English to "hold her own," she related that when she had first opened her store, she spoke "not a word of English." She stressed her initial lack of English-speaking skills in constructing a narrative of her own economic mobility and progress as a migrant in the U.S.: she had not known even a word of the language, but had been determined to learn it; likewise, she had only spoken Spanish, yet was able nonetheless to start a successful small business. Ironically, although she claimed that other Latinos had outdone Puerto Ricans because they immediately went about the task of learning English, Awilda's own story appeared nonetheless to suggest that being bilingual or, more specifically, speaking English was not quite necessary for the economic advancement of Latino migrants. Awilda depicted Puerto Ricans as upstaged or even undermined by the achievements of other Latino groups— namely, Cubans and Mexicans—but she attributed this disparity to what she perceived to be Puerto Ricans' crisis of identity—"the Puerto Rican is not sure of what he is"—as manifested in an anti-assimilationist ambivalence about embracing an "American" identity and learning the English language.

Among effectively bilingual Puerto Ricans who had grown up migrating back and forth between Puerto Rico and Chicago, Spanish frequently became a language that was decidedly marginal from their public involvements in institutional settings. Thus, bilingualism tended to serve as a hallmark of Puerto Ricans' U.S. citizenship through the active expression of their political participation. Nevertheless, precisely those Puerto Ricans who were more fully bilingual tended to emphasize the great psychological significance of retaining their Spanish—an act in which they took great pride, which they sometimes explicitly construed to be an expression of political resistance to the assimilationist pressures of colonization. Indeed, struggles over the inclusion of Spanish into hegemonic institutions, especially those of the U.S. nation-state, such as public schools, also were prominent in the production of a distinctive political identity among older Puerto Rican migrants with longer histories of involvement with the English-dominant institutions of the U.S. mainland.

For many of the Puerto Rican women that Ramos-Zayas met in Chicago, bilingual education was a site of political struggle and was critical in the development of a civic and political identity. For instance, Haydée Colón, a Puerto Rican woman who first arrived in Chicago in the early 1970s, talked about her experience as an advocate of bilingual education. Having grown up in a "very sheltered" and gender-segregated household in Puerto Rico, Haydée arrived in Chicago with her husband and daughter, not quite knowing "how things worked." Haydée's first experience of public institutional involvement and political activism was motivated by her insistence on having her daughter learn Spanish in school and not be penalized for her language. Haydée recalled:

> Back in the 1970s we lived at Kedzie and Madison [in the soon-to-be almost homogeneously African American East Garfield Park neighborhood], around there. Around here [in Chicago], everything is by neighborhoods. There was where I stayed when I arrived and there it was where my struggle started, when I put my daughter in school. They wanted to lower her a grade. I put her in a private school on the South Side. I fought to have someone who spoke Spanish in that school. Since my cousin worked as a teacher there, they assigned her to be my daughter's teacher. From then on, when I knew that someone's son or daughter, that they wanted to move them to a lower grade because of language, I would intervene. I would not stand for that.

Echoing many other Puerto Ricans' complaints, Haydée continued by contending, "Other Spanish-speaking groups don't recognize the work that we, Puerto Ricans, have done. They reject bilingual education. And there are problems with bilingual education, sure, it could be improved. But they want their children to speak *only* English, to learn English. They don't care if they continue to speak Spanish or not! They want to be more American than the Americans—because now, even Americans want to learn Spanish!" Along with the pervasive perception that Mexicans spoke more Spanish than Puerto Ricans, then, came the paradoxical belief that "other Spanish-speaking groups" generally did not care to promote the proper place of the Spanish language in the "public" realm, specifically failed to honor the historical leadership of Puerto Ricans in struggles for language rights, such as bilingual education, and thus were more willing to submit to the assimilationist demands of Anglo hegemony.

Bilingualism, then, had multiple meanings but functioned as a fundamentally double-sided sign in these debates over language. Bilingualism was never really a self-evident and stable "thing in itself" that rested at some presumably neutral point of convergence between the two opposite poles of English and Spanish. Instead, bilingualism supplied a flashpoint where it was possible to clearly identify language as a site of struggle. From one perspective, bilingualism signaled the defense of Latinos' language rights, and at least implicitly, their cultural integrity as well, through the audacious assertion of Spanish into the public realm of U.S. institutions as a disruptive challenge to Anglo hegemony. From the opposite vantage point, bilingualism was always already no better than a euphemistic veil for the subordination of Spanish, overshadowed by the menacing incursions of English into the mouths of Latino youth.

Good English/Bad English

In both Mexican and Puerto Rican migrant discourses concerning bilingualism, there was commonly an analogous generational sensibility that was preoccupied with the social reproduction of each group's distinctive community through their U.S.-born children. The premier concern—to guard the sanctity of Spanish and to ensure that the younger generation spoke their parents' language—was often accompanied by a desire for the kind of well-ordered bilingualism that would simultaneously enable the cultivation of vibrant Latino communities that could engage in a perfectly smooth and effective intercourse with the broader English-speaking U.S. social system. This implied the acquisition of a "good" or "proper" English.

Among Mexican migrants, the opinion that Puerto Ricans spoke "bad" Spanish and the vulnerability they sometimes felt about Puerto Ricans' relatively greater bilingualism, were commonly resolved in the sense that the English that Puerto Ricans spoke was ultimately "bad" English. Much like his coworker Lino Pacheco, discussed above, another Mexican migrant working at Liberty Carton named Antonio Valdés, who was thirty-nine years old and had been in the U.S. eighteen years, informed De Genova, "I think that I don't want to be in a class— it's a form of discrimination against us because we're Latinos—because it's only going to be for some people, and not everyone has to go. There are Puerto Ricans who laugh at us, but they speak very bad English—street English [*callejero* English]—and I see what they write on the [job] orders, and it's wrong; they make lots of mistakes, so why won't they have to go to classes? I told them [the management] that I don't want to go to school, but they told me that I have to do it. Why?!? That's discrimination!" Here, Antonio expressed an acute sense of the stigma for many Mexican migrants, especially men, attached to having to attend English classes, whereby their Spanish language was produced as a "lack" of English. Indeed, this was a workplace like countless others that had functioned quite well predominantly in Spanish for many years (by relying upon a small number of bilingual intermediaries in lower management). Thus, especially at this historical moment, in the aftermath of the passage of Proposition 187 in California, a new regime in the factory that seemed to be mandating that Spanish-speaking workers (the vast majority) start speaking English, seemed, plainly enough, to be discriminatory. Indeed, insofar as this inequality pertained directly to the question of Spanish language, Antonio identified the aggrieved group not as Mexicans but as Latinos. Yet, this was a Latinidad articulated to the exclusion of Puerto Ricans, whose bilingualism was perceived to garner them unfair advantages. Despite the bilingualism attributed to Puerto Ricans, however, Mexican/migrant men like Antonio and Lino disqualified the English that Puerto Ricans spoke as "bad," full of mistakes, and little more than slang—in short, a degraded expression of the language of the street.

While many Mexicans believed that Puerto Ricans spoke "bad" English, similar to the "street" English attributed to African Americans, Puerto Ricans often made fun of Mexicans' attempts to learn English. Puerto Ricans often had the impression that Mexicans placed a great importance on learning English, and learning it fast. In December of 1994, various Puerto Rican members of a high school salsa band in West Town revealed their shared perception that Mexicans were willing to go to great lengths to learn English, and also their sense of the vulnerability of not knowing the language for Mexicans and other Latinos. Following a discussion of whether the salsa band would sing in both English and Spanish or only in English, Mayra, a Puerto Rican singer, proposed that they sing mostly in English, since many of the band members (including herself), most of whom were U.S.-born Puerto Ricans, did not speak Spanish well. Pablo reminded Mayra that Mariela, a Mexican band member, and another new student, spoke better Spanish. Mayra began to laugh, responding, "Yeah, Mexicans learn English with 'Fa-louuu Mi'!" Through her exaggerated Spanish phonetic pronunciation of its title, Mayra was referring to "Follow Me," a program of audio cassettes and videos for learning English at home, which was advertised on Spanish-language television channels and public billboards in Latino communities. The other students laughed at Mayra's joke, and she added, "Hey, I'm serious! We had this woman that we knew in our building. She was Mexican or Colombian or something and her *whole family* had cassettes to learn English— like 'Learn English in 2 Days,' and stuff like that!" Everybody laughed, and in jest, Ramos-Zayas asked, "So, the programs to learn English—did they work?" Mayra replied, still joking, "I don't know, I think they moved back to Mexico— or Colombia? . . . no, it was Mexico—so I guess they didn't!" Besides revealing that she did not have a distinct sense of the differences among other Latino groups, confusing Mexicans and Colombians, Mayra marveled at what she perceived to be Mexican and other Latino migrants' virtual desperation to learn English. Furthermore, Mayra's comments also suggested that Mexicans were gullible—easy prey for the unrealistic promises of false advertising. In some sense, Mayra's joke reflected her belief that Mexicans were required to learn English in order to succeed in the U.S., and failure to do so would culminate in the apparent defeat of their eventual return home. Nevertheless, Mayra—who was herself English-dominant—deployed the joke to deflect her own vulnerability; she insisted that the group sing in English so as to secure her own place as a lead singer, against competitors such as Mariela, a Mexican/migrant peer and native speaker of Spanish.

In an ESL course in a Pilsen community organization called Casa del Pueblo, Claudio Barrajas, a young Mexican migrant who had been in the U.S. only three years and was indeed quite eager to learn English, wanted to know what the word "da" was, as it was a word he was seeing repeatedly in reference to the Chicago Bulls professional basketball team. The advertisements in question ironically transliterated a stereotypical (white working-class) Chicago accent, to say "da Bulls," and here was an inquisitive learner of the English language who wanted to know what this peculiar word meant. After De Genova had explained that this was an improper spelling of the word "the," intended to more closely resemble how some people actually spoke, Barrajas said, "Like the Blacks [los morenos], for example, you can tell that they don't speak well." Olga Mendoza responded, more emphatically, "It's that they speak badly [feo, literally 'ugly']—they don't know how to speak well." De Genova tried to dispute the characterization of Black English as "bad" [feo] and persuade the class to see these differences as related to class-based and often racialized inequalities of social power, suggesting that those with wealth and power had both the means to impose their own standards in the continuous production and reconfiguration of notions of "proper" or "standard" English, as well as privileged access to the most elite educational institutions through which those standards were reproduced and enforced. Barrajas, however, was not apparently touched by this line of argument; he continued, "Yeah, like when Puerto Ricans or Dominicans speak Spanish, I can't even understand them—because they don't speak well—although I understand people from any other country in South America or Central America." Faustino Galarza, a much older man who had been in Chicago for much longer, pointed out that "they also think that Mexicans speak funny—they ask why Mexicans are always singing when they talk." Nevertheless, most of the others seemed fairly convinced that African Americans spoke "bad" English, in much the ways that they judged Puerto Rican Spanish to be simply "bad" Spanish. The explicit analogy that Claudio made here between Puerto Rican Spanish and Black English, furthermore, was quite telling.

A similar discussion had arisen in an ESL class at the DuraPress factory in January of 1994. This factory was located in an industrial suburb of Chicago, and many of the mainly Mexican/migrant workforce there lived nearby. In a discussion of the differences between living in the surrounding suburbs as opposed to living in the city, Ricardo began to comically mimic his idea of how people in the city speak, saying, "Hey, whassup" in a deliberately exaggerated way. Carmen simply remarked, "Like the Blacks [*como los negros*]." Eudoro, however, responded by complicating Carmen's generalization, adding, "But Tejanos [Texas Mexicans] and Puerto Ricans speak that way, too." Carmen replied abruptly, with great seriousness, "Well, it's because they're ill-bred [*son malcriados*]." Eudoro laughed, lightheartedly agreeing, "Yes, it's bad upbringing [*mala educación*]." Carmen, however, did not share his levity. Seriously, definitively, she pronounced again, "That's right—they're badly brought up [*mal educados*]." This severe judgment on Carmen's part retained none of the playful teasing that she had shown just two weeks earlier during the discussion of holiday foods (discussed above), when her Puerto Rican coworker Yadira had been present. Carmen's utter lack of irony in this instance established that she concealed a more conclusively negative opinion about Puerto Rican Spanish, and about "Chicano" (here, specifically Tejano) Spanish as well. But these were not merely appraisals of their language; they were condemnations of what she presumed to have been the shortcomings of their upbringing. Indeed, her initial remark that Puerto Ricans and Tejanos were "*malcriados*" might also be glossed as a more general allegation of "rudeness." Likewise, this exchange hinged upon the prior identification of Ricardo's performance of a distinctively "urban" slang, which Carmen immediately resorted to racialize, explicitly, as "Black." What was identified as the "bad" English of Puerto Ricans (and also some Mexicans raised in the U.S.), therefore, was "bad" precisely in that it could be racialized as "Black," and what it signaled was not only an improper habit of speech but a more generally debased condition of rudeness that reflected having been badly raised.

Some Puerto Rican migrants not only bemoaned the lack of Spanish among younger, U.S.-born Puerto Ricans (as discussed above), but also decried their English as virtually indistinguishable from Black English, in ways that sometimes resembled the negative judgments of Mexican migrants concerning Puerto Ricans' English (as well as that of some Mexicans raised in the U.S.). The preoccupation of older generations of Puerto Ricans was not only that the younger generations were not speaking Spanish or not speaking "proper" Spanish, but also that these Puerto Rican youth were presumably embracing an "improper"— i.e., Black—English. For instance, after chatting with Ramos-Zayas for about twenty minutes, Willie Pérez, a Puerto Rican migrant in his early thirties and a staff member at a local ESL program, asked her in Spanish, "*¿Cuál es tu raza?*" Ramos-Zayas was perplexed by Pérez's question, as it meant, most literally, "What's your race?" but could also be taken to mean, "What is your nationality?" or even more broadly, "What is your heritage?" Presuming that it would have been fairly obvious to another Puerto Rican, with whom she was conversing in Spanish, that she was herself Puerto Rican, Ramos-Zayas asked him what he meant. Pérez responded, "I mean, are you Puerto Rican? Are you from Puerto Rico or from New York?" The ambiguity in the question was therefore clarified, only then to be unsettled again by the second question which insinuated a decisive difference—a difference of *raza*—between Puerto Ricans from Puerto Rico and those from New York. When Ramos-Zayas explained that she had been raised in Puerto Rico, but had lived in the U.S. for over a decade, Pérez remarked, "Yes, it figures you're from Puerto Rico, because your Spanish is very good." Willie mentioned that, unlike other Puerto Ricans living in the area, he valued the Spanish language and felt that not enough was being done to maintain the language among younger generations. He then added, jokingly, "Me, the more years I spend in the U.S., the worse my English gets!" When Ramos-Zayas asked he what he meant, Pérez added, "People here don't speak English well. They don't. They speak street English, not correct English. The Puerto Rican or Mexican who comes here learns English from the streets and from TV. They speak like Blacks." In Willie's view, then, not only was there a fundamental difference between Puerto Ricans from the Island and those from the Mainland, but also the longer a migrant spent in the U.S., the more he or she exchanged the Spanish language for only the most corrupted and debased kind of English—that which was racialized in terms of Blackness. In this sense, Puerto Ricans and Mexicans were seen to share the same fate—not only to inevitably witness the demise of their Spanish and come under the pressure to become English-dominant, but also to have access only to an unrefined "street" English that located them on a shared racial ground approaching that of African Americans; furthermore, if this was true of Latino migrants, their children— U.S.-born or -raised Mexicans and Puerto Ricans—were, in Willie's view, even more irretrievably "like Blacks." Willie contended that they were actively neglecting and thus losing "proper" Spanish, and he conflated this "loss" of Spanish language competency with the claim that these barrio youth were moving toward a racial condition akin to Blackness by speaking Black English. In this sense, largely premised on a reverence for fluency in both a "standard" English and a "proper" Spanish, Puerto Rican and Mexican migrants, and especially their U.S.-born progeny, were drawn together by a Latinidad that actually derived not from shared Spanish language but rather a shared erosion of Spanish, supplanted by a "street" English signaling the advent of a racialized status approximating that of African Americans. Notably, while Willie principally concerned himself with language, he had begun with the ambiguous question of "race" or "nation" that differentiated being from Puerto Rico in opposition to being from the U.S., and concluded by positing racial Blackness as a sign of degeneracy that threatened all Latinos in the U.S.

Most of these discourses around the politics of language invariably reinforced the association between the younger generation's U.S.-born identity, "improper" (disorderly) language, and racial Blackness in connection with mass-mediated popular culture, particularly rap music and hip-hop styles. A Puerto Rican man in his late forties, Justino Ramírez had lived in Chicago for over ten years. Ramos-Zayas met Ramírez through his daughter, Brenda, a worker at a health clinic in Humboldt Park. When Justino Ramírez asked Ramos-Zayas about her research, she mentioned that she was interested in learning more about the cultural experiences of young people in Humboldt Park. Almost indignant, Justino responded, "What kind of culture are the [U.S.-born Puerto Rican] kids going to have? That's something you have to take into account in your work, when you interview people. The younger generations don't know Spanish! They are into rap music. What's going to happen with them?" By implication, for Justino, not speaking Spanish and English-dominance was uncontestably associated not only with a lack of cultural authenticity, but also with the cultural corruption of Puerto Ricanness by a popular culture viewed as distinctly "Black."[4] Similarly, Eugenio Martínez, a Puerto Rican man in his late forties who worked as a part-time custodial worker at a public high school in Humboldt Park, was aggravated upon learning that the school's student council wanted to invite a rap group to perform at a school activity. A very expressive man, Martínez, immediately upon hearing the news, interrupted a conversation that Ramos-Zayas was having with two other Puerto Rican teachers, in order to object to the students' choice of entertainment. He complained: "That rap, that music—if you can call it music— is disgusting! That's all these kids want to listen to. Maybe they want to be Black!" Since Eugenio had a reputation for being very irritable and short-tempered, one of the Puerto Rican teachers immediately explained to him that "Puerto Rock," the New York rap group that the students wanted to invite, "play[ed] songs in Spanish, too," emphasizing, "They're Puerto Rican." The teacher who responded to Eugenio thus upheld the legitimacy of maintaining the distinction between Blackness and Puerto Ricanness, insofar as she treated the rappers' presumed credentials as Puerto Rican and Spanish-speaking as evidence that they ought to be considered more acceptable and appropriate than an African American rap group. Eugenio's objections, of course, were hardly alleviated. Like other older Puerto Rican migrants, Justino and Eugenio conflated rap music with Blackness and with Black English and viewed such youth cultural formations among U.S.-born Puerto Ricans as antagonistic to the Spanish language and the preservation of "Puerto Rican culture."[5]

If Mexicans and Puerto Ricans alike disparaged what they perceived to be "bad" or "improper" English, there was one elementary and fundamental preoc-cupation that they shared. It concerned the unseemly prospect of their respective communities' social reproduction getting derailed into a condition of abjection associated with the subjugated and loathsome racial status of U.S. "minority," for which Blackness was the iconic exemplar and template. Thus, it was only with chagrin that these Latino migrants witnessed some of their U.S.-born children's acquisition of distinctively African American–identified language, modes of expression, and creative forms. Nonetheless, in the intermediate and equivocal space between whiteness and Blackness, where most frequently they were respectively racialized simply as "Mexicans" or as "Puerto Ricans," and in the specific context of Anglo hegemony in the U.S., to be monolingual Spanish-speaking ("Latino") "foreigners" may have supplied one basis for their racialization, but to become speakers of "Black" English was readily presumed to be much worse.

Spanglish

The allegation, on the part of many Puerto Rican migrants (as well as many Mexicans), that U.S.-born Puerto Ricans spoke "Black" English was often coupled with the related charge that their Spanish was so thoroughly corrupted by their English-dominance that it was no longer even recognizably Spanish at all.[6] Francisco González, a Puerto Rican who had lived in Chicago for five years when Ramos-Zayas met him in the summer of 1995, commented with disdain, "Some Puerto Ricans from here do not even speak Spanish or, if they do, they speak a dialect, Spanglish. They don't speak English well either. They speak Black English, not the English we learn in school in Puerto Rico or in college." By regarding Spanglish as "a dialect," Francisco insinuated that it was merely a derivative of the true language. Rather than see Spanglish as a creative fusion, a syncretistic innovation, Francisco viewed Spanglish as evidence that U.S. Puerto Ricans could not really speak Spanish at all.[7] In effect, class-stigmatized Spanglish was a corollary to "Black" English, and for Francisco, the two debased derivatives traveled hand in hand: those Puerto Ricans who spoke "Black" English were presumed to inevitably also be speakers of Spanglish.[8]

Although Spanglish was often associated with Puerto Ricans in general (cf. Flores et al., 1987), Spanish-dominant Puerto Ricans were commonly as critical of "Spanglish" as were any other Latino migrants. On one occasion at Ester García's beauty salon in Logan Square, a mixed group of Puerto Rican, Mexican, and Guatemalan women were talking about their favorite Spanish-language soap operas from years past. The conversation turned to a Mexican soap opera, *Dos Mujeres y Un Camino* (*Two Women, One Road*), which had starred U.S.-born Puerto Rican actor Erik Estrada in the lead male role, torn between two women, played by two Mexican actresses Bibi Gaitán and Laura León. Although she had migrated from Puerto Rico to Chicago nearly three decades prior, Ester had remained perfectly fluent in Spanish; expressing her frustration about the casting of Estrada, she commented, "I never understood why they would choose Erik Estrada for that role. He couldn't even speak! He would make so many mistakes when he tried to speak Spanish! He really spoke Spanglish. Because—even though his mother was from Ponce, my hometown—he was born in the U.S." When Ramos-Zayas asked García why she thought Erik Estrada had been chosen for the role, one of the Mexican beauty school students hypothesized that it was because *Patrulla Motorizada* (as the television program originally titled *CHiPs* had been translated for Spanish-speaking audiences) had been very popular in Mexico. She added, joking, "Maybe they thought that the Spanish he spoke on [the dubbed version of] *Patrulla Motorizada* was his real voice! I didn't even know he was Puerto Rican. I just thought he had some speech problem." Now more defensively, embarrassed by the association of Puerto Rican Spanish with Estrada's linguistic difficulties, Ester immediately replied, "In soap operas in Puerto Rico, everyone speaks very good Spanish—but they had to go and choose someone from here [the U.S.] to play that role?? I just don't understand. And you know how it is with those soap operas, they all speak perfect Spanish [un español fino]. They [the actors] may be Mexican, but you can't even tell if they are or not." Clearly, by suggesting that all soap opera actors spoke a standardized and generically refined Spanish that served to homogenize any differences of national accent, Ester underscored the singularity of this example, and, already aware of many Mexicans' negative appraisals of Puerto Rican Spanish, sought to distance the U.S.-born Puerto Rican actor's incompetence in Spanish from the genuine language of Puerto Ricans. In Ester's account, Estrada's fumbling efforts exposed the fact that "he couldn't even speak" Spanish, and that what he "really" spoke was Spanglish. For many Puerto Rican migrants like Ester, even after having spent half her life in the U.S., Spanglish was merely the abject language of U.S.-born Puerto Ricans whose linguistic hybridity signaled that they were uneducated, incompetent, inauthentic, and basically an embarrassment.

Spanglish, figured as a kind of unwholesome hybridity that revealed other kinds of disorder and excess, also became a racialized stigma attached to Puerto Ricans in the commentaries of some Mexicans. During an interview in her Pilsen apartment in 1995, María Gaitán described her experience several years earlier of having just arrived in Chicago for the first time as an adult migrant from Mexico (although she had spent many years growing up partly in California). It is significant that her memory came to focus upon a Puerto Rican woman. María recounted:

> I got off the bus, we got off on California [Avenue] . . . that stop there [in Little Village]. It was, like, "Oh shit, it's so ugly." I kept thinking, "It's so ugly and gray." And then my brother came to pick us up with a friend of his in the car. The guy in his car, some guy, his roommate, really, like, not friendly at all, kind of like, "Oh shit, I have to give him a ride to pick up his sister." So you could kind of feel the bad vibes. We got to where my brother lived. He lived on Grand Avenue and Western [in West Town]. So I got there and like, "Oh my God, what is this?" I expected a neighborhood or something. I don't know what I expected because I had never been to Chicago or seen pictures or anything, so I didn't really know what to expect. (Actually, I *had* seen pictures—of Downtown!)
>
> That same evening I was in my brother's apartment, it was a basement and all the tile was this ugly plastic kind of tile where you just cut out the thing and you put it on a tile floor. That was really strange, when I was used to the hard floors in Mexico, and the cement walls. Now everything was wood and seemed . . . like paper, everything seemed like cardboard. And there were so many people living in that little apartment too! And it was really bizarre. By that time, I hadn't spoken English in a long time. I was mainly speaking Spanish so my English was really rusty and I wasn't speaking English to anyone. I was speaking Spanish. I remember being in the basement and people coming

into my brother's apartment [. . .] people were coming in and out and . . . just listening to the people talk, in Spanglish!—Puerto Rican women, and that was another thing! In California, we were all Mexicans. And here, Puerto Ricans. And in California it was just Mexicans and whites . . .

De Genova asked, "So your brother was living with Puerto Ricans?"

"No, I remember that night a Puerto Rican woman came in because she was married with someone there, but they were Mexicans."

"Was that the first time you had encountered any Puerto Ricans?"

"[. . .] If I encountered them in California, they probably never said they were Puerto Ricans and I probably never . . ." María paused for a moment, and then recollected; "You know—the hair and the black mouth [referring to the woman's lipstick] and all of that. Really gaudy. I was just amazed, looking at this woman speak, speak, speak. She was like a caricature. That's how I saw her. It was like looking at a movie. Seeing people walk down into the basement, seeing them walk back up. 'What does all this mean?'"

Even though she had spent significant portions of her childhood and adolescence in California, this depiction recounts what was, nonetheless, an alienating shock of arrival from Mexico to Chicago. In addition to the post-industrial bleakness of the physical environs of these impoverished working-class neighborhoods, and the sense that everything was made of inexpensive and makeshift materials, however, María fixed upon the incessant and hybrid language, as well as the fashions (hairstyle, cosmetics, clothing), of a Puerto Rican woman as a complex sign of what she had encountered, at least initially, as the irreducible and uncanny difference of Chicago from all that she had known previously. Whereas, growing up in California, the racial order of the U.S. that María had known was simply comprised of "Mexicans and whites," her arrival in Chicago immediately confronted her with a Puerto Rican woman as the embodiment of a new racialized category to apprehend, and this woman was inseparable from the disorienting cacophony of Spanglish.

When Mexican migrants reflected upon Spanglish, however, they were at least as likely to identify it with Mexicans raised in the U.S. as to project it onto Puerto Ricans, and thus, much like Puerto Rican migrants, tended to discuss Spanglish as an issue internal to their own community. The same Mexican migrant, Lino Pacheco, who was enthusiastic about the ESL course but disdained the prospect of participating in an English class that would include his Puerto Rican coworkers, whose bilingualism he discounted due to what he considered their "bad" English (discussed above), also had very pronounced opinions about Spanglish. Speaking to De Genova in English, Pacheco explained:

I always try to practice my English and learn more, but in Mexico I don't speak English—I say this is my country, here I speak Spanish. But what I hate is when people come here [to the U.S.] and then mix the English and Spanish, and you can't understand them. In movies, you see Chicanos speaking only English, except they curse in Spanish—why is that the only thing they can say?? If I could meet that Edward James Olmos, I'd tell him—"Do it in English or do it in Spanish, but don't mix the words, goddammit!"

Although he had been only fourteen years old when he migrated, and he had been in the U.S. for eighteen years, Lino maintained a definitive sense of himself as Mexican and clearly differentiated himself from "Chicanos." Likewise, although he was extraordinarily fluent in English in comparison with his Mexican/migrant coworkers at Liberty Carton, and was very earnest about further improving his English, Lino remained an adamant linguistic purist.

Despite a general aversion expressed by many Mexican migrants to Spanglish, there were nonetheless innumerable words from English that had been incorporated as Spanish neologisms into the mundane discourse of most Mexicans in Chicago. New Spanish words—such as *carro* ["car"], *troca* ["truck"], *un raid, un rait* ["a ride"], *parquear* ["to park," as in parking a car], *un core* ["a quarter," as in a 25-cent coin], and *lonchar* ["to have lunch," or more precisely, "to take a lunch break" (in a workplace)]—proliferated in the language of everyday life of Mexican Chicago. At the Caustic Scrub tank-cleaning facility, Mateo Valdivia always referred to these Spanish versions of English terms as "Tex-Mex," ironically adopting that marketing phrase as his own peculiar marker of linguistic syncretisms in the Mexican/migrant context. On one occasion in the fall of 1995, when Valdivia invoked the phrase "Tex-Mex," but was referring to something particular to California, De Genova sought to clarify that "Tex-Mex" referred specifically to Texas, or Tejanos (Texas Mexicans), and that the more general term for U.S. Mexicans was "Chicano." Smiling knowingly, Mateo added, "Or you can say, '*pocho*' too, right?" In an overly earnest pedagogical spirit, unreceptive to Valdivia's humor, De Genova clarified that the term "Chicano" is not negative, but that words like *pocho* or *cholo* are derogatory. Upon hearing the word *cholo*, Manuel began to chuckle, and responded in English: "*Cholos,* that's the ones who say '*wátchale!*' to the *mojados* who are running across the border with their little plastic bags slung over their shoulders and their heads ducked down to hide from La Migra."[9]

In conclusion, then, the presumed commonality of Spanish language, which is frequently considered to supply an automatic bond and source of unity among Latino groups, tended to offer no such guarantees in many of the everyday life scenarios where Latinos confronted one another. As we have seen in this chapter, the value of Spanish as a ground for the production of Latinidad remained persistently problematic, and in fact was as likely as not to contribute to the highly charged and delicate circumstances that often undermined the formation of a shared Latino identity. Mexicans and Puerto Ricans in Chicago not only drew distinctions between themselves based on the identifiable type and "quality" of Spanish spoken by each group—particular words and idiomatic expressions used, spoken accents, and the overall "correctness" of their respective ways of speaking Spanish—but also evaluated and hierarchically ranked each other's English. While "proper" or "good" Spanish was recognized as a symbol of being culturally "authentic" and was embraced as the ideal for each group's distinctive Spanish, the "Spanglish" or "bad English" of U.S.-born and -raised Mexicans and, more often, Puerto Ricans was likewise disparaged as an undesirable kind of "Americanization" by which "Latinos" became mere U.S. "minorities," and were racialized as approximating the degraded status of Blackness by speaking a type of English associated with African Americans. In this sense, the discourses of language difference between Mexicans and Puerto Ricans, as well as between migrants and the U.S.-born within each group, were hierarchically organized and forcefully racialized, often explicitly in relation to Blackness, and thus, always also at least implicitly with respect to white supremacy. Given the highly divergent and inherently conflictual ways in which Mexicans and Puerto Ricans deployed discourses of language—the one element commonly presumed to *unify* both groups—in order not to find common ground but rather to fortify the racialized difference between them, we are required to confront this complex question: What might be the conditions under which the formation of a shared "Latino" identity—a mutual sense of Latinidad that could provide a viable and reliable basis for community and collaboration—becomes possible? This, finally, is the question that has inspired so much attention to the circumstances that have undermined that possibility in these foregoing chapters, and is the question that we now must examine more directly in chapter 7.

CHAPTER 7

Latino Rehearsals: Divergent Articulations of Latinidad

In the preceding chapters, antagonistic divisions frequently presented palpable obstacles to the possibility of a shared sense of Latino identity between Mexicans and Puerto Ricans in Chicago. Indeed, as we have seen, the differences between Mexicans and Puerto Ricans often themselves came to be racialized as divisions that situated each group differently in relation to the hegemonic polarity of whiteness and Blackness. Nevertheless, as we suggested at the outset, in the introduction to this book (chapter 1), it is not only possible but also politically necessary to contend that Mexicans and Puerto Ricans do indeed have a shared historicity—one that they share with various other Latin American groups as well. This shared historicity has taken shape, in its most general outlines, in relation to global capitalism, but in its specific political forms, more evidently in relation to the U.S. state, its nationalism, as well as its colonial and imperialist relations to Latin America as a whole. Furthermore, this shared historicity has been racialized virtually since its very inception. Thus, while Mexicans have certainly been racialized as "Mexicans," and Puerto Ricans, likewise, have been racialized as "Puerto Ricans," there have been and are increasingly powerful forces that contribute to their racial formation as "Latinos" or "Hispanics." A wide range of expressions and invocations of Latinidad, or a Latino identity in common, did indeed emerge at times among Mexican migrants and Puerto Ricans in Chicago in a variety of divergent contexts. Especially in light of such a complex array of potential sources of racialized division between these two groups, it becomes crucial, finally, to examine with care and precision the particularities of these various formulations of Latino commonality, and their distinct anticipations or rehearsals of potential forms of Latino community and communion.

"Latino" as a Racial Category

Whatever else various people with origins in Latin America may attribute to or claim for the substantive meanings of the terms "Latino" or "Hispanic," it was quite commonplace in our respective research projects to find that Latinos understood and explicitly deployed these terms in order to delineate a category of racialized distinction that located them in relation to whiteness and Blackness. One revealing instance occurred when De Genova interviewed Gloria Encino, a Mexican/migrant worker whom he had taught at the DuraPress factory, with several of her siblings. When De Genova asked Juanita León (Gloria's sister), what kind of people [*qué tipo de gente*] there were at the restaurant where she worked, she responded, "all kinds of people, namely Americans, Blacks, uhmm, Latinos [*de todo tipo de gente, o sea, americanos, morenos, este, latinos*]." Whereas this very general question had been deliberately asked in an open-ended fashion, Juanita's reply was revealing of the extent to which her experience as a migrant in the U.S. had conditioned her to readily identify racialized distinctions as immediately salient categories by which to sort different types of people. As we have discussed already, "American" was routinely and ubiquitously posited by Mexican migrants as well as Puerto Ricans as a name for racial whiteness, consistently juxtaposed to Blackness. In Juanita's formulation, the category "Latinos" was an equivalent category of meaningful differentiation that belonged alongside of these other two racialized terms. At the risk of overspeculation, furthermore, it is not entirely unreasonable to posit that her momentary hesitation, signaled by her use of the verbal place-holder "*este*" to mark her pause, prior to the addition of the word "Latinos," can be taken to suggest that she was still engaged to some extent in a deliberation about that term. Conceivably pausing for a second to weigh the relative merits of one term ("*latinos*") against another (perhaps, for example, "*hispanos*"), or considering whether or not to specifically identify Mexicans or to opt instead for the more inclusive category "Latinos"—in retrospect, we really cannot know—Juanita nonetheless seemed to be thoughtfully selective and deliberate about her choice of words. In any case, she was indisputably positing Latinidad as a *racial* formation.

What ensued immediately thereafter was also quite revealing. De Genova followed Juanita León's remark with a question of clarification about whether she was referring to the workers employed with her at the restaurant. Juanita clarified that she had been referring to the customers, and that the workers were all Latinos. She paused for a moment, explaining, "They're ... Mexicans," and then paused again before adding, "[there's] one Ecuadorian, who for sure has very different customs than one's own, many different words [*los trabajadores son latinos, son ... mexicanos ... una ecuatoriana que por cierto tiene muy diferentes costumbres con uno, muchas palabras diferentes*]." Remarkably, in a manner that confirms again many of the themes in chapter 6 concerning the viability of a notion of Latinidad premised upon language in common, Juanita here formulated a Latinidad shared between Mexicans and Ecuadorians that was immediately differentiated internally by divergences of language, rather than any presumed sameness. As soon as she grouped the two together as Latinos, she specified their distinct linguistic "customs" or divergent idiomatic usages. Juanita continued, "Another thing, very different that ... even while we are Latinos, we are very different; we're not all the same [*Otra cosa, muy diferente que ... aún cuando somos latinos, somos muy diferentes; no todos somos iguales*]." De Genova then asked, "Well, how do you mean? How do you explain that?" León explained further that the differences of vocabulary between these two Latino groups' distinct Spanish languages contributed to confusion, misunderstandings, and even offense: "She's Ecuadorian, I'm Mexican. She has more . . . some words that [re-fer to] food, and for me, it offends me, they're offensive words . . . and for us Mexicans, those words offend us, right? There are words they have that are an in-sult for us, and in turn, we . . . there are words that are insults for them." Clearly, a presumed Spanish language in common was not always or automatically suf-ficient to sustain Latinidad, and even became a source of fragmentation among Latinos, but what is crucial here is to recognize that these differences of language or "custom" that Juanita identified were subsumed within and encompassed by a definite sense of Latinidad. On the one hand, she stated plainly, "Even while we are Latinos, we are very different." On the other hand, the durable meaning-fulness of that Latino commonality of identity or interest was derived, first and foremost, from its location within a racialized social order in the U.S. that was defined by the placement of Latinos in relation to whites and Blacks.

The racialized condition that attained to a commonality as "Latinos" or "Hispanics" was likewise routinely asserted and reinforced by the everyday workings of white supremacy itself, as articulated notably by many of the whites with whom Latinos sometimes interacted. Many white Chicagoans, confronted with a variegated Latino reality whose internal diversity they did not necessarily understand or even trouble themselves to comprehend better, frequently were inclined to adopt the terms "Latino" or "Hispanic" as presumably neutral and polite racial categories. The following incident is exceptionally revealing. De Genova's friend Rafael Jiménez, a Mexican in his early twenties born in Chicago to migrant parents, related the story of how he had encountered two white male acquaintances in a bar where all three regularly went to drink and socialize. On this occasion, one of the whites casually inquired, "Hey, you're Mexican, right?" His counterpart immediately interrupted the exchange, however, cor-recting his friend with the admonition, "Don't say that! He's Latino!" Bemused by this peculiar performance of what appeared to be simple white ignorance, Rafael refuted the second speaker's correction of the other's presumed insen-sitivity; assuming a pedagogical posture, he explained simply, "But that's what I am—I am Mexican." Now, however, the second white interlocutor made his own assumptions more clear; he replied, "But still, I'd never call you that! He shouldn't say that!" Compounding his ignorance with a kind of liberal racial condescension, the young white man revealed something even more profound about the economy of racialized meanings and distinctions at play in this ex-change. For him, "Mexican" was an irreducibly racialized term, indeed an intrin-sically derogatory racist slur, and it was offensive to call someone that; likewise, "Latino" was the preferable term, because it was a presumed to be a compa-rable and effectively synonymous racial category, but one that appeared to be neutral, a racial euphemism, and thus inoffensive. Similarly, MaryAnn Weber, a white college student who had grown up in a white working-class Chicago suburb that neighbored predominantly African American working-class sub-urbs, but whose mother had been raised in Texas and still had numerous family connections there, once admitted very candidly, "I still can't quite bring myself to say 'Mexican'; even though I know it's not, I can't hear it as anything but a racist insult."[1] In contexts where "Mexican" and "Puerto Rican" have themselves served as racialized group identifiers, often equated for whites with an already degraded, subordinate racial status, the viability of "Hispanic" or "Latino" as parallel categories for labeling specifically *racial* group identities has been, in effect, an inevitable outcome.

Latinidad as the "American" Abjection of the U.S.-Born

While often guarding a robust sense of their own particularities as Mexicans or Puerto Ricans, and thereby *not* embracing a notion of their own Latinidad, Mexican and Puerto Rican migrants did nevertheless sometimes project an idea of shared Latino identity onto the younger generations, Mexican or Puerto Rican, who had been born and raised in the U.S. Most commonly, these articulations of Latinidad projected "Latino" commonalities as a kind of debased homogenization alleged to prevail among the U.S.-born generations of all Latino groups. Such a perceived loss among the U.S.-born of their respective "Mexican" or "Puerto Rican" specificity, moreover, was inevitably conjoined to assumptions of the more generic racial abjection attributed to the status of a U.S. "minority group."

In September of 1995, for instance, during an ESL course at the Pilsen community organization called Casa del Pueblo, a group of Mexican migrants revisited the equation of street gangs and other figures of abjection with Mexicans raised in the U.S. (discussed in chapter 4). On this occasion the discussion was concerned with the rising tide of anti-immigrant politics associated with the passage in California of the ballot initiative known as Proposition 187. Claudio Barrajas was twenty years old, and had been in Chicago for four years after migrating from the medium-sized city of Irapuato in the Mexican state of Guanajuato. He worked cutting glass in a mirror factory for shifts ranging from ten to eleven and a half hours. With regard to the new anti-immigrant legislation, Claudio posited, "I think the whites [*los güeros*] are reacting to the problems caused by the ones who are born here and grow up here, because it's mainly not us immigrants who go on welfare and get involved in gangs—it's the children of the immigrants, the ones who are from here, and then the problems they cause are blamed on immigrants." There was an ambiguity and open-endedness that is instructive for our purposes here in Claudio's articulation of a critical distinction between (im)migrants and those who were born and raised in the U.S. in a manner that potentially transcended the particularities of *Mexican* migrants and *their* children raised in the U.S. and instead could refer more generally to migrants and U.S.-born Latinos. Claudio proposed that the persecution of Mexican (or more generally, Latino) migrants was really a misplaced backlash that might more appropriately be directed, not against migrants, but rather against Mexicans raised in the U.S. (and perhaps other U.S.-born Latinos), who, he claimed, were the ones who caused problems by collecting welfare and engaging in the criminality associated with street gangs. In response, De Genova sought specifically to challenge Barrajas's apparent allegation that people who collected public aid were causing some kind of problem. In an effort to suggest that there is always a necessary relationship between the actual labor of workers employed for wages and the unemployed who are required by capitalism as a reserve of potential labor, De Genova contended that the politicians were "trying to cut welfare for the poor who can barely survive on the little they're already getting, but in reality there's plenty of wealth in the U.S., and really they [the government] should be providing *more* welfare, not less." Another course participant, Andrea, who came from a lower-middle-class background in Mexico City and had only been in the U.S. for three months, was employed by a private social service agency, working with children with disabilities. She had already in only three months acquired a remarkably strong opinion about "welfare," and challenged, "But I can tell you, there are some people who get welfare and they don't need it, so that's the problem they [the politicians, the government] should work on!" Although Andrea did not identify what she perceived to be welfare "abuse" with any particular group, Claudio had indeed linked this substantive entitlement associated with U.S. citizenship to "the ones who are born here and grow up here," or "the children of the immigrants," whom he perceived to be the source of social problems otherwise blamed upon implicitly more honorable migrants.

There was, then, a chain of associations that connected the substantive entitlements of citizenship to the criminality of those Latino U.S. citizens who, by implication, were least deserving of such privileges, in clear juxtaposition to the hardworking and thus, by implication, more "deserving" migrants, especially the undocumented, who were systematically denied such benefits. While this is revealing for our more general argument about how the politics of citizenship shaped relations between Mexican migrants and Puerto Ricans (see chapter 3), it is particularly instructive here, in revealing how the figure of Mexicans raised in the U.S. (sometimes called "Chicanos"), especially in its most abject equation with street gangs and criminality, supplied an important bridge that served to connect the two groups, if only by way of the abjection ascribed to both of their U.S.-born generations.

Many migrants, both Mexican and Puerto Rican, accentuated the distinctions between themselves and their respective U.S.-born generations, and posited an explicitly "Latino" identity as the embodiment of negative stereotypes associated with the generic racial condition of U.S. "minority." Thus, many migrants perceived Latinidad as an identity that fundamentally pertained to "second-generation" youth as the effect of a kind of racially subordinate "Americanization." This type of "American" abjection was generally considered to be a degeneration of the "good" or "proper" values that migrants prized, and was readily conflated with "laziness" and welfare system "dependency." This debased Latinidad projected onto the second generation was likewise characterized by a loss of cultural authenticity, evidenced not only by a demise of fluency in the Spanish language and a reliance upon "Spanglish," but perhaps even more troubling, by the adoption of "bad" (Black-identitifed) English, as discussed in chapter 6. Hence, the processes that might be called "American-ization" in the second generation were widely disparaged as a movement away from the presumed integrity of "Mexican"-ness or "Puerto Ricanness," in the direction of a Latinidad apparently inseparable from the racialized status of U.S. "minority" that was synonymous with Blackness. As "Latinos" or "Hispanics," the U.S.-born generations were viewed not as genuine "Americans" (namely, whites) but rather as mere "minorities," who did not speak any language "prop-erly," were criminalized and associated with gang activity, and embodied values or behaviors more stereotypically associated with poor African Americans.

Melvin Rodríguez, a second-generation Puerto Rican resident of Humboldt Park, noted the tensions that arose between Puerto Ricans "from the Island" and Puerto Ricans like himself who were "from the Mainland," in his recollec-tions describing ESL teachers who had been hired directly from Puerto Rico to teach at Roberto Clemente High School. When Ramos-Zayas asked Melvin to further elaborate these distinctions between "Islanders" and "Mainlanders," he explained:

> Here in the U.S. I don't see that as much [status distinctions among U.S.-based Puerto Ricans]. But I see that with other Puerto Ricans that come to the U.S. I don't see it so much with Puerto Ricans from here looking at other Puerto Ricans as lowlifes or anything. Some of the Puerto Ricans from Puerto Rico, particularly those teaching at Clemente, make those distinctions. They say things to students even if they are Puerto Rican too. They'd say *muchacho de arrabal* [kid from the slum] and stuff like that. Puerto Ricans from here don't see that as much, because we have to look to each other to defend each other.

Some Islanders, especially those from relatively privileged backgrounds, avoided the distinctly racialized "minority" identity of Puerto Ricans in the U.S. in an effort to uphold the prestige of their Island "authenticity" and guard the status that they had enjoyed in Puerto Rico, and thereby enforced the social distance between themselves and the U.S.-based Others. Chicago, for them, was treated largely as a transitory space in which they were not substantively located, a space associated with the presumably temporary character of their employment and occupational mobility as professionals. Thus, the Island's elite, once in the U.S., sought to maintain their class and status dominance in spite of the fact that the racial order of the U.S. tended to consign them to the same debased "minority" status as their barrio counterparts. Island Puerto Ricans' associations of U.S.-born Puerto Ricans with rudeness, marginality, and pathology—the ultimate "underclass"—were not significantly different from those that other Latino migrants, such as Mexicans, often harbored of Puerto Ricans as a group. On the other hand, these Island-versus-Mainland Puerto Rican distinctions were also analogous to the views that many Mexican migrants held of U.S.-born Mexicans whom they ambivalently disavowed as inauthentic, undeserving of the benefits of citizenship, or simply criminal.

U.S.-born Mexicans and Puerto Ricans often grappled with their various and varying degrees of cultural "authenticity," as measured and monitored by their respective migrant counterparts. Among Puerto Ricans in Chicago, there was a definite sensitivity to the negative connotations attached to the term "Nuyorican" (discussed in chapter 4). Puerto Ricans overwhelmingly rejected the term "Nuyorican" as evocative of a derogatory stereotype, used on the Island to signify an uncouth U.S.-born, Spanglish-speaking, Puerto Rican criminal. In Chicago, most Puerto Ricans insistently retained their identity as "Puerto Ricans," and repudiated the identity of "Nuyorican" as pertaining to "those from the Bronx." Nevertheless, as a generational identity that distinguished between migrants and the U.S.-born, "Nuyorican" came to be understood as equivalent or analogous to the identities of U.S.-born Mexicans, and thus contributed to the formulation of an incipient notion of a generationally delimited Latinidad that was spatially grounded within the U.S. Return migrants to Puerto Rico, like Allan Rivera, whose life was characterized by back-and-forth migration between various towns in Puerto Rico and Chicago, described the ways in which his lack of belonging or marginality from a "culturally authentic" Puerto Ricanness was analogous to that of U.S.-born Mexicans, in what implicitly suggested a sense of pan-Latino commonality. Allan remarked:

> The Puerto Rican who leaves the United States to go back to Puerto Rico, they immediately call them "gringos" or "gringas." The puertorriqueños already see you as being an American. They don't see you as puertorriqueño. Lots of negative images. Stuff like "your Spanish is not even good . . . it's different." "Nuyorican" is a divisive term, similar to Tejano or Chicano and all that. I guess I'd be an "Illinoisrican" [he remarked, laughing]. It's all about trying to create a new group and obviously, your experiences are different in reality. But, instead of trying to come together and make it cohesive, it's more about, "You are different now. You're not quite like us."

In Allan's comments, the characterization on the Island of U.S.-identified Puerto Ricans as "gringo" or "American" was quite distinct from the use of the term "American" among Puerto Ricans in Chicago to identify the social power of whites. Rather, the conflation of Puerto Ricans with "American"-ness in Puerto Rico, as Allan has experienced it, summoned "lots of negative images." These images of abjection, including not speaking proper Spanish, became a basis for division, with which Islanders differentiated themselves from U.S.-born or U.S.-based Puerto Ricans, and at least implicitly disavowed them as "American," but only in the sense of a mere U.S. "minority."

Among Puerto Rican migrants, limited Spanish-language competence often-times served as a generational marker that reinforced Puerto Rican migrants' views of Puerto Rican youth as similar to Mexicans raised in the U.S., and the U.S.-raised children of other Latino migrants more generally. In this sense, migrants invoked a Latinidad that could be projected onto the U.S.-born generations of both Puerto Ricans and Mexicans, while positioning themselves outside the parameters of this identity. This became evident when Ramos-Zayas spoke casually with Eugenio Martínez, a Puerto Rican man in his early fifties who worked as a part-time custodial worker at the public high school in Humboldt Park, at a bus stop in front of the school. Calling attention to the many Spanish-language billboards and storefront advertisements of a variety of everyday products, Eugenio commented that his grandchildren would not even be able to understand the Spanish-language signage. Ramos-Zayas mentioned that it was ironic that much of the advertising was aimed primarily at young Latinos, but that many of them seemed to speak more English than Spanish. Eugenio responded, "Well, that's more true of Puerto Ricans. Guatemalans, Central Americans, even Mexicans—they speak more Spanish. Well, they do if they just got here, or their parents only knew Spanish . . . But," he then interrupted himself, "their kids, and the ones that have been here for a while, they don't speak any Spanish either." Surrounded by Puerto Rican and other Latino high school students every day, Eugenio had a reputation for always being unsympathetic to English-dominant Puerto Rican youth and their parents, whom he viewed as the responsible for the children's "Americanization." Eugenio often denounced the "assimilation of Puerto Rican youth" whenever he wanted to complain of the students' "bad behavior," "loudness," or "lack of respect for their elders." Eugenio's commentary about the younger generation's lack of proficiency in Spanish initially portrayed Puerto Ricans as distinct from other Latino groups, whom he perceived as more effective at sustaining and cultivating the continuity of their language. However, Eugenio immediately qualified his judgment by foregrounding a generational commonality to the demise of Spanish-speaking among all U.S.-raised Latinos, positing that the younger generation of Latinos, regardless of nationality, could not speak the language. By implication, Eugenio invoked a Latinidad that was distinguished fundamentally by its deficiency, a debased kind of identity formation invariably associated not only with a loss of Spanish, but also with poor upbringing and "Americanization."

Ironically, Pedro Alvarez, one of the same U.S.-born generation to whom Eugenio had referred, presented a different side of the "Americanization" projected onto him, by illustrating how white supremacy and its institutions worked to fragment or subvert the possibilities for Latino coalitions based upon the Spanish language from very early on. A Puerto Rican artist in his early thirties who lived in Logan Square with his mother and sister, Pedro talked about his experiences of the ways in which Latinidad was interrupted in the context of a public elementary school. After having been in Puerto Rico for seven years, Pedro returned to Chicago where he continued elementary school in the 1970s. When

Ramos-Zayas asked him about his experience readjusting to life in Chicago as a child, Alvarez commented that his most salient memories of that time were related to schooling and language, explaining:

> In school with me back then, there was one Cuban and three Puerto Ricans and one African American in the third grade. At home ... it was a mental mess [*despelote*], because at home Spanish was always spoken. I always grew up with Spanish. English was spoken outside of home, but it was to obtain something. Once, in second grade, I'll never forget, there were two Greeks in front of me. So, assuming they spoke Spanish, I go and speak to them in Spanish. I would speak Spanish to them, one by one. The teacher would tell me "in English!" Imagine, I would get home and it was a big frustration. At that time—this was the early seventies—bilingual programs were very primitive, you could say.

When Pedro tried to reach out to his classmates by speaking Spanish, the teacher would reprimand those attempts by presenting English, a language relatively foreign to Pedro, as the only potential basis of communication in the classroom. In Pedro's eyes, his Greek classmates had appeared as though they should "naturally" be able speak Spanish. Ramos-Zayas asked Pedro if he also tried to speak Spanish to the Cuban or the Puerto Rican classmates, and he mentioned, "Well, the Cuban kid wouldn't even want to talk to me!" In subsequent conversations, Pedro drew from his childhood experiences to note that he had always considered Cubans to be preoccupied with "being with the whites, not wanting to speak Spanish in school." Pedro had made his primary friendships with the other Puerto Ricans in the class, relationships largely based on the linguistic marginality that they all felt. Nevertheless, Pedro also mentioned that any efforts on his part to speak Spanish with other Latinos had been vigilantly interrupted by teachers in charge of the "very primitive" bilingual programs of the 1970s. As Pedro recalled, "Spanish-speaking kids would be deliberately seated apart from each other so they couldn't talk in Spanish. I remember the teachers always complaining to our parents that they didn't want us to segregate, but they wanted to integrate us with the white kids. The thing is, when you are that age, you don't understand any of this. You just view it as, 'I want to be with my friends and my friends happen to speak Spanish.'" Hence, the similarities and compatibilities that drew Pedro closer to other children were racialized in juxtaposition to whiteness and immediately perceived as an undesirable manifestation of linguistic self-segregation. In this sense, this particular group of schoolchildren's incipient Latinidad as Spanish speakers and the prospect of cultivating their bilingualism were promptly interrupted by a policy of public schooling aimed at forming appropriately English-speaking citizens.

Latinidad through Migrant "Illegality"—a Latinidad without Puerto Ricans

Latinidad was sometimes explicitly formulated by Mexican migrants in opposition to the U.S. state and its politics of citizenship. This perspective posited a shared Latino identity that was inextricable from common experiences of migrant "illegality" and border crossing. During the group interview with Gloria Encino and her siblings in 1994 (discussed above), Gloria's brother Adán León posited a robust sense of Latinidad on this basis. "Among all the Latinos, it's the same," he asserted, "because it's the same border—so we all encounter the same problems there...the Mexican police, the drug traffickers, the U.S. Border Patrol [La Migra]." To this claim of a common Latino identity based upon the shared travails of undocumented border-crossing, Adán added, "But for the Guatemalans, it's worse—because they have to cross two countries! For us Mexicans, it's easier." In 1997, in the Pilsen home of Ramiro and Rosa Tejada, who both worked at Imperial Enterprises, when De Genova was tutoring their daughter Rosita in math, the same sentiment was expressed in virtually the same language. Upon hearing her uncle Seferino mention some Guatemalans with whom he worked, Rosita asked, "Uncle, the Guatemalans—are they Hispanics like us? [*¿son hispanos como nosotros?*]. Seferino explained simply, "Yes, but they're from another country—they have to cross three borders!" This distinctively Mexican/migrant sensibility formulated an empathetic Latinidad that recognized the plight of other undocumented Latino migrants to be still more arduous than their own because of a compounding of nation-state borders to cross. Indeed, this understanding of Latino commonalities underscored the profound link in Mexican migrants' experiences between their racialization and the juridical status of "illegal alien." Notably, however, here was a Latinidad in which Puerto Ricans, as U.S. citizens, did not take part at all and could not be included.

Latinidad in Opposition to African Americans

Especially as Mexican migrants sought to account for the unequal politics of citizenship that had demarcated such starkly diverging relations on the part of Mexicans and Puerto Ricans to the U.S. state's allotment of social welfare benefits, as the two groups vied for position within the larger social order of white supremacy, Blackness (as we have seen in previous chapters) was the degraded racialized extreme toward which Mexican migrants in Chicago were frequently inclined to demote Puerto Ricans. There were, however, various occasions and contexts in which Mexican migrants and Puerto Ricans nonetheless aspired toward a mutual recognition through their shared sense of Latino identity. One noteworthy way in which Latinidad came to be invoked, however, was precisely in opposition to African Americans. In one interview, a Mexican migrant named Olivia discussed how, when she had first come from Mexico, her aunt had been very intent to impress upon her the belief that she should avoid Black people at all costs.[2] When she consulted a Puerto Rican coworker, however, Olivia had her aunt's opinions reaffirmed:

> What my aunt was telling me about Black people [*la gente negra*], for example... she was saying that, that they're very bad, that they're thieves, and that

they rape ... and that they shoot guns, and above all that they rob you. [...] I recall one time chatting with a coworker of mine, saying how it bothered me that people, you know, would make these comments, and she was telling me, "Yes, well look, you know what?"—she is Puerto Rican—she says, "When I arrived here, I was saying that to my husband, you know, because my husband was always telling me, 'Be careful with the Blacks [*los negros*],' [...] and I was always telling him, 'I think that they're exaggerating,' you know, 'that there's good people and bad in every race [*en todas las razas*]'" she says. "But," she says, "it happened to me, you know, that a Black (man) [*un negro*] assaulted me, me and my daughter, it was a very bad experience, and now I can't help it, you know, I have a lot of reservations with Black people [*la gente negra*]."

It is striking that Olivia's Puerto Rican coworker had been tutored much as Olivia herself was being coached to distrust and fear African Americans. When Olivia sought a confirmation of her own anti-racist impulses against her aunt's insistences, however, the Puerto Rican woman produced a certain racialized commonality of concern between the two of them by affirming her own distrust of Black people (in effect, in solidarity with Olivia's aunt).

This kind of Latinidad produced between Mexican migrants and Puerto Ricans also became apparent at Imperial Enterprises, a workplace where the two groups not only found themselves employed together but also worked alongside African American workers. In September of 1993, De Genova had met the union steward, a Black woman named Josie. For her own part, Josie was not particularly suspicious of the ESL class, but said that she wanted to be sure that the workers' performance in class, or conceivable lack of improvement in English, would not be used against them by the company, as a pretext to fire them. A week later, Josie appeared in class unannounced during her lunch break for a brief twenty-minute visit. Because there were fairly contested contract negotiations underway, with rumors of a possible strike and company threats to relocate the factory, De Genova proposed that the union steward be interviewed by the Latino workers as an English exercise. Given the legal constraints imposed upon her as a low-level official of the union bureaucracy, Josie was careful to dutifully refrain from answering the workers' inquiries about the negotiations. As a result, the Latino workers interviewed her about her life history. The workers learned that, similar to themselves, Josie had also migrated to find work in Chicago— from a region of Louisiana with a predominantly agricultural economy based on sugar cane, rice, and cotton, where many people were poor for lack of work or low pay. What ensued was a long discussion about each of the workers' respective reasons for migrating from each of their specific places of origin, motivated by De Genova's hope that this might encourage some recognition of a potential analogy between their own Latino experiences and those of African Americans.

When the Latino workers in the class teased her, Josie admitted to being considered "too slow" among the workers on Second Shift. (As it turned out,

Josie ordinarily worked during the day shift and was only temporarily on Second because she needed dental treatments that required her days to be free.) She explained that on First Shift there was consistently lower productivity, in spite of (or perhaps because of) the presence of more managerial supervision and more stringent labor discipline. The predominantly Latino Second Shift was more productive with fewer bosses and less monitoring of workers' compliance with various rules governing the labor process. To illustrate this apparent laxity of regulation on Second Shift, Fernando, a Mexican migrant, gave the example of workers not being allowed to keep coffee at their respective workstations during the First Shift, whereas this was permissible on Second. Nonetheless, Fernando himself described how workers on Second Shift could be disciplined for getting tired and slowing down at the end of a shift of continuously high production. Indeed, later that same evening, one of the participants in the course, a Mexican migrant named Tomás, whom the company had recently celebrated as a "model" worker for his long record of efficient high productivity without accidents, was summarily issued a warning ticket for allegedly operating a punch press carelessly. (This was no minor event, because three such warning tickets during one year's time would have cost a worker his or her job.)

Despite the management's demands that they maintain such an intense work routine, the Second-Shift Latino workers took pride, during the conversation with Josie, in the fact that they worked harder and maintained higher productivity ratings than their counterparts on the daytime shift. After Josie left the training room, several Latino workers laughed as they criticized her for being "too slow." Victoria quickly added, in a more serious tone, that in fact, Josie was "lazy." This remark opened up a whole discussion about the Black workers in general. It became apparent that the Mexican/migrant and Puerto Rican workers bonded around their shared opinion that the African American workers were all "lazy," as well as their shared distrust of their Black coworkers. They resented what they perceived to be the Black workers' license to get away with anything and freedom from having to follow the rules. Furthermore, they considered the Black workers to be dangerous, claiming that they carried weapons, and readily threatened the life of any boss who menaced the security of their jobs. The Latino workers in the class also believed that the management indulged the African American workers because the company feared that the Black employees would charge them with discrimination since there were really very few Blacks employed there. Similarly, they claimed that, because Josie and other union officers were Black, the union provided African American workers with privileged protection, but that the union did not look out for the interests of the Latino workers. As a result of these reputed advantages, the Latino workers charged that the Black workers were permitted to sleep during work hours and also to leave work early, saying that their time cards were missing or lost, and leaving the foreman to sign their cards for them as if they had completed the shift.

Rather than recognizing the Black workers' insubordination as a potential example of resistance that they might emulate, however, the Latino workers at Imperial Enterprises tended to perceive only "laziness." While the Latino workers certainly had sound reasons for resenting the unresponsiveness of their union officials—including the failure to conduct union meetings with Spanish translation, and using the existence of ESL classes as an excuse, saying, "You're in the class, you should speak English"—it turned out nonetheless that at least one of the other union stewards was Puerto Rican. Likewise, shortly before Josie had visited the class, earlier that same evening, Fernando (who was Mexican) and Ramón (who was Puerto Rican) had together enthusiastically related how they had themselves threatened their boss (albeit only indirectly, by insinuation)— precisely what they claimed African American coworkers routinely did with impunity.

About a year and a half later, during an interview in the home of Alfredo Reynosa, another Mexican/migrant worker from the same ESL group at Imperial Enterprises, similar themes emerged about the unfair advantages of the Black workers as opposed to the Latinos:

> Okay, look: sometimes there are problems...a problem happens to you on a machine—you get cut, you get bruised [...] there's one thing that one (who's a worker, a factory worker) notices...very, very much over many other things— that being Latino, being Latino, you're a little...neglected in many things. Nevertheless—I hope it's not bad what I'm saying, but there is one thing— that should a Black, a white, get bruised or get cut, get injured—a Puerto Rican, the Puerto Rican is still almost, almost, almost the same as us—but should he be Black, it's as if it were God [*que se lastima un moreno, un güero, un portorriqueñ— todavía el portorriqueño es casi, casi casi igual que nosotro—pero que sea moreno es como si fuera Dios*]. Okay, but you also have to take into account that the Blacks [*los morenos*]...had...a long spell of slavery, but because of that we're not going to repeat it—may they give me a punch in the mouth if I'm saying that, if I'm sneering at that—no-o-o, me, my respect is for all people—but yes, there is one thing that one notices that whatever may happen to the Latino, what may happen to him is very different than...than other people—I'm referring to Blacks or whites, right [*morenos o güeros*]. There is where there begins—such a kind of impotence in the sense that...why, why those things occur, but they occur—who can explain them?

It is striking here that Alfredo explicitly invoked a Latino identity, premised on the sense that "the Puerto Rican is still almost, almost, almost the same" as "us" Mexicans. Alfredo's excessive qualifying of "the Puerto Rican" as similar but not quite the same as Mexicans, clearly, underscored a distinct ambivalence about the Latinidad he invoked. But he most certainly did nevertheless invoke that Latinidad, and he did so in contradistinction to both whites and Blacks, but most forcefully in opposition to Blacks. This was true even while Alfredo admirably tried to distance his own sense of Latino disadvantage from any conclusively negative judgment of Blacks as a group.

In spite of Alfredo's more delicate observations, however, the Mexican/ migrant and Puerto Rican workers at Imperial had seemed singularly united in their allegation that Blacks were "lazy." Perhaps a month after Josie's visit to the ESL class, De Genova had introduced enlarged photographs taken on the factory floor, as a pedagogical device intended to evoke classroom conversation about the labor process in the plant. There were a variety of relatively benign jokes about the coworkers visible in the photos—this one works too hard, that one works too slow, another talks too much, etc. But then, one of the Puerto Rican workers, Ramón, declared, "Oh, and there's Jimmy [one of the African American workers]—he's sleeping just behind [machine #] 709!" The claim that Jimmy was sleeping on the job had been intended to be sufficient in and of itself, but De Genova gullibly examined the photo more closely, and demanded, "Where is Jimmy?" As if to make the racialized content of the joke more blatant, Ramón replied, "Here he is!...Oh, no—it's just a black oil drum!" The group broke into loud laughter. This inspired Héctor (another Puerto Rican worker) to relate, "You know what was the first word I learned in English? The first word I learned in English is 'nigger.' You know why? Because I was working with a Black guy." De Genova asked, "Did you learn it from him?" Héctor responded emphatically, "No, but that's the first word I learned—because I was *working* with him." It was abundantly evident in these comments that the equation of African Americans with laziness (and the implicit valorization of "hard work") became conjoined with the denigration of racial Blackness, and that this conjuncture became one kind of condition of possibility for the sense of a shared (racialized) identity—as "Latinos"—to be mutually invoked by Mexican migrants and Puerto Ricans.

Another context in which Mexican migrants and Puerto Ricans aspired toward a mutual recognition through their shared sense of Latino identity emerged in relation to sharing physical space, and avoiding residential proximity to African Americans. Haydée Colón, a resident of Logan Square, invoked Latinidad in opposition to African Americans when she was describing the reason why she and her family had moved out of her previous neighborhood. When Ramos-Zayas interviewed Colón in October of 1994, Haydée explained why she moved from the South Side neighborhood where she had first lived after arriving in Chicago in the 1970s. Haydée mentioned:

> We moved to the North because of work convenience, housing, always seeking specific areas, wherever there were Latinos. The area where we used to live before then was getting spoiled with all the Blacks [*prietos*] moving in. It was customary that, when one Puerto Rican would move, all others would follow.

Haydée implied that the origins of a Puerto Rican community were principally cemented through a movement away from Blackness. Haydée recognized that, in addition to seeking general convenience (closeness to work, housing), the combined concerns of having "Latinos" as neighbors and avoiding Blacks were the leading motivations for Puerto Ricans to migrate to the North Side. Haydée's reference to African Americans as "*prietos*" (rather than "*morenos*" or "*negros*," for instance) accentuates the derogatory tone of her comment.[3] By reserving the term "*prieto*" for African Americans, many Puerto Rican barrio residents (regardless of phenotype) were intent to avoid being racialized as "Black," a term reserved for African Americans. This denigration of Blackness was further reiterated by the allegation that once African Americans moved in, the neighborhood would "get spoiled." In this sense, Latinidad emerged as a strategy for the avoidance of Blackness, the results of which have been especially perilous for Puerto Ricans, who often have themselves been racialized by other Latinos as equivalent to "the Blacks."

A critical aspect of Puerto Ricans' will to deflect being racialized as "Black" included commonplace invocations of the racial triad mythology of Puerto Rican national origin, originating in the history of the Spanish colonization of the Antilles, according to which Puerto Ricans are the product of a mixture of Spanish, indigenous Taíno, and African "bloods." These three "racial" components of the Puerto Rican "nation" tended to be weighted differently, according to context and the particular agendas being promoted, but generally were depicted in ways that privileged "whiteness" (the Spanish) and downplayed "blackness" (the African). In principle, Puerto Ricans' invocation of this racialized national-origin myth in Chicago may have tended to emphasize Puerto Ricans' racial uniqueness, not only in contrast to African Americans, but also vis-à-vis Mexicans, and thus would seem to have favored Puerto Rican nationalism over Latinismo. However, Puerto Rican assertions of the racial triad in fact tended to enable the incorporation of Puerto Ricans into a broader Latinidad, precisely by subordinating the African as merely one of three elements in the triad, and by maintaining that this constitutively "racially mixed" Puerto Ricanness was conclusively distinct from African American Blackness. While most Puerto Ricans in Chicago (and perhaps in other areas of the U.S. as well) would readily recite the racial triad in discussions of Puerto Rican identity—"We have Spanish, African, and Taíno Indian blood"—the Spanish element in the triad of Puerto Rican racial identity was given precedence in those instances when the deployment of a shared Latinidad between Mexicans and Puerto Ricans could serve to affirm their shared difference from African Americans.

Puerto Rican youth did, indeed, embrace a sense of Latino commonality with Mexicans in racially mixed contexts that brought them together with African Americans. This became strikingly evident when Ramos-Zayas and other teachers, staff, and students from various Chicago alternative high schools attended a "cultural diversity" festival at Foundations Alternative High School, a predominantly African American high school on the North Side. Latino Heritage, a predominantly Mexican alternative high school, along with a predominantly Puerto Rican and a mixed Latino high school, were all invited to the festival. One of the main events of the celebration consisted of poetry readings by students and staff. Some Mexican students stood in one corner of the large classroom, where the activities were to take place, while the Puerto Rican students gathered in the middle and the rear. The Black students were at the opposite end of the room. Almost as soon as a young Mexican woman had begun reading an autobiographical poem in Spanish, her classmates became frustrated and offended by the behavior of some of the other students in the audience who were visibly and disruptively ignoring the Mexican student's recitation. One of the Mexican teachers reprimanded a group of African American students and told them that it was disrespectful not to listen to the young woman reading the poem. She addressed her comments to a group of Black students who had been evidently surprised when the poem was recited in a language that they did not understand, and had begun to giggle. Some of the African American students complained or made jokes about the fact that they simply did not understand the language. One student declared, "They should speak English. We're in America." Confronted with the Black students' adversity, many of the Puerto Rican students who had avoided sitting next to the Mexican students from Latino Heritage High School (with whom they had had an ongoing rivalry throughout the academic year) began listening more attentively to the poems, despite the fact that many of them did not understand any more Spanish than did the African American students. A symbolic claim to the Spanish language, even among English-dominant U.S.-born Puerto Ricans, enabled the Puerto Rican students to demonstrate a solidarity with the Mexican woman reading the poem, as well as her Mexican classmates and teacher who were requesting the audience's attention to the Spanish poem. In this instance, the Spanish language, which had not ordinarily been a particularly compelling source of commonality, became the shared "cultural" element around which Puerto Rican and Mexican youth developed a sense of Latinidad in racialized opposition to the Black students. Among English-dominant Puerto Ricans, in this instance, the Spanish language was mobilized symbolically for the purposes of an identity formation process in which Puerto Ricans and Mexicans felt compelled to distinguish themselves from African Americans.

Ironically, throughout the putative "cultural diversity" activity, Puerto Ricans aligned themselves with Mexicans and upheld a notion of their shared Latinidad precisely as a way of distancing themselves from Blacks. The Mexican student's poetry recitation in Spanish was followed by a monologue by an African American performer from an Afrocentric cultural center located near Foundations High School. One of the lines in the performer's monologue declared, "All of us are one race: the African race . . . of different shades." Mexican and Puerto Rican students alike immediately expressed their disagreement with that phrase by sighing, rolling their eyes, frowning, and talking among themselves. Vanessa, a sophomore at one of the predominantly Puerto Rican high schools, quickly approached one of the young Puerto Rican teachers standing next to Ramos-Zayas to remark disdainfully, "These people don't know anything about our heritage."

The students' discomfort became so obvious and disruptive that some of the teachers began telling the students to be quiet, that they could express their opinions later. A few days after the incident, some of the Puerto Rican students at the alternative high school where Ramos-Zayas volunteered seemed to agree with Alicia, a junior at the high school, when she remarked, "I think the Blacks were disrespectful of us. Because you know, I don't know Spanish either, but I was paying attention to what that Mexican girl was saying. Because I know that Spanish is part of our heritage, and I respect that. But those Black girls that were sitting behind me, they were making comments up and down, they were saying negative things about the language and making fun of it." Elena Colón, a teacher who had not attended the activity, but who was listening to the students' descriptions of the event, teased the students by saying, "At least you guys didn't fight with Latino Heritage." In the hope of provoking the students to recognize the counterproductive or even self-defeating dimensions of their own antagonism toward the Mexican students, Elena was reminding them of the ongoing rivalry—involving basketball competitions exacerbated by gang feuds—that had recurred throughout the school year between the students of the Puerto Rican alternative high school and the predominantly Mexican students of Latino Heritage. In response to Elena's comments, however, Mario Figueroa, a senior at the high school, reaffirmed his distrust and resentment of the Mexican students: "If it had been one of us up there doing the poetry, I don't know if they [the Mexican students] would have stood up for us like we stood up for that Mexican girl." He added that a group of Mexican students from Latino Heritage had assumed that he was a student at the predominantly African American high school. A Puerto Rican with curly hair who was not particularly dark-skinned, Mario interpreted the Mexican students' incorrect assumption about which school he attended to indicate that Mexicans were generally inclined to diminish or disregard the "racial" differences between African Americans and Puerto Ricans. Invoking the Puerto Rican racial triad, Mario remarked, "Neither Mexicans nor Blacks understand that Puerto Ricans are a mixture of three races, not just African, but also Taíno Indian and Spanish." Despite these U.S.-born Puerto Ricans' claim to the Spanish language, and the selective instances in which a Latinidad was deployed among Mexicans and Puerto Ricans, particularly vis-à-vis African Americans, their Latinismo proved nonetheless to be quite fragile. Although Mario was proud of himself and his classmates for having supported the Mexican girl who had been ridiculed for reading her poem in Spanish, he also questioned the Mexicans' potential for reciprocity, particularly in light of the fact, as he saw it, that some of the Mexican students had "insulted" him—or implicitly excluded him from their own notions of "Latino" identity—by assuming that he was Black. Mario's insistence on the Puerto Rican "racial triad"—in spite of its African component—sought to deflect any possible identification of his identity as "Puerto Rican" with the Blackness of African Americans.

The proposition that there was an "Indianness" which Puerto Ricans and Mexicans both could claim might have provided another plausible if improbable commonality between the two groups. However, in our research, no articulation of Latinidad among Puerto Ricans and Mexicans was ever sustained on the basis of claims of a shared "Indianness." The mythological Taíno Indian ancestry was resurrected in Mario's remarks in concert with Spanish "blood," but ultimately in a way that subordinated the indigenous element of the triad to the dominant European. Thus, in a manner characteristic of the underlying Eurocentrism of many Latin American nationalist ideologies of racial mixture (*mestizaje*), the assertion of the Puerto Rican racial triad was deployed in the service of a process that implicitly privileged racial whitening (*blanqueamiento*). Puerto Ricans' claims to a Taíno Indian heritage tended to be figured as a symbolic or mythic feature rather than a salient social identity in everyday life.[4] Above all, it served to reaffirm that Puerto Ricans, as a people, were not merely a combination of white and Black.

Puerto Ricans in Chicago confined their "Taíno"-ness to the triadic origin myth, and thus differentiated it from the "real" Indianness attributed to other Latinos, especially Mexicans and Central Americans. In fact, the Taíno Indians—reclaimed retrospectively as a symbol of "Puerto Rican" resistance to colonialism and figured as the revered third "bloodline" in the national origin myth—were conceptualized as markedly distinct from the contemporary social reality of indigenous populations in Mexico. When the Puerto Rican students in Ramos-Zayas's class visited a predominantly Mexican middle school on the South Side, for instance, they made numerous comments about a mural that depicted Spanish conquest motifs alongside an insignia of the Zapatista (EZLN) rebellion and a presumably more contemporary landscape of indigenous life in a rural community in Mexico. One of the students joked that the "Indians" in the mural resembled the Taínos. To this, another student replied, "But Mexicans have real Indians. We [Puerto Ricans] have Indian blood in our heritage, but we are not *Indian* Indian." This student at some level recognized the subjugation of indigenous communities in Mexico; his claim that "the Mexicans have real Indians," moreover, suggested that indigenous populations in Mexico are not quite "Mexican," but rather are merely a possession, a subordinated population that Mexicans "have." Furthermore, he also comprehended to some extent the racialized denigration among Mexicans of their own "Indian"-ness. The racialized figure of "Indian"-ness, therefore, did not supply Mexicans and Puerto Ricans with a common ground for their Latinidad based upon indigeneity in the Americas, but it did nonetheless serve to reconstitute a racialized middle ground between whiteness and Blackness that both groups navigated in contradictory ways.

The perception among many Puerto Ricans that Mexicans were racially "more Indian" did, furthermore, occasionally find expression in terms of differences between the two groups' gendered bodies. Puerto Rican youth and even adult teachers, working in the popular-education programs where Ramos-Zayas volunteered, readily racialized certain female body types in ways that routinely bestowed greater sensual qualities upon Puerto Rican women. For instance, a few weeks prior to the announcement that Selena would be played by Jennifer López, a group of Puerto Rican students had been invited to a reopening ceremony at the Rudy Lozano School, a predominantly Mexican public middle/high school in the West Town neighborhood. At one point, Ramos-Zayas asked Steve O'Neil, a white teacher who worked at Excel High School, an alternative high school sponsored by a not-for-profit organization in West Town, if a particular group of students standing in the back of the auditorium were Puerto Rican. Overhearing the conversation, Mike, a student visiting from the alternative high school, interrupted, explaining, "You can tell if someone is Mexican or Puerto Rican by looking at their ass." A group of students sitting nearby started giggling, and Héctor, a Junior at Excel High School added, "Yeah, you see, Puerto Ricans have an ass and Mexicans are flat-assed—they have an Indian ass." Noticing that O'Neil and Ramos-Zayas were uncomfortable with the boys' explanation, another student, Adela, in an effort to problematize Mike and Héctor's comments, while still participating in the joke, asserted, "Selena had a big ass..." Referring to the popular Mexican singer, Héctor agreed: "Yeah, Selena was real pretty. She looked Puerto Rican, you know. She had an ass." The conversation about the relative merits of each group's presumably characteristic asses became more definitively gendered when Héctor contended further that "women who have big tits have flat asses. If you really want to know if a woman has a flat ass, you just look at her chest. That's why you have a lot of Mexican women who are big on top and have no ass." This exchange among these Puerto Rican adolescents was perhaps the most explicit claim of a biological notion of racial difference between Mexicans and Puerto Ricans that Ramos-Zayas ever encountered. In contrast to their own pronounced sense of a "racial" difference between themselves and Mexicans' purported "Indian"-ness, however, this particular group of students frequently discussed their sense that white people, in particular, were unable to distinguish between Puerto Ricans and Mexicans (or other Latinos). They recognized that both whites and African Americans frequently assumed that Puerto Ricans and all Latinos were simply "Mexican," or tended to homogenize them together under the generic racialized labels of "Hispanic" or "Latino," which delineated a racial category that was neither white nor Black.

Latinidad as an Articulation of Working-Class Solidarity

If Latinidad sometimes emerged as a basis of racialized solidarity among Mexican migrants and Puerto Ricans, specifically against African Americans, it nevertheless tended to be fractured by class divisions generated through contentious relations of labor subordination. In the DuraPress factory, the Mexican/migrant majority of the workforce commonly called a Puerto Rican supervisor "Boricua," marking his Puerto Ricanness, whereas they tended to not differentiate themselves strongly from their Puerto Rican coworkers (who were rather few). As we saw in chapter 6, even when Carmen teased Yadira about how Puerto Ricans speak Spanish, she reserved her more blunt opinions about Puerto Ricans' "bad" English (which she racialized as "Black") for when Yadira was not present. In the same factory, the personnel boss was a Puerto Rican woman named Rita, who prided herself on the paternalistic rapport she cultivated with the mainly Mexican/migrant workforce. The workers, for their part, acknowledged this condescension sarcastically by referring to her as "Mamá" and "Tía" (Aunt), but ultimately rejected her specifically cross-class overtures of Latinidad, especially during a protracted period of conflict when the workers were engaged in a struggle to certify a union in the plant, when they began to refer to her as "La Cucaracha," the cockroach.[5]

In the interview with Alfredo Reynosa from Imperial Enterprises (discussed above), similar themes emerged, simultaneously foregrounding a Latinidad grounded in the shared plight of Latino workers and lamenting the tenuousness of such Latino solidarity due to the fractures of class:

> Many times, the bosses...if it's a Latino, if it's a Latino, well—you don't feel the support very fully, a good support, no-o-o; on the contrary, there are [...] Latino supervisors who...who put you down. Many times, I think, it's because of how they feel that, "No, if I let him rise higher, most likely, he passes me up—and he's going to replace me." But I don't think that's true, because [...] we are people—the majority—[people] of good sentiments to the effect that with work...you complete your job—and then some! [...] But what's also missing is unity—because of that, there's no strength. [...] But why, I wonder, don't we have a compatriot ideal, so to speak, here in this country? Because if we were, ooh, more united, with more patriotic feeling to the effect that one should say, "No, this happened to so-and-so, let's go help him, yes, if we help them, yes, we help ourselves." But in any case, there's a lack of that—and with those who give us orders in our jobs, that's how it is automatically—it's like nothing...because you cut yourself, you get injured, "nah, nah, nah, you work, get going, and if not..."—it's happened many times—"and if you don't like your job, there's the door."...Nevertheless, to a white, to a Black, they don't do that. Why? Because it's a white, because it's a Black [*Sin embargo a un güero, un moreno no le hacen eso. ¿Por qué? Porque es güero, porque es moreno*].
>
> And as I say, the Puerto Rican and the Central American is the same as us— overworked to death, mistreated. [...] We arrive and we do jobs that the white [*el güero*] doesn't do, Blacks [*morenos*] don't do it...and nevertheless, how one feels in the flesh as if he were a type of beast...as if he's screwed over so that he can just be screwed over some more. Aah, Nico, how lacking is a little humanity for each person. Maybe I'm wrong...but no, because...because the things you see, they're felt, they touch you at every moment. [...] In the workplaces, for not knowing the language.... I say, "If I leave my job, I'm going to struggle to find another one, although here I have such-and-such problems..." In any event, it's...it's like...like a long aftertaste of impotence...that...[here, Alfredo let out a deep sigh] doesn't let us express that feeling because they bridle you, they silence you. [...] Ohh, so many things, so difficult sometimes to explain, in the system of one who is an immigrant.

While Alfredo here again invoked a Latinidad produced in racialized opposition to whiteness and Blackness, he now asserted an unequivocal sameness or equivalence between Mexicans and Puerto Ricans (and also Central Americans)—as workers and finally, as (im)migrants—in a class-inflected opposition, above all, to specifically Latino bosses. Notably, while this shared Latinidad was invoked among coworkers who all continued to be identifiable according to their national or regional particularities, in this instance, Alfredo applied the more generic label "Latino" only to those whose class difference was seen to subvert the possibility of a specifically working-class Latino community.[6] The lack of "unity," "patriotic feeling," and "a compatriot ideal" that served to undermine a genuine Latino solidarity in Alfredo's account, were particularly symptomatic of a perceived betrayal, on the part of those Latinos who had achieved some measure of greater power in the U.S. (specifically in relation to the white owners and upper management of the factories where they were employed), against those other Latinos who were their subordinates in the workplace. Indeed, Latino bosses seemed to Alfredo to be committed above all else to demonstrating their greater loyalty and devotion to whites and Blacks.

Against Latino politicians and professionals, poor Puerto Rican residents of the Humboldt Park barrio similarly invoked a commonality of interest among Latinos in class-specific terms. In the summer of 1995, Roberto Clemente High School was in the media spotlight for the controversial involvement of Puerto Rican nationalist activists in school curriculum development and an alleged misuse of state funds (Flores-González, 2002; Ramos-Zayas, 1998). This high-profile controversy, fueled by front-page articles in the major Chicago newspapers which charged that the high school had "terrorist links," became a critical instance in which Puerto Ricans in Humboldt Park and West Town embraced a class-specific Latinidad, that implicitly downplayed local markers of Puerto Ricanness in favor of a more inclusive Latino identity, but restricted Latino solidarity to poor and working-class barrio residents. During this controversy, Latino-identified not-for-profit and research agencies, such as the Latino Institute, stepped forward to act as spokespersons on behalf of the high school staff, parents, and students, by proclaiming that "Latinos" were outraged by allegations of "terrorist links" (Espinosa, 1995). In this sense, the media's accusations that Roberto Clemente High School was a bastion of specifically Puerto Rican–identified corruption, unconcerned parents, and promiscuous or violent youth were countered with an explicit Latinismo deployed as the official response of "the community." At a more grassroots level, however, the alliances that parents such as Alma Juncos drew as a consequence of these media attacks were based on a spatially inflected class solidarity, rather than a generic cross-class Latinismo. For instance, in a conversation among Alma, her Puerto Rican best friend, Elda, and Claudia, a Guatemalan parent, Alma explained that the attacks on Roberto Clemente High School reflected Latino professionals' disrespect for the involvement in the school of "people who are poor." Claudia and Elda agreed, and Claudia affirmed that she had heard that the latest article criticizing Roberto Clemente High School had been written by a Latino. When asked whether they knew if the Latino in question had been a Puerto Rican, Elda replied, "No, not Puerto Rican, some other race." A distinction between Puerto Ricans and other Latinos was sustained, even as the spatially specific class category of barrio "poor" could encompass people from all Latino groups. Rather than prioritizing any overt notion of Latinidad as the basis for this solidarity, social inequalities of wealth and power were evoked. However, nationality-based distinctions among Latinos were notably downplayed all the same. For these poor and working-class Puerto Ricans, then, to the extent that it became viable, Latinismo was understood through a complex conflation of class identities and racialization processes. Local Latino politicians who harbored aspirations of developing broader Latino electoral constituencies, moreover, later piggybacked on these events, precisely by recapitulating a class- and space-specific language of Latino solidarity.

Latinidad as a Strategy of Middle-Class Formation

When Ramos-Zayas asked Tamika Miranda and Brenda Ramírez, two college-educated Puerto Ricans, and Marisol Lozano, their U.S.-born Mexican coworker at Horizons Youth Initiative, a national "Puerto Rican/Latino" not-for-profit social service agency in West Town, about the perceived lack of unity between Mexicans and Puerto Ricans in Chicago, they emphatically denied that the frictions or antagonisms between Mexicans and Puerto Ricans were as serious as was often claimed, for example, in reporting by the news media. These upwardly mobile, college-educated women in their mid-twenties deployed a rather pious Latinismo as a middle-class politics of coalition. Their distinctive way of upholding their identity as Latinas had been produced in very specific institutional contexts that were inseparable from promoting upward social mobility, namely, their own higher education as well as their place of employment, a not-for-profit organization concerned with educational and career opportunities, explicitly devoted to serving all Latino groups.

Admitting that Chicago was a highly segregated city and aware of the rifts these particular urban patterns caused between Mexicans and Puerto Ricans, Marisol asserted, "Latinos have learned how to stand together when they need to." Marisol mentioned that there had been problems in the workplace instigated by a Puerto Rican woman named Carmen Vargas, a worker at Horizons who believed that the revered, late founder of the youth organization, a Puerto Rican woman, had not intended for Horizons Youth Initiative to be "for Mexicans," but rather only "for Puerto Ricans." Vargas had argued that that they needed to revisit Horizons' original philosophy and mission to ensure that the organization was genuinely fulfilling the needs of Puerto Rican youth in particular, and not embracing the "Latino" label as a requisite convenience simply to secure state funding. This created some divisions within Horizons Youth Initiative, since many of the agency's clients, as well as some of its employees, were Mexican. Implicitly referring to this context of contentious Puerto Rican resistance to the broader "Latino"-identified mission of the organization, and teasing her Puerto Rican coworkers, Marisol added, "At the Horizons Youth Initiative, the Mexicans are the ones who are more devoted to the [Latino] cause. Although for some of the Puerto Ricans who work there, Horizons Youth Initiative is just their job, for the Mexicans it's a way of fighting for the cause." At this point, however, despite her playful claim that Mexicans were more sincere and committed "Latinos," Marisol was careful to qualify her own role as a Mexican in relation to the plight of Puerto Ricans; she continued, "That's not to say that I think I'm better-qualified than a Puerto Rican to help the Puerto Ricans. If a Puerto Rican came along and could do my job, I would understand that the job was given to him or her instead of to me. I'm an ally of the Puerto Rican community, but I understand that it's not my community."

Committed to an explicit politics of Latino-identified coalition, therefore, these women were nevertheless quite aware of the distinct and sometimes contentious claims of their respective Mexican and Puerto Rican "communities." Brenda Ramírez, who had been Marisol's college roommate and was not only her coworker but also a very close friend, reaffirmed that the Mexican employees at Horizons Youth Initiative were working for "the Puerto Rican cause" as allies. When Ramos-Zayas asked her what she meant by "the Puerto Rican cause," Ramírez clarified that she was referring to both the cause of educational advancement for Puerto Ricans in the U.S. and also the political goal of national self-determination for Puerto Rico. Brenda also expressed her opinion that the internal conflicts in the organization were in fact "external attempts by white society to set us off against each other." Marisol added, "I wish we could convey this message to others, but these things are so subtle that it's hard to do." These young women were unusually politicized and aware of the ways in which white supremacy worked to systematically undermine many possibilities for the formation of Latinidad or the advancement of Latinismo. Furthermore, they emphasized the specifically *racial* politics of the Latinidad they promoted. Their self-conscious deployment of "Latino" identities, and the explicit positing of Latinidad as a racial formation counterpoised to "white society," however, also involved a recognition of class differences within Latinidad. They mobilized a fairly self-conscious position of their own relative privilege as college-educated, upwardly mobile or newly "middle-class" Latinas, and an acute sense of their own consequent responsibilities, as indicated by a persistent emphasis on "giving back" to their communities. Becoming upwardly mobile and navigating the educational and occupational institutions that enabled such class mobility, however, contributed to a shifting process of racial identification among these women. In a sense, while retaining and accommodating their more elementary identities as "Mexican" and "Puerto Rican," primarily based in the working-class experiences of their childhoods and pre-college years, these young women's political orientations and actions tended to confirm a sense that exclusively identifying with Mexicanness or Puerto Ricanness would fail to fully satisfy the requirements of their upward social mobility. The process of becoming "middle-class" was consonant with "becoming Latino."

On one occasion, while driving through Downtown Chicago with Tamika, Marisol, and Brenda, Tamika Miranda called Ramos-Zayas's attention to a particular nightclub that, she explained, was emblematic for her of "the buppy social scene." Tamika was a light-skinned Puerto Rican woman who was romantically involved with an African American man; she was also a part-time law student. Referring to the elite African American–identified nightclub, she remarked, "Only 'beautiful people' go there. If you don't look like Whitney Houston or Denzel Washington, forget it! To get reservations there, you probably have to be Oprah or Michael Jordan." Tamika's comment revealed both an awareness of the material achievements as well as what she perceived to be the elitist exclusivity of the African American middle class. Indeed, Brenda, Marisol, and Tamika deployed an upwardly aspiring middle-class Latinismo as an identity formation in explicit contradistinction to the example they perceived among many middle-class African Americans whom they considered "sellouts." Marisol, a Mexican who had grown up in the U.S. Southwest and had come to Chicago for college, but had stayed and chose to live on the North Side of Chicago after graduating from the University of Illinois, viewed upwardly aspiring middle-class Blacks as materialistic and likely to desert their presumably poor or working-class communities of origin. She believed that, unlike many affluent African Americans, Latinos did not tend to abandon "the community," but rather tried to stay close to their roots and create services for their poorer counterparts. "Logan Square is a diverse community," she affirmed. "Many of the people who live in Logan Square are Latinos, even Latino professionals, who have settled there so that they can be close to their jobs in social service agencies in Humboldt Park and the poorer areas of the community." When Marisol and Brenda had decided to room together, they deliberately looked for an apartment in Logan Square.

The neighborhood where Marisol and Brenda chose to live accentuated their self-consciously middle-class sense of Latinidad, which had been cultivated both during their college experience and further through their employment in a Latino not-for-profit agency. In a housewarming party they held, Marisol and Brenda were happy to be living in an area that they positively described as "working-class" and "Latino," but which they also considered to be very socially mixed. Indeed, such constructions of Latinidad facilitated the formulation of a middle-class identity among college-educated Latinos from working-class backgrounds. This way of being both "middle-class" and "Latino"—rooted in an affirmative sense of "giving back" or "serving the community," and "remembering where you came from" without "selling out"— appeared to couple politically committed goals and middle-class aspirations in a manner that were

presumed to be significantly different from the allegedly materialistic preoccupations of the African American "buppies." The emphasis that Brenda and
Marisol, and to a lesser extent Tamika, placed on "staying in the community"
and being suspicious of a potentially seductive world of corporate careers that
presumably became available with college degrees, suggested the possibility of a
Latinidad among Mexicans and Puerto Ricans with higher educational credentials and middle-class aspirations grounded in a middle-class formation that
was distinguished in racialized terms, in contradistinction to both the Black
and white middle classes, as well as the hegemony of "white society" more
generally.

Ricardo Pérez, a Puerto Rican executive at the same not-for-profit organization where Marisol, Brenda, and Tamika worked, nonetheless complained that
professional Puerto Rican women seemed increasingly to be marrying middle-
class African American men. When Ramos-Zayas asked him why he thought this
to be the case, he replied, "Well, Puerto Rican women have on average higher
educational levels than Puerto Rican men. And if you look here in Chicago,
those men who have the better jobs and more education are African American."
Ricardo proceeded to give examples of college-educated Puerto Rican women
who worked in his agency, one of whom was Tamika, who were either married
to or dating African Americans. Notably, marriage to middle-class white men—
who likewise "have the better jobs and more education"—seemed nonetheless to
be largely beyond the realm of possibility in Ricardo's appraisal of what he constructed to be an interracial gendered strategy of upward class mobility. The view
that Puerto Rican women were "marrying up" by marrying professional African
American men was fairly common and somewhat counterintuitive, given the
marginality and poverty otherwise ubiquitously associated with Black people.
This by no means suggests that upwardly mobile Puerto Ricans in Chicago harbored no prejudice toward African Americans, but rather that these middle-class
Puerto Ricans tended to see African Americans in more complex ways that appreciated the socially differentiated contexts in which class and racial identities
were mutually constituted.

Tamika had been dating her African American boyfriend, Robert, for over
three years. A successful businessman in his early thirties, Robert owned a
fashionable duplex loft apartment near Downtown Chicago. On one occasion,
Brenda, who at this point was working in a Humboldt Park health clinic, and
Marisol, who continued to be employed as Tamika's coworker at Horizons,
asked Tamika if she did not miss having a boyfriend with whom she could speak
Spanish. By implication, these two Latinas appeared to presuppose that shared
Spanish language was a premier basis for Latinidad. Tamika responded:

> Well . . . I did have a Mexican boyfriend when I was in college. He used to go
> to Harvard and now works for General Motors. But we never spoke Spanish
> among ourselves. It's not that important for me to speak Spanish with Robert.

I have my culture and Robert has his. This is not something we have to share.
Each one can keep his [sic] individuality.

Tamika did not consider her relationship with her Mexican ex-boyfriend as
having been based on a Latinidad derived from any linguistic commonality;
instead, she emphasized their shared social and educational context, and, by
implication, their presumably similar class mobility aspirations. The commonalities as Latinos that they had shared and that she had appreciated, it became
more evident, were those that she attributed to the possibility of participating in
each other's extracurricular and social activities in college, such as collaborating
in inviting Latino authors to campus and publicizing events through common
groups of friends, Puerto Rican and Mexican alike. Although Spanish language
could be deployed symbolically as a marker of Latino difference, it was more
likely that similar Latino social networks and college experience, rather than the
Spanish language, served as a common ground among many second-generation,
upwardly mobile Latinos.

While Brenda and Marisol seemed to consider language as an important aspect of their intimate relations, they nevertheless did not explicitly contend that
language was necessarily critical in the formation of a Latinidad. Indeed, even
though these three young women espoused an overt politics of Latinismo which
foregrounded the importance of shared Spanish language for the consolidation
of a Latino political identity in institutional contexts, as second-generation
Latinas, they acknowledged that Spanish langauge was not at all paramount.
In fact, Marisol concurred with Tamika's reply and revised the implications of
her original question. Marisol responded that what mattered most for her was
not even finding an intimate partner who spoke Spanish, but rather that she
wanted to find someone who shared her Mexican background, and would be
willing to return with her to the Southwest as well. Despite her declared politics of
Latinismo, Marisol was not finally inclined to subsume altogether her particular
"national" or "cultural" specificity as a "Mexican" under a broader construction
of Latino identity. More importantly for our purposes here, however, Marisol's
recourse to a specifically Mexican "cultural" particularism reframed her original
question about Tamika's African American boyfriend as one that was not really
about Spanish language at all, as such, and was, in effect, much more about the
fact that Tamika's boyfriend was Black rather than Puerto Rican (or at least,
Latino). In this light, Marisol's initial concern about shared Spanish language
may have appeared to be suggestive of a Latino "cultural" identity, but once
language came to be so readily deemphasized in both Tamika's and her own
ensuing remarks, it became more evident that her Latinismo in this instance
more forcefully articulated a Latino *racial* formation.

Some Latinos in managerial positions at not-for-profit agencies in the Puerto
Rican community, such as Jorge Irizarry, a middle-class Puerto Rican man in
his mid-forties, who was the assistant director at Horizons, would routinely

emphasize the sense that Puerto Ricans and Mexicans should identify as "Latinos" or "Hispanics":

> Among Latino groups, including Puerto Ricans and Mexicans, there should be stronger ties. Because here, we're either white, black, or Latino ... not white, black, Puerto Rican, or Mexican. That unity [between Puerto Ricans and Mexicans] is not there and I don't think it's being promoted, nor do I think that it's going to be there in the future.

Like other Puerto Rican professionals, Jorge sponsored a politics of Latinismo, which conformed and responded to dominant racial categories. Still, Jorge had to admit that such a Latino unity between Mexicans and Puerto Ricans seemed unlikely. Indeed, as managers and professionals like Jorge saw it, the Latinidad that their organizations promoted was at odds with more working-class and barrio-identified groups who overtly endorsed various expressions of Puerto Rican nationalism. Jorge believed that such recalcitrant particularisms were an obstacle to consolidating the necessary political unity among Latinos that might adequately advance the best common ("racial") interests of Mexicans and Puerto Ricans. In Jorge's account, the creation of a viable Latinidad was, therefore, the presumed duty of the upwardly mobile educated professionals. Such a Latinidad was a beleaguered proposition, however, not only because it always existed in tension with the more "nationalist" or "chauvinistic" pursuits of grassroots activists, but also because once a Latino attained a position of political or occupational authority, the prevailing tendency was nonetheless to advocate narrowly for his or her own national-origin group.

Within their institutions, however, program managers like Jorge also had to contend with the pressure that they consciously hire mixed Latino personnel who could be representative of and responsive to a diverse Latino reality in the West Town and Humboldt Park neighborhoods. This was true even in cases where the "community" that their organizations primarily or originally served was conceptualized in national terms—as "Puerto Rican." The executive director of the National Puerto Rican Forum at the time, for instance, insisted, "We have every group represented here [at the agency]. We have Puerto Ricans, Argentines, Colombians, Mexicans ... and we like it that way." Latinismo had become a more or less official position for the middle-class professionals charged with conducting the affairs of these social service agencies and not-for-profit community organizations.

Frank Rivera, who also worked for Horizons Youth Initiative, the same organization that Jorge directed, exuded the concomitant tendency of Puerto Rican professionals to blame barrio residents—and grassroots Puerto Rican "nationalist" politics in Humboldt Park, in particular—for subverting efforts to advance the cause of Latinidad.[7] Prior to starting his position at Horizons, Frank had had minimal contact with the Puerto Rican barrio. His parents, having grown up in a very poor neighborhood in Gary, Indiana, had later made deliberate efforts to raise their children "in the suburbs" and "away from the ghetto." Frank's professional contact with Roberto Clemente High School in the West Town–Humboldt Park barrio, and his role as coach for a local boys' basketball team, had occasioned his first encounters with the Puerto Rican flag monuments that had been first unveiled on Division Street in January of 1995, marking the commercial area of Humboldt Park (Ramos-Zayas, 1997). Ramos-Zayas asked Rivera what he thought of the flags:

> *Rivera:* That's the Puerto Rican community. The community there is Puerto Rican, predominantly. But I've noticed other cultures in there too. I've noticed other Latinos, Guatemalans or Colombians. But, to be honest with you, I really feel that they shouldn't have put the flag there. The reason why, because of the different cultures. You have a diverse number of groups. The Mexican area, Little Village . . . the entrance says "*Bienvenidos a la Villita.*" But they don't display the [Mexican] flag over there. They just have that "Welcome to Little Village." There's not a flag being displayed—which means that this is not Mexico; this is Chicago. But when you are putting a *flag* out there, you're almost saying, "This belongs to us."
> *Ramos-Zayas:* Would it have been different if instead of the flag they had something else . . . a *garita*, a *coquí*, something like that?
> *Rivera:* It probably would. Because it would have said that there's an influence of the [Puerto Rican] culture in that sector. It would have less of an effect on people. You see, your initial view, when you see a flag right away . . . that's telling you "this is a country." You're able to go ahead and label that area right away: "This is Puerto Rico."

Frank questioned the appropriateness of the double-gateway monuments to the Puerto Rican flag. Like other professionals, Frank suggested that Mexicans showed ethnic pride "respectfully," in accordance with an hegemonic ideology of "multiculturalism" or "ethnic pluralism" that was not exclusionary. To Frank and other white-collar workers in the Humboldt Park barrio, expressions of Mexicanness were perceived as primarily "cultural," and thus conceivably complementary to a presumably broader and more inclusive identity as "American." Puerto Ricanness and the display of the Puerto Rican flag, by contrast, were perceived as openly confrontational and an oppositional repudiation of the prospect of integration into a presumed U.S. "mainstream." In addition to the perception of Mexicans as more "cultural" and Puerto Ricans as more "political" (discussed in chapter 4), Frank's disapproval of an overtly nationalist symbol—the Puerto Rican flag—was related to his conception of Humboldt Park not as a conclusively Puerto Rican space, but as an area with a diverse Latino population. Puerto Rican barrio residents and grassroots groups were blamed for promoting a nationalist politics that, in effect, sabotaged the Latinidad that these professionals sought to forge. Moreover, in this instance, displaying the Puerto Rican flag was perceived as a willful act of presumptuous entitlement, incompatible with the "multiculturalist" discourse of pluralism endorsed by U.S. nationalism.

Puerto Rican professionals such as Jorge and Frank subscribed to the idea that, in order to ultimately achieve the privileges of the white middle class in the United States, groups with origins in Latin America must unite as a "Latino" racial or "ethnic" constituency for the purposes of securing their effective integration into the U.S. social formation. Concerning "the construction of Latino social movements," or "Latinismo," Suzanne Oboler has suggested, "It is important to incorporate the idea that they [middle-class Latinos] may also share class backgrounds and status, racial and ethnic prejudices and values that . . . can unite middle class people beyond their nationalities" (Oboler, 1995:163). These middle-class-specific values and attitudes may facilitate a sense of Latino solidarity that nevertheless serves to undermine efforts to foster unity among Latinos across class lines. In the context of a multiplicity of competing identity formations, to identify as "Latino," Oboler rightly contends, is "more than solely a culturally dictated fact of life. Identifying oneself as Latino or Latina and participating in a Latino social movement is also a *political* decision, one that aims to strengthen *la comunidad* in those terms" (Oboler, 1995:163).

The dynamic ways in which Puerto Rican barrio residents and activists, on the one hand, and middle-class professionals variously conceptualized Latinidad was linked to the spatially inflected class tensions between them. While the professional middle class in the not-for-profit sector asserted their middle-class Latinismo precisely by contending that nationalist grassroots politics associated with the barrio poor tended to corrupt possibilities for pan-Latino identification, Latinidad nonetheless became emblematic of class solidarity *within* the middle class among the suburban Latino professionals whom Ramos-Zayas interviewed. A tall, light-skinned woman in her early thirties, Ingrid Font grew up in Puerto Rico, the daughter of the general manager of a large U.S. corporation on the Island. After finishing a bachelor's degree at Northwestern University, Ingrid married Miguel, a man of Cuban descent who had been her high school sweetheart in Puerto Rico. When Miguel graduated from an engineering college in Puerto Rico, he was recruited on-campus by a leading telecomunications company that offered him a job at the company's Chicago headquarters. Miguel, Ingrid, and their two children resided in a middle-class southwestern suburb of Chicago. When asked about her community involvement, Ingrid, replied that "all the Latin Americans we know, we've met through the company's Club de Hispanos. . . . It's a very mixed group, not just Puerto Ricans. . . . I never hang out with Puerto Ricans from here [the U.S.]. Where I live is more mixed. We see ourselves as 'Hispanos.' Not 'Puerto Ricans,' but 'Hispanos.' I guess this is a loss of identity or something." Ingrid's invocation of an "Hispano" identity, despite her having only recently migrated to the U.S. from Puerto Rico, was more related to her husband's corporate affiliations than to her own relations with the

204 • Latino Crossings

other Latinos in the suburban neighborhood where she was living. Since she was also married to a man who considered himself Cuban, the Hispano label served as common "cultural" ground between them as well. Moreover, deploying an identity as "Hispanos" allowed Ingrid and Miguel to sustain their status as middle-class Puerto Ricans in a U.S. context where Puerto Ricans are stigmatized as "underclass" and racialized as nonwhite. Indeed, Ingrid was quite explicit about the distance she maintained from U.S. Puerto Ricans. In this sense, identifications as "Hispano" or "Latino" became a cherished status distinction that signaled a markedly middle-class racial formation that sustained one kind of racialized identity ("Hispano") while it repudiated and supplanted another ("Puerto Rican") that was inextricably more entangled with lower-status class connotations.

Among the upwardly mobile or upwardly aspiring middle class, identifying as "Latino" or "Hispanic" presented an alternative to the most stigmatized aspects of "Mexican" or "Puerto Rican" identity by affirming substantive affiliations with less stigmatized groups of Latin American descent, such as Cubans, Argentines, and other South American groups. Hence, while the negative discourse associated with constructions of "Latinos" or "Hispanics" are predominantly built upon dominant stereotypes of U.S.-born Mexicans and Puerto Ricans, or the poorest Latin American–origin groups most commonly associated with undocumented migration, such as Mexicans and some Central Americans, the "Latino' or "Hispanic" labels serve nonetheless to dilute specific stereotypical characterizations of any of the particular national-origin categories they purport to encompass.

Fractured Latinidad: Institutional Contexts, Whiteness, and Power

Within the hegemonic bipolarity of whiteness and Blackness that characterizes white supremacy within the space of the U.S. nation-state, groups that come to be racialized as neither white nor Black must inevitably be constituted in relation to both. If, as we have demonstrated, a racialized Latinidad that could be invoked to comprise Mexican migrants and Puerto Ricans in Chicago consistently tended to be conjoined with the hegemonic racist denigration of Blackness, such pan-Latino identifications tended to be rather more tenuous and selective in relation to a dominant whiteness. The fact that social interaction between Latinos and whites occurred for the most part in institutional contexts is indicative of how, for many Mexicans and Puerto Ricans in Chicago, whiteness was localized in sites of power. Those Mexicans and Puerto Ricans who had access—however unequal and subordinate—to such institutional contexts, deployed various expressions of Latinidad in relation to whites.

Carlos Flores, a young Puerto Rican man who was teaching at an elementary school in West Town, believed that the relationship between Latinos of different nationalities flourished and was transformed in institutional contexts, such as higher education, that were related to upward social mobility and the social power of racial whiteness. In an interview with Ramos-Zayas in March of 1995, Carlos described his experience of relocating from a predominantly Mexican suburban neighborhood to becoming a student in a predominantly white college in rural Illinois:

> The Latinos where I lived were mostly Mexican. The Mexicans, you see, they iden-tified themselves as being culturally different from us [Puerto Ricans] . . . The dialect . . . They didn't like our dialect. They *detested* it. We knew that indirectly they would say slurs at you and try to push you down. [. . .] In college, I hung out with all the Latino groups on campus. Immediately, the first semester, I became part of the Latin American Student Association. It was a good experience. There we didn't have friction at all, because we knew we were a very small percentage. Therefore, even more, we created a bond.

Carlos also recalled that white students at the rural college appeared to be afraid of Latinos, whom they perceived as menacing, "ghetto," and dangerous. As Carlos explained, the white college students "were stereotyping that everybody that was from Chicago came from a very hardcore environment. They thought that Latinos coming from Chicago were dangerous. You don't mess with them, because they can pull a knife on you." Like Carlos, the other young, upwardly mobile Puerto Ricans whom Ramos-Zayas interviewed referred to their college experience as a decisive turning point that not only made them more aware of their own Puerto Ricanness, but also facilitated common bonds with other Latinos—and, to a lesser extent, African Americans and other "minority" stu-dents in general.

"You talk badly about Mexicans now," argued María Echevarría, a recent graduate of the University of Illinois visiting her family in Humboldt Park, in reply to a Puerto Rican student at the alternative high school where Ramos-Zayas was teaching, "but those are the people who'll stand by you when you go to college and everyone else is white."[8] The incipient Latinidad that Carlos and María each depicted was deployed in overt relation to whiteness. In an institutional context traditionally associated with ideas of "mobility," "assimilation," and "mainstreaming" (i.e., college), Latinidad became a form of racial identification that held the promises of coalition and solidarity for the sake of contesting the dominant racializations of "Mexicans" and "Puerto Ricans" that both groups had to confront.

Perfectly aware of the incompatibility and contradictions between the as-similationist expectations of "college" as a social institution and the pervasive racialization of Latinos as nonwhites by predominantly white student bodies at such institutions of higher education, many of the upwardly mobile Puerto Rican college students whom Ramos-Zayas interviewed described their col-lege experiences as a continuous and unrelentingly intense project of "learning about one's culture." Like other Puerto Rican college graduates from Humboldt Park, María Echevarría had taken "Latino Studies" courses, joined Latin

American/Latino student associations, and read Latino authors, as she put it, "to learn more about my culture, about myself." Similarly, Tony Santiago's experience with Black fraternities and Latino groups on campus triggered a process of self-awareness, which situated reading books—not only about Puerto Ricans, but also about Mexicans/Chicanos and other Latinos—at its center. A middle school teacher in his late twenties, Tony explained:

> I started to go through stages of self-awareness. I started reading a lot. That was my stage in life to read about our [Puerto Rican] culture. Piri Thomas had a big influence on me. [I was also reading] books by Mexican authors, Chicano poetry. I was reading anything I could get my hands on. We also brought down speakers like Jaime Escalante, César Chávez. We got more radical. I saw the process of my change.

Since most college courses dealing with Latino issues had tended to survey the particular experiences of various national-origin groups, these college-educated Puerto Ricans were necessarily exposed to a cross-fertilization of Puerto Rican, Mexican/Chicano, and other Latino intellectuals' endeavors.[9] Not only did Tony perceive Puerto Ricanness as something that had to be actively and deliberately "learned," but he also embraced Latinidad as a self-consciously racialized, radical political identity that facilitated the transformations associated with his upward social mobility without requiring an assimilationist movement toward an always unattainable "whiteness."

In contrast to these institutionally mediated assertions of Latinidad in opposition to whiteness, Ricky Rosa, a young Puerto Rican man who had just moved to Humboldt Park, described the area where he had previously lived by saying, "In the area where I lived there were a lot of Puerto Ricans and poor whites... you had ethnic whites and poor whites that are Appalachians, so it's almost like two different groups." Interestingly, while Puerto Ricans and Mexicans in Chicago routinely conflated "white" with "American," Ricky's comment revealed that Latinos, especially those living or working in close proximity to poor or working-class whites, also sometimes challenged the normalized invisibility and monolithic character of an undifferentiated whiteness (Ramos-Zayas, 2001). In this instance, the category of "poor whites" became further modifiable as "ethnic" or "Appalachian," as two distinct groups that were both racialized as white but virtually distinct from one another, and each somehow differentiable from some presumed "real" or "pure" normative whiteness that might otherwise go unmarked as simply "American." Moreover, Ricky's characterization of these people as poor Appalachian or "ethnic" whites, rather than as unproblematically "American," implicitly posited a tenuous yet plausible space of class-specific commonality between Puerto Ricans and their (impoverished, ethnicized) "white" neighbors.

A quite different example of a Latino identity produced between Mexicans and Puerto Ricans, in juxtaposition with white neighbors, emerged at the

DuraPress factory. One of the few Puerto Rican workers, Yadira, was married to a Mexican/migrant coworker named Eduardo. They lived in the predominantly white working-class industrial suburb of Marshall Park, where the factory was located. Unlike many of their coworkers who lived in the thoroughly segregated and enclosed Mexican/migrant space known as La Selva ("The Jungle"), however, Yadira and Eduardo lived in a predominantly white area. When Eduardo was asked about the place where he lived, he declared, "Marshall Park is nice because I live by Americans; they're quiet—Mexicans and Puerto Ricans like to listen to music and drink beer, they make too much noise." In this comparatively simple example, a Latinidad that encompassed both Mexicans and Puerto Ricans was enabled in contrast to whites, but in a way that diminished the collective dignity of both.

There were several instances, on the other hand, when Mexican migrants articulated a sense of their Latinidad in opposition to whites, but did so selectively, in a manner that repudiated their commonalities with Puerto Ricans. It is useful to revisit an excerpt from the interview with Leobardo Sandoval (presented in chapter 3). After denouncing Puerto Ricans as "lazy" (along with both Blacks and whites, but specifically in conjunction with Blacks), Leobardo invoked a selective Latinidad: "So now we're taking it [North America] back. You go to Miami, it's all Cubans. Texas, it's all Mexicans. California, all Mexicans. Chicago, all Mexicans." Leobardo's proclamation quite noticeably included Cubans with Mexicans, but excluded Puerto Ricans, and therefore also omitted New York City altogether from his projected image of a Latino reconquest of the U.S. Although Leobardo's additional remarks clearly privileged Mexico with respect to Latin America and favored Mexicans in relation to other Latinos, there was for him the possibility of a Latinidad that might accommodate Cubans but not Puerto Ricans. Similarly, in the discussion of "Chicanos" and gangs among Mexican migrants at DuraPress (examined in chapter 4), it became conceivable for some that the children of Central American migrants might be included among those ranked as "Chicano," but it was unthinkable to include Mainland-born Puerto Ricans in that group. Likewise, when, in chapter 6, Antonio argued that ESL courses mandated by the Liberty Carton management would be, in effect, a form of discrimination against "Latinos," he nevertheless specified Puerto Ricans as the relatively advantaged group whose "bad" English would shield them from the persecution of being obliged to attend the classes. Precisely when he posited the basis of his own oppression in terms of Latinidad, Antonio was most adamantly disarticulating that Latino identity from any sense of commonality with Puerto Ricans. In all of these examples, then, various formulations of pan-Latino commonality proved nonetheless to be persistently fractured.

Whereas a variety of institutional contexts served to enable the emergence of a racialized Latinidad, furthermore, it has always also been the larger-scale institutional frameworks of the U.S. state apparatus that have simultaneously homogenized Latinos as "Hispanics" while also differentiating and hierarchically sorting and ranking them. One of the most glaring illustrations of this may be found in the divergent histories of Mexican/migrant "illegality" and Puerto Rican citizenship, discussed in chapter 1. This kind of production of difference between Mexican migrants and Puerto Ricans in Chicago through the mediation of state institutions, however, also transpired in much more localized and everyday forms. One quite revealing instantiation of such emerged in an ESL-classroom discussion at the Casa del Pueblo, a Pilsen community organization. "One time," Claudio (who lived on the South Side) recounted, "the police stopped me on the North Side, and they asked me, 'Where are you from?'" When Claudio responded that he was from Mexico, the cop went on to explain, "If you were Puerto Rican, you'd be in trouble, but since you're Mexican, I'll let you go." Claudio concluded with the remark, "He was a white." One cannot underestimate the significance in this episode of police racism that it transpired on the North Side of Chicago, where Puerto Ricans were most spatially concentrated. This can be understood to be salient in either of two distinct but complementary ways. In one plausible interpretation, the racialization of that space as a Puerto Rican one—where this young Mexican migrant was effectively considered by the white cop to be "out of place"—provided the white police officer an occasion to exercise his racist discretion in a manner that appeared to be doing Claudio a favor, a magnanimous gesture of (not-quite) "benign" neglect, with regard to a Mexican migrant. In another conceivable scenario, Claudio may have been presumed to be one of the growing number of Mexicans living in those same historically Puerto Rican neighborhoods. In either case, the white cop's overall message seemed to communicate to the teenaged Mexican migrant that Puerto Ricans were presumed criminals toward whom he would show no mercy, whereas Mexicans were deserving of his leniency, and therefore, since Claudio was judged more favorably as a Mexican, he had better not get mixed up with any Puerto Ricans because, next time, he might not be so lucky. Indeed, in this episode, Claudio's undocumented status as a Mexican migrant mattered less to a local representative of the U.S. state than the prospect of "criminal" citizenship, had he been a Puerto Rican. This encounter demonstrates how police racism has an expressly *pedagogical* dimension, as it participates in the genesis and reproduction of antagonistic divisions among racially subordinated groups and the spaces that they inhabit and move through. Indeed, there was a racialized ambiguity that required the white police officer to inquire about Claudio's origins. For the cop, Claudio's generically "Hispanic" racialized character demanded further sorting among distinct national-origin Latino identities. Precisely this racial ambiguity in the face of power might otherwise have been productive for Claudio of a certain Latinidad, were it not so bluntly interrupted and subverted by the policeman's very materially efficacious privileging of a difference between Mexicans and Puerto Ricans.[10]

The white policeman's initial question ("Where are you from?") revealed the way that a "Latino" identity became possible in a racialized space of indeterminacy and ambiguity: Claudio's Hispanic or Latino "race" was visible whereas his Mexicanness or not inconceivable Puerto Ricanness were not sufficiently legible to the white policeman. Likewise, the cop's forceful interruption of an incipient occasion for Latinidad exposed the extent to which the institutions of the U.S. nation-state serve to simultaneously impede those Latino possibilities as well as generate them. It seems fitting, finally, that this chapter should have explored so many disparate expressions of pan-Latino identification between Mexicans and Puerto Ricans, only then to confront anew a stark demonstration of the unequal politics of citizenship and racialization between Mexican migrants and Puerto Ricans. Indeed, the conditions of possibility for the emergence of a shared sense of Latinidad between these two groups have been framed at each juncture by these two defining axes of inequality in the United States.

In conclusion, despite many tenacious obstacles, a variety of distinct formulations of a shared sense of Latino identity and commonality did indeed emerge among Mexicans and Puerto Ricans in Chicago. According to one "migrant" sensibility—one shared by Mexicans as well as Puerto Ricans—a common and largely homogenized Latino identity could be discerned not among the migrants themselves, who remained irreducibly particular and associated with their countries of origin, but rather among their U.S.-born generations. This, however, was a Latinidad constituted by perceived cultural deficiencies, which was equated with the degraded condition of a U.S. "minority" group, and connoted a kind of racialized abjection approximating Blackness. Latinidad was also posited in relation to the shared "migrant" status, and especially that of undocumented migrants, which located many Latinos within the space of the U.S. nation-state as "illegal" border-crossers, but which notably tended to exclude Puerto Ricans altogether—due to their U.S. citizenship. One very prominent form of Latino identity arose as a racial formation in explicit opposition to African Americans and racial Blackness. Another important modality of Latinidad articulated class-specific forms of solidarity between Mexicans and Puerto Ricans (and also, other Latinos)—as workers, in express opposition to specifically Latino overseers in workplaces where members of the two groups were employed together, or as poor people sharing the same urban space, or on the other end of the social spectrum, as upwardly aspiring or upwardly mobile middle-class professionals seeking to secure entitlements, privileges, and status in juxtaposition to other racialized constituencies. Yet another form of Latino identity came to be evoked in various institutional contexts, in a manner that was more or less overtly juxtaposed to whites and social institutions that were understood to enact white power within the U.S. nation-state. Indeed, such formulations of Latino commonalities tended to be quite fractured and selective, in ways that exposed the invidious workings of a racialization process whereby some Latinos were nonetheless excluded from other Latinos' assertions of a pan-Latino identity. If much of our research confirms that racialization processes often undermined the possibilities for Latinidad, what was most revealing in these instances, however, was the way that pan-Latino identifications, when they did arise, did so precisely as racial formations. To the varying degrees that a shared sense of Latino identity became possible, this consistently tended to be already posited in overt or implicit relation to the hegemonic racial polarity of whiteness and Blackness, and also fractured by class and confounded by the politics of citizenship. In the next and concluding chapter of this book, we will situate this ethnography in the wider context of its particular sociopolitical and historical moment of anti-immigrant restrictionism and anti-welfare restructuring during the mid-1990s, and consider the broader implications of our study for the ongoing project of theorizing and mobilizing across the fault lines of racialization and the unequal politics of citizenship.

CHAPTER 8

Conclusion: Latino Futures?

The research for this book was conducted during a specific historical moment with a particular political climate, above all distinguished by the clear correlation between the passage of the so-called "Welfare Reform" under the self-righteous and hypocritical title of the Personal Responsibility and Work Opportunity Reconciliation Act (signed August 22, 1996), which itself included extensive anti-immigrant stipulations, and the passage five weeks later of the Illegal Immigration Reform and Immigrant Responsibility Act of 1996 (signed September 30, 1996). These pronouncedly punitive legislations together represented a major material and practical culmination of the protracted onslaught against the poor that had been defining of the broader ideological climate of hostility against both "welfare" and "immigrants," especially the undocumented. The nativism of the mid-1990s was clearly distinguished by anti-immigrant racism, and was disproportionately directed against Mexican migrants in particular, due to the hegemonic conflation of Mexicans with "illegal aliens," and especially against Mexican/migrant women who came to be equated with Mexican/migrant long-term settlement, families, and therefore the dramatic growth of a U.S.-citizen racial "minority group" (Chock, 1996; Coutin and Chock, 1995; Lowe, 1996:159–60; Roberts, 1997). Increasingly, undocumented migrant families also came to be persistently hounded with allegations that they were primarily motivated by the desire to avail themselves of social services in the U.S. and were, in effect, abusing the beneficence of the public welfare infrastructure. Rather than highly exploited workers, undocumented migrants were prominently refigured as a fiscal "burden" and an overall "drain" on state resources. This exacerbated anti-immigrant racism operated in tandem with what was, in effect, the combined racism and sexism of the more general assault against "welfare"— inasmuch as it was disproportionately identified with African Americans and Puerto Ricans, and likewise, especially Black and Puerto Rican women and their children.

Thus, the anti-immigrant politics of the period was very forcefully coupled, both discursively and in its implementation, with the dismantling and wholesale liquidation of the social welfare safety net for impoverished U.S. citizens. Both can be seen as disciplinary measures intended to intensify the subordination of labor in general in the U.S. by rendering more vulnerable, and thus more tractable and flexible, precisely the poorest of working-class people (whether they were more or less permanently unemployed and underemployed U.S.

citizens, or the consistently overemployed migrant working poor). That groups not racialized as white were disproportionately represented among *both* of these social categories, is hardly necessary to point out. In this context, these hegemonic projects partly relied on effectively articulating the desperation of impoverished U.S. citizens in the terms of a nativist resentment for the "cheap labor" of migrants who were purportedly displacing "American" workers from "American" jobs. On the other hand, migrant (and especially undocumented) workers' legal vulnerability meant that they always had only a tenuous hold on their own employment. This climate of insecurity therefore could quite readily inspire undocumented migrants to denigrate (as unproductive, or "lazy") the labor-power that was the commodity for sale on the part of their most proximate competitors in the labor market—namely, impoverished U.S. citizens. Other racially subordinated "minorities," such as African Americans and Puerto Ricans (but also Mexicans born in the U.S.), who often could marshal various other potential labor-market advantages, such as U.S. citizenship, English-language fluency, and higher levels of formal schooling, thus became prime targets for Mexican migrants' accusations of "laziness." These parallel processes served as a kind of double-disciplining, of course. Employers, and indirectly the state, used both the U.S.-born poor and the migrant working poor as disciplinary mechanisms, one against the other. Furthermore, inasmuch as migrant workers were always at pains to demonstrate to their overseers that they were hardworking and not "lazy," they were compelled to participate in their own intensified exploitation. Michael Kearney has characterized this kind of double-disciplining as "jujitsu politics." In effect, the momentum of migrant workers' and impoverished U.S. citizens' respective efforts at self-defense is used to subvert their own resistance (1996:156; 1998:29). As we have seen, discourses of "welfare" among Mexican migrants always signaled the unequal politics of citizenship, and were inherently concerned with access to such benefits as substantive entitlements of U.S. citizenship. Thus, the combined legislative onslaught in the mid-1990s against both "immigration" and "welfare" exacerbated the invidious distinctions and the palpable difference between what it meant for Mexican migrants to be "immigrants" and what it meant for Puerto Ricans to be U.S. citizens.

The unequal politics of citizenship, therefore, was mobilized in particularly forceful ways to intensify the subordination and discipline of both Mexican migrants and Puerto Ricans during the period of our study, and in ways that tended to aggravate divisions between the two groups' understandings of their respective experiences. Mexican migrants' and Puerto Ricans' perceptions of these substantive divergences in one another's relations to the U.S. state and the labor market, as we have seen throughout much of this book, were very commonly manifested in terms of racialized difference. The "jujitsu politics" that converted both of their efforts at self-defense into self-defeat, therefore, was inseparable in everyday life from the translation of the inequalities structured by the institutions of citizenship and immigration law into a racialized language of apparently intrinsic and inherently antagonistic group differences.

Our collaborative ethnography, then, supplies a kind of archive of the history that Mexican migrants and Puerto Ricans in Chicago were actively implicated in producing in a particular sociopolitical climate during a specific historical moment. It is precisely the irreducible historical specificity of all racialization processes which ought to remind us that racial meanings and distinctions are eminently situated in ongoing struggles. Over the course of their respective historical relations to the U.S. nation-state and its imperial projects, Mexicans' and Puerto Ricans' relations to U.S. citizenship have been formulated and institutionalized in divergent ways, and, likewise, have often been racialized in historically contingent and necessarily distinct ways. Mexican migrants' and Puerto Ricans' contrasting sociopolitical locations within the field of citizenship inequalities have contributed to the production of distinct and competing racial formations of "Mexican"-ness and "Puerto Rican"-ness that frequently came to be juxtaposed as mutually exclusive. While both groups suffered the consequences of the U.S. nation-state's naturalized conceptions of citizenship and deservingness—criminalizing and exploiting undocumented Mexican migrants' "illegality" and demonizing endemic Puerto Rican poverty through the ideological figures of welfare "dependency" and "abuse" in order to legitimize each group's subjugation—these parallel processes of domination often generated opposition and division between the two groups, rather than analogy and coalition.

While much of our research foregrounds the ways that the two groups were positioned, and positioned themselves, in relation to one another, it would be impermissible not to draw conclusive connections between these processes and the wider sociopolitical conflicts of this particular historical period. The two groups' distinct racializations, and the divergences between their respectively racialized particularities, have historically corresponded to specific material needs and political requirements. The U.S. state produces and continually refines and reformulates a politics of citizenship that hierarchically orders and regulates juridical differences that facilitate the creation and subordination of highly disciplined and tractable subjects. The institution of citizenship itself, therefore, generates substantial inequalities that have readily supplied an elusive material and practical basis for each group's racialization, and thus also their racialized constructions of one another.

Our argument about the inherently *unequal* and ultimately racializing character of U.S. citizenship deliberately disrupts and directly challenges the hegemonic mythologies of citizenship as a neutral framework for the equality of individuals in relation to the U.S. nation-state and, more generally, in relation to the rule of law in all "democratic" and "republican" systems of government. Indeed, a rigorous and critical scrutiny of the institution of citizenship and its unequal politics provides a crucial material foundation to critiques of U.S. nationalism itself as a racial formation of white supremacy. While this study makes only a modest contribution to the much-needed scholarship and research that substantiates such a critique, our focus on the racialization of Mexicans as

"Mexicans" and Puerto Ricans as "Puerto Ricans," rather than a taken-for-granted and naturalized presupposition of their racialization as "Hispanics" or "Latinos," provides important insights into the often implicit but enduring racialization of "American"-ness itself as essentially white. This equation of "American" national identity, belonging, and deservingness with racial whiteness, of course, has profound ramifications not only for securely relegating Latinos to an implied or overt racial category of nonwhiteness and thus subordination, but also for perverting the equal citizenship of *all* people who come to be racialized as not-white and thus the disqualification of *all* racial "minorities" in the U.S. from the entitlements of genuine or legitimate "American"-ness.

If indeed U.S. nationalism has been historically devised in a manner that is persistently entangled with white supremacy, it is not difficult to identify the defining ideological significance of the figure of racial Blackness as a requisite emblem for the opposite extreme of social power, prestige, and value. In our research, various acts of racialized demotion perpetrated between Mexicans and Puerto Ricans therefore served the purposes of a kind of self-promotion in that agonistic and contradictory space between white and Black. The examples in this study of Mexican migrants' and Puerto Ricans' often conflicted relations are instructive for analyses that take racial oppression in the U.S. seriously enough to confront without temerity how racially subordinated groups are compelled to vie with one another for position on this bitterly antagonistic terrain. Furthermore, our study reveals something decisive about the intermediate space between the hegemonic poles of whiteness and Blackness—namely, that space which encompasses the various and often divergent conditions of those racialized as *neither* white nor Black. As an effect of the overwhelming salience of racism in all aspects of everyday life in the U.S., Mexican migrants' and Puerto Ricans' competing efforts to position themselves in relation to the inequalities of citizenship tended to readily construct their sociopolitical differences as racialized ones that made explicit reference to a social order defined in terms of whiteness and Blackness. Furthermore, given the rigid hierarchical ordering of racial meanings in U.S. society, these intra-Latino divisions seemed always to be entrenched in the hegemonic denigration of African Americans.

Racialization, as we have repeatedly emphasized, is a dynamic and intrinsically contradictory and conflicted process. Thus, it is fundamentally counterproductive and potentially complicit with the workings of racial oppression to seek stability and coherence in something as constitutively open-ended and mutable as racialization. Acts of racial distinction and definition are inherently implicated in the ongoing work of racial oppression itself, and the more fixed and stable they become, the more racist hegemony tends to be sustained. In this book, therefore, we have simultaneously examined the ways that Mexicans and Puerto Ricans were racialized in separate and divergent ways and often themselves participated in the production of racialized differences between each other, while also examining the emergence of a parallel process of their racial homogenization, together, as generically "Hispanic" or "Latino."

In chapter 7, we considered the variety of ways in which Mexicans and Puerto Ricans did indeed formulate a series of divergent perspectives on their commonalities as Latinos. These discrepant conceptualizations of Latinidad, however, consistently tended to be already framed within the conjunctures of race and citizenship. In this light, one of our central concerns has been to comprehend what precisely is at stake in various formations of Latino identity and commonalities and thereby to theorize more rigorously what exactly Latinidad truly entails. Thus, if we have taken such great pains and gone to such extraordinary lengths to analyze the bases for Latino division, it has been motivated by a more fundamental desire to explore the possibilities for effectively sustaining various ideas of Latino community and coalition that could viably serve to promote counterhegemonic sociopolitical projects formulated in terms of Latinismo.

In circumstances where two Latino groups tended to be more inclined to emphasize their differences than their commonalities, and to cast those differences moreover in the blunt and even brutal language of "racial" distinctions, culturalist notions of Latino "ethnic" identity and community formation seem misplaced, if not misguided. Indeed, as we have seen, even when Mexican migrants and Puerto Ricans in Chicago did come to formulate various ideas of Latinidad, they seldom pretended to anything resembling a collective sense of cultural sameness or similarity. Rather, "Latino" identifications emerged precisely as *racial* formations, more often than not in explicit relation to a social order of inequality defined by the hegemonic polarity of whiteness and Blackness. Latinidad became most viable as an articulation of certain commonalities of experience and interest that operated within the context of the entrenched institutional white supremacy of the U.S. nation-state.

If Latinidad is fundamentally a racial formation, then we can only explore the implications of such a premise in relation to a social and political order that produces "racial" difference as a basis of racialized inequality. Therefore, as a racial formation, Latinidad is preeminently a *political* formation. When commonalities were articulated between Mexicans and Puerto Ricans, they were never self-evident or easily presumed; rather, they were actively and purposefully produced in historically specific and contextually situated ways. Such gestures toward "community" were always and inevitably contingent; they were never permanent or secure but rather fleeting moments of possibility or fragile achievements. Hence, our ethnographic examination of moments of Latino possibility necessarily has had to be coupled with an unflinching analysis of the fragmentations of Latinidad by racialized divisions between Latinos. By considering the relations between Mexicans and Puerto Ricans through the critical lens of racialization and the politics of citizenship, we have underscored the *political* character of these productions of *both* Latino identity and difference.

Ultimately, the stakes of our research concern the possibility for mobilizing Latinidad as a principle of racialized political organization. In various ways, commonalities of Latino identity and interest are already widely and routinely deployed in the more mundane and limited sense of electoral representation and the hegemonic coalescence of political constituencies. If these strategies have succeeded, and to whatever extent that they do prove to be effective, it is precisely because they correspond to and in some fashion articulate the sense among many Latinos that they share a significant disproportionately working-class experience as a racialized "minority" within the U.S. social order. Nevertheless, such strategies can as likely as not serve to organize Latinos for the purposes of their own subjection to a dominant and disempowering status quo. The complex and often contradictory lessons of our research, however, make clear that Latinidad likewise has the potential to acquire unprecedented salience in the production of an *oppositional* political identity. Such a political formation of Latinidad might serve the purposes of effectively struggling for substantive citizenship rights and entitlements, albeit within the predictably treacherous constrictions of the U.S. nation-state, but its hemispheric frame of reference could conceivably facilitate transnational anti-capitalist and anti-imperialist struggles as well. Latinidad's oppositional and even counterhegemonic possibilities, however, are inseparable from a forceful articulation of the shared historicity of struggle by Latinos as a racial formation with a diverse range of irreducibly particular but analogous experiences of subordination to global capitalism and concomitant colonization or imperial domination throughout Latin America, as well as parallel circumstances of class exploitation and racialized oppression within the space of the U.S. nation-state.

If we began this conclusion by highlighting the specificity of the sociopolitical climate attacking "illegal immigration" and "welfare dependency" in the U.S. during the mid-1990s when we each realized our respective research projects in Chicago, it is impossible finally to not address the very palpable reconfiguration of the politics of nativism, race, and nationalism that prevails in the U.S. in the aftermath of September 11, 2001. The so-called "war on terrorism" has dramatically exacerbated anti-immigrant suspicion, coupled with racist harassment, intimidation, and violence against Arabs and Muslims in particular, as well as anyone who might be confused with such. Spearheading this climate of intensified nativism, notably, has been the U.S. state's mass detention and deportation of suspected "terrorists," and the more widespread subversion of elementary civil liberties for citizens and "aliens" alike by the implementation of a new "homeland security" apparatus.

The declaration of a "war on terrorism," explicitly formulated as a war without borders, definitions, or limits, has not only culminated in U.S. war drives against Afghanistan and Iraq but has likewise promised an indefinite and expanded militarization of U.S. border policing and countless other dimensions of governance within the U.S. The concomitant propagation of a militaristic U.S. nationalism that openly endorses imperial warfare and military invasions has likewise reinforced and reconfigured already naturalized nativist constructions of who may be counted as "real Americans" and which nonwhite "foreigners" are to be racialized as intrinsically under suspicion.

In addition to the widespread and indirectly state-sanctioned targeting of migrant communities with origins in the Middle East, however, Latinos have not been redeemed of the allegations of "foreign"-ness, "illegality," or "criminality" that were already prominent features of their racialization in the years immediately prior to September 11, 2001. The escalation of immigration raids against undocumented Mexican migrants and other Latinos, especially those employed in airports, in the name of "homeland security" and the "war on terrorism," as well as the heightened policing of the U.S.-Mexico border, remind us that the pervasive racialized equation of Mexicans in particular with the figure of the "illegal alien" that prevailed during the 1990s has hardly been suspended or diminished. Likewise, we are haunted by the arrest in Chicago's O'Hare International Airport and effective disappearance of José Padilla, a Puerto Rican U.S. citizen from a poor background in Chicago's Logan Square neighborhood, alleged to have been a former street-gang member, and accused of conspiring to carry out a "terrorist" bombing in the U.S. as an Al-Qaeda operative. Without any of the purportedly sacrosanct due process of law to which his U.S. citizenship ought to have entitled him, Padilla has been indefinitely imprisoned under military jurisdiction as an "enemy combatant." Despite a flagrant refusal by the U.S. government to publicly present any formal charges or evidence against him whatsoever, Padilla has been stripped of any semblance of juridical personhood. Popularly stigmatized in the mass media as "the Dirty Bomber" and "the Puerto Rican Taliban," the case of José Padilla is instructive, especially in juxtaposition to that of John Walker Lindh, "the *American* Taliban," a white middle-class U.S. citizen captured in Afghanistan as a Taliban combatant, and later charged and convicted for his alleged "crimes" only after abundant public consideration of his rights as a U.S. citizen and careful public legal proceedings.

In light of this book's examination of the decisive conjuncture of race, citizenship, and national identity in the U.S., it is not difficult to discern in the divergent fortunes of John Walker Lindh and José Padilla the workings of a racialized sociopolitical order in which the presumed benefits of U.S. citizenship are allotted unequally according to the naturalized logic and discriminations of white supremacy. José Padilla's racially subordinated (Puerto Rican) U.S. citizenship has been effectively subjected to the protocols otherwise so systematically reserved for "illegal aliens," whether simply Mexican workers, or other undocumented migrants suspected of "foreign" and "anti-American" allegiances. Whether as U.S.-citizen "minorities" or migrants racialized as nonwhite "aliens," Puerto Ricans, Mexicans, and all of the racially oppressed within the U.S. nation-state's system of white supremacy remain permanently liable to be brought under suspicion as irreducibly "foreign," essentially "un-American," potentially mere "enemies within," and thereby denied even the most fundamental civil or human rights.

Notes

Chapter 1

1. "Hegemony" is a category of analysis inspired by the work of Antonio Gramsci (1971[1929–35]). As a concept, hegemony encompasses state power within a wider field of sociopolitical domination that emphasizes the necessary relationship between organized violence and coercion, on the one hand, and the more diffuse and inevitably contradictory operations of ideologies, on the other, that serve to legitimate political projects of rule by eliciting consent and enlisting those who are ruled and oppressed into either active or passive support of their own domination. Thus, this concept posits that it is ultimately a requirement for any oppressive system, no matter how brutal its exercise of power, to persistently seek to defend and secure its rule and justify its authority, precisely because its domination rests upon an inherently unstable and always precarious basis of social struggle and conflict, and thus is always problematic, contested, and never guaranteed. Relations of domination and subordination, in other words, are constituted through antagonistic social relations that always also entail resistance and insubordination. Similarly, when we refer specifically to the *racist* hegemony of the U.S. nation-state, we are not positing a monolithic, fixed, or enduring sociopolitical order but rather a relentlessly dynamic project of white supremacy whose domination is always challenged to reconsolidate its power and must enlist various racialized subjects or constituencies to passively accept or actively participate in upholding various forms of racial oppression.

2. U.S. Immigration and Naturalization Service, "Illegal Alien Resident Population" (Estimates of the Undocumented Immigrant Population Residing in the United States: October 1996; Updated December 2001).

3. Article 11 of Mexico's decree of April 6, 1830, stated: "it is prohibited that emigrants from nations bordering on this Republic shall settle in the states or territory adjacent to their own nation" (Moquin and Van Doren, 1971:193).

4. Throughout the ensuing text, the term "Mexican/migrant" refers to people who have migrated from Mexico to the United States, in contradistinction to "Mexicans raised in the United States." When the category "migrant" is deployed here, it should not be confused with the more precise term "migratory"; rather, the term "migrant" is intended to do a certain epistemological work—i.e., to serve as a category of analysis that disrupts the implicit teleology of the more conventional term "immigrant," which is posited from the standpoint of the U.S. nation-state (see De Genova, 1999; in press). Among those designated here as "Mexican/migrant," there is a remarkable heterogeneity of experiences ranging from seasonal migration to long-term settlement, and from undocumented legal status to U.S. citizenship.

   Regardless of their various legal statuses and heterogeneous migration histories, Mexican migrants in Chicago virtually never use the terms "Mexican American" or "Chicano/a" for self-identification; the pervasive categories are "*mexicano/a*" in Spanish or "Mexican" in English. Similarly, among those designated here as "Mexicans raised in the United States," the pervasive category of self-identification is likewise "Mexican," rather than either "Chicano/a" or "Mexican American." Thus, due to the ways that both migrants from Mexico and U.S.-born or -raised Mexicans in Chicago would be equally inclined to self-identify as simply "Mexican," we use the term "Mexican" to refer to both, modified either as "migrant" or "raised in the United States."

5. The "Bracero" accords were effected unceremoniously by a Special Committee on Importation of Mexican Labor (formed by the U.S. Immigration Service, the War Manpower Commission, and the Departments of State, Labor, and Agriculture) through a bilateral agreement with Mexico. The U.S. Department of Agriculture was granted primary authority over the coordination of the program. Ostensibly an emergency wartime measure at its

inception in 1942 (Public Law 45), the program was repeatedly renewed and dramatically expanded until its termination in 1964.

6. Approximately 4.8 million contracts were issued to Mexican workers for employment as braceros over the course of the program's 22 years, and during that same period there were more than 5 million apprehensions of undocumented Mexican migrants. Both of these figures, of course, include redundancies, and thus are not indicative of absolute numbers, but they are revealing nonetheless of the more general complementarity between contracted and undocumented migration flows (Samora, 1971:19–20). Indeed, as early as 1949, U.S. employers and labor recruiters were assisted with instantaneous legalization procedures for undocumented workers (Calavita, 1992).

7. Based on pooled estimates from the U.S. Census Bureau's Current Population Survey (March 1998, March 2000), 36.5% of the Mexican population were "foreign-born" and 49.3% of the latter were "recent arrivals" (Logan, 2001). The lower estimate reflects the foreign-born percentage (36.5%) of the total Mexican population, as derived from U.S. Census Bureau data; the higher figure reflects the same percentage for the adjusted population total, estimated by researchers at the Lewis Mumford Center for Comparative Urban and Regional Research at the State University of New York at Albany (cf. Logan, 2002).

8. U.S. Immigration and Naturalization Service, "Illegal Alien Resident Population" (Estimates of the Undocumented Immigrant Population Residing in the United States: October 1996; Updated December 2001); Jeffrey Passel, "New Estimates of the Undocumented Population in the United States," Migration Policy Institute, Migration Information Source, May 22, 2002.

9. Notably, the first major community of Puerto Ricans outside of their homeland was comprised of contract-labor migrants transported to Hawaii in 1900 and 1901 (N. Carr, 1989; cf. Gonzalez, 2000:62).

10. A combination of factors, including the Island's reputed "overpopulation," the labor needs of the U.S., and the strategic location of Puerto Rico during the Cold War, have been cited as explanations for the Operation Bootstrap project. For a detailed account of Operation Bootstrap and industrialization in Puerto Rico, see History Task Force (1979) and Wagenheim and Jiménez de Wagenheim (1994).

11. In fact, the Puerto Rican government had proven itself to be remarkably eager to coordinate efforts with Mainland employers, by creating organizations such as the Office of the Commonwealth of Puerto Rico in order to "ease the transition of Puerto Rican workers into the new environment." Ironically, while potential Puerto Rican migrants to the U.S. were exhorted to "integrate harmoniously" into the receiving society and "to contribute to the betterment and enlargement of the American nation," those who stayed in Puerto Rico were instructed to "affirm and expand their way of being Puerto Rican" ("Emigración," 1966; pamphlet originally published in the 1950s, cited in Dávila, 1997:37).

12. The social phenomenon of back-and-forth migration between Puerto Rico and the United States has been described by such terms as "the airbus" (Sánchez, 1994), "the Neo-Rican Jetliner" (Carrero, 1965), the "commuter nation" (Torre et al., 1994), the "air bridge" (Sandoval-Sánchez, 1998), the "vaivén" ["come-and-go"] (Duany, 2000), and "the U-Turning Oxcart" (Laviera, 1981).

13. Data compiled by researchers at the Lewis Mumford Center for Comparative Urban and Regional Research at the State University of New York at Albany, based on pooled estimates from the U.S. Census Bureau's Current Population Survey (March 1998, March 2000); (cf. Logan, 2002).

14. Throughout the text of this book, for reasons of racial politics, we capitalize "Black" and "Blackness" as they refer to the social condition and historical specificity of African Americans, whereas we deliberately do not capitalize "white" or "whiteness." Ralph Ellison, for example, referred to the capitalization of the term "Negro" as "one of the important early victories of my own people in their fight for self-definition" (Ellison, 1958[1964:253]). In contrast, as David Roediger explains, "It is not merely that whiteness is oppressive and false, it is that whiteness is *nothing but* oppressive and false. . . . Whiteness describes not a culture but precisely . . . the empty and therefore terrifying attempt to build an identity based on what one isn't and on whom one can hold back" (Roediger, 1994:13).

15. By appearing to bridge differences of "culture" *and* "race," the term "ethnicity" actually serves to obscure and confuse matters further; "ethnicity" is an analytic category that effectively "distracts attention from the continuing power of racism, and trivializes more complex

processes of nationalism" (R. T. Smith, 1996:187; cf. B. Williams, 1989). The elision and effective equation of the categories "immigrant" and "ethnic" has a long genealogy in U.S. social science (cf. De Genova, 1999; in press). This conflation is a characteristic feature, for example, of the work of W. Lloyd Warner and his research associates (Warner, 1962[1953]; Warner and Srole, 1976[1945]). While Warner was always careful to underscore the distinction between the social status of "ethnic groups" (which he associated principally with European migrant groups who came to be racialized as white) and the "racial caste" status of African Americans, he nonetheless readily subsumed Mexicans and Puerto Ricans into the "ethnic" category, attributing their low social status merely to the recentness of their migrations 1962[1953], Thus, the analytic category of "ethnicity" became an obstacle to identifying and critically examining the proliferation of racialized distinctions and the extension of what Warner called "racial caste" status to migrant groups who did not come to be racialized as white.

16. See Madrid-Barela (1976) for an attempt to produce a genealogy for the term "Chicano," which reveals that the term originally referred to Mexican migrants and was largely derogatory, despite its contemporary connotation of Mexicans born in the U.S. based on political efforts in the 1960s to reappropriate the term and positively revalorize it. For discussions of the political radicalism of the Chicano Movement across the Southwest in the late 1960s and early 1970s, and the subsequent intellectual formulation and academic institutionalization of Chicano Studies, see Muñoz (1989).

17. For a Chicano perspective on Nixon's "Hispanic" strategy, see Acuña (2000:389); for a comparative discussion of the discrepant nationalisms of Chicanos and Puerto Ricans, see Klor de Alva (1989).

18. Whereas the notion of *Hispanidad* was actively promoted in the Americas during the nineteenth century by Liberal Spain (cf. Pike, 1971), parallel ideological formulations of *Latinidad* can be similarly traced to France's political ambitions in the Americas during the era of Napoleon III (cf. Davis, 2000:13). In contrast, throughout the era of "Latin" American independence struggles and thereafter, hemispheric internationalist formulations of *Americanismo* were explicitly juxtaposed to the Anglo-Saxonist usurpation of "American"-ness by the United States (cf. De la Campa, 1999; Saldívar, 1991), ranging from Simón Bolívar's contention in the late 1810s that "for us, the fatherland is America" [*Para nosotros la patria es América*] (cited in Oboler, 1995:181n2; cf. F. Padilla, 1990), to José Martí's conception of *Nuestra América* (1979[1891]; cf. Saldívar, 1991), to the revitalization of Martí's hemispheric anti-imperialist vision by the Cuban Revolution of 1959, perhaps most forcefully articulated in the "Second Declaration of Havana," February 4, 1962 (Casa de las Américas, 1979:179–207), and reworked in Ernesto "Che" Guevara's Third Worldist "tricontinentalism" as a reconceptualization of "Nuestra América" as the Latin American "continent" (e.g., Guevara, 1987[1967]; cf. Fernández Retamar, 1976; 1981, 1989).

19. Unlike many working-class people in Suzanne Oboler's research (1995) who frankly rejected the Hispanic label as a strategy to facilitate their subordination, many upwardly aspiring middle-class Latin Americans embraced the more inclusive category as a way to mobilize together and coordinate their efforts in order to achieve the privileges of the white middle class.

20. A major shortcoming of Padilla's study (1985) is its general neglect of any critical consideration of class formation or the politics of citizenship as such. In Michael Jones-Correa's study (1998) of Latino politics among predominantly South American (noncitizen) migrants in New York City, however, transnational commitments and the reluctance to relinquish citizenship in their countries of origin, coupled with the exclusions of U.S. citizenship, produced a redoubled political marginalization. Such a sociopolitical condition of indefinite disenfranchisement was nevertheless effectively mediated by a dual sense of identity that could enable "Latino"-identified coalitions with respect to local politics in the U.S. alongside of enduring national identities and transnational commitments (cf. Jones-Correa and Leal, 1996).

21. In an effort to problematize narrowly state-centric notions of politics, the analytical concept of "Latino cultural citizenship," initially articulated by Renato Rosaldo (1994; cf. Flores and Benmayor, 1997), has emphasized the need to formulate how Latino "cultural" specificity— in its divergence from the normative ideals on which U.S. citizenship and "American" national identity are premised—may be upheld as a vital and enduringly visible dimension of Latinos' struggles for political empowerment and social incorporation. Given that, even as U.S. citizens, Latinos have not reaped the purportedly universal benefits afforded by citizenship, but

actually have been rendered suspect as a potential menace to national unity, the claims of cultural citizenship are presented as an alternative medium for Latinos to demand recognition, expand entitlements, and deepen the meanings of social and political membership, without succumbing to assimilationist mandates to surrender their specific "cultural" identities. A serious potential shortcoming of this perspective is that it ultimately seems to sustain rather than subvert the basic premises by which racialized inequality is organized and managed through the multiculturalist rhetoric of the U.S. state, whereby the effective normalization and subordination of "difference" is facilitated through its accommodation. Nevertheless, the "cultural citizenship" argument has important potential advantages for simultaneously addressing the racialized subjugation of both citizen and noncitizen Latinos. It affirms the possibility and necessity of political agency that is not confined to the state's formal constructions of juridical citizenship and rights, and resituates virtually every aspect of Latino community formation within a broadly conceived understanding of the political.

22. As Juan Flores (2000:141–65) argues, the viability of pan-Latino categories of identification hinges on their inclusiveness toward the full range of social experiences, including the divergence between contemporary configurations of Latino "immigrant" groups in contradistinction to the "native born." In the context of the "New Nueva York," for instance, the possibility for a tenable Latinismo faces the significant challenge of extending notions of language and cultural authenticity to include the experience of English-dominant Puerto Ricans, in particular, as well as long-term U.S.-resident Puerto Ricans, more generally, whose social identities, in addition to being formulated in relation to Puerto Ricans "over there" on the Island, have partly taken shape in relation to African Americans as well as other Francophone and Anglophone Caribbean communities (Flores, 2000:164).

23. One prominent formulation of the instrumentalist approach to Latino identity is Felix Padilla's concept of "situational ethnic identity" (1985:3–4). Emphasizing the significance of Latinidad as an innovative identity that ought not to be taken for granted as naturally or automatically encompassing all "Spanish-speaking groups," Padilla contends that "Latino ethnicity is an emergent expression of shared structural and cultural feelings, excited as a strategic, wider-scale unit by disadvantaged people as a new mode of seeking political redress in American society" (1985:155). Despite his insistence on the contextual variability of "ethnicity," Padilla nonetheless reverts to an explicitly semiprimordialist perspective (1985:151), retreating to an analytic privileging of the Spanish language as the presumed symbolic, if not practical, basis for Latinidad. Undoubtedly, there is an obvious validity to the claim that the convenience for Spanish-speaking Latin American migrants to relate to other Spanish speakers on the basis of language without regard to national origins holds a simple and inevitable practical appeal in everyday life. But as we have already suggested, such presuppositions must be problematized in relation to the increasing significance of English-language dominance among many U.S.-born Latinos (cf. Flores, 2000; Zentella, 1997). To his credit, Padilla acknowledges that "Latino ethnic identity is related more to the symbol of the Spanish language than to its actual use by all members of the various groups" (1985:151), and rightly recognizes that the "primordial" basis of Latino identification may be largely mythic. Still, Padilla's instrumentalist approach requires that he take recourse to the primordialist assertion that "the unique potential of Latinismo or Hispanismo for mobilizing Spanish-speaking people as a collective 'political force' must stem from its appeal to sentiments of 'common origin.' . . . Latino ethnic identity, then, needs to be based upon the reality or myth of unique culture ties which serve to demarcate them from other groups or populations" (1985:148).

24. For further discussion of these issues, see De Genova (in press).

25. For further discussion of these issues, see Ramos-Zayas (2003).

Chapter 2

1. This company name and all others that appear in the ensuing text, as well as all personal names, are fictive. Some of the people who have been interlocutors in De Genova's research are vulnerable to the punitive legal recriminations that could be brought to bear upon their undocumented immigration status. Likewise, some of the people who have been interlocutors in Ramos-Zayas's research might be vulnerable to the repressive political recriminations that could be directed against their community activism. Thus, in the interests of protecting the anonymity of the people depicted here, we have deliberately obfuscated or altered various

descriptive details deemed to be inconsequential for the analysis, but that nonetheless could potentially serve to identify particular persons. Likewise, in the interests of protecting himself legally against any possible charges of breach of contract or confidentiality on the part of the companies where he was employed, De Genova has also opted to exclude or alter any extraneous details that could serve to identify particular companies or workplaces.

2. According to the U.S. Census 2000, the city of Chicago has the third largest Latino population in the U.S. However, as with virtually every prior census, there have been serious concerns about a very probable undercount of Latinos in Chicago by Census 2000 (Williams, 2000). According to calculations based upon the 2000 Census data by researchers at the Lewis Mumford Center for Comparative Urban and Regional Research at the State University of New York at Albany, the Chicago primary metropolitian statistical area (PMSA) is the second largest concentration of Mexicans and the third largest area of Puerto Rican settlement, but also represents the third largest Guatemalan population, and ranks among the top ten areas of U.S. settlement for Cubans, Ecuadorians, Hondurans, Argentines, Chileans, Bolivians, and Paraguayans; likewise, Chicago is among the top fifteen cities for Panamanians, Colombians, and Peruvians, and among the top twenty for Salvadorans, Dominicans, Nicaraguans, and Costa Ricans. (Cf. "Latinos here are epitome of diversity," *Chicago Sun-Times*, September 16, 1992).

3. Among the sixty most segregated U.S. metropolitan areas (PMSAs), Chicago ranked first for Latino/Asian segregation, tied for first for Black/Asian segregation, third for Black/Latino segregation, fifth for white/Black segragation, sixth for white/Latino segregation, and eighteenth for white/Asian segregation, according to measures of residential dissimilarity scores in U.S. cities, calculated from the 2000 Census by researchers at the Lewis Mumford Center for Comparative Urban and Regional Research at the State University of New York at Albany (cf. Harrigan and Vogel, 2000; Hirsch, 1983; Squires et al., 1987).

4. Following the Los Angeles metropolitan area (either consolidated with, or without the inclusion of the Riverside–San Bernardino and Orange County primary metropolitan statistical areas [PMSAs]), metropolitan Chicago's Mexican population represents the second largest concentration in absolute numbers (whether counting the Chicago PMSA alone, or the Chicago–Kenosha, WI–Gary, IN, consolidated metropolitan statistical area [CMSA]). According to estimates by researchers at the Lewis Mumford Center for Comparative Urban and Regional Research at the State University of New York at Albany, intended to correct undercounting by the U.S. Census for 2000, the Houston, TX, San Antonio, TX, and Phoenix, AZ, metropolitan areas rank third, fourth, and fifth, respectively, or fourth, sixth, and seventh if the Riverside–San Bernardino, CA, and Orange County, CA, PMSAs are counted separately from the Los Angeles PMSA. Although they are numerically smaller, the Mexican populations of the cities of Houston, San Antonio, and Phoenix each represent larger percentages of their total municipal populations than Chicago's Mexican population: according to the U.S. Census 2000, whereas Chicago's population is 18.3% Mexican, Los Angeles's population is 29.5% Mexican; Houston's population is 27% Mexican; San Antonio's population is 35.9% Mexican; and Phoenix's population is 28.4% Mexican.

5. These percentages are calculated from U.S. Census 2000 data.

6. By 2000, Mexican migrants comprised 46.5% of the total "foreign-born" population in the city of Chicago, 40% in Cook County (comprising the city and its closest suburbs), and 41% in the greater metropolitan area. These percentages are calculated from U.S. Census 2000 data.

7. The Back of the Yards (or "Packingtown") neighborhood, historically, encompassed all of the "New City" community area (Barrett, 1987; Jablonsky, 1993; Slayton, 1986). Since the demise of the meatpacking industry in Chicago during the 1950s, the New City area has been radically partitioned by racial segregation; the predominantly Mexican northern half has continued to be identified as the "Back of the Yards," whereas the almost homogeneously African American southern half has come to be largely dissociated from its historical relation to the stockyards and packing houses.

8. Caruso and Camacho, 1985:6.

9. Latino Institute Research, cited in Rob Paral, "NAFTA and Chicago's Latinos," in *Latino: A Publication of the Latino Institute*, Vol. 6, No. 1 (August 1993).

10. Predictably, the Illinois report reductively equated the category "illegal alien" with the act of "illegal entry" (Illinois Legislative Investigating Commission, 1971:1, 11, 43). Even for the purposes of a proposed bill intended to implement employer sanctions for the hiring

of undocumented workers, the Commission defined "illegal alien" as "any alien . . . who has not obtained permission from the United States Government to be admitted to this country" (Appendix 2, p. 43), thereby overlooking altogether the possibility of overstaying a visa, or working in violation of a visa, that otherwise would constitute undocumented labor in spite of having obtained "permission to be admitted." This construction of migrant "illegality" is an effect of a long-established pattern of INS enforcement practices aimed disproportionately against "surreptitious entry" (precisely the profile of Mexican undocumented migration in particular) rather than other manifestations of undocumented status (cf. De Genova, 2002; in press).

11. These arrests took place in a period of heightened workplace raids, following the passage of the Illegal Immigration Reform and Immigrant Responsibility Act of 1996, which allocated additional resources to the Chicago-area INS for worksite enforcement. The number of investigators nationwide had been more than doubled from 317 to 701 during 1996. At the time, the Chicago office alone had 107 investigators and support personnel. See Gordon, 1997.

12. In the immediate aftermath of the African American "riots" in Chicago following Martin Luther King, Jr.'s assassination in 1968, between 1969 and 1974 the city of Chicago lost 212,000 manufacturing jobs (a decline of 12%), while overall employment in the suburbs increased by 18%, comprising 220,000 jobs (Preston, 1982:92; cf. Betancur et al., 1993:124–25).

13. The findings of the Illinois Legislative Investigating Commission's report on the "The Illegal Mexican Alien Problem" (1971) specifically identified an industrial working-class *suburb*, Chicago Heights, to the south of the city, as having "a particularly serious problem" with undocumented Mexican migration (Illinois Legislative Investigating Commission, 1971:6; cf. 3–6, 13–17).

14. This figure has been estimated by researchers at the Lewis Mumford Center for Comparative Urban and Regional Research at the State University of New York at Albany, intended to correct undercounting by the U.S. Census for 2000. The comparable U.S. Census 2000 figure is nearly 438,000.

15. On this score, Mike Davis's characterization of Chicago's Latino urban spaces as "polycentric barrios" is insufficient; in fact, there is a much more viable analogy to be drawn between Latino Chicago (or more precisely, Mexican Chicago) and Davis's model of Latino Los Angeles as a "city within a city" (cf. Davis, 2000:39–49).

16. Notably, the South Lawndale neighborhood to the southwest of Pilsen (soon to be better-known as Little Village) was growing rapidly—already 32% Mexican by this point (Belenchia, 1982:126).

17. "Alderman" is the title for the elected members of Chicago's City Council; each of the city's fifty electoral wards is represented by an alderman.

18. Rosenfeld (1993:5) suggests that Lozano came within 37 votes of a runoff, whereas Maria de los Angeles Torres (1991:171) claims that the margin was a mere 17 votes, and the Commission for Justice for Rudy Lozano (Taller de Estudios Comunitarios, n.d.:79) contends that he missed the runoff by only 7 votes.

19. For discussions of the fragmantation of the Latino coalition in Chicago city politics during the late 1980s that led to Latino support for Richard M. Daley, see Rivlin (1992); M. Torres (1991).

20. About 2,000 Puerto Ricans were recruited through private employment agencies in the 1946–47 period, and approximately 15,000 more were hired as seasonal farm workers. Ultimately, the bulk of Puerto Rican migration to Chicago did not come from these contract laborers; they did, however, serve as an important catalyst and resource for relatives and friends migrating to the region (Welfare Council of Metropolitan Chicago, 1957:17). As Maldonado (1979), Senior and Watkins (1966), and Isham Jones (1955) have noted, the seasonal farm labor system both augmented already existing Puerto Rican communities and prompted the emergence of new ones. Some agricultural workers stayed beyond the determined employment season and sought work in better-paid industrial jobs. This was the case for many early Puerto Rican agricultural workers in Wisconsin, Michigan, Indiana, and Illinois, who first had been contracted to harvest field crops and later found employment in foundries (Maldonado, 1979:117). Thus, labor shortages in steel mills after World War II provided fertile terrain for new Puerto Rican communities to develop and for already existing Puerto Rican areas to flourish during the early stages of migration to Chicago.
Castle, Barton, and Associates was a Chicago-based private employment agency that had opened offices in various cities throughout the United States and Puerto Rico (M. Martínez,

1989:93; Welfare Council of Metropolitan Chicago, 1957). In agreement with Puerto Rico's Department of Labor, this private employment agency recruited Puerto Rican women to be domestics in general household service and enlisted Puerto Rican men for foundry work at the Chicago Hardware Foundry Company in the far northern suburb of North Chicago. Thereafter, workers were brought to work on midwestern farms as well. (Welfare Council of Metropolitan Chicago, 1946; 1957:16). Government and private agencies recruited contract or seasonal workers directly from Puerto Rico and placed them in steel mills and factories in Lorraine, Ohio, and Gary, Indiana; in agriculture around Milwaukee, Wisconsin; and domestic service jobs in Chicago.

21. Notably, the percentage of Puerto Rican women who were employed in Chicago in 1960 as operatives and kindred workers, mainly in manufacturing, was 63%, considerably highter than the rate for men (cf. F. Padilla, 1987:114).

22. Official letter from Mr. Waitstill H. Sharp, director of Chicago Council Against Racial and Religious Discrimination, to Miss Hagel Holm of Maryville College, Tenn., in reference to Anthony Vega's policy to integrate Puerto Ricans; dated January 25, 1951 (Chicago: Chicago Historical Society).

23. The large majority (329) of the 396 Puerto Ricans first contracted in 1946 by Castle and Barton were young women who originally migrated as domestic workers and whose social activities were partly coordinated through the YWCA in Chicago; although there were some married couples contracted for domestic service, most of the Puerto Rican men were contracted for foundry work and were settled in the far northern suburb of North Chicago. Notably, when Puerto Rican men and women socialized together in a north suburban nightclub called the Happy Hour, frequented by foundry workers as well as Mexican braceros, the interrelations of Puerto Ricans and Mexicans tended to be more limited and sometimes conflictual (E. Padilla, 1947:84–86). Nevertheless, as the Puerto Rican foundry workers moved out of the barrack-like accommodations provided for them in converted freight cars, most relocated to rent rooms, either as individuals or married couples, in the homes of Mexicans in a small Mexican section of North Chicago (E. Padilla, 1947:86–87, 90). Likewise, whereas some of the Puerto Rican women eventually entered into "consensual unions" with Mexican men, many of the Puerto Ricans who first came into contact with Mexicans at the Rancho Grande "usually" resented "the disorganizing effect that contacts between Mexican men and Puerto Rican girls have had" (E. Padilla, 1947:90).

24. The careless recruitment and deplorable working conditions of contracted Puerto Rican workers in Chicago became a source of widely publicized controversy. As stipulated in a study by Elena Padilla and Muna Muñoz (1946), the Department of Labor did not require any proof of age or medical certificates from any of the workers, thus hiring extremely young and oftentimes physically ill Puerto Ricans to perform strenuous work. Charges of mistreatment of Chicago's Puerto Rican workers—including 15-hour workdays, substantially lower wages than other Chicago workers, unannounced transfering of domestic workers between worksites, etc.—triggered a storm of controversy, which occupied the front pages of Island newspapers. (*El Mundo* [San Juan], December 19, 27, 31, 1946, and January 4, 15, 18, 23, 24, 25, 28, and February 9, 1947; cited in Maldonado, 1979:114; cf. E. Padilla, 1947:92–93). As a consequence, Puerto Rican workers abandoned their labor contracts at extremely high rates (E. Padilla, 1947:87–89).

25. The theme of social distance in juxtaposition with geographical proximity was prominently developed in Harvey Warren Zorbaugh's classic sociological monograph *The Gold Coast and the Slum* (1929), which examined Chicago's Gold Coast in relation to the neighboring impoverished Italian slum.

26. One explanation for the Puerto Rican exodus from the racially mixed but predominantly Italian Near West Side community area advanced by Felix Padilla (1987:84), following Gerald Suttles (1968), is the interracial friction and the intensity of street gang violence between Italian, Mexican, Puerto Rican, and Black youth residing in various sections of the larger neighborhood.

27. Only days before the riot, the Chicago police superintendent, Orlando Wilson, had ordered a special report on racial tensions in both the Puerto Rican and Mexican communities, and the investigation had shown no signs whatsoever of unrest in either community (F. Padilla, 1987:149).

28. The racist stereotypes of criminality and violence had already been extended to the Chicago Puerto Rican community in 1960, when the *Saturday Evening Post,* a prominent national publication, ran a piece entitled "Crime without Reason" (November 5, 1960), with a yellow

tag attached to newsstand copies that read "Racial Violence in Chicago," relating the story of two Puerto Ricans who allegedly murdered a man they had never met for the simple reason that he was Italian, thus identifying the source of "racial violence" in the irrational criminality attributed to Puerto Ricans. The same article depicted Chicago's Puerto Ricans as "noisy" and "nervous," living on the streets and sidewalks during the warm-weather season, and having no social organizations or civic institutions other than taverns (F. Padilla, 1987:61).

29.   Whereas the New York Young Lords included a variety of Latino nationalities and class backgrounds in its constituency, the Chicago Young Lords were decidedly Puerto Ricans from poor barrio backgrounds. Many Chicago activists have pointed out that "the Young Lords originated in Chicago, but most people mistakenly think they began in New York." In fact, the Chicago Young Lords and their New York counterparts attempted to develop parallel strategies to address problems common to all U.S. Puerto Ricans, but the partnership between the two groups was short-lived due to differences in the class and educational backgrounds of the members. The New York Young Lords Organization (who later called themselves the Young Lords Party) had emerged among college-educated Puerto Rican youth. By contrast, the Chicago organization consisted largely of Puerto Rican high school dropouts more concerned with immediate barrio needs (Browning, 1973:25).

30.   Since these individuals had been renowned community activists prior to their arrests, various sectors of the community—not only those self-identified as *nacionalistas,* or advocates of Puerto Rican independence—devoted considerable energy and resources to their release. In September of 1999, most of these prisoners were given presidential pardon. Most of the released prisoners decided to relocate to Puerto Rico, rather than come back to their neighborhood in Chicago, for fear of retaliation by the Daley administration and local surveillance agents. In Chicago, nationalist activists recognized the prisoners' release as a bittersweet victory after fifteen years of amnesty campaigns. The victory was bittersweet not only because the release had not been unconditional (it was criminalized, rather than a recognition of the purely political character of the charges), but also because two of the most revered prisoners were not considered for presidential pardon. The two prisoners who remained in jail, considered the "masterminds" of the FALN, were the brother of a renowned Chicago activist and the son of the reverend of a local church. For various accounts of the individual or collective motivations which led to the creation of the FALN, see Fernández (1994); cf. Zwerman (1994; 1995).

31.   Not surprisingly, when José Padilla was arrested in Chicago's O'Hare International Airport in 2002 on allegations of his involvement with the Al Qaeda "terrorist" network, even the most sympathetic reporters tried to explain his "anti-American" sentiments in light of his upbringing in Chicago, particularly searching for elements of his youth as a "typical Puerto Rican" in the area—growing up in the Logan Square neighborhood, belonging to a street gang, being raised by a single mother—that might have become explosive in the midst of the politically charged atmosphere of Puerto Rican Chicago during the 1980s and '90s.

32.   J. E. Cruz, "Puerto Rican Poverty," pp. 2–11 in *Advocacy Notes,* National Puerto Rican Coalition (October 1991–December 1992).

33.   The index of dissimilarity is a percentage; it indicates that percentage of the total population which would have to physically relocate in order for their group to be distributed across the particular geography's census tracts in the same way as members of the comparison group. The higher the value (on a scale from 0 to 1.00) reveals the degree to which the two groups compared tend to live in separate census tracts.

34.   These measures of residential dissimilarity scores in U.S. cities were calculated from the 2000 Census by researchers at the Lewis Mumford Center for Comparative Urban and Regional Research at the State University of New York at Albany. Whereas the overall segregation of Latinos from African Americans had ranked Chicago highest among all U.S. cities in 1980, and second highest in 1990, these figures ranked Chicago third highest for the year 2000; the comparative ranking among the sixty most segregated U.S. cities for overall segregation of Latinos from whites in Chicago had actually risen from nineth highest in 1990 to sixth highest in 2000.

35.   The higher figures have been estimated by researchers at the Lewis Mumford Center for Comparative Urban and Regional Research at the State University of New York at Albany, intended to correct undercounting by the U.S. Census for 2000. The lower figures come from U.S. Census 2000. "Metropolitan area" here refers to the Primary Metropolitan Statistical Area (PMSA).

36. These six neighborhoods are West Town, Humboldt Park, Logan Square, Avondale, Hermosa, and Belmont Cragin.
37. These figures are compiled from U.S. Census 2000 data. The comparable figures for 1990 actually revealed somewhat higher percentages of Puerto Ricans in three of the four South Side neighborhoods, but were rather similar overall: Pilsen (92.4% Mexican; 2.7% Puerto Rican); Little Village (92.7% Mexican; 3.2% Puerto Rican); Back of the Yards (88.2% Mexican; 5.6% Puerto Rican); South Chicago (85.8% Mexican; 7.2% Puerto Rican). The 1990 figures are based on U.S. Census data for Chicago Community Areas, compiled by the Latino Institute, June 1991.
38. For further discussion of these "nationalist performances," see Ramos-Zayas (2003).
39. An important (and widely celebrated) precursor for our study is Felix Padilla's work (1985) on the emergence of Latino "ethnic consciousness" and political mobilization among Mexican American and Puerto Rican community organizers in Chicago in the 1970s. Padilla sought to problematize the naturalization of the "Latino" or "Hispanic" labels within conventional social science research, and rightly emphasized the situational character of Latinismo as it emerged in shared political contexts as a new "ethnic group identity," distinct from specific Latin American national-origin group identities. Much of the merit of Padilla's study, however, derives from the relative uniqueness of the historically specific situation of Latinos in Chicago, i.e., the roughly comparable size of the Mexican and Puerto Rican communities in the early 1970s. In 1970, when Puerto Rican migration had already peaked, however, Mexican migration was at the threshold of a new period of accelerated growth. At that particular historical moment, nonetheless, the size of the two communities was nearly comparable: 79,000 Puerto Ricans (comprising 32% of Chicago's Latino population), and an estimated, but very probably undercounted, 83,000 Mexicans (accounting for 43% or more of Chicago's Latinos) (cf. F. Padilla, 1985:56). Despite the roughly comparable numbers of the two groups in Chicago in 1970, however, both the earlier as well as the subsequent periods are distinguished, in fact, by the numerical preponderance of Mexicans. Therefore, the appearance of a kind of numerical parity between the two groups during the 1970s, on which important aspects of Padilla's arguments are premised, has been misleading. Padilla's study of "Latino ethnic consciousness in Chicago" is also impaired by its rather selective focus on a very small number of specifically Latino-identified political organizations and their activists, which necessarily imposed limits on the relevance of his study for considerations of the possibilities for Latinidad in everyday life.
40. In contrast, by 1979, there were fourteen African American aldermen on Chicago's fifty-member City Council (Preston, 1982:100–101).
41. Latino Institute, *Al Filo/At the Cutting Edge: The Empowerment of Chicago's Latino Electorate* (Chicago, 1986).

Chapter 3

1. These statistics for "foreign-born" Mexican migrants as a whole are less extreme but still rather high. In 1990, 18.4% of all Mexican migrants in Illinois were living below the poverty level, and for noncitizen Mexicans the poverty rate was 19.2% (Paral, 1997:Table 21).
2. These statistics, based upon U.S. Census Bureau data, U.S. Immigration and Naturalization Service surveys, and research by the National Immigration Law Center, were compiled by the Legal Center of the Hermandad Mexicana Nacional (1994).
3. For instance, although the Illinois Legislative Investigating Commission's report on the "The Illegal Mexican Alien Problem" (1971) was explicitly interested in establishing that undocumented Mexican migrants represented a fiscal burden to the state, the Commission's random survey to determine the scope of unemployment benefits and public aid payments made to undocumented Mexicans was able to identify only two migrants (representing only 1.05% of the sample) who had received any form of public assistance payment whatsoever (Illinois Legislative Investigating Commission, 1971:36–37).
4. While comparable figures for U.S.-born Mexican women were considerably higher—13.9% of teen mothers and 16.6% of young mothers receiving welfare payments, respectively—their participation in these public assistance programs was nevertheless significantly lower than that of their Puerto Rican counterparts (Kahn and Berkowitz, 1995:Tables A.6, B.5).

5. It is ironic for our purposes that Oscar Lewis's "culture of poverty" thesis (1959; cf. 1970) was originally formulated on the basis of his research among both Mexicans (in Mexico) and Puerto Ricans (in both Puerto Rico and New York City). Lewis posited that "poverty . . . creates a subculture of its own," and that "one can speak of the culture of the poor, for it has its own modalities and distinctive social and psychological consequences . . . [that cut] across regional, rural-urban, and even national boundaries" (1959:2); furthermore, he contended that "once [the culture of poverty] comes into existence, it tends to perpetuate itself from generation to generation [such that] by the time the slum children are age six or seven they have usually absorbed the basic values and attitudes of their subculture and are not psychologically geared to take full advantage of changing conditions or increased opportunities which may occur in their lifetime" (1966:xlv). Thus, Lewis pathologizes the behaviors and values of poor people, regardless of their particular cultural milieus, but by culturalizing these pathologies, his position encourages the view that poor people become trapped in endemic poverty because of their "culture." Such concepts have continued to be remarkably influential in much of contemporary hegemonic social science research, as evidenced by the "underclass" theories of the 1980s and '90s.

6. It may be useful to emphasize here that it is not at all unusual for Mexican migrants to begin working at such a young age (and younger) in U.S. agriculture.

7. For a more extended treatment of the gendered dimensions of Mexican migrants' racialized constructions of "laziness," see De Genova (1999:287–356; in press).

8. This joke is also gendered in a manner that parallels Evangelina's remarks, inasmuch as the figure of Pancho Villa is a premier symbol, not merely of a romanticized nationalist Mexicanness, but more accurately, of an heroic, popular-nationalist, Mexican masculinity (cf. Paredes, 1971[1993:234]).

9. For a discussion of Pancho Villa jokes as a distinct genre, see Reyna (1984). For a more extended discussion of this joke, especially in relation to Blackness, see De Genova (1999:287–356; in press).

10. It is possible to identify the same distinctions, deployed fairly consistently, in the transcripts of ethnographic interviews with Mexican migrants compiled by Jorge Durand and his collaborators, and published in Spanish (1996). One encounters the phrase "*americanos o negros*" (p. 217), as well as an operative mutually exclusive juxtaposition of "*gringos*" and "*negros*" (pp. 92–93, 106), or "*gabachos*" and "*negros*" (p. 57).

11. In Mexican Spanish, the term "*¿Mande . . . ?*" supplies a polite but ubiquitous way of asking the question "What?"—especially when requesting that someone repeat what they have already said. Literally, the word is the polite form of address for the imperative of the verb *mandar,* hence glossed here by a Puerto Rican observer to mean "Order me . . ." or something akin to "At your service . . ."

Chapter 4

1. The Puerto Ricanization of "salsa" began with its very genesis as a distinct musical genre in a manner that must be problematized in relation to salsa's antecedents in Cuban *son*. The popularity of Cuban-identified musical forms among U.S. audiences had been based upon extensive U.S. tourism and economic interests in Cuba, prior to the Cuban Revolution of 1959. While there are diverse and conflicting accounts of the history of salsa, it is indeed instructive to situate these debates in relation to the historical moment following the Cuban Revolution when Cold War–era imperatives increasingly sought to discredit any cultural forms that could be claimed as expressions of the vitality of Cuban nationalism. Thus, in an era when Cuban-born musicians in the U.S. were often persecuted as "communists," the refashioning of *son* into salsa, and the Puerto Ricanization of salsa as a distinct musical form originating in New York City, arguably provided a "good citizen" alternative to the politically problematic (Cuban-identified) genre from which it was being differentiated. While salsa is commonly celebrated as something distinctly "Puerto Rican," its historical relationship with Cuban music has also been a significant inspiration for pan-Caribbean culturalist expressions of Latinidad, especially in the U.S., in ways that notably exclude other Latinos, such as Mexicans.

2. The Puerto Ricanization of Cuban *son* that established salsa as a distinct and originally New York–identified musical form was itself a parochialization of a musical genre that had already

enjoyed considerable transnational publicity. Once salsa had become pronouncedly Puerto Rican–identified and associated through its lyrical content with the specific experiences of Puerto Rican communities in New York City, however, salsa was poised again to be globalized in new ways in the 1980s and '90s.

3. For instance, the local 26th Ward alderman Billy Ocasio, born and raised in Chicago, launched a successful electoral campaign in the barrio wearing a straw hat and emphasizing his "*jíbaro*" background. In Puerto Rico, the image of the *jíbaro,* when deployed in the context the electoral politics, is a widely recognized symbol of the Partido Popular Democratico, the pro-Commonwealth party. In Chicago, and many other diasporic Puerto Rican communities, however, the *jíbaro* is a more generic symbol of authenticity and considered a lowest common denominator, useful in political campaigning. Hence, the *jíbaro* in Chicago is not associated with a specific political party, but is a fairly ubiquitous strategy common to Puerto Rican–identified urban politics.

4. Terms like "nigger" and "ghetto" were casually invoked among students at the alternative school were Ramos-Zayas volunteered, as well as at the local public high school. In this instance, rather than indicating any truly volatile animosity, this form of name-calling, and recourse here to an otherwise racist epithet, often functioned to signify the close friendship between the parties to the exchange. Although David clearly felt compelled to reply to William's insult with another insult, he nonetheless also reinforced his closeness to William by using a language that in any other context (or with people other than close friends) would be considered degrading and a cause for serious conflict. William was only slightly darker-skinned than David, and he was not especially dark by the standards of other youth at the school. The racialized name-calling in this case was clearly affectionate, despite its aggressive masculinist form. Elsewhere, Ramos-Zayas (1997) discusses the counterintuitive uses of racialized terms in apparently nonracial contexts, when she describes the ways in which Puerto Ricans used terms like "*rubia*" or "*colorá*" to describe beauty, even when the person (usually a woman) to whom the terms were applied was not a blonde or redhead.

   Discussing the intimate, affectionate, often diminutive uses of "*negro/negrito*" in Colombia to address people not otherwise readily classifiable as "Black," Wade suggests that the potency of these gestures of affection derives "precisely from the contravention of a more basic meaning: intimacy is implied by the ability to use a potentially derogatory term without derogation" (Wade, 1993:260). Likewise, De Genova (1999; in press) discusses the use of the word "*negro*" in Spanish, as well as "*nigger*" in English, as terms of endearment (regardless of whether or not the person referenced was actually dark-skinned by specifically Mexican standards of reference), in relation to Mexican migrants' more frankly derogatory racialized discourses about African Americans.

5. As Edna Acosta-Belén (1992) explains, the "Nuyorican" or "Neorican"—a hybrid word from "New [York]" and "[Puerto] Rican"—originally had negative connotations, especially as it was used on the Island. In its inception, the term suggested an undesirable cultural "impurity" produced among uneducated younger generations of Puerto Ricans from "the New York ghetto." "Nuyorican" is the first term coined to articulate distinctions between Puerto Ricans "from the Island" and Puerto Ricans "from the mainland U.S." (specifically, New York), and suggests a difference which transcends place of birth to focus on distinctive sociocultural identitities. Through the cultural and literary achievements of Puerto Ricans artists in New York, the term was adopted by younger Puerto Rican generations to describe a new "identity consciousness" and "cultural syncretism" (Flores, 1993), as well as to designate a growing Puerto Rican literary canon illustrative of their unique migration and barrio life experiences. As Acosta-Belén explains, "Regardless of its implied geographic limitations, since not all U.S. Puerto Rican writers are from New York, the label is now generally accepted by many of the writers themselves as a word that defines a collective Puerto Rican identity stemming from the migrant experience and thus differentiated from that of the island" (Acosta-Belén, 1992:980). Hence, "Nuyorican" or "Neorican" was conceived primarily as a classification for the literature produced in the emerging Puerto Rican enclaves of New York.

6. Even as the term became a sign of pride (rather than a pejorative term) among New York Puerto Ricans, "Nuyorican" continues to suggest a degraded kind of "assimilation" and "inauthenticity" to Puerto Ricans on the Island. In Puerto Rico's popular culture and media (especially on television sitcoms), the Nuyorican is generally portrayed as dark, young, and embodying mannerisms and dress styles that some Puerto Ricans on the Island associate with

Black American youth. Regardless of age, the Nuyorican is always negatively stereotyped as eternally adolescent, loud, irresponsible, immature, and disrespectful to the elderly by using the informal form of "you" (*tú* instead of *usted*) to address older people.

7. The term "migration" often evokes the imagery of the massive migrations of the 1940s, '50s, and '60s. In the collective imaginary, the most pervasive type of "migrant" is the one who left the Island escaping poverty to settle in the New York Puerto Rican barrios; the one whose patriotic love would always be tempting him back; the one who attempted to attain the American Dream, as long as it would enable him to buy a parcel of land and return to his beloved Island; and, ultimately, the one who died poor and still "exiled" on the streets of Spanish Harlem. For instance, in the movie *La guagua aérea*, Island-based cinematographer Luis Molina satirizes a 1940s trip of Puerto Rican migrants carrying live crabs that break loose through the airplane floor, to the North American flight attendant's dismay; of people pulling out *fiambreras* (lunch pails) of rice and beans when the airplane food is unsavory, unseasoned, or simply unrecognized; and of a typical applause as the airplane lands successfully. Flashes of the passengers' "past" life, the one they are now leaving behind in their towns in Puerto Rico, and visions of a future in the U.S., provide the bittersweetness and intensely emotional dimensions to this otherwise comic movie. Similarly, *nueva trova* songs like Roy Brown's "Boricua en la Luna" narrate the story of the expatriate migrant who dies in the streets of the U.S. These images are complicated by competing discourses of the migrant as an urban "underclass," with all the racializing and colonialist projections that implies.

8. "Gang-banger" was the ubiquitous term used in English to refer to street gang members in Chicago, and will be deployed in the ensuing text as the most appropriate category to convey the colloquial sense of words like "*ganguero*," "*cholo*," or "*pandillero*" that appear in Spanish-language quotes.

9. The term "*pocho*" is a widely used derogatory term for Mexicans raised in the U.S., deployed by Mexicans in Mexico and migrants in the U.S. Its literal meaning is "pale" or "pale-faced," implying that such U.S.-born and -raised "Mexicans" have been sapped of their natural strength and vigor, that their Mexican inheritance has been diluted, that they have been "whitened" or even perhaps that they have tried to whiten themselves in spite of their Mexican inheritance (cf. Maciel, 1991; Madrid-Barela, 1976; Monsiváis, 1987). Figuratively, then, the term connotes cultural inauthenticity, if not outright abjection, but in a way that also exposes the contiguity of culturalist and racialist assumptions.

10. Here it is important to recall that this usage of the category "American" ("*americano*") is discrepant with the more ubiquitous Mexican/migrant equation of that term with racial whiteness, in a way that would very seldom include Puerto Ricans. For a further discussion, see De Genova (1999:287–356; in press).

11. As we have indicated previously, the term "Chicano" actually has very little currency in Chicago; very few Mexicans raised in the U.S. would identify themselves as "Chicanos" in Chicago; for most, the pervasive category of self-identification was simply "Mexican," rather than "Chicano/a" or "Mexican American." In the particular instance discussed above, recourse to the term "Chicano" on the parts of David and Benito is best understood in light of their long prior experiences in California. In general, this important sociocultural distinction tended to be otherwise more commonly expressed descriptively, e.g., in terms of those "who were born here," "who grew up here," "who are from here," etc.

12. For a related discussion of this incident, see De Genova (1999:260–65).

Chapter 5

1. Later, during that same ESL session, Benito Vásquez turned the inquiry back upon the anthropologist, demanding, "Nick, what's your story? Tell us about Italy." De Genova replied, "But I'm not from Italy; I was born and grew up in Chicago." David Villanueva then persisted, grinning: "Were you born in Cook County Hospital?"—a joke that everyone understood because of the stigma attached to the county hospital as the last resort for healthcare among only the most desperate of poor people. When De Genova replied, however, that he had been born at St. Elizabeth's Hospital [on the border between West Town and Humboldt Park], it is noteworthy that Villanueva's immediate response was, "Oh—in the Puerto Rican neighborhood!"

2. The Moynihan Report (1965) popularized and racialized much of the "culture of poverty" notions that were current in academic social science through its pathologization of African American "female-headed households," effectively equating endemic poverty with "dysfunctional families" and the presumed absence of strong male role models. While the stigma of "divorce" and "dysfunctional" families has frequently been attached to Puerto Rican women's welfare "dependency," in ways that are juxtaposed with purportedly "traditional" (and, by implication, properly functioning) Mexican families, this distinction has often also taken the form of a more generic opposition between the family structures or patterns of "Hispanics" in contradistinction to African Americans, in a manner that elides the specificities of Puerto Rican experiences altogether (e.g., Taub, 1991); some social scientists recapitulate this perspective by upholding "underclass" theory for Blacks, but disavowing the relevance of "underclass" theory for "Hispanics" (e.g., Moore and Pinderhughes, 1993).

3. Pérez (2003) depicts the ironic contrast between two women interviewed in her study: a Mexican/migrant woman who accused Puerto Rican women of being "*rencorosas*" [unforgiving], and attributed this shortcoming to the high incidence of divorce among Puerto Ricans, despite the fact that she herself had not forgiven two previous husbands whom she had divorced; and a Puerto Rican woman who characterized Mexican women as "*sufridas*" [inured to their own suffering], despite the fact that she herself would routinely welcome her abusive husband back after repeated conflicts. By reappropriating as positive qualities the stereotypes projected upon their respectively racialized gender positions, these women engaged in a process of defensive self-racialization, through which they reconstituted their gendered identities in light of their respective racializations as "Mexican" and "Puerto Rican."

4. By examining the children of unions between Mexicans and Puerto Ricans, Rúa (2001) eloquently demonstrates how Mexicanness is Puerto Ricanized and how Puerto Ricanness is Mexicanized in the deployment of "PortoMex" and "MexiRican" identities in Chicago. Puerto Ricans often perceived these romantic unions between Mexicans and Puerto Ricans with considerable suspicion, as unions of legal convenience in which the Mexican partner was seeking to acquire U.S. legal residency or access to U.S. citizenship by marrying a Puerto Rican. Rúa's ethnographic examination of upwardly mobile "bicultural" Latinos examines the ways that romantic liaisons between Mexicans and Puerto Ricans often developed at the margins of community sanctions, and thus carved out spaces of resistance to internal racialization processes among Latinos. The dissolution of these romantic unions, however, was also critical in the tendency of their offspring to resume nationality-based, rather than mixed, identifications, with most claiming the racialized identity of the parent that was more present in their lives. While this tendency was also apparent in Ramos-Zayas's research, the impact of neighborhood affiliation was also critical in the identity deployed by children of mixed (Mexican and Puerto Rican) parentage, as in Mercedes's case.

5. It is unknown what specific forms of public assistance benefits, and during what specific time period, that Luisa Zambrano had been able to access, in spite of the restrictions on her eligibility as a migrant.

Chapter 6

1. For a further discussion of the racialized politics of language in relation to a methodological critique of ethnographic research, see De Genova (1999:129–204; in press).

2. Although recent work in the field of Cultural Studies has examined how Puerto Ricans and African Americans in New York participate in overlapping and intersecting artistic and popular cultural expressive forms and genres (e.g., Flores, 2000), the autobiographical work of Piri Thomas (1967), for example, also underscores the important ways in which Thomas, as a Black Puerto Rican, deployed the Spanish language in public spaces to mark his "Puerto Ricanness" and avoid being mistaken for African American.

3. Rodríguez-Morazani (1998a) has forcefully criticized Clara Rodríguez's (1989) "Rainbow People" thesis, which contends that, by being considered "neither black nor white" and by being positioned "between black and white," but more importantly, by spanning the phenotypic spectrum from white to Black, the "racial" hybridity of Puerto Ricans in the U.S. effectively disrupts and challenges the hegemonic Black-white racial binary. Rodríguez-Morazani notes that the "Rainbow People" metaphor—in all its colorfulness—continues

to view "race" in essentialist terms that privilege "color," while undermining or altogether overlooking the historically contingent and colonial context in which Puerto Ricans have come to be racially marked in the United States.

4. In Puerto Rico, as Santos-Febres (1996) notes, rap performers and fans are frequently constructed as delinquents, and are identified as those responsible for deploying discourses of Latinidad and Blackness on the Island and for promoting "a new identity designated with the epithet la raza [the race]" (1996:229). Rap music continues to be associated specifically with Mainlanders who return to the Island. As Santos notes, rappers are generally characterized as "young men, blacks and mulattos, between the ages of 14 and 25 from the 'lower' classes of the unemployed and underemployed" (1996:229). Likewise, they are assumed to have been born in New York and thus, by conventional definition, are Nuyorican Others. The fact that rap music participates in a well-articulated popular cultural system that includes identifiable social groups, forms of linguistic expression, distinctive fashions, a discourse of identities, and symbolic economies of violence, further accentuates the contrast between Nuyorican Otherness and the Island elite's preferred distinctions of status and "taste." Knowledge of the streets is the implicit social knowledge valued by Mainland youth, and it is this same knowledge that allows Mainlanders to be rendered as violent outsiders in the eyes of the Islander elite. For extensive analyses of the role of salsa, hip-hop, and Latin/Boricua rap in Puerto Rico and the United States, see Aparicio (1997); Santos-Febres (1996); Glasser (1995); Quintero Rivera (1991); Flores (2000).

5. While many of working-class and poor Puerto Ricans, such as Eugenio, in Humboldt Park and West Town frequently associated "Black culture" with rap music, oversized hip-hop fashions, and "bad" English, many of the Puerto Rican middle-class professionals who worked in white-collar jobs at various not-for-profit organizations in Humboldt Park frequently noted the existence of a significant African American professional middle class, whom they perceived as having higher rates of upward social mobility than most Puerto Ricans (Ramos-Zayas, 2003). These more affluent African Americans tended to be disassociated from the "Black English" that many Puerto Rican migrants associated with the degraded status of impoverished U.S.-born "minority," for which Blackness was the template, that they were intent to reject among their own younger generation. Thus, there were class-inflected contexts in which "Black English" was divorced from some Black people, and in which African Americans were viewed as comparatively more "privileged" than Latinos.

6. As Urciuoli (2003) convincingly argues, the major language issue faced by working-class New York Latinos is not conveyed in the question "Do they speak English?" but rather, by the ways in which their English is subject to judgment by non-Latinos, particularly when those judgments are backed up by institutional prestige. Perceptions of linguistic "disorder" signal a transposition of racial judgment onto linguistic practices. Upwardly mobile bilinguals thus often found themselves monitoring how they enacted their identities. For many Latino, and especially Puerto Rican, students at the elite liberal arts college where Urciuoli conducted her study, Spanish was supposed to be part of their racialized "multicultural" personae, but that only worked, semiotically, "if Spanish and English stay[ed] neatly compartmentalized. Otherwise the performance may be judged as disorderly, may be racialized."

From their sociolinguistic research in New York's Barrio (East Harlem), Flores et al. conclude that the linguistic abilities of Puerto Ricans (of all generations) have to be placed in a Spanish-English continuum, with most Puerto Ricans speaking some combination of both languages—Spanglish (1987:228). Drawing upon these findings, the authors argue that assimilation is neither a "fatal assault on the national culture of a colonially-oppressed people" (as Seda Bonilla [1972], Maldonado-Denis [1976], and Nieves-Falcón [1975] have variously argued), nor is it reducible to "the problematic insertion of another ethnic subculture into a variegated current of the North American immigrant experience" (1987:230). Flores et al. contend that analyses which polarize U.S. Puerto Ricans' identities into one or the other national alternative—Puerto Rican or U.S. ("American")—are inadequate to address the constitutive duality of the Puerto Rican experience, as is shown in the adoption of Spanglish to convey a hybrid and dynamic cultural identity. This argument is further developed by Quintero Rivera (1991), who emphasizes that "language-transformation is an important element in the symbolic infusion of new meanings into identities that is part of many social movements throughout the continent" (1991:101). For an analysis of the ways in which cultural "authenticity" is invariably measured in relation to creative language practices among families in Puerto Rico and in East Harlem, see Zentella (1990; 1997).

7. The emergence of explicitly Nuyorican-identified poets and writers has inspired some critics to herald "the development of a new language, of a new form of communication emerging out of a collective reality and as part of an ethnic struggle, [turning] the individual act of creation into a social process" (Quintero Rivera, 1991:101). Hence, Spanglish, as a dynamic linguistic form in its own right, becomes an essential instrument in the construction of collective identities among Puerto Ricans specifically identified with New York City and other U.S. mainland locations.

8. Despite Francisco's conflation of the two, speaking Spanish and bilingual code-switching, historically, have been linguistic strategies deployed by Puerto Ricans in the U.S. to separate themselves from African Americans. As Wakefield noted in his 1950s study, "speaking only Spanish identifies [Puerto Ricans] as foreign and therefore not just a Negro" (1957:41). Given this crucial racialized context, the "loss" of the Spanish language among subsequent U.S.-born generations has often become a preoccupation not only for migrants in the U.S., but also for Puerto Ricans on the Island. Discourses surrounding the stereotypical image of the "Nuyorican"—the U.S.-born Puerto Rican who is presumed to speak neither Spanish nor English but only Spanglish—provide a crucial example of this anxiety on the Island (Acosta-Belén 1991–92; Attinasi, 1983; Flores, 1987; F. Padilla, 1987; Quintero Rivera 1991; Zentella, 1990).

9. For further discussion of various forms of distinctly Chicano Spanish, see Anzaldúa (1990); cf. Mendoza-Denton (1999).

Chapter 7

1. For discussions of the long history by which the term "Mexican" itself has been reduced to a racist epithet in the formerly Mexican territories of what has come to be known as the U.S. "Southwest," often with the distinctively Texan inflection "Meskin," see De León (1983); Foley (1997:8); Mirandé (1987:3); Vélez-Ibáñez (1996:71–77, 86, 91, 268); Vila (2000:81–165).

2. For a more extended discussion of this interview excerpt, see De Genova (1999:394–405; in press).

3. Among Puerto Ricans, the term "*moreno*" is used in reference to middle-class or socially prominent/well-respected Blacks, whereas "*prieto*" is used in reference to the most marginalized segments of a Black community. See also Arlene Torres (1998). (This usage is distinctly different from that of Mexicans).

4. "Taíno"-ness was deployed only symbolically in Chicago, unlike in some communities in the northeastern U.S. where an active "Taíno"-ness has emerged as a modality of self-identification, and some Puerto Ricans have become invested in tracing their genealogy and phenotype to actual Taínos. As Duany and Jiménez Román have each argued, the renewed interest in tracing one's roots to the Taíno Indians is an attempt for Puerto Ricans to create an unbalanced racial triad by focusing on a long-deceased indigenous population as a disavowal and movement away from Blackness (cf. Duany, 1990; Jiménez Román, 1990).

5. For a more extended discussion, see De Genova (1999:227–53).

6. We are grateful to Carlos Vargas for calling our attention to this discrepancy in Alfredo's usage.

7. For an extended dicussion of these grassroots political efforts, see Ramos-Zayas (1997).

8. Maria echoes the role of context in political conscientization and identification in ways that resonate with Winddance Twine's study of biracial women at the University of California–Berkeley. Raised in white suburbs, once these women moved to another context—in this case, the University of California at Berkeley—spaces and possibilities for new political expressions and alliances complicated their previous self-identifications (Winddance Twine, 1997: 214).

9. As Oboler notes, "instead of recognizing diversity, [upwardly mobile Latino college students] opt to emphasize a nebulous definition of Latino group identity—creating, for example, the 'ideal Latina' or 'Latino,' the stereotyped version of a homogenized Latino or Latina self" (Oboler, 1995:172). These "upwardly mobile" or "college identities" invariable relied on the creation of essentialized and bounded notions of a singular "Latino culture" grounded in ideas of the "authentic Latino." In this sense, they participated in the larger process whereby whites enjoy the privilege of individuality, but people racialized at the margins of white power tend to be constructed as mere "representative specimens" of their collective categories of racialized social being.

10. This episode ought not to be misunderstood to suggest that police in Chicago were otherwise lenient toward Mexican migrants. Indeed, what followed was an extended discussion of how undocumented Mexican migrants routinely found themselves harassed by police who extracted bribes from them whenever the vulnerability that defined their generally undocumented condition became exposed, e.g., not having a driver's license. For further discussion of the "illegalities of everyday life," see De Genova (2002; cf. 1999:471–76).

References

Acosta-Belén, Edna. "Ethnicity, Gender, and Cultural Revitalization in the Nuyorriqueña Literature." *Homines* 15, no. 2–16, no. 1 (1991–92):338–57.

Acuña, Rodolfo. *Occupied America: A History of Chicanos.* 2nd ed. New York: Harper and Row, 1981.

——*Occupied America: A History of Chicanos.* 3rd ed. New York: HarperCollins, 1988.

——*Anything but Mexican: Chicanos in Contemporary Los Angeles.* New York: Verso, 1996.

——*Occupied America: A History of Chicanos.* 4th ed. New York: Addison-Wesley Longman, 2000.

Allen, Theodore. *The Invention of the White Race, Vol. 1: Racial Oppression and Social Control.* New York: Verso, 1994.

Almaguer, Tomás. *Racial Fault Lines: The Historical Origins of White Supremacy in California.* Berkeley: University of California Press, 1994.

Alonso, Ana María. *Thread of Blood: Colonialism, Revolution, and Gender on Mexico's Northern Frontier.* Tucson: University of Arizona Press, 1995.

Anderson, Alan B., and George W. Pickering. *Confronting the Color Line: The Broken Promise of the Civil Rights Movement in Chicago.* Athens, GA: University of Georgia Press, 1986.

Año Nuevo Kerr, Louise. *The Chicano Experience in Chicago, 1920–70.* Ph.D. dissertation, Department of History, University of Illinois at Chicago, 1976.

Anzaldúa, Gloria. "How to Tame a Wild Tongue." In *Out There: Marginalization and Contemporary Culture,* ed. Russell Ferguson, Martha Gever, Trinh T. Minh-ha, and Cornel West, pp. 203–11. New York and Cambridge, MA: New Museum of Contemporary Art and Massachusetts Institute of Technology Press, 1990.

Aparicio, Frances R. "On Sub-Versive Signifiers: Tropicalizing Language in the United States." In *Tropicalizations: Transcultural Representations of Latinidad,* ed. Frances R. Aparicio and Susana Chávez-Silverman, pp. 194–212. Hanover, NH: Dartmouth College/University of New England Press, 1997.

Aparicio, Frances R., and Susana Chávez-Silverman. "Introduction." In *Tropicalizations: Transcultural Representations of Latinidad,* ed. Frances R. Aparicio and Susana Chávez-Silverman, pp. 1–17. Hanover, NH: Dartmouth College/University of New England Press, 1997.

Arias Jirasek, Rita, and Carlos Tortolero. *Mexican Chicago.* Chicago: Arcadia/Tempus Publishing, 2001.

Attinasi, John J. "Language Attitudes and Working Class Ideology in a Puerto Rican Barrio of New York." *Ethnic Groups* 5, nos. 1–2 (1983):55–78.

Baker, Anthony. *The Social Production of Space of Two Chicago Neighborhoods: Pilsen and Lincoln Park.* Ph.D. dissertation, Department of Sociology, University of Illinois at Chicago, 1995.

Balderrama, Francisco, and Raymond Rodríguez. *Decade of Betrayal: Mexican Repatriation in the 1930s.* Albuquerque: University of New Mexico Press, 1995.

Barrera, Mario. *Race and Class in the Southwest: A Theory of Racial Inequality.* Notre Dame, In: University of Notre Dame Press, 1979.

Barrett, James R. *Work and Community in the Jungle: Chicago's Packinghouse Workers, 1894–1922.* Urbana: University of Illinois Press, 1987.

Bederman, Gail. *Manliness and Civilization: A Cultural History of Gender and Race in the United States, 1880–1917.* Chicago: University of Chicago Press, 1995.

Belenchia, Joanne. "The Latino Communities." Chapter 2 (pp. 12–40). In *The Political Organization of Chicago's Latino Communities,* by John Walton and Luis M. Salces. Evanston, IL: Center for Urban Affairs, Northwestern University, 1977.

—— "Latinos and Chicago Politics." In *After Daley: Chicago Politics in Transition,* ed. Samuel K. Gove and Louis H. Masotti, pp. 118–45. Urbana: University of Illinois Press, 1982.

Betancur, John, Teresa Córdova, and María de los Angeles Torres. "Economic Restructuring and the Process of Incorporation of Latinos into the Chicago Economy." In *Latinos in a Changing U.S. Economy: Comparative Perspectives on Growing Inequality,* ed. Rebecca Morales and Frank Bonilla, pp. 109–32. Newbury Park, CA: Sage, 1993.

Bowden, Charles, and Lew Kreinberg. *Street Signs Chicago: Neighborhood and Other Illusions of Big-City Life.* Chicago: Chicago Review Press, 1981.

Browning, Frank. "From Rumble to Revolution: The Young Lords." In *The Puerto Rican Experience: A Sociological Sourcebook,* ed. Francesco Cordasco and Eugene Bucchioni, pp. 231–45. Totowa, NJ, New Jersey: Littlefield, Adams & Co., 1973.

Burnett, Christina Duffy, and Burke Marshall, eds. *Foreign in a Domestic Sense: Puerto Rico, American Expansion, and the Constitution.* Durham, NC: Duke University Press, 2001.

Cabán, Pedro. "Redefining Puerto Rico's Political Status." In *Colonial Dilemma: Critical Perspectives on Contemporary Puerto Rico,* ed. Edwin Meléndez and Edgardo Meléndez, pp. 19–39. Boston: South End Press, 1993.

———*Constructing a Colonial People: Puerto Rico and the United States, 1898–1932.* New York: Westview, 1999.

Cabranes, José A. *Citizenship and the American Empire.* New Haven: Yale University Press, 1979.

———"Some Common Ground." In *Foreign in a Domestic Sense: Puerto Rico, American Expansion, and the Constitution,* ed. Christina Duffy Burnett and Burke Marshall, pp. 39–47. Durham, NC: Duke University Press, 2001.

Calavita, Kitty. *U.S. Immigration Law and the Control of Labor: 1820–1924.* New York: Academic Press, 1984.

———*Inside the State: The Bracero Program, Immigration, and the I.N.S.* New York: Routledge, 1992.

———"The New Politics of Immigration: 'Balanced Budget Conservatism' and the Symbolism of Proposition 187." *Social Problems* 43, no. 3 (1996):284–299.

Camarota, Steven A. *Immigration from Mexico: Assessing the Impact on the United States.* Washington, DC: Center for Immigration Studies, 2001

Cardoso, Lawrence. *Mexican Emigration to the United States, 1897–1931.* Tucson: University of Arizona Press, 1980.

Caruso, Jorge, and Eduardo Camacho. *Hispanics in Chicago.* Reprints from the *Chicago Reporter.* Chicago: Community Renewal Society, 1985.

Carr, Raymond. *Puerto Rico: A Colonial Experiment.* New York: Vintage/Random House, 1984.

Carr, Norma. *The Puerto Ricans in Hawaii, 1900–1958.* Ph.D. dissertation, University of Michigan, 1989.

Carrero, Jaime. *Jet Neorriqueño: Neo-Rican Jet Liner.* San Germán, Puerto Rico: Universidad Interamericana, 1965.

Casa de las Américas. *Tres documentos de nuestra América.* Havana: Casa de las Américas, 1979.

Chavez, Leo R. *Covering Immigration: Popular Images and the Politics of the Nation.* Berkeley, CA: University of California Press, 2001.

Chock, Phyllis Pease. " 'Illegal Aliens' and 'Opportunity': Myth-Making in Congressional Testimony." *American Ethnologist* 18, no. 2(1991):279–94.

———"No New Women: Gender, 'Alien,' and 'Citizen' in the Congressional Debate on Immigration." *PoLAR: Political and Legal Anthropology Review* 19, no. 1 (1996):1–9.

Clark, Victor S. "Mexican Labor in the United States." Department of Commerce and Labor, Bureau of Labor Bulletin, Number 78. In *Mexican Labor in the United States,* ed. Carlos E. Cortés. New York: Arno Press, 1974/1908.

Cockcroft, James D. *Outlaws in the Promised Land: Mexican Immigrant Workers and America's Future.* New York: Grove. 1986.

Coutin, Susan Bibler, and Phyllis Pease Chock. " 'Your Friend, the Illegal': Definition and Paradox in Newspaper Accounts of U.S. Immigration Reform." *Identities* 2, nos. 1–2 (1995):123–48.

Cronon, William. *Nature's Metropolis: Chicago and the Great West.* New York: W.W. Norton, 1991.

Cruz, J. E. "Puerto Rican Poverty." In *National Puerto Rican Coalition, Advocacy Notes* (October 1991–December 1992):2–11.

Davalos, Karen Mary. *Ethnic Identity among Mexican and Mexican American Women in Chicago, 1920–1991.* Ph.D. dissertation, Department of Anthropology, Yale University, 1993.

Dávila, Arlene. *Sponsored Identities: Culture and Politics in Puerto Rico.* Philadelphia: Temple University Press, 1997.

————*Latinos Inc.: The Marketing and Making of a People.* Berkeley: University of California Press, 2002.

Davis, Mike. *Magical Urbanism: Latinos Reinvent the U.S. Big City.* New York: Verso, 2000.

De Genova, Nicholas. "Race, Space, and the Reinvention of Latin America in Mexican Chicago." *Latin American Perspectives,* Issue 102; 25, no. 5 (1998):87–116.

————*Working the Boundaries, Making the Difference: Race and Space in Mexican Chicago.* Ph.D. dissertation, Department of Anthropology, University of Chicago, 1999.

————"Migrant 'Illegality' and Deportability in Everyday Life." *Annual Review of Anthropology* 31 (2002) :419–47.

———— *Working the Boundaries: Race, Space, and 'Illegality' in Mexican Chicago.* Durham, NC: Duke University Press, in press .

De la Campa, Román. *Latin Americanism.* Minneapolis: University of Minnesota Press, 1999.

De León, Arnoldo. *They Called Them Greasers: Anglo Attitudes toward Mexicans in Texas, 1821–1900.* Austin: University of Texas Press, 1983.

Díaz-Quiñones, Arcadio. *La memoria rota.* Río Piedras, Puerto Rico: Ediciones Huracán, 1993.

Dietz, James L. *Economic History of Puerto Rico: Institutional Change and Capitalist Development.* Princeton, NJ: Princeton University Press, 1986.

Dinwoodie, D. H. "Deportation: The Immigration Service and the Chicano Labor Movement in the 1930s." New Mexico Historical Review 52, no. 3 (1977):193–206.

Domínguez, Jorge I., ed. *Race and Ethnicity in Latin America. Essays on Mexico, Central and South America: Scholarly Debates from the 1950s to the 1990s.* Vol. 7. New York: Garland. 1994.

Drinnon, Richard. *Facing West: The Metaphysics of Indian-Hating and Nation Building.* Norman: University of Oklahoma Press, 1980.

Duany, Jorge. "Making Indians Out of Blacks: The Revitalization of Taíno Identity in Contemporary Puerto Rico." In *Taíno Revival: Critical Perspectives on Puerto Rican Identity and Cultural Politics,* edited Gabriel Haslip-Viera, pp. 31–55. New York: Centro de Estudios Puertorriqueños, 1990.

————"Nation on the Move: The Construction of Cultural Identities in Puerto Rico and the Diaspora." *American Ethnologist* 27, no. 1 (2000):1–26.

Durand, Jorge, ed. *El Norte es como el mar: Entrevistas a trabajadores migrantes en Estados Unidos.* Guadalajara, México: Universidad de Guadalajara, 1996.

Ellison, Ralph. *Shadow & Act.* New York: Random House, 1958.

Espinosa, Leticia. "El cierre de HIMRI." *La Raza,* July 27–August 2 (1995):4.

Estades-Font, María Eugenia *La presencia militar de Estados Unidos en Puerto Rico 1898–1918. Intereses estratégicos y dominación colonial.* Río Piedras, Puerto Rico: Ediciones Huracán, 1988.

Fernandez, Ronald. *Prisoners of Colonialism: The Struggle for Justice in Puerto Rico.* Monroe, ME: Common Courage Press, 1994.

Fernández Retamar, Roberto. "Nuestra América y Occidente." In *Casa de las Américas* 98 (1976):36–57.

————"Calibán: Apuntes sobre la cultura en nuestra América." In *Para el perfil definitivo del hombre,* pp. 219–90. Havana: Editorial Letras Cubanas, 1981.

————*Caliban and Other Essays,* ed. Edward Baker. Minneapolis: University of Minnesota Press, 1989.

Flores, Juan. "Rappin, 'Writin', & Breakin." *Dissent* 34, no. 4 (1987):580–84.

————*Divided Borders: Essays on Puerto Rican Identity.* Houston: Arte Público Press, 1993.

————*From Bomba to Hip-Hop: Puerto Rican Culture and Latino Identity.* New York: Columbia University Press, 2000.

Flores, William V., and Rina Benmayor, eds. *Latino Cultural Citizenship: Claiming Identity, Space, and Rights.* Boston: Beacon. 1997.

Flores-González, Nilda. *School Kids/Street Kids: Identity Development in Latino Students.* New York: Teachers' College Press, 2002.

Foley, Neil. *The White Scourge: Mexicans, Blacks, and Poor Whites in Texas Cotton Culture.* Berkeley: University of California Press, 1997.

————"Becoming Hispanic: Mexican Americans and the Faustian Pact with Whiteness." In *Reflexiones 1997: New Directions in Mexican American Studies,* ed. Neil Foley, pp. 53–70. Austin: Center for Mexican American Studies/University of Texas at Austin, 1998.

Franco, Jean. *Plotting Women: Gender and Representation in Mexico.* New York: Columbia University Press, 1989.

Friedlander, Judith. *Being Indian in Hueyapán: A Study of Forced Identity in Contemporary Mexico.* New York: St. Martin's. 1975.

Galarza, Ernesto. *Merchants of Labor: The Mexican Bracero Story.* Charlotte, NC: McNally & Loftin. 1964.

Gamio, Manuel. *Mexican Immigration to the United States.* Chicago: University of Chicago Press. New York: Dover, 1971/1930.

García, Juan Ramón. *Operation Wetback: The Mass Deportation of Mexican Undocumented Workers in 1954.* Westport, CN: Greenwood. 1980.

García, Mario T. *Desert Immigrants: The Mexicans of El Paso, 1880–1920.* New Haven: Yale University Press, 1981.

Glasser, Ruth. *My Music Is My Flag: Puerto Rican Musicians and Their New York Communities, 1917–1940.* Berkeley: University of California Press, 1995.

Gómez, Dante. "Una poca de gracia ... y otra cosita." In *La Bamba Cultural: México en Chicago,* pp. 248–52. Chicago: Instituto Mexicano de Cultura y Educación de Chicago, 1999.

Gómez-Quiñones, Juan. *Mexican American Labor, 1790–1990.* Albuquerque: University of New Mexico Press, 1994.

Gonzalez, Juan. *Harvest of Empire: A History of Latinos in America.* New York: Viking Penguin, 2000.

González, Nacho. "Latino Politics in Chicago." *CENTRO: Journal of the Center for Puerto Rican Studies* 2, no. 5 (1990):47–57.

González, Rosalinda Méndez 1981 *Capital Accumulation and Mexican Immigration to the United States: A Comparative Historical Study of the Political Economy of International Labor Migrations.* Ph.D. dissertation, Department of Comparative Culture, University of California at Irvine.

Gordon, Danielle. "INS Aims at Businesses, Hits Mexicans." *Chicago Reporter,* July/August, 1997. <www.chicagoreporter.com>

Gramsci, Antonio. *Selections from the Prison Notebooks.* New York: International Publishers, 1971[1929–35]

Grimshaw, William J. "The Daley Legacy: A Declining Legacy of Party, Race, and Public Unions." In *After Daley: Chicago Politics in Transition,* ed. Samuel K. Gove and Louis H. Masotti, pp. 57–87. Urbana: University of Illinois Press, 1982.

————*Bitter Fruit: Black Politics and the Chicago Machine, 1931–1991.* Chicago: University of Chicago Press, 1992.

Griswold del Castillo, Richard. *The Treaty of Guadalupe Hidalgo: A Legacy of Conflict.* Norman: University of Oklahoma Press, 1990.

Grosfoguel, Ramón. "Puerto Ricans in the USA: A Comparative Approach." *Journal of Ethnic and Migration Studies* 25(2) (1999):233–49.

Grosfoguel, Ramón, and Chloé S. Georas. "The Racialization of Latino Caribbean Migrants in the New York Metropolitan Area." *CENTRO: Journal of the Center for Puerto Rican Studies* 8, nos. 1& 2 (1996):191–201.

Guerin-Gonzáles, Camille. *Mexican Workers and American Dreams: Immigration, Repatriation, and California Farm Labor, 1900–1939.* New Brunswick: Rutgers University Press, 1994.

Guevara, Ernesto "Che." *Che Guevara and the Cuban Revolution: Writings and Speeches of Ernesto Che Guevara.* New York: Pathfinder. 1987[1967].

Guterbock, Thomas M. *Machine Politics in Transition: Party and Community in Chicago.* Chicago: University of Chicago Press, 1980.

Gutiérrez, David G. *Walls and Mirrors: Mexican Americans, Mexican Immigrants, and the Politics of Ethnicity.* Berkeley: University of California Press, 1995.

Gutiérrez, Ramón A. *When Jesus Came, the Corn Mothers Went Away: Marriage, Sexuality, and Power in New Mexico, 1500–1846.* Stanford, CA: Stanford University Press, 1991.

Gutmann, Matthew C. *The Meanings of Macho: Being a Man in Mexico City.* Berkeley: University of California Press, 1996.

Harrigan J., and R. Vogel. *Political Change in the Metropolis.* 6th ed. New York: Longman, 2000.

Hietala, Thomas. *Manifest Design: American Exceptionalism and Empire.* Ithaca, NY: Cornell University Press, 1985.

Hirsch, Arnold R. *Making the Second Ghetto: Race and Housing in Chicago, 1940–1960.* New York: Cambridge University Press, 1983.

History Task Force. *Labor Migration under Capitalism: The Puerto Rican Experience.* New York: Centro de Estudios Puertorriqueños, 1979.

Hoffman, Abraham. *Unwanted Mexican Americans in the Great Depression: Repatriation Pressures, 1926–1939.* Tuscon: University of Arizona Press, 1974.

Honig, Bonnie. "Immigrant America? How Foreignness 'Solves' Democracy's Problems." *Social Text* 56 (1998):1–27.

Horsman, Reginald. *Race and Manifest Destiny: The Origins of American Racial Anglo-Saxonism.* Cambridge, MA: Harvard University Press, 1981.

Illinois Legislative Investigating Commission. *The Illegal Mexican Alien Problem.* Springfield: State of Illinois Printing Office, 1971.

Institute for Puerto Rican Policy. *Datanote.* New York: Institute for Puerto Rican Policy, March 1993.

Jablonsky, Thomas J. *Pride in the Jungle: Community and Everyday Life in Back of the Yards Chicago.* Baltimore: Johns Hopkins University Press, 1993.

Jacobson, Matthew Frye. *Barbarian Virtues: The United States Encounters Foreign Peoples at Home and Abroad, 1876–1917.* New York: Hill and Wang, 2000.

Jiménez-Román, Miriam. "The Indians are Coming! The Indians are coming!: The Taíno and Puerto Rican Identity." In *Taíno Revival: Critical Perspectives on Puerto Rican Identity and Cultural Politics,* edited Gabriel Haslip-Viera, pp. 75–107. New York: Centro de Estudios Puertorriqueños, 1990.

Johnson, Kevin R. "The New Nativism: Something Old, Something New, Something Borrowed, Something Blue." In *Immigrants Out! The New Nativism and the Anti-Immigrant Impulse in the United States,* ed. Juan F. Perea, pp. 165–89. New York: New York University Press, 1997.

Jones, Anita Edgar. *Conditions Surrounding Mexicans in Chicago: A Dissertation.* M.A. thesis, University of Chicago. San Francisco: R and E Research Associates, 1971/1928.

Jones, Isham. *The Puerto Rican in New Jersey: His Present Status.* New Jersey: State Department of Education, Division Against Discrimination, 1955.

Jones-Correa, Michael. *Between Two Nations: the Political Predicament of Latinos in New York City.* Ithaca: Cornell University Press, 1998.

Jones-Correa, Michael, and David L. Leal. "Becoming 'Hispanic': Secondary Panethnic Identification among Latin American–Origin Populations in the United States." *Hispanic Journal of Behavioral Sciences* 18, no. 2 (1996):214–54.

Kahn, Joan R. and Rosalind E. Berkowitz. "Sources of Support for Young Latina Mothers." Washington, DC: The Urban Institute, 1995.

Kearney, Michael. *Reconceptualizing the Peasantry: Anthropology in Global Perspective.* Boulder, CO: Westview. 1996.

——— "Peasants in the Fields of Value: Revisiting Rural Class Differentiation in Transnational Perspective." Unpublished manuscript, Department of Anthropology, University of California–Riverside, 1998.

Klor de Alva, Jorge. "Aztlán, Borinquen and Hispanic Nationalism in the United States." In *Aztlán: Essays on the Chicano Homeland,* ed. Rudolfo Anaya and Francisco Lomeli. Albuquerque, NM: Academia/El Norte Publications, 1989.

——— "The Postcolonization of the (Latin) American Experience: A Reconsideration of 'Colonialism,' 'Postcolonialism,' and 'Mestizaje.'" In *After Colonialism: Imperial Histories and Postcolonial Displacements,* ed. Gyan Prakash, pp. 241–75. Princeton, NJ: Princeton University Press, 1995.

Kornblum, William. *Blue Collar Community.* Chicago: University of Chicago Press, 1974.

Lancaster, Roger N. *Life Is Hard: Machismo, Danger, and the Intimacy of Power in Nicaragua.* Berkeley: University of California Press, 1992.

——— "Guto's Performance: Notes on the Transvestitism of Everyday Life." In *Sex and Sexuality in Latin America,* ed. Daniel Balderston and Donna J. Guy, pp. 9–32. New York: New York University Press, 1997.

Latino Institute. *Al Filo/At the Cutting Edge: The Empowerment of Chicago's Latino Electorate.* Chicago: Latino Institute, 1986.

———*Chicago's Working Latinas: Confronting Multiple Roles and Pressures.* Chicago: Latino Institute, 1987.

———*Chicago Community Areas.* Latino Institute Research. Chicago: Latino Institute, June 1991.

——— Latino Institute Research. Chicago: Latino Institute, May 3, 1993.

——— Latino Institute Research Datanote. Chicago: Latino Institute, July 1995.

Laviera, Tato. *La Carreta Made a U-Turn.* Houston: Arte Público, 1981.

Lefebvre, Henri. *The Production of Space*. Cambridge, MA: Blackwell, 1991[1974].

Levinson, Sanford. " Installing the *Insular Cases* into the Canon of Constitutional Law." In *Foreign in a Domestic Sense: Puerto Rico, American Expansion, and the Constitution*, ed. Christina Duffy Burnett and Burke Marshall, pp. 121–39. Durham, NC: Duke University Press, 2001.

Lewis, Oscar. *Five Families*. New York: Basic Books, 1959.

———*La Vida*. New York: Random House, 1966.

———*Anthropological Essays*. New York: Random House, 1970.

Littlewood, Thomas. *The Politics of Family and Fertility in Puerto Rican Population Control*. Notre Dame, IN: University of Notre Dame Press, 1977.

Logan, John R. "The New Latinos: Who They Are, Where They Are." Press Conference Advisory, Lewis Mumford Center for Comparative Urban and Regional Research, State University of New York at Albany, 2001.

———"Hispanic Populations and Their Residential Patterns in the Metropolis." Press Conference Advisory, Lewis Mumford Center for Comparative Urban and Regional Research at the State University of New York at Albany, 2002.

Lomnitz-Adler, Claudio. *Exits from the Labyrinth: Culture and Ideology in the Mexican National Space*. Berkeley: University of California Press, 1992.

———*Deep Mexico, Silent Mexico: An Anthropology of Nationalism*. Minneapolis: University of Minnesota Press, 2001.

Lowe, Lisa. *Immigrant Acts: On Asian American Cultural Politics*. Durham, NC: Duke University Press, 1996.

Maciel, David. "Mexico in Aztlán and Aztlán in Mexico: The Dialectics of Chicano-Mexicano Art." In *CARA—Chicano Art: Resistance and Affirmation, 1965–1985*, ed. Richard Griswold del Castillo, Teresa McKenna, and Yvonne Yarbro-Bejarano, pp. 109–19. Los Angeles: Wright Art Gallery, University of California, Los Angeles, 1991.

Madrid-Barela, Arturo. "Pochos: The Different Mexicans, An Interpretive Essay, Part I." *Aztlán* 7, no. 1 (1976):51–64.

Maldonado, Edwin. "Contract Labor and the Origins of Puerto Rican Communities in the United States." *International Migration Review* 13, no. 1 (1979):103–21.

Maldonado-Denis, Manuel. "Cultura y educación: el problema de la asimilación cultural." In *Puerto Rico y Estados Unidos: Emigración y Colonialismo*. Mexico: Siglo XXI, 1976.

Martí, José. "Nuestra América." In *Tres documentos de nuestra América*. Havana: Casa de las Américas, 1979[1891].

Martínez, Manuel. *Chicago: Historia de nuestra comunidad Puertorriqueña*. Photographic documentary published independently by the author, 1989.

Martínez, Vilma S. "Illegal Immigration and the Labor Force." *American Behavioral Scientist* 19, no. 3 (1976):335–349.

Massey, Douglas S., and Nancy A. Denton. "Residential Segregation of Mexicans, Puerto Ricans, and Cubans in Selected U.S. Metropolitan Areas." *Social Science Research* 73, no. 2 (1989):73–83.

Mendoza-Denton, Norma. "Sociolinguistics and Linguistic Anthropology of U.S. Latinos." *Annual Review of Anthropology* 28 (1999):375–95.

Mirandé, Alfredo. *The Chicano Experience: An Alternative Perspective*. Notre Dame, IN: University of Notre Dame Press, 1985.

———*Gringo Justice*. Notre Dame, IN: University of Notre Dame Press, 1987.

Monsiváis, Carlos. *Entrada libre: Crónicas de la sociedad que se organiza*. México, DF: ERA, 1987.

Montejano, David. *Anglos and Mexicans in the Making of Texas, 1836–1986*. Austin: University of Texas Press, 1987.

Moore, Joan, and Raquel Pinderhughes, eds. *In the Barrios: Latinos and the Underclass Debate*. New York: Russell Sage Foundation, 1993.

Moquin, Wayne, and Charles Lincoln Van Doren. *A Documentary History of the Mexican Americans*. New York: Praeger, 1971.

Mora, Juan. "A Brief History of Chicago's Mexican Community." In *Rudy Lozano: His Life, His People*. Chicago: Taller de Estudios Comunitarios, n.d.

Morris, Nancy. *Puerto Rico: Culture, Politics, and Identity*. New York: Praeger Publishers, 1995.

Moynihan, Daniel P. *The Negro Family: The Case for National Action*. Washington, D.C.: Office of Planning and Research, U.S. Department of Labor, 1965.

Muñoz, Jr., Carlos. *Youth, Identity, Power: The Chicano Movement*. New York: Verso, 1989.

Nagengast, Carole, and Michael Kearney. "Mixtec Ethnicity: Social Identity, Political Consciousness, and Political Activism." *Latin American Research Review* 25, no. 2 (1990):61–91.

Negrón-Muntaner, Frances. "Jennifer's Butt." *Aztlán* 22, no. 2 (1997):181–94.
Nelson, Dana. *National Manhood: Capitalist Citizenship and the Imagined Fraternity of White Men.* Durham, NC: Duke University Press, 1998.
Neumann, Gerald L. "Constitutionalism and Individual Rights in the Territories." In *Foreign in a Domestic Sense: Puerto Rico, American Expansion, and the Constitution,* ed. Christina Duffy Burnett and Burke Marshall, pp. 182–205. Durham, NC: Duke University Press, 2001.
Newman, Katherine. *No Shame in My Game: The Working Poor in the Inner City.* New York: Russell Sage Foundation, 1999.
Ngai, Mae M. "The Architecture of Race in American Immigration Law: A Reexamination of the Immigration Act of 1924." *Journal of American History* 86, no. 1 (1999):67–92.
——— *Illegal Aliens and Alien Citizens: Immigration Restriction, Race, and Nation, 1924–1965.* Princeton, NJ: Princeton University Press, in press.
Nieves-Falcón, Luis. *El emigrante puertorriqueño.* Río Piedras, PR: Editorial Edil, 1975.
Oboler, Suzanne. *Ethnic Labels, Latino Lives: Identity and the Politics of (Re)Presentation in the United States.* Minneapolis: University of Minnesota Press, 1995.
Oclander, Jorge. "Public School's 'Pathetic' Use of Poverty Funds." *Chicago Sun-Times,* June 15 (1995a):A1.
——— "Latinos Split over Keeping Their House District." *Chicago Sun-Times,* December 13 (1995b):A22–23.
Orfield, Gary, and Ricard M. Tostado. "*Latinos in Metropolitan Chicago: A Study of Housing and Employment.*" Latino Institute Monograph No. 6. Chicago: Latino Institute, 1983.
Omi, Michael, and Howard Winant. *Racial Formation in the United States: From the 1960s to the 1980s.* New York: Routledge, 1986.
Padilla, Elena. *Puerto Rican Immigrants in New York and Chicago: A Study in Comparative Assimilation.* M.A. thesis, University of Chicago, 1947.
Padilla, Elena, and Muna Muñoz. "Preliminary Report on Puerto Rican Workers in Chicago." November 25. Chicago: Chicago Historical Society Archives, 1946.
Padilla, Felix. *Latino Ethnic Consciousness: The Case of Mexican Americans and Puerto Ricans in Chicago.* Notre Dame, In: University of Notre Dame Press, 1985.
———*Puerto Rican Chicago.* Notre Dame, In: University of Notre Dame Press, 1987.
———"Latin America: The Historical Basis of Latino Unity." *Latino Studies Journal* 1, no. 1 (1990):7–27.
Paral, Rob. "NAFTA and Chicago's Latinos." *Latino: A Publication of the Latino Institute* 6 [August 1, 1993]):1, 6.
Perea, Juan. "Fulfilling Manifest Destiny: Conquest, Race, and the Insular Cases." In *Foreign in a Domestic Sense: Puerto Rico, American Expansion, and the Constitution,* ed. Christina Duffy Burnett and Burke Marshall, pp. 140–66. Durham, NC: Duke University Press, 2001.
Paredes, Américo. "The United States, Mexico, and Machismo." Chapter 9 (pp. 215–34) in Paredes, *Folklore and Culture of the Texas-Mexican Border.* Austin: Center for Mexican American Studies/University of Texas Press, 1993[1971].
——— "The Problem of Identity in a Changing Culture: Popular Expressions of Culture Conflict along the Lower Rio Grande Border." Chapter 2 (pp. 19–47) in Paredes, *Folklore and Culture of the Texas-Mexican Border.* Austin: Center for Mexican American Studies/University of Texas Press, 1993[1978].
——— *Folklore and Culture of the Texas-Mexican Border.* Austin: Center for Mexican American Studies/University of Texas Press, 1993.
Pérez, Gina. "Puertorriqueñas rencorosas y mexicanas sufridas: Gendered Ethnic Construction among Chicago Puertorriqueñas." *Journal of Latin American Anthropology* 8, vol. 2 (2003).
Pike, Frederick B. *Hispanismo, 1898–1936: Spanish Conservatives and Liberals and Their Relations with Spanish America.* Notre Dame, IN: University of Notre Dame Press, 1971.
Piña, Francisco. "His Life." In *Rudy Lozano: His Life, His People.* Chicago: Taller de Estudios Comunitarios, n.d.
Pitt, Leonard. *The Decline of the Californios: A Social History of the Spanish Speaking Californians, 1846–1890.* Berkeley: University of California Press, 1971.
Preston, Michael B. "Black Politics in the Post-Daley Era." In *After Daley: Chicago Politics in Transition,* ed. Samuel K. Gove and Louis H. Masotti, pp. 88–117. Urbana: University of Illinois Press, 1982.
Price, Glenn W. *Origins of the War with Mexico: The Polk-Stockton Intrigue.* Austin: University of Texas Press, 1967.

Quintero-Rivera, Angel G. "Culture-Oriented Social Movements: Ethnicity and Symbolic Action in Latin America and the Caribbean." CENTRO: Journal of the Center for Puerto Rican Studies. 3, no. 2 (1991):97–104.

Rakove, Milton. *Don't Make No Waves—Don't Back No Losers: An Insider's Analysis of the Daley Machine.* Bloomington: Indiana University Press, 1975.

Ramírez de Arellano, Annette, and Conrad Scheipp. *Colonialism, Catholicism, and Contraception: A History of Birth Control in Puerto Rico.* Chapel Hill: University of North Carolina Press, 1983.

Ramos-Zayas, Ana Y. *"La patria es valor y sacrificio": Nationalist Ideologies, Cultural Authenticity, and Community Building among Puerto Ricans in Chicago.* Ph.D. dissertation, Department of Anthropology, Columbia University, 1997.

———"Nationalist Ideologies, Neighborhood-Based Activism, and Educational Spaces in Puerto Rican Chicago." *Harvard Educational Review* 68, vol. 2 (1998):164–92.

———"Racializing the 'Invisible' Race: Latino Constructions of 'White Culture' and Whiteness in Chicago." *Urban Anthropology* 30, no. 4 (2001):341–80.

———*National Performances: The Politics of Class, Race and Space in Puerto Rican Chicago.* Chicago: University of Chicago Press, 2003.

Reilly, Phillip. *The Surgical Solution: A History of Involuntary Sterilization in the United States.* Baltimore: Johns Hopkins University Press, 1991.

Reisler, Mark. *By the Sweat of Their Brow: Mexican Immigrant Labor in the United States, 1900–1940.* Westport, CN: Greenwood, 1976.

Reyna, José R. "Pancho Villa: The Lighter Side." *New Mexico Humanities Review* 7, no. 1 (1984):57–62.

Rivera Ramos, Efrén. *"The Legal Construction of Identity: The Judicial and Social Legacy of American Colonialism in Puerto Rico."* American Psychological Association: Law and Public Policy Series, 2001.

Rivlin, Gary. *Fire on the Prairie: Chicago's Harold Washington and the Politics of Race.* New York: Henry Holt and Co., 1992.

Roberts, Dorothy E. "Who May Give Birth to Citizens? Reproduction, Eugenics, and Immigration." In *Immigrants Out! The New Nativism and the Anti-Immigrant Impulse in the United States,* ed. Juan F. Perea, pp. 205–19. New York: New York University Press, 1997.

Rodríguez, América. "Racialization, Language, and Class in the Construction and Sale of the Hispanic Audience." In *Reflexiones 1997: New Directions in Mexican American Studies,* ed. Neil Foley, pp. 29–52. Austin: Center for Mexican American Studies/University of Texas at Austin, 1998.

Rodríguez, Clara. *Puerto Ricans Born in the U.S.A.* Boston: Unwin Hyman, 1989.

Rodríguez-Morazzani, Roberto. "Beyond the Rainbow: Mapping the Discourse on Puerto Ricans and 'Race.'" In *The Latino Studies Reader: Culture, Economy and Society,* ed. Antonia Darder and Rodolfo Torres, pp. 143–62. Malden, MA: Blackwell, 1998a.

———"Political Cultures of the Puerto Rican Left in the United States." In *The Puerto Rican Movement: Voices from the Diaspora,* ed. Andrés Torres, José Velázquez, and Emilio Pantoja-García, pp. 25–47. Philadelphia: Temple University Press, 1998b.

Roediger, David R. *Toward the Abolition of Whiteness: Essays on Race, Politics, and Working Class History.* New York: Verso, 1994.

Ropka, Gerald William. *The Evolving Residential Pattern of the Mexican, Puerto Rican, and Cuban Population in the City of Chicago.* New York: Arno. 1980.

Rosaldo, Renato. "Cultural Citizenship and Educational Democracy." *Cultural Anthropology* 9, no. 3 (1994):402–41.

Rosaldo, Renato, and William Flores. "Identity, Conflict, and Evolving Latino Communities: Cultural Citizenship in San Jose, California." In *Latino Cultural Citizenship: Claiming Identity, Space, and Rights,* ed. William V. Flores and Rina Benmayor, pp. 57–96. Boston: Beacon. 1997.

Rosales, Francisco Arturo. *Mexican Immigration to the Urban Midwest during the 1920s.* Ph.D. dissertation, Department of History, Indiana University, 1978.

———*Pobre Raza! Violence, Justice, and Mobilization among México Lindo Immigrants, 1900–1936.* Austin: University of Texas Press, 1999.

Rosen, George. *Decision-Making Chicago Style: The Genesis of a University of Illinois Campus.* Urbana: University of Illinois Press, 1980.

Rosenfeld, Michael. "Who Killed Rudy Lozano?" *Grey City Journal,* October 15 (1993):1, 4–6.

Ross Pineda, Raúl. *Los Mexicanos y el voto sin fronteras.* Chicago: Salsedo, 1999.

Rúa, Mérida. "Colao Subjectivities: PortoMex and MexiRican Perspectives on Language and Identity." *CENTRO: Journal of the Center for Puerto Rican Studies* 8, no.2 (2001): 116–33.

Saldívar, José David. *The Dialectics of Our America: Genealogy, Cultural Critique, and Literary History.* Durham, NC: Duke University Press, 1991.

———*Border Matters: Remapping American Cultural Studies.* Berkeley: University of California Press, 1997.

Samora, Julian. *Los Mojados: The Wetback Story.* Notre Dame, IN: University of Notre Dame Press, 1971.

Sánchez, Luis Rafael. *La guagua aérea.* Río Piedras, Puerto Rico: Editorial Cultural, 1994.

Sandoval-Sánchez, Alberto. "Puerto Rican Identity up in the Air: Air Migration, Its Cultural Representations, and Me 'Cruzando el Charco.'" In *Puerto Rican Jam: Essays on Culture and Politics,* ed. Ramón, Grosfoguel, and Frances Negrón-Muntaner, pp. 189–208. Minneapolis: University of Minnesota Press, 1997.

Santos Febres, Mayra. "A veces moro mi vida." *Dialogo,* October 1993, p. 42. Cited in Raquel Rivera's "Rapping Two Versions of the Same Requiem." In *Puerto Rican Jam,* Frances Negrón-Muntaner and Ramón Grosfoguel, editors. pp. 243–256. Minneapolis: University of Minnesota Press, 1997.

Seda-Bonilla, Eduardo. *Requiem por una cultura.* Río Piedras: Ediciones Bayoán, 1972.

Senior, Clarence, and Donald O. Watkins. "Towards a Balance Sheet of Puerto Rican Migration." In *Status of Puerto Rico: Selected Background Studies for the United States–Puerto Rico Commission on the Status of Puerto Rico,* pp. 715–16. Washington, DC: U.S. Government Printing Office, 1966.

Skirius, John. "Vasconcelos and México de Afuera (1928)." *Aztlán* 7, no. 3 (1976):479–97.

Slayton, Robert A. *Back of the Yards: The Making of a Local Democracy.* Chicago: University of Chicago Press, 1986.

Smith, Carol A. "The Symbolics of Blood: Mestizaje in the Americas." *Identities* 3, no. 4 (1997):495–521.

Smith, Raymond T. *The Matrifocal Family: Power, Pluralism, and Politics.* New York: Routledge, 1996.

Smith, Rogers M. *Civic Ideals: Conflicting Visions of Citizenship in U.S. History.* New Haven, CN: Yale University Press, 1997.

——— "The Bitter Roots of Puerto Rican Citizenship." In *Foreign in a Domestic Sense: Puerto Rico, American Expansion, and the Constitution,* ed. Christina Duffy Burnett and Burke Marshall, pp. 373–88. Durham, NC: Duke University Press, 2001.

Squires, Gregory D., Larry Bennett, Kathleen McCourt, and Phillip Nyden. *Chicago: Race, Class, and the Response to Urban Decline.* Philadelphia: Temple University Press, 1987.

Stark, Robert. *Religious Ritual and Class Formation: The Story of Pilsen, St. Vitus Parish, and the 1977 Via Crucis.* Ph.D. dissertation, School of Divinity, University of Chicago, 1981.

Suttles, Gerald D. *The Social Order of the Slum: Ethnicity and Territory in the Inner City.* Chicago: University of Chicago Press, 1968.

Takaki, Ronald. *Iron Cages: Race and Culture in 19th-Century America.* New York: Oxford University Press, 1979.

Taller de Estudios Comunitarios. *Rudy Lozano: His Life, His People.* Chicago, n.d.

Taub, Richard. "Differing Conceptions of Honor and Orientations Toward Work and Marriage Among Low-Income African-Americans and Mexican-Americans." Paper presented to the Chicago Urban Poverty and Family Life Conference, October 10–12, Chicago, 1991.

Taylor, Paul S. *Mexican Labor in the United States: Chicago and the Calumet District.* University of California Publications in Economics 7, No. 2 (1932). Berkeley: University of California Press.

Teaford, Jon C. *Cities of the Heartland: The Rise and Fall of the Industrial Midwest.* Bloomington: Indiana University Press, 1993.

Thomas, Piri. *Down These Mean Streets.* New York: Vintage, 1967.

Thornburgh, Richard. "Puerto Rican Separatism and United States Federalism." In *Foreign in a Domestic Sense: Puerto Rico, American Expansion, and the Constitution,* ed. Christina Duffy Burnett and Burke Marshall, pp. 349–72. Durham, NC: Duke University Press, 2001.

Torre, Carlos Antonio, Hugo Rodríguez-Vecchini, and William Burgos, eds. *The Commuter Nation: Perspectives on Puerto Rican Migration.* Río Piedras: Universidad de Puerto Rico, 1994.

Torres, Andres. "Introduction: Political Radicalism in the Diaspora—The Puerto Rican Experience." In *The Puerto Rican Movement: Voices from the Diaspora*, ed. Andrés Torres, José Velázquez, and Emilio Pantoja-García, pp. 1–24. Philadelphia: Temple University Press, 1998.

Torres, Arlene. "La Gran Familia Puertorriqueña Ej Prieta de Beldá" (The Great Puerto Rican Family Is Really Really Black). In *Blackness in Latin America and the Caribbean, Volume II*, edited by Arlene Torres and Norman E. Whitten, Jr, pp. 285–306. Bloomington: Indiana University Press, 1998.

Torres, María de los Angeles. "The Commission on Latino Affairs: A Case Study of Community Empowerment." In *Harold Washington and the Neighborhoods: Progressive City Government in Chicago, 1983–1987*, pp. 165–87. New Brunswick, NJ: Rutgers University Press, 1991.

Torruella, Juan R. *The Supreme Court and Puerto Rico: The Doctrine of Separate and Unequal*. Río Piedras, Puerto Rico: Universidad de Puerto Rico, 1985.

—— "One Hundred Years of Solitude: Puerto Rico's American Century." In *Foreign in a Domestic Sense: Puerto Rico, American Expansion, and the Constitution*, ed. Christina Duffy Burnett and Burke Marshall, pp. 241–50. Durham, NC: Duke University Press, 2001.

Trías Monge, José. *Puerto Rico: The Oldest Colony in the World*. New Haven: Yale University Press, 1997.

—— "Injustice According to Law: The *Insular Cases* and Other Oddities." In *Foreign in a Domestic Sense: Puerto Rico, American Expansion, and the Constitution*, ed. Christina Duffy Burnett and Burke Marshall, pp. 226–40. Durham, NC: Duke University Press, 2001.

Urciuoli, Bonnie. *Exposing Prejudice: Puerto Rican Experiences of Language, Race, and Class*. Boulder, CO: Westview Press, 1996.

—— "Boundaries, Language and the Self: Issues Faced by Puerto Ricans and Other Latino/a College Students." *Journal of Latin American Anthropology* 8, no. 2 (2003).

Vélez-Ibáñez, Carlos G. *Border Visions: Mexican Cultures of the Southwest United States*. Tucson: University of Arizona Press, 1996.

Vila, Pablo. *Crossing Borders, Reinforcing Borders: Social Categories, Metaphors, and Narrative Identities on the U.S.-Mexico Frontier*. Austin: University of Texas Press, 2000.

Wade, Peter. *Blackness and Race Mixture: The Dynamics of Racial Identity in Colombia*. Baltimore: Johns Hopkins University Press, 1993.

——*Race and Ethnicity in Latin America*. Chicago: Pluto. 1997.

Wagenheim, Karl, and Olga Jiménez de Wagenheim. *The Puerto Ricans: A Documentary History*. Princeton, NJ: Markus Wiener, 1994.

Wakefield, Dan. *Island in the City*. New York: Corinth Books, 1957.

Wald, Priscilla. "Terms of Assimilation: Legislating Subjectivity in the Emerging Nation." In *Cultures of United States Imperialism*, ed. Amy Kaplan and Donald E. Pease, pp. 59–84. Durham, NC: Duke University Press, 1993.

Walton, John, and Luis M. Salces. *The Political Organization of Chicago's Latino Communities*. Evanston, IL: Center for Urban Affairs, Northwestern University, 1977.

Warner, W. Lloyd. *American Life: Dream and Reality*. Rev. ed. Chicago: University of Chicago Press, 1962[1953].

Warner, W. Lloyd, and Leo Strole. *The Social Systems of American Ethnic Groups*. New York: Greenwood, 1976[1945].

Weber, David S. *Anglo Views of Mexican Immigrants: Popular Perceptions and Neighborhood Realities in Chicago, 1900–1940*. Ph.D. dissertation, Department of History, Ohio State University, 1982.

Welfare Council of Metropolitan Chicago and Office of the Department of Labor. "Preliminary Report on Puerto Rican Workers in Chicago." Presented on November 25. Chicago: Chicago Historical Society Archives, 1946.

—— "Minutes of the Welfare Council of Metropolitan Chicago." April 9. Chicago: Chicago Historical Society Archives, 1954.

—— "Puerto Rican Americans in Chicago." Report presented on February 12. Chicago: Chicago Historical Society Archives, 1957.

Weiner, Mark S. "Teutonic Constitutionalism: The Role of Ethno-Juridical Discourse in the Spanish-American War." In *Foreign in a Domestic Sense: Puerto Rico, American Expansion, and the Constitution*, ed. Christina Duffy Burnett and Burke Marshall, pp. 48–81. Durham, NC: Duke University Press, 2001.

Williams, Brackette F. "A Class Act: Anthropology and the Race to Nation across Ethnic Terrain." *Annual Review of Anthropology* 18 (1989):401–44.

Williams, Stephanie. "Sluggish Returns in Latino Neighborhoods Raise Concerns about Undercount." *Chicago Reporter,* July/August, 2000. <www.chicagoreporter.com>

Winant, Howard. *Racial Conditions: Politics, Theory, Comparisons.* Minneapolis: University of Minnesota Press, 1994.

Winddance Twine, Frances. "Brown-Skinned White Girls: Class, Culture, and the Construction of White Identity in Suburban Communities." In *Displacing Whiteness: Essays in Social and Cultural Criticism,* edited by Ruth Frankenberg, pp. 214–243. Durham, NC: Duke University Press, 1997.

Zentella, Ana Celia. "Returned Migration, Language, and Identity: Puerto Rican Bilinguals in Dos Worlds/Two Mundos." *International Journal of the Sociology of Language* 84 (1990):81–100.

———*Growing Up Bilingual: Puerto Rican Children in New York.* New York: Blackwell, 1997.

Zorbaugh, Harvey Warren. *The Gold Coast and the Slum: A Sociological Study of Chicago's Near North Side.* Chicago: University of Chicago Press, 1929.

Zwerman, Gilda. "Mothering on the Lam: Politics, Gender Fantasies and Maternal Thinking in Women Associated with Armed, Clandestine Organizations in the United States." *Feminist Review* 47 (1994).

———"The Identity Vulnerable Activist and the Emergence of Post–New Left Armed, Underground Organizations in the United States." Working Paper Series, Center for Studies of Social Change, New School for Social Research. Working Paper No. 218 (1995).

Index

U.S.–born children of, 7, 35, 87, 103, 105, 120, 149; undocumented, 2, 3, 7, 37, 60–61, 75, 78, 213, 224n. 13, 234n. 10; welfare and, 60–61; whites and, 207; work ethic of, 81, 88; working poor, 61
Mexican migrants and Puerto Ricans: authenticity issues and, 105; coalition-building between, 19, 29, 54–56, 196–97; commonalities between, 21–22, 193, 209, 215; competing moral economies and, 57–82; competing notions of civility and modernity and, 28; conflicts between, 74, 214, 225n. 27; differences between, 22, 32, 61–63, 77, 94–95, 108, 208, 215; gendered differences between, 107–43; histories of, 17, 213; ideological contrasts between, 83–106; intermarriage between, 56; language differences between, 29, 143–74 (see also Spanish language); racialized differences between (see racialized differences between Mexicans and Puerto Ricans); segregation of, 50; sociopolitical relations between, 1; solidarity between, 193–96; U.S. citizenship and, 2, 16
Mexican migrants in Chicago: acceleration of, 36–37, 223n. 6; community formation on the South Side, 34–42; cultural forms of, 86–88; experiences of, 72, 95; history of, 34–37, 39; Inland Steel and, 34–35; mass, 39; meatpacking and, 35, 37; poverty of, 227n. 1; railroads and, 35, 37; steel plants and, 34–37; undocumented, 38; unemployment and, 35
Mexican migration, 2, 227n. 39; and illegality, 3–7, 12; quotas on legal, 4; transnational, 90; undocumented, 3
Mexican Revolution, 4
Mexican stereotypes about Puerto Ricans, 57–58, 80–82, 83; aggressiveness, 94; criminality and violence, 96, 101, 109; laziness, 28, 80–82; racialized, 83, 94, 99–100; welfare and, 57
Mexican women (see also Latinas), 91; arranged marriages and, 132; celebrities, 91; divorce and, 141; domestic violence and, 107, 138–41; familial ideal and, 28; gender relations of, 128, 130, 132–34, 137–42; marital experiences of, 124–26, 138–41, 231n. 3; martyrdom of, 108; single mothers, 125–26; stereotypes about, 161; teen mothers, 61; traditional marriages and, 130; U.S. born, 227n. 4;

U.S. citizenship and, 108; welfare and, 227n. 4
Mexican-ness: as a transnationality, 73; equation of illegality and, 38; ideal of, 76–80, 86–87; identity of, 198, 202; Mexican men and, 113; of South Side barrios, 42; racial formation of, 15, 42, 209, 213; stereotypes of, 96, 102; work ethic of, 88
Mexicans: arrest rates for, 35; as illegal aliens, 32, 34, 36, 56, 57; as permanent outsiders, 6; criminality associated with, 101–104; cultural authenticity of, 103; domestic violence and, 107, 110, 112; in Illinois, 35; in the Southwest, 35; Latinidad and, 21; Latinismo and, 78; negative stereotypes about, 32, 34, 57, 75, 81; parochialism among, 85; perceived submissiveness of, 81; police violence against, 35, 39; racial formations and, 16–22; racialization of (see racialization of Mexicans); relations with United States, 33; U.S. citizens, 5, 7; U.S. population, 220n. 7; U.S.-born (see U.S.-born Mexicans); U.S.-raised (see U.S.-raised Mexicans); work ethic of, 79–81
Mexico: -U.S. border, 5, 217; -U.S. history, 2, 3–4, 11–13, 15; 1848 war with United States, 11, 13; civilization in, 85; elections in, 41; elite, 85; linkages with United States and, 150; Spanish conquest and colonization of, 83
migrants, 219n. 4; Central American, 31, 53, 58; cultural integrity of, 28; culture, 28; Latin American, 31; Latino, 78, 80, 162, 168–69, 180, 182, 183–84; Mexican (see Mexican migrants); Puerto Rican (see Puerto Rican migrant workers; Puerto Rican migrants); recent, 78; undocumented, 184, 211, 217
migration, 230n. 7; Bracero Program and (see Bracero Program); legal contract-labor, 5–6; Mexican (see Mexican migration); Puerto Rican (see Puerto Rican migration); seasonal, 42; transnational, 41, 120, 126, 150; undocumented, 5–6, 37–38
minorities: abjection and, 178–83; Latinos as, 17, 21; racialized, 60, 97, 169, 174, 180, 212, 214, 216; U.S.-citizen, 78, 169, 211, 217
modernity, 83–95; racialized notions of, 85
Molina, Luis, 230n. 7

127, 133, 138–41; gang, 225n. 26;
legitimate, 109; masculine, 108, 109–15;
racialization and spatialization of,
95–106; street, 113
visa fees, 4
voting rights, 15
Voting Rights Act, 54

W
War on Poverty, 47
Warner, W. Lloyd, 221n. 15
Washington, Harold, 40–41, 54
welfare: abuse, 65, 69, 179, 213; African
Americans and, 7; assault against, 60, 210,
211; complexities of, 65–66; dependency,
7, 32, 57, 75, 78, 213, 216; discourses of,
57, 65; immigrants and, 178–79;
Mexicans and, 75, 141, 227n. 4; moral
economy of, 65–69, 74, 78–79, 160;
programs, 60; Puerto Ricans and, 7, 32,
34, 57, 65, 213, 227n. 4; racial economy
of, 74–78, 83; reform, 211; stigma of, 57,
68, 73; teen pregnancy and, 67–68; the
permanently poor and, 62; undocumented
migrants and, 60–61; use, 65
Welfare Reform legislation of 1996, 60
white supremacy, 21, 30, 47, 174, 204, 217;

Americanization and, 182; social order of,
161, 177; U.S. nationalism and, 30, 73,
213, 215
whiteness, 220n. 14; American-ness and, 73,
77; and Blackness polarity, 170, 175, 210,
215; dominance of, 204; Latinidad and,
204–10; Latino groups and, 16; non-, 146,
214; privileged, 189; racial, 60, 131, 157,
176, 205, 230n. 10
whites: as Americans, 77, 84–85; Blacks and,
187; middle-class, 199, 203; racial
categories used by, 177–78
Wilson, Orlando, 225n. 27
work: ethic, 79; moral economy of, 69–74;
racial economy of, 74–78, 83
World War I, 4, 8; Mexican migration to
Chicago during, 34
World War II: contract-labor migration
initiatives during, 10; labor shortages of,
5, 35, 224n. 20

Y
Young Lords Organization: Chicago, 47,
226n. 29; New York, 29, 226nn. 28

Z
Zorbaugh, Harvey Warren, 225n. 25